RNLI
motor lifeboats

The history and development of the Royal National Lifeboat Institution's motor lifeboats

Nicholas Leach

Published by
Landmark Publishing Ltd
Ashbourne Hall
Cokayne Avenue
Ashbourne
Derbyshire DE6 1EJ
England
Tel 01335 347349
Fax 01335 347303
landmark@clara.net
www.landmarkpublishing.co.uk

ISBN 978-1-84306-341-1
Updated edition
© Nicholas Leach 2007

1st edition ISBN 978-1-84306-201-4

British Library Cataloguing in Publication Data: a catalogue
record for this book is available from the British Library.

Printed by Gutenberg Press Ltd, Malta

Cover designed by James Allsopp
Book design and layout by Nicholas Leach

*Cover photograph: Ballycotton's 14m Trent Austin Lidbury (ON.1233) on
exercise in Youghal Bay. See table 38/25. (Nicholas Leach)*

*Back cover main picture: Holyhead's 17m Severn Christopher Pearce
(ON.1272) rounds Point Lynas off Anglesey as she heads back to station. See
table 37/41. (Nicholas Leach)*

*Back cover, top left: Dunbar's 14m Trent Sir Ronald Pechell Bt (ON.1207)
puts out from her Torness base on a blustery winter day. See table 38/9.
(Nicholas Leach)*

*Back cover, top centre: Wells' 12m Mersey Doris M. Mann of Ampthill
(ON.1161) breaks through a short sea off the entrance to the harbour.
See table 36/5. (Nicholas Leach)*

*Back cover, top right: Relief 47ft Tyne Voluntary Worker (ON.1146) from
Moelfre with Holyhead lifeboat Christopher Pearce (ON.1272) off Point Lynas.
See table 35/31. (Nicholas Leach)*

*Frontispiece: The prototype 16m Tamar lifeboat Peter and Lesley-Jane
Nicholson (ON.1280) off Sennen Cove. See table 39/2. (Tim Stevens)*

Acknowledgements

This book has been very much a collaborative effort and my
grateful thanks are due to Tony Denton, Jeff Morris and Phil Weeks
for thoroughly checking the facts and figures at various stages of
the project. Tony Denton was particularly helpful and enthusiastic
to see the project succeed, while Jeff Morris's vast knowledge of
the lifeboat service has been drawn upon and I am very grateful
to them both. The records of the late Grahame Farr, held at the
RNLI Headquarters in Poole, were also consulted extensively and
proved to be of considerable assistance. I am grateful to successive
members of staff at the RNLI for the facilities afforded me for
research, and must mention in particular Barry Cox, honorary
librarian, who provided much additional information. Liz Cook,
Eleanor Driscoll and Brian Weed, also at the RNLI, assisted in
various ways. The photographs have come from a range of sources,
and individual images are credited. I am grateful to all who are
named and have very kindly supplied me with photographs. All
drawings and plans are published courtesy of the RNLI. I also
acknowledge the assistance and generous hospitality given at the
many lifeboat stations I have visited, with coxswains and volunteer
crews providing much help in enabling me to take many of the
photographs used in this book. This edition includes corrections to
the first edition, brings the tables up-to-date, and the opportunity
has also been taken to include some new photographs. Lastly, my
thanks to Sarah for her patience, undertsanding and comments
which always help to improve and refine my writing and research.

Nicholas Leach, Birmingham, July 2007

RNLI Motor Lifeboats

Contents

Aran Islands 17m Severn lifeboat David Kirkaldy (ON.1217) shows her speed off the west coast of Ireland as she heards into the Atlantic swells. The 17m Severn is the RNLI's largest all-weather lifeboat. (Nicholas Leach)

Port St Mary 14m Trent lifeboat Gough-Ritchie II (ON.1234) passing the Chicken Rock lighthouse off the Calf of Man at the southern end of the Isle of Man. The 14m Trent is one of two twenty-five knot lifeboat designs built to operate from a berth or mooring. (Nicholas Leach)

Part 1
Development of the motor lifeboat

The Royal National Lifeboat Institution's (RNLI) largest all-weather class of lifeboat, the 17m Severn, powering along at twenty-five knots, is an extremely impressive sight. The modern technology employed throughout the lifeboat's advanced design provides its volunteer crew with a safe and sophisticated sea rescue tool that is equipped to deal with a wide range of casualties, often in the worst of weathers. Looking at twenty-first century technology in isolation makes it hard to imagine how, a century ago, the RNLI tentatively began the first experiments with motor power for lifeboats. Indeed, comparing the Severn with the early motor lifeboats might lead to the conclusion that they have little or nothing in common. But in fact, the Severn is the culmination not only of more than two centuries of lifeboat development, as designers have sought to find a coastal lifeboat that best fits the purpose of saving 'those in peril on the sea', but also of a century of motor lifeboat development. During this century, technology has been harnessed to provide a rescue vessel for Britain's volunteer lifeboat crews that is second to none.

Steam power

Since its foundation in 1824, the RNLI has been constantly seeking to design and build the best possible lifeboat for service off the coasts of the United Kingdom and Ireland. For over a century prior to the first powered lifeboats, lifeboatmen using pulling and sailing lifeboats performed remarkable feats of life-saving. Crews would often row small lifeboats through heavy seas to reach a casualty. Then, during the latter years of the nineteenth century, the first mechanical lifeboats, powered by steam engines, were introduced. Steam had been used to power vessels since the 1820s and steam packets had become an increasingly common sight in Britain's ports as steam was more widely used. Although the use of steam power in a lifeboat would provide definite advantages over a lifeboat relying on sails, oars or a combination of the two, not until almost the end of the century did a steam lifeboat see service with the RNLI. Designing and building a steam-powered lifeboat presented designers with a different set of problems to those of pulling lifeboats. Since 1825 the idea of a steam lifeboat had been discussed, but all the suggestions put forward had been rejected.

At a number of the major ports, pulling and sailing lifeboats worked in conjunction with the local steam tug, notably Ramsgate, Gorleston and Lowestoft on the east coast. Many coxswains and crews regarded this as an ideal arrangement as the close-quarter manoeuvrability of a pulling lifeboat when attending a wreck was better, they believed, than that of a larger and more cumbersome steam tug. The benefits of the steam tug and lifeboat combination were clearly demonstrated during the service to the barque *Indian Chief*, one of the most famous rescues in the RNLI's history. The barque went aground on the Long Sand at the mouth of the Thames at 2am on 6 January 1881 and slowly began to break up forcing the crew to take to the rigging. Both Harwich and Clacton lifeboats were launched but neither found the casualty despite many hours searching. Just after midday, Ramsgate's lifeboat *Bradford*, a large 44ft self-righter intended primarily for sailing, set out. She was towed by the steam-paddler *Vulcan* for thirty miles until reaching the casualty, by when it was dark. Throughout the passage, the lifeboat crew had been exposed to biting winds and heavy seas as their open lifeboat offered no shelter from the elements. As the steamer and lifeboat cruised between the Sands amidst the full fury of the storm, the steamer sustained some damage to her deck housing. In the morning, under her own sail, the lifeboat negotiated the seas around the wreck and succeeded in rescuing the remaining survivors. She then sailed back across the Sands to *Vulcan* and both vessels returned to Ramsgate having been away for more than twenty-four hours. The Gold medal was awarded to Coxswain Charles Fish and other awards went to his crew for a remarkable rescue which no pulling and sailing lifeboat could have performed on its own.

But however good tugs were at getting a lifeboat to the scene of a wreck, considerable effort was still required on the part of the lifeboat crews to complete a rescue and the outcome was not always successful. The inadequacies of the pulling lifeboat were demonstrated in 1883 during a rescue off the coast of Anglesey.

The first steam lifeboat, Duke of Northumberland *(ON.231), on trials. (RNLI)*

The 1897-built steam lifeboat Queen *(ON.404). (RNLI)*

RNLI Steam Lifeboats

ON	Year Builder	Length Breadth	Name Donor	Engines	Station (Launches/lives saved)
231	1889 R. & H. Green	50' 14'3"	Duke of Northumberland RNLI Funds.	1x170hp water pump single screw	Harwich 1890-92 (15/33); Holyhead 1892-93 (6/9); New Brighton 1893-7 (29/14); Holyhead 1897-1922 (125/239)
362	1894 R. & H. Green	53' 16'	City of Glasgow City of Glasgow Lifeboat Fund.	1x200hp scoop single screw	Harwich No.2 1894-97 (23/4); Gorleston 1897-98 (1/0); Harwich 1898-1901 (5/28)
404	1897 J. I. Thornycroft	55' 16'6"	Queen RNLI Funds.	1x198hp water pump single screw	New Brighton No.2 1897-1923 (81/196)
420	1898 J. S. White, Cowes	56'6" 15'9"	James Stevens No.3 Legacy of James Stevens, Birmingham.	1x180hp compound single screw	Grimsby 1898-1903 (6/0); Gorleston 1903-08 (37/30); Angle 1908-15 (12/5); Totland Bay 1915-19 (6/0); Dover 1919-22 (5/1); Holyhead 1922-28 (20/18)
421	1899 J. S. White, Cowes	56'6" 15'9"	James Stevens No.4 Legacy of James Stevens, Birmingham.	1x180hp compound single screw	Padstow 1899-1900 (4/9) Capsized and wrecked on service, 11.4.1900, eight lost
446	1901 J. S. White, Cowes	56'6" 15'9"	City of Glasgow City of Glasgow Lifeboat Fund.	1x180hp compound single screw	Harwich 1901-17 (98/87)
478	1901 Ramage & Fergusun	95'6" 19'6"	Helen Peele Legacy of Mr C. J. Peele, Chertsey.	2x331hp compound twin screw	Padstow 1901-29 (steam tug working in conjunction with pulling & sailing lifeboat, 19/10 on own account)

On 31 April 1883, the Greenock barque *Norman Court* went ashore on rocks in a heavy gale and sunk, forcing her crew to take to the rigging. At dawn the following day, the Rhosneigr lifeboat *Thomas Lingham*, a small 30ft self-righting type, was launched but failed to save the wrecked crew after being nearly overwhelmed in terrible conditions and forced to return to station. Later in the day, a second launch was attempted but in the heavy breakers the boat could not get to sea. As tugs were on hand at Holyhead, a few miles round the coast, the lifeboat *Thomas Fielden*, a larger 37ft self-righter, was towed to the scene by the steam tug *Challenge*. The lifeboat was brought to within a mile of the wreck, at which point she cast off. But in the severe weather, under oars and sail, the lifeboat could not get close enough to save the stranded men and was forced back. A third attempt was therefore made to launch the Rhosneigr lifeboat. Manned by a Holyhead crew, she finally got away and succeeded in saving twenty people from the barque after considerable exertion. Holyhead Coxswain, Thomas Roberts, was awarded the Silver medal for this arduous rescue.

The *Norman Court* incident showed the difficulties of rescue work using not only pulling lifeboats but also steam tugs, and within five years the RNLI's Committee of Management was considering building a steam-powered lifeboat. Although doubts remained about the efficiency of a steam lifeboat, the potential advantages it offered over the pulling and sailing boats convinced the RNLI to go ahead with construction. Advances in engineering techniques during the 1880s meant that building a steam-powered lifeboat was feasible and, in June 1888, plans submitted by R. & H. Green, shipbuilders of Blackwall, were taken up by the RNLI which ordered Green to build a steam lifeboat. The new lifeboat, named *Duke of Northumberland* (ON.231), was launched from her builder's yard on the Thames and made her first trial trip on 31 May 1889. The Thornycroft engine with which she was fitted, with its 'patent tubulous pattern' boiler, produced 170hp and drove hydraulic pumps, which were in effect water jets. On 4 August 1890, she was taken to the Maplin measured mile for speed trials when she averaged more than nine knots. With a full bunker of three tons of coal, her radius of action was 254 miles at eight and a half knots. She was sent to Harwich in September 1890 and

undertook her first service less than a month later, on 8 October. She towed the station's 38ft self-righting lifeboat *Reserve No.3* to the Cork Sand and stood by the brigantine *Ada*, of Faversham, which was aground.

During the next decade, the RNLI had further steam lifeboats built. The next, completed in 1894, was larger than *Duke of Northumberland* at 53ft in length. A third, named Queen to mark Queen Victoria's 60th anniversary, was launched in June 1897 and these two vessels were both driven by hydraulic pumps. The RNLI ordered three more steam lifeboats but, having reviewed the method of propulsion, employed screws rather than hydraulic pumps because it was found that the hydraulic propulsion did not give the boats sufficient speed. Screw propulsion had originally been rejected because of the possibility of the propeller being damaged but a tunnel was designed to provide the necessary protection. Two 56ft 6in boats, named *James Stevens No.3* (ON.420) and *James Stevens No.4* (ON.421), were ordered in January 1898. The first was sent to Grimsby, to cover the Humber estuary, and the other to Padstow for working off the treacherous Cornish coast. A sixth and final steam lifeboat, identical to the other two screw-powered boats, was ordered in 1901 to serve Harwich, an important station which covered the outlying sandbanks at the northern end of the Thames Estuary.

Steam lifeboats offered many benefits. Not only were they able to head into the wind, they could also tow a pulling lifeboat to the scene of a casualty and stay at sea for longer. But they had their drawbacks. Their size, 50ft in length and more than thirty tons in weight, restricted the number of places where they could be stationed. They had to be kept afloat at a time when lifeboats were operated from moorings only as a last resort as anti-fouling paints were not as effective as now. Getting the necessary steam up before setting out could take twenty minutes and even then they were comparatively slow, making no more than seven knots in practice despite higher speeds achieved during trials. Manning was also problematic as they required specialist engineers to service the boiler whilst their relatively large draught meant they were not ideal for shallow water operation. And construction costs were higher, working out at more than three times greater than the cost of an average Watson sailing lifeboat. But despite their difficulties, steam lifeboats remained in use for almost three decades, saved more than 600 lives and performed some excellent rescues.

At Gorleston, the much-travelled *James Stevens No.3* which went to the station in 1903, undertook an outstanding service on 15 January 1905 that proved steam lifeboats could operate in the worst of weathers. She went to a vessel in distress four miles south of Gorleston in a severe south-easterly gale with freezing temperatures. In charge was Coxswain Sydney Harris, who later said that he had never before experienced seas as bad. But in spite of the horrendous conditions, the steam lifeboat battled her way out of harbour, frequently disappearing from view in mountainous seas, and found the brig *Celerity*, of Lowestoft, dragging her anchors and in grave danger. With outstanding seamanship, Coxswain Harris manoeuvred the lifeboat up to the brig and, despite their vessel rolling and heaving, the lifeboat crew got a line aboard. The brig's crew of six were then brought to safety, the line was cut and the lifeboat pulled clear. When the lifeboat arrived at the harbour entrance, extremely heavy seas were breaking across it so Coxswain Harris dropped anchor in the Roads to await better conditions. On the lifeboat, rescuers and rescued endured repeated soakings as waves swept over them with water freezing on the decks. Eventually, shortly after 2am, Coxswain Harris took the lifeboat through the harbour entrance with tremendous skill. For his outstanding seamanship, Harris was awarded the Silver medal, but the rescue could not have been achieved without the skill of the boat's engineers and firemen. They had to remain in the engine room throughout and in recognition of his courage, determination and fine leadership, the Chief Engineer, James Sclanders, was awarded the Silver medal.

The first steps to motorisation

As the shortcomings of steam power when applied to lifeboats were so numerous, the newly-invented internal combustion engine offered greater possibilities. Petrol-driven engines, developed during the second half of the nineteenth century, had powered motor vehicles since the 1880s and by the 1900s, it was inevitable that motor power, in the form of the internal combustion engine, would be applied to sea rescue. The RNLI's Committee of Management, according to *The Lifeboat* (journal of the RNLI) of 1 August 1904, 'for many years had the problem . . . of the successful employment of a motor in a Life-boat, so as to assist by mechanical means, and thus relieve some of the tremendous work entailed by getting a Life-boat to a wreck against wind and sea.'

By this time, the Committee believed that the motor had been developed from a 'more or less unreliable and often capricious machine' to one with 'nearly all its previous faults eliminated, and ready for use afloat'. So preparations were made for its intro-duction into the lifeboat fleet when, in the autumn of 1903, George Lennox Watson, the RNLI's Consulting Naval Architect, was asked to determine the best way to develop a motor lifeboat. Watson, who had already formulated a successful sailing lifeboat design and produced plans on which several steam lifeboats were based, decided that an existing lifeboat should be motorised.

The conversion project was entrusted to Captain E. du Boulay, of Thellusson & Co, who had experience of fitting engines to yachts. The Folkestone lifeboat *J. McConnell Hussey* (ON.343), a 38ft self-righting type built in 1893 and pulled by twelve oars, was chosen to be converted and was taken off station to go to Guy's yard at Cowes where the motor was fitted. The work necessitated major alterations to the boat, starting with the fitting of a watertight mahogany box amidships to house the 11hp two-cylinder Fay & Bowen petrol engine and its associated equipment. The motor drove a three-bladed propeller through a long shaft via a disconnecting clutch. The petrol was held in a metal tank inside the forward end box and sufficient fuel was carried for over ten hours of continuous running.

The technical problems to be overcome to successfully operate an engine on board a lifeboat were complex and numerous. The engine had to start easily under any conditions and be capable of surviving potentially severe motion as well as operating in heavy seas when the propellers might be out of the water. It had to be housed in a casing that was watertight, in case of capsize, but not airtight because the carburettor needed a supply of air. The risk of fire had to be minimised and the engine's lubricating system had to be self-maintaining. The propellers themselves had to be carefully considered so that they were located in a position on the hull which would prevent their damage during launching and when working either in shallow waters or round floating wreckage.

Once these problems had been solved, however, lifeboats powered by the internal combustion engine represented the future for lifeboat design and powered lifeboats offered considerable advantages over their pulling counterparts. They could sail into the wind giving them a far greater and more flexible operational scope, approach a casualty from any direction (not just to windward), had considerably better manoeuvrability and could be operated by fewer men. Another benefit, albeit in the long term, was the gradual removal of sails which took up valuable space on board and required considerable expertise to deploy.

Once converted, *J. McConnell Hussey* was subjected to a series of trials during April 1904, including using the engine as auxiliary to the sails. Her speed on the measured mile, with full crew and stores on board, was just over six knots. She was capsized four times and each time successfully righted herself with the motor automatically stopping after the boat had heeled over just beyond 'her beam ends'. In November 1904, she was sent to Newhaven for station evaluation where she spent six months under operational conditions. Although she was not called upon to perform any services, the coxswain and crew were so impressed by her performance that they asked for their own lifeboat, *Michael Henry* (ON.407), to be converted to motor. The RNLI acceded to

The first motor lifeboat, J. McConnell Hussey (ON.343), during her self-righting trials after being fitted with an engine in 1904. The box housing the motor can be seen amidships. (From an old photo loaned by Jeff Morris)

the crew's wishes and, on 5 July 1905, ordered an engine from Thornycroft at Chiswick so *Michael Henry* could be motorised. Two further engines were also ordered so that two other lifeboats could be similarly converted. On 19 July 1905, a 30bhp engine was ordered from Tylor for the 42ft self-righter *Bradford*, built in 1893, recently replaced at Ramsgate and then renamed *Reserve No.2*. And on 5 August 1905, a 40bhp motor was ordered from Blake for the 43ft Norfolk & Suffolk boat at Walton-on-the-Naze.

The conversion to motor of these four lifeboats during the 1904-06 period proved to be a difficult process. The engines proved unreliable at almost every stage and the RNLI's engineers had their work cut out to repair them, find improvements necessary to make them function properly, as well as contend with working on the engines at sea, often in bad weather. During the trials, almost every aspect of the engines broke down at some time. In the Walton-on-the-Naze boat, the crank-shaft and gear-casing were found to be faulty during installation and this delayed the completion of the conversion. While on trials out of Harwich in November 1906, the Newhaven boat's sparking and air supply went wrong causing the engine to stop. And the *Reserve No.2* boat's first trials in June 1906 proved unsatisfactory when the reversing gear failed and the carburettor was found to be of the wrong type. Worse was to come for this boat after her self-righting trial on 2 August 1906. She righted after being deliberately turned over but, when the engine was restarted, an explosion ripped through the engine casing and the hatches were blown open. The explosion had been caused by petrol from the carburettor igniting, but fortunately no one was hurt in the incident.

Although making the engines work reliably and efficiently in the conversions involved considerable effort, the RNLI's engineers and naval architects persevered and the boats were eventually returned to service. The first, *J. McConnell Hussey*, went to Tynemouth after her trials at Newhaven and here a new problem had to be faced – crew mistrust of a motorised lifeboat. The Tynemouth crew was made up of local fishermen and pilots who were very reluctant to man the motor boat and so, for the first eight months of her time at Tynemouth, she was crewed by soldiers stationed at the nearby Clifford Fort in North Shields and commanded by Lieut. Herbert Burton, an Officer of the Royal Engineers and an experienced yachtsman. But gradually, after seeing the motor boat prove herself in action, the local men offered their services although

The Newhaven lifeboat Michael Henry *(ON.407) which was fitted converted to motor during 1907-8. (From and old photo loaned by Jeff Morris)*

Burton remained in charge as Superintendent of the lifeboat.

After trials and tests of the converted boats and their engines, and in spite of these proving rather temperamental and unreliable initially, the RNLI's Committee of Management decided to meet the next challenge, that of constructing from scratch a motor lifeboat. As early as 1905 it had been decided that the lifeboats destined for Fishguard, Stronsay, Stromness and Thurso would be built as motor lifeboats. In the event, the Thurso boat was competed without an engine, and the motor intended for her was placed into the Broughty Ferry boat instead. *The Lifeboat* of November 1905 explained that 'fitting these lifeboats for motors entails considerable structural alterations, which have occupied a considerable time in carrying out, but as soon as all is completed, and the engines installed, a very interesting series of trials is anticipated.' Protecting the propeller from damage was a major concern for the RNLI's designers, so a tunnel was built to house it as far forward along the hull as possible.

The new motor lifeboats, all over 40ft in length, were built to either Watson's plans or the standard self-righting design with high end boxes and a narrow beam. The work of construction and testing lasted throughout 1908 and not until 1909 did the Fishguard boat, the 40ft self-righter *Charterhouse* (ON.563), arrive at her station. Following this, the two boats destined for the Orkney stations of Stromness and Stronsay, *John A. Hay* (ON.561) and *John Ryburn* (ON.565), were sent north from the Thames in company with the Thurso pulling lifeboat. The crew at Stromness were keen to have a motor lifeboat because the conditions they faced in the Pentland Firth, and often in just getting out of the harbour at Stromness, would be better tackled using a powered lifeboat. That two motor lifeboats were sent to stations in Orkney suggests a far-sightedness in realising that motor lifeboats would be particularly effective in areas where heavy seas were frequent and often considerable distances – well beyond the range of a pulling lifeboat – had to be travelled to reach casualties.

John Ryburn and *John A. Hay*, together with the pulling lifeboat, left London Docks on 15 April 1909 and began an epic journey north under their own power. Hitherto, new lifeboats had usually been delivered to their station by steamship or railway, and so a sea voyage as far as Orkney was a major undertaking. It was, perhaps, the ultimate proving test for the new motor lifeboats. Although the boats eventually reached their stations safely, the passage had not been without incident, with the motors breaking down on several occasions and at one port of call, Aberdeen, the boats needing assistance from the local steam tug to reach harbour. But the RNLI's positive account of the journey in spite of the difficulties was part of the Institution's campaign to get motor

Motor lifeboat conversions

ON	HP Cyl	RPM Weight	Engine maker Reverse gear	Max speed Fuel consumed	Stations
343	11hp 2	500 24cwt	Fay & Bowen Durham Churchill	5.9 knots 12 pints/hr	Tynemouth Sunderland
350 (1907)	40hp 4 35hp 4	900 8cwt 900 18.5cwt	Briton Tylor Buffalo	 6.75 knots 18.5 pints/hr	Seaton Snook Teesmouth
407 (1913)	24hp 4 20hp 4	1,000 20cwt 1,000 12.25cwt	Thornycroft Thornycroft Gardner Gardner	6.8 knots 15.6 pints/hr	Newhaven Dunmore East
432	40hp 4	600 22.5cwt	Blake Caledonia	7.42 knots 20.4 pints	Walton & Frinton
463	40hp	700 32cwt	Tylor Gardner No.4	7.63 knots 40 pints/hr	Clacton-on-Sea Arranmore

One of the first purpose-built motor lifeboats to go on station, the 42ft self-righter John A. Hay (ON.561), alongside the slipway at Stromness. She sailed to Orkney from the Thames in convoy with another new motor lifeboat and a pulling boat. This photo shows how similar the first motor boats were to their pulling equivalents. See table 1/4. (Orkney Photographic Archives)

lifeboats accepted around the coasts and, over the next few years as more motor craft entered service, local opposition diminished considerably. Indeed many crews requested a motor lifeboat.

Two years after the convoy had reached Orkney, a similar passage was undertaken by three motor lifeboats travelling together up the east coast. The boats were destined for Tynemouth, Seaham Harbour and St Abbs, with the new motor boat opening the station at St Abbs. As with the earlier convoy, the engines proved a little unreliable and a day had to be spent at Gorleston after one of the motors failed to start. As a result, doubts about the boats remained and, throughout the first ten years of motor lifeboat service, the RNLI's Committee of Management found it necessary to constantly restate the positive advantages of the motor lifeboat, while also explaining that the motor was in fact an auxiliary to sails and oars. The Lifeboat of February 1913 stated that 'should the motor in a Life-boat break down, the boat, with her masts, sails, and oars is really no worse than if she had gone to sea without a motor. This is an important point which should always be brought to the notice of local committees and crews at those stations where a question of supplying a motor Life-boat has come to the front.'

By 1914 the number of motor lifeboats in service was well into double figures although the engines had still not reached the degree of reliability required, and up to 1918 non-motorised lifeboats were still being built. In 1910, motor lifeboats had been ordered for a new station at Donaghadee, at the entrance to Belfast Lough, and Wicklow, a key station on Ireland's east coast to the south of Dublin. In 1911, three 43ft Watson type motor boats were ordered for Campbeltown, Beaumaris and Peterhead, almost the largest motor lifeboats built to date and, fitted with a 60hp engine, the most powerful. But if doubts about the motor lifeboat's capabilities remained at the outbreak of World War I in 1914, the events of the war involving, most notably, the motor lifeboats on the east coast proved beyond doubt that motor-powered lifeboats could outperform pulling boats every time and accomplish feats hitherto unachievable.

The Tynemouth station at North Shields at the mouth of the Tyne operated the first motor lifeboat, J. McConnell Hussey until 1911. During her six years at the station she saved eight lives. She was replaced by a new, purpose-built motor lifeboat, a 40ft self-righter named Henry Vernon (ON.613) which was powered by a single 40bhp Tylor petrol engine. Built on the Thames by Thames Ironworks, she sailed to her new station in April 1911 under her

own power in company with two other new motor lifeboats. This lifeboat performed many rescues and in less than seven years of service on the Tyne is credited with saving over 200 lives. Her most notable achievement came during one of the most famous incidents in the history of the RNLI, the wreck of the hospital ship Rohilla in 1914, which, according to James Barnett, the Consulting Naval Archtitect who played a major role in motor lifeboat development, 'cannot be recalled too often, for that rescue clearly demonstrated that what is impossible for a pulling and sailing boat can be accomplished by a motor-lifeboat'.

On 30 October 1914, shortly after the outbreak of War, the hospital ship Rohilla, with 229 people on board, was wrecked near Whitby. Huge waves were breaking over the vessel, and many people were washed overboard and drowned. Frantic efforts were made to help and the Whitby No.2 lifeboat was launched, with considerable difficulty. In two trips, she saved thirty-five lives but was so badly damaged during these that she could not go to sea again. Another lifeboat was brought through the town from the neighbouring station at Upgang and lowered down the steep cliffs opposite the wreck. But in the terrible seas breaking on the cliffs, it was impossible to launch her until the following morning. After many attempts, she got to within fifty yards of the wreck, only to be swept back. The Teesmouth lifeboat was then summoned, but got badly damaged attempting to cross the Tees Bar in mountainous seas and a tug had to help her. The Scarborough lifeboat, and another from Whitby, were towed out by tugs but neither could get close to the wreck.

The only hope was the motor lifeboat Henry Vernon at Tynemouth and so an urgent telegram was sent north requesting assistance. As soon as the message was received, she left the Tyne at 4.30pm, as darkness was falling, under Coxswain Robert Smith and arrived in Whitby harbour after midnight having travelled over forty miles contending with horrendous weather and, because of the war, navigating without any lights to guide her southwards. She was met at Whitby by Lieut. Basil Hall, the Inspector of Lifeboats, who had several barrels of oil loaded on board.

At daybreak on 1 November, she set out from Whitby harbour, made to windward of the wreck, getting to within 200 yards of it before discharging the oil to smooth the breaking waves. With the oil flattening the waves, Coxswain Smith swung the lifeboat round and made straight for the wreck, heading past the stern of Rohilla at full speed to reach the lee side of the vessel, below the bridge. Ropes were lowered and all fifty people were taken off. Perhaps the most dangerous part of the rescue was getting away from

Launch of General Farrell (ON.614) at St Davids. Completed in 1911, she was a 40ft motor self-righter and one of the few motor lifeboats to enter service before 1914. See table 4/4. (From a postcard supplied by a Shoreline member)

the wreck. As the lifeboat cleared the casualty, she was struck by a huge wave that threatened to upset her. But she withstood this and battled through a wall of water to reach the open sea. She made for the harbour, where she landed the survivors and was greeted by tremendous cheers from thousands of people lining the quays and cliffs.

This prolonged and difficult rescue, which lasted for two and a half days and involved lifeboatmen and helpers from several stations, is one of the most famous in the history of the RNLI. Gold medals were awarded to Coxswain Smith of Tynemouth, as well as Whitby Coxswain Thomas Langlands for their efforts, while the Second Coxswain of the Tynemouth lifeboat received the Silver medal, and additional monetary awards were made to the rest of the intrepid Tynemouth crew. The delay in sending for the motor lifeboat had not in the end proved fatal, but it highlighted the continuing mistrust at lifeboat stations of the motor craft despite their becoming increasingly numerous. The rescue, though, did prove that motor lifeboats could work in worse weathers and provide lifeboat crews with a far better means to effect rescues than they were used to. The next challenge was to rebuild the fleet once war had ended and continue implementing advances and improvements to the motor lifeboat.

Twin engines and diesels

The World War of 1914-18 affected the lifeboat service in many ways, the most serious of which was a significant loss of revenue. Lifeboat operations themselves were made more difficult by the removal of navigation aids while the conflict also delayed further advances in motor lifeboat development. A year to the day after war broke out, 4 August 1915, the new Fraserburgh motor lifeboat *Lady Rothes* (ON.641), a 42ft self-righter with a single 40bhp Tylor engine, was christened by Lady Rothes. The new boat had been provided as a 'thank offering' from the donor for the survival of his daughter, the Countess of Rothes, a passenger when the liner *Titanic* had sunk. But more than three years passed before another new lifeboat was named as new construction halted.

Following the cessation of hostilities, the RNLI adopted a policy of renewal, building many new motor lifeboats to modernise the fleet and replace the pulling, sailing and steam lifeboats. An ambitious building programme for the completion of fifty new motor lifeboats was announced and as motor lifeboats became increasingly widespread, they had a significant impact on the number of lifeboat stations in operation. Motor lifeboats had a greater range than pulling boats, so a motor boat could effectively cover a coastline that, during the nineteenth century, had been covered by several pulling lifeboats. At their peak, more than 300 pulling lifeboats were in service with some stations, mainly those on the east coast, operating two or in some cases more boats. The motorisation of the fleet therefore resulted in a significant reduction in the number of stations. With a motor lifeboat at one station, it was often found that the neighbouring stations could be closed yet rescue coverage of the area still improved.

Hitherto, motor lifeboat designs had been basically pulling and sailing lifeboats fitted with a single engine, driving a single propeller. But as the RNLI gained greater experience in the operation of motor lifeboats, more reliable and powerful engines were developed so larger boats with a greater range could be built. The largest of the early motor lifeboats was the 45ft Watson which weighed about fifteen tons, and was powered by a single 60bhp engine. The prototype of the class, *Elsie* (ON.648), was launched in 1919 and placed on station at St Mary's (Isles of Scilly). Between 1919 and 1925, more than twenty 45ft Watsons were completed and proved to be a most successful design. Another early motor lifeboat type was the Norfolk & Suffolk, 46ft 6in in length, of which three were built during the early 1920s. While these designs proved very capable and were clearly better than pulling lifeboats, the first time motor power was fully utilised in lifeboat design came in 1922 when James Barnett, the RNLI's Consulting Naval Engineer, designed a 60ft lifeboat that employed twin engines, in separate watertight engine rooms, driving twin propellers.

The introduction of twin engines to lifeboat design was the most significant inter-war development. The impressive 60ft lifeboat was a ground-breaking design in many ways and the first of many contributions Barnett made to motor lifeboat design during more than half a century of designing lifeboats. His pioneering development moved lifeboat design forward with the twin engine arrangement eliminating the need for auxiliary sails carried by single-engined motor lifeboats. Several other advances were incorporated in the 60ft boat including, for the first time in a lifeboat, shelters for crew and survivors, a feature taken for granted on modern lifeboats. With a displacement of forty tons, a lifeboat of such size had never been seen before. The design reflected a new era as the RNLI, preparing to celebrate its centenary, entered the second century of its existence with confidence and assurance after the difficulties of operations during World War I.

The first of the new 60ft type, *William and Kate Johnston* (ON.682), was allocated to the New Brighton station at the mouth of the river Mersey, guarding one of the busiest shipping lanes in the country. During a career of more than twenty-five years, she saved almost 250 lives and performed several outstanding rescues, perhaps the most notable of which began in the early hours of 24 November 1928 when she went to the aid of the French steamer *Emile Delmas*, of La Rochelle. The steamer had been dragging her anchors in violent seas and a strong gale four miles west-north-west of the Bar Lightvessel while trying to make for Holyhead. The lifeboat put to sea at 7.45am with a crew of eight. It proved to be a particularly difficult rescue carried out in a very heavy gale, high seas, blinding rain squalls and 100 mile per hour gusts of wind.

Once the lifeboat reached the casualty, Coxswain George Robinson had difficulty in getting the lifeboat close due to the steamer's violent motion. However, with outstanding seamanship,

38ft motor self-righter Frederick H. Pilley *(ON.657) outside Saunders' boatyard. Based on a standard pulling lifeboat design, she was typical of the early motor lifeboats. See table 1/7. (From a photo in the author's collection)*

The ground-breaking 60ft Barnett *William and Kate Johnston (ON.682)*, the first twin-engined motor lifeboat to enter service, pictured on trials. See table 7/1. (From an old postcard in the author's collection)

45ft Watson motor *Duke of Connaught (ON.668)* on service at Peterhead. The 45ft Watson was one of the early deep-water single-engined motor designs which were completely open boats with auxiliary sails. See table 5/3. (RNLI)

courage, and teamwork amongst the lifeboat's crew, he succeeded in bringing *William and Kate Johnston* alongside so that twenty-three of the steamer's crew could be brought to safety. Although the lifeboat was damaged, Coxswain Robinson was able to bring her safely clear of the steamer and set course for New Brighton. During the return journey, extreme seas were encountered and one huge wave which swept over the lifeboat washed two of the lifeboat crew overboard, as well as the Chief Engineer from the steamer. The wave flooded the engine rooms and only with great difficulty was Robinson able to bring the lifeboat round. Although the two lifeboatmen were picked up, the lifeboat was unable to reach the Chief Engineer who drowned. After more than six hours at sea in the worst conditions imaginable, *William and Kate Johnston* arrived back at her station. For this outstanding service, Robinson was awarded the Silver medal and Bronze medals went to the rest of the lifeboat crew. The French Government awarded Gold medals to Coxswain Robinson and to the two men who had been washed overboard, George Carmody and Samuel Jones.

Rescues such as this, and the others described above, helped to overcome the prejudice shown by lifeboat crews when the first motor lifeboats were introduced. Many of the crews who saw the powered boats at first hand had been sceptical about their capabilities and particularly suspicious of the benefits an engine would bring. But by the 1920s such suspicions seemed to have disappeared with some crews, such as that at Sennen Cove in Cornwall, expressing their desire for a new motor lifeboat with the Coxswain writing in 1921, 'don't delay the new boat.' His new boat, a 40ft self-righter named *The Newbons* (ON.674), arrived on 1 May 1922 after a three-day journey from Cowes in company with another 40ft motor self-righter, the new Appledore lifeboat *V. C. S.* (ON.675). A number of boats of this 40ft self-righting type were built during the 1920s and gave good service at their stations.

The 40ft self-righters were towards the smaller end of the motor types planned during the 1920s as the inter-war years saw motor lifeboats getting ever larger. The debate over whether self-righting or non-self-righting craft were preferable had been ongoing since the end of the nineteenth century when Watson had first introduced his non-self-righting sailing design. This was more stable than the self-righters with their narrow beam, but of course if turned over would not come upright. After the introduction of Watson's design in the 1890s, the RNLI built lifeboats to the two basic designs, deployed according to local conditions and local preferences: the self-righter and Watson's non-self-righter.

Designers had been unable to produce a lifeboat which was self-righting and yet retained the same lateral stability as the non-self-righting designs of Watson. Barnett favoured the non-self-righting principle and his designs for large twin-engined non-self-righting boats, such as the 60ft type described above, became the mainstay of the lifeboat fleet for many decades.

The 'deep-water boats', as he termed them, built from his plans, were all over 45ft in length with ample beam, large cockpits and shelters. They were kept afloat or launched from a slipway but, for stations where carriage launching was practised, a lighter type was necessary. Getting an engine small enough to fit into a boat that was easily manhandled across a beach and hauled onto a carriage was the next challenge for the RNLI's engineers. Plans for such a design had first been drawn up before 1914 and in 1915 a small 15hp engine was being developed by Tylor & Sons for a light motor lifeboat. But not until 1921 did a carriage-launched motor boat enter service when a 35ft self-righter, *Priscilla MacBean* (ON.655), was completed with a 15hp Gardner engine. Although small, carriage-launched motor boats were effective rescue tools and their development meant that all stations, no matter which method of launching they employed, could operate a motor lifeboat. Three 35ft self-righting motor lifeboats were built, and subsequently the type was enlarged and improved. A non-self-righting carriage-launched type was also developed, the Liverpool class, for crews preferring a more stable but not self-righting boat.

Of the three prototype motor self-righters, the third, *L. P. and St Helen* (ON.703), remained in service for the longest. Throughout World War II she operated from the Newcastle station in Co Down, and in 1942 was involved in one of the most famous services of the war. On 21 January, she went to the steamship *Browning*, of Liverpool, which went ashore off Ballyquinton Point, twenty miles from Newcastle. She launched just after 5am into gale force winds and, after overcoming confused seas off Strangford Bar, forced her way against the weather until, at 10.30am, she reached the scene to find seven ships from the convoy ashore with *Browning* stern first on the rocks. Trying to take the lifeboat alongside proved impossible and at one point she was nearly flung on the steamer's deck by the seas. So Coxswain Pat Murphy went to the lee side of the vessel and steered between casualty and rocks through a channel only 20ft wide. In the relative calm, it was a straightforward task to rescue the steamer's crew. The small self-righter could carry a maximum of twenty-eight in rough weather but thirty-nine men had to be saved. After assessing the situation, the coxswain decided he had no choice but take them all as he could not return to the steamer.

Once the men were all aboard the lifeboat, getting away was a major problem as the channel was too narrow for the lifeboat to turn round. So Coxswain Murphy decided to cross the reef on which the steamer had been wrecked but any mistake in doing so would have capsized the lifeboat and thrown all on board into the sea. But, as three big seas washed over the reef, the boat successfully crossed it with the Coxswain driving her at full speed. The lifeboat was still twenty miles from her station by now but as it was impossible to return against the gale, she was taken north. Nine hours after setting out, she reached the safety of the small harbour at Portavogie to land the survivors. For this outstanding rescue, which consisted of a series of episodes of superb seamanship, Coxswain Murphy was awarded the Gold medal while Silver and Bronze medals went to the other members of the crew.

Although the carriage-launched self-righters were built to what was basically a standard design, standardisation was not the rule at the time and a number of unusual types were developed of which only a few examples, and sometimes only one, were built. The RNLI consulted coxswains and crews about their preferences, and the result was a fleet of motor lifeboats that had extreme variations. Lifeboats were built for the unique conditions of a specific station where the sea conditions justified the building of a one-off type. They included a special design for working in estuaries, known as the Ramsgate class; a motorised version of the Norfolk & Suffolk sailing lifeboat for service at Gorleston and Lowestoft; variations of the 41ft Watson lifeboat with a broader beam than the standard and strengthened hull for launching over skids laid on a beach; a fast 64ft vessel for air-sea rescue in the English Channel; and in the mid-1930s, a light Surf lifeboat intended for carriage launching and working close inshore. With the latter design, the RNLI ventured into new territory as several of the boats were driven by an early form of water jet, but this did not prove to be particularly successful and only nine Surf lifeboats were constructed.

At the opposite end of the scale from the small Surf boats were the 60ft Barnetts, of which four were built during the 1920s. But these large lifeboats proved a little too big to be practical everywhere. As they had to be kept afloat, they were restricted to where a sheltered mooring could be found. Consequently, a smaller 51ft Barnett was introduced in 1928, known as the 'Stromness' class after the station at which the first one served. Like the larger 60ft type, twin engines and twin screws were incorporated into the design but, because it was smaller and lighter, it could serve at a wider range of stations. Able to be slipway launched, the 51ft Barnett became one of the RNLI's standard heavy weather lifeboats during the 1930s and 1940s, operating from stations where a large sea area had to be covered.

While the power of the motor lifeboat had resulted in the closure of stations situated close together, it also enabled lifeboats such as the 51ft Barnett type to operate effectively at more remote places where rescue work involved travelling distances far in excess of anything a pulling lifeboat could manage. Stations in the Channel Islands and Orkney were equipped with lifeboats that could at last meet the challenges presented by the seas there after pulling lifeboats had proved to be inadequate for the job. In almost fifty years down to 1929, the pulling lifeboats operated from the Guernsey station at St Peter Port performed just thirteen effective services. In the eleven years of service by the 51ft Barnett *Queen Victoria* (ON.719) down to 1940, she completed forty-five rescue missions – more than three times as many as the pulling boats

The small self-righter L. P. and St Helen *(ON.703) on her carriage inside the boathouse at Newcastle, from where she performed some notable services.*

had managed in total. On the west coast of Ireland, at Valentia, Galway Bay and Baltimore, new stations were established with motor lifeboats where lifeboat operations had been hitherto more or less impossible due to the nature of the seas on the country's Atlantic seaboard. Meanwhile, two new stations were established in Shetland in the 1930s, at Lerwick and Aith, places where a pulling lifeboat could not have operated.

Before the Shetland stations had been established, a difficult service took place involving the 51ft Barnett at Stromness, *J. J. K. S. W.* (ON.702). This long service, during which the boat's range and the endurance of her crew were tested to the extreme, was one of the most tragic incidents to take place in the Northern Isles. On the night of 28 March 1930, the Aberdeen trawler *Ben Doran* ran aground off Shetland. But in the gale force winds and heavy seas, nothing could be done to assist those on board. The nearest lifeboat was at Stromness and so, late on the afternoon of 30 March, *J. J. K. S. W.* was called to help. She fought her way north through the heavy seas and gale force winds until she reached Scalloway, 134 miles from Stromness, to where a telegram was sent asking for food, fuel and a local pilot to be ready.

She reached port at 7.30am on 31 March after a passage of almost fifteen hours in atrocious conditions and, after refuelling, set out with the pilot. On reaching the scene, only the top of the trawler's mast could be seen above the waves and, despite a thorough search of the area, no survivors were found. The lifeboat returned to Scalloway where the crew grabbed a few hours sleep. Early on 1 April they headed south but the journey back to Orkney took over sixteen hours and *J. J. K. S. W.* reached Stromness after more than fifty-five hours away having travelled nearly 260 miles. This, according to the RNLI account, was 'the longest journey on service which has been made by any Motor Lifeboat', and proof if it were needed of the capabilities of Barnett's design. Coincidentally, the RNLI had announced plans in March 1930 for establishing a lifeboat station at Lerwick, and if *Ben Doran* had been wrecked a year later her crew would probably have been saved.

The 51ft Barnett design proved itself on many other occasions and some amazing rescues carried out during the inter-war years enabled lifeboat crews to demonstrate that their bravery, skill and stamina allied to a powered rescue craft was a formidable combination. One of the most extraordinary rescues of all, which would have been inconceivable in lifeboats operated just two decades earlier, took place off the coast of County Cork in 1936 when the Ballycotton lifeboat went to aid the Daunt Rock Lightvessel. The Lightvessel, with eight men on board and usually anchored twelve miles off in Ballycotton Bay, broke her moorings on 11 February and began to drift during a severe gale which had been blowing for several days. Conditions were so bad that it was not thought possible to launch the lifeboat. However, Coxswain Patrick Sliney managed to board the 51ft Barnett *Mary Stanford* (ON.733), which was kept at moorings in the harbour, and with a full crew succeeded in taking her through the narrow harbour entrance. The station's watching Honorary Secretary, Robert Mahony, 'did not believe it was possible for the coxswain to get aboard the lifeboat. . . [but] to my amazement the lifeboat headed out between the piers. . . As I watched the lifeboat, I thought every minute she must turn back. At one moment a sea crashed on her; the next she was standing on her heel. But she went on.'

Despite the mountainous seas, the lifeboat cleared the harbour and set course for the drifting vessel, reaching her at noon, a quarter of a mile south-west of the Daunt Rock and only half a mile from the shore. The crew would not leave the lightvessel, knowing the danger to shipping of an abandoned lightvessel out of position. As towing the lightvessel was impossible, the lifeboat stood by until darkness and then made for Queenstown to refuel. On 12 February, *Mary Stanford* returned to the casualty to stand by throughout the day in horrendous conditions. At daylight on 13 February, Coxswain Sliney again went to Queenstown to refuel. Despite being swept constantly by breaking seas for over twenty-five hours and having had no food, the lifeboat crew set out again as soon as the lifeboat was refuelled. That evening, as the weather worsened, the lightvessel's situation became increasingly perilous. As she was in serious danger of striking the Daunt Rock, Coxswain Sliney decided to take the lightvessel's crew off and, in a dangerous manoeuvre that risked the lifeboat itself, took *Mary Stanford* alongside the drifting vessel several times.

With seas sweeping over the wildly plunging lightvessel, the lifeboat had to make numerous passes to take off the eight men with the last two being dragged to safety by the lifeboat's crew.

Some had suffered injuries during their ordeal, while the lifeboat crew had also endured extreme hardship. *Mary Stanford* had been away from station for seventy-six hours, at sea for forty-nine and the crew had been without food for twenty-five; all were suffering from the cold and had salt water burns. For what was a truly remarkable rescue, the Gold medal was awarded to Coxswain Sliney, Silver medals to Second Coxswain John Lane Walsh and Motor Mechanic Thomas Sliney, and Bronze medals to the rest of the crew. The motor lifeboat proved its worth during this gruelling service, and the extra power and endurance it offered enabled the successful completion of an extraordinary rescue, one of the most outstanding ever performed by an RNLI lifeboat crew.

At the time of the Daunt Rock rescue, attempts were underway to improve motor lifeboats' endurance through the use of diesel engines and indeed the rescue highlighted the relative lack of range afforded by petrol engines. Although petrol engines had been refined and developed since being first used, the introduction of diesel engines during the 1930s was a significant step forward. The former Tenby and Barra Island lifeboat *John R. Webb* (ON.684, later renamed *684RM*) was the first lifeboat to receive a diesel engine. In 1932, she was taken off station and in September 1934 fitted with a single six-cylinder 85hp diesel to a design by the Ferry Engine Co. The trials, during which she was compared with the Portpatrick boat, the CE.4 petrol-engined *Jeanie Speirs* (ON.788), proved that diesel engines outperformed their petrol counterparts. ON.684 could travel at full speed for 118 miles using just under thirty pints of fuel an hour whereas the Portpatrick boat could travel just fifty-seven miles at full speed yet consumed almost sixty-five pints an hour. The difference in consumption at cruising speed was even greater. These trials concluded in 1936 as the first lifeboat built with a diesel engine, *S. G. E.* (ON.787) destined for Yarmouth, was completed. Unfortunately, *S. G. E.* was destroyed by fire at Groves & Guttridge boatyard at Cowes in June 1937 after less than a year of service but in that time she had proved that diesel engines represented the future for lifeboat power.

By the outbreak of World War II, almost the whole of the fleet had been motorised and just fifteen pulling and sailing boats remained in service. But even with motor lifeboats, lifeboat crews were severely tested by the events of the conflict. They were forced to operate in conditions more hazardous than ever and even routine services were more difficult than in peacetime. But during the course of the war, some of the most outstanding rescues and courageous acts ever performed by lifeboat coxswains and crews

The prototype Ramsgate lifeboat, Prudential *(ON.697), at Ramsgate, the station after which the class was named, where she served for almost thirty years. See table 8/1. (From an old postcard in the author's collection)*

51ft Barnett Mary Stanford *(ON.733) in the harbour at Ballycotton with the crew led by Coxswain Patrick Sliney who rescued the survivors from the Daunt Rock lightvessel in 1936. See table 10/7. (Supplied by Brendan O'Driscoll)*

35ft 6in Liverpool Oldham IV *(ON.894) built for Hoylake in 1952. She was a typical non-self-righting motor lifeboat for carriage launching. Crews at some stations preferred the non-self-righting types to the less stable but self-righting boats. See table 13/1. (From a postcard in the author's collection)*

46ft Watson cabin motor Julia Park Barry of Glasgow *(ON.819) which served at Peterhead from 1939 to 1969. The 46ft Watsons were one of the most numerous lifeboat classes built and many variations of the type were produced. See table 19/16. (RNLI)*

took place with nobody more courageous than the coxswain of the Cromer lifeboat, Henry Blogg. In the Cromer lifeboat, the 46ft Watson motor *H. F. Bailey* (ON.777), he helped to save many lives on numerous occasions during some daring rescues.

One of the most extraordinary was that to six vessels forming part of Convoy 559 which went ashore on the Haisborough Sands on 5 August 1941 in a severe gale and heavy seas. The Cromer lifeboat launched at 8am on 6 August with Blogg at the helm and found the vessels close together but breaking up rapidly. In a series of daring manoeuvres, the lifeboat was taken alongside or, in some cases, driven over the decks of the ships to save those on board. In total eighty-eight lives were rescued during what was later described as 'one of the finest feats of seamanship . . . ever seen'. When *H. F. Bailey* returned, she was found to be severely damaged having been driven over sunken decks, bumped severely on the sands, and at one point run aground, with three holes punched in her bow. Much of her port fender had been torn off and her stem had been damaged, but she survived as the strength of the Watson

motor lifeboat contributed to the rescue's successful outcome. Blogg was awarded the Gold medal for this service, his third such award, with Silver and Bronze medals to the rest of the crew.

As well as Blogg, many other lifeboatmen carried out remarkable rescues during the war including Coxswain Robert Cross of the Humber lifeboat station on Spurn Point. On 7 January 1943, he was in command of the lifeboat *City of Bradford II* (ON.709), a 45ft 6in Watson motor, when she went to HM trawler *Almondine* which was stranded on a sandbank, lying on her side, and being swept by heavy seas. The lifeboat was taken alongside the casualty twelve times and nineteen men were rescued. Several times the lifeboat was smashed against the hull of the trawler, causing her stem to be splintered and some planking to be holed. But she survived her ordeal and made it back to station to land the survivors. For this service, made possible only by fine seamanship and great determination, the Gold medal was awarded to Cross, the Silver medal to Reserve Mechanic George Richards and Bronze medals to five other members of the crew

Rebuilding after World War II

Although many gallant rescues were performed during World War II, lifeboat construction and development effectively ceased. Therefore, after 1945, new lifeboats were needed urgently. Embarking on an ambitious building programme for new boats, all of which had twin engines and twin propellers, the RNLI shared the optimism for a better and brighter future that swept the nation in the immediate post-War years. New motor boats were soon completed and entered service, with the pulling and sailing lifeboat phased out completely during the 1950s.

As far as technical advances were concerned, the introduction of midship steering, fully enclosed cockpits and commercial diesel engines were the most significant. Midship steering was first proposed during the early years of the war. In the April 1940 edition of *The Lifeboat*, Barnett announced his ideas for the next stage in lifeboat development by noting that, as future lifeboats would be built with twin engines, sails were no longer necessary. As long as sails were required, the coxswain had to steer from aft to keep an eye on them but without sails Barnett believed 'the proper place for the steersman in a power vessel . . . is amidships. He would have a much better view not only forward, but all round, and that position is much better for controlling his crew.' Barnett designed a 46ft lifeboat which embodied this new feature. A cockpit forward

of the engines was provided for the wheel, just forward of which sat the mechanic with the instrument panels under a shelter. Instead of a cabin below deck, a large cockpit and shelter was provided aft, with room beneath the shelter for at least two stretchers.

Although the design was never built owing to the outbreak of war, Barnett's ideas were not wasted but employed in many of the larger boats designed after the war. The 46ft 9in Watson was the first new post-war lifeboat type and, fitted with twin 40bhp four-cylinder diesel engines, was the first to be diesel-powered. Boats of this class built after 1948 all had midship steering. The next Watson type, slightly larger at 47ft, also had midship steering as did the 52ft Barnett type, first built in 1950. Subsequently, the cockpit on these designs was enclosed so as to provide a degree of shelter for crew and survivors.

The use of diesel engines became widespread after the war. Not only were they more economic, but diesel was less flammable than petrol so its use reduced the risk of fire. The first boats to be diesel-powered before the war were the 46ft Watsons, fitted with twin 40hp Ferry diesels, and 46ft 9in Watsons and 52ft Barnetts after the war. These large lifeboats were powered by what were basically modified bus engines weighing almost a ton. Such size and weight was unsuitable for the smaller classes of lifeboat and a more suitable lightweight diesel engine was required. Various units were assessed in the late 1940s, including the Admiralty Coventry Kadenacy four-cylinder supercharged two-stroke engine, which was made watertight and manufactured in a three-cylinder version to suit RNLI requirements, developing 20hp at 1,600rpm. The Ferry Kadenacy FKR.3 engine was also used, first fitted in the Rhyl lifeboat *Anthony Robert Marshall* (ON.869) of 1949. It proved to be a reliable engine and more than twenty other lifeboats were subsequently fitted with similar units.

Another advantage of the diesel engine over its petrol counterpart was its relatively cheap construction cost. The petrol engines had largely been bespoke units specifically designed for use in the lifeboat in which they were fitted. Such specialised manufacturing was, inevitably, extremely expensive, so in 1950 the RNLI considered using commercial engines. Adopting an engine in daily use in the commercial world, which was made in a range of power and cylinders, with standard parts easily obtainable, and proven reliability had considerable appeal. So, in 1954, for the first time a commercial diesel engine was fitted to a new lifeboat with the new 42ft Watson for Coverack, *William Taylor of Oldham* (ON.907), built with 48hp Gardner 4LW diesel engines. A similar boat was later sent to Troon and all 42ft, 47ft and 52ft boats were then fitted with Gardner engines of varying power that proved to be ideal for lifeboat work.

The success of the Gardner diesels during the 1950s resulted in a major re-engining programme after it had been determined that re-engining existing petrol-driven lifeboats would be both possible and beneficial. Trials were undertaken with the 1939-built 41ft Watson motor *Matthew Simpson* (ON.823) from Port Erin which, in 1961, was fitted with twin 47hp Ford Parsons Porbeagle diesels, more powerful than the petrol engines provided when built. The diesel engines increased the boat's maximum speed from 8.12 to 8.57 knots and the radius of action from sixty-four to ninety-four miles. The success of *Matthew Simpson's* trials led the RNLI's Superintendent Engineer, Cmdr. R. A. Gould, to conclude: 'there is now no room for doubt that the policy of fitting commercial diesel engines has been a momentous and outstanding success and will result in a marked financial saving in running and upkeep.'

Several other modifications were introduced to new lifeboats during the 1950s which, although relatively minor, were nevertheless important. They included stainless steel propeller shafts and water-cooled side exhausts in place of stern exhausts,

while equipment carried on board also became more sophisticated. Wireless had first been introduced in the 1920s and increasingly advanced radio transmitters had been employed ever since. Other electronic equipment, such as echo sounders, was also used for the first time in the 1950s and the first radar was fitted in 1963 to the 48ft Oakley *Earl and Countess Howe* (ON.968).

The next major advance came in the mid-1950s. Despite the many improvements in design and advances in equipment, lifeboats were still failing to cope in the worst of conditions and, more importantly, lifeboat men were losing their lives as a result. In April 1947, catastrophe overtook the Mumbles lifeboat *Edward, Prince of Wales* (ON.678), a 45ft Watson type, when she went to the aid of the steamship *Santampa*. The ship was on the rocks at Sker Point and, in trying to approach in heavy surf, the lifeboat overturned and her entire crew was lost. In February 1953, the lifeboat at Fraserburgh on Scotland's north-east coast, *John and Charles Kennedy* (ON.790), was overwhelmed and capsized close to the harbour entrance, with the loss of six of her seven crew. Further capsizes occurred at Bridlington in 1952, Arbroath in 1953 and Scarborough in 1954, all with fatal consequences. And in November 1962, the 35ft 6in Liverpool type non-self-righting lifeboat at Seaham Harbour capsized only thirty feet from the harbour pier, resulting in the loss of five of her crew.

As a result of the tragedies, the RNLI reviewed its policy on self-righting lifeboats and made increased efforts to find a design of lifeboat with a self-righting ability. The situation that existed in the 1950s was the result of a combination of historical preferences and an inability to overcome the problem of designing a self-righting lifeboat that was as stable as a non-self-righting boat. Crews wanted stable, seaworthy lifeboats with a high degree of lateral stability. This was provided by the Watson and Barnett motor lifeboats, based on Watson's non-self-righting hull design of the 1890s. But designing such a boat that would also self-right if capsized had challenged naval architects for well over a century and the problem remained unsolved. In seeking an answer to the challenge, Richard Oakley, the RNLI's Consulting Naval Architect, designed a 37ft lifeboat that employed a system of water ballast transfer which would right the boat in the event of a capsize. Although the use of water ballast tanks had originally been intended just to provide extra ballast for the relatively light carriage-launched type, his design, the 37ft Oakley which entered service in 1958, became the first lifeboat with a high degree of

The first 42ft Watson motor to be built, William Taylor of Oldham (ON.907), before the addition of her wheelhouse. She was the first lifeboat to be built with commercially-developed twin diesel engines which were tested during extensive trials around the coasts of the UK. She remained in service for more than thirty years. See table 22/1. (From a photo supplied by Jeff Morris)

Field Marshall and Mrs Smuts (ON.846), the second of two 46ft Watsons completed in 1945 and 1946 with midship steering. They were the first motor lifeboats with this feature, and served at Cromer and Beaumaris. During the late 1940s, a slightly larger Watson design, 46ft 9in in length, was introduced and later examples of this type had the cockpit amidships. See table 19/28.

52ft Barnett Ramsay-Dyce *(ON.944) was one of the last of the large non-self-righting lifeboats to be built. During the course of her service career, she was fitted with a self-righting air-bag. See table 21/16. (RNLI)*

47ft Watson Margaret *(ON.947) as built with no radar or air-bag. The 47ft Watson was the last design of displacement non-self-righting lifeboat. See table 23/3. (From an old postcard in the author's collection)*

inherent stability yet which was also self-righting.

But although a new self-righting design was available, and the water ballast principle was subsequently applied to a larger 48ft type, existing non-self-righting lifeboats remained vulnerable and tragically further capsizes occurred. At Longhope and Fraserburgh in 1969 and 1970 respectively, non-self-righting lifeboats capsized in very heavy seas with heavy loss of life. The entire crew of eight from the Longhope boat was lost, while at Fraserburgh the 1970 capsize was the station's second lifeboat disaster in less than two decades. The change to self-righting lifeboats became more urgent and the disasters prompted the RNLI to find a way to provide Watson and Barnett lifeboats with a self-righting capability. An air-bag system was therefore developed by RNLI designers working in conjunction with technicians from the British Hovercraft Corporation. Fitted on the aft cabin, the air-bag automatically inflated if the boat rolled over more than 100 degrees and acted as a giant buoyancy chamber to right the boat. Having solved the problem of self-righting, the RNLI declared that the entire fleet of offshore lifeboats would be entirely self-righting by 1980. All subsequent lifeboat designs have been inherently self-righting and since 1982 no lifeboat crewmembers have been lost on service.

The new self-righting lifeboats in the fleet proved their worth during the 1970s and 1980s when several capsized on service but righted successfully. Only once was a life lost when the 37ft Oakley at Kilmore Quay, *Lady Murphy* (ON.997), capsized and righted twice on service on 24 December 1977 during a search of

Bannow Bay. When she righted herself after the second capsize, four crew members had been washed overboard. Three were recovered, but the fourth, Finton Sinnott, was not found despite a thorough search. Although one life had tragically been lost, the self-righting system saved the rest of the crew.

The fitting of air-bags to the larger Watsons and Barnetts also saved lives on two other occasions. Firstly, in November 1979, the Barra Island lifeboat *R. A. Colby Cubbin No.3* (ON.935) capsized on service and was righted by her air-bag. Secondly, less than four years later, on 10 April 1983, Salcombe lifeboat *The Baltic Exchange* (ON.964) capsized in heavy seas. She had put out in a force nine southerly gale and forced her way through solid water at the harbour entrance. However, she cleared this and set course for the southern end of Start Bay where it was reported two divers were hanging on to their upturned boat. The gale force nine winds, at times gusting to force eleven, caused the lifeboat to roll heavily. The lifeboat crew eventually sighted the casualty but as the lifeboat approached, a huge breaking wave about fifty feet high hit her port quarter. She rolled heavily to starboard and one crew member, who was attaching his lifeline, was washed overboard. The lifeboat righted herself from that knockdown but a second enormous wave then struck her and she capsized while travelling at full speed. As the lifeboat heeled beyond the point of no return, the air-bag inflated automatically and righted the boat. The excess water drained away and all of the crew, except the one washed overboard who saw the capsize from the water, were found to be

52ft Barnett R. A. Colby Cubbin No.3 *(ON.935) from Barra Island with air bag inflated after capsizing in November 1979. The air-bag deployed successfully and almost certainly saved the lives of the crew. See table 21/11. (RNLI)*

The 37ft Oakley Ernest Tom Neathercoat *(ON.982) on her launching carriage outside the lifeboat house at Wells. The 37ft Oakley was the first lifeboat design to be both self-righting and inherently stable. See table 24/15. (Paul Russell)*

safe. The crewman in the water was recovered and the lifeboat sheltered under the lee of Start Point. The divers were eventually recovered by helicopter and *The Baltic Exchange* made for Brixham, being escorted part of the way by the Torbay lifeboat. The air-bag system proved its worth during these two incidents and with no lives lost in either showed the importance of having lifeboats with a self-righting capability.

The quest for speed

During the 1960s, the RNLI began to introduce faster all-weather lifeboats starting with a 44ft steel-hulled self-righting type purchased from the United States Coast Guard for trials around Britain, was a giant step forward for the RNLI. For the first time, the Institution had acquired a design not conceived by its own designers and showed faith in radical ideas for a rescue craft rather than the tried and trusted technology of post-war Britain. This boat, self-righting by virtue of its watertight cabins, was faster – at about fifteen knots – than conventional displacement-hulled lifeboats then in service and completely different from traditional British lifeboat designs. The US boat, numbered 44-001 by the RNLI, went around the British Isles visiting lifeboat stations so that crews' opinions of the new design could be gauged. The reaction of lifeboat crews who saw the boat at first hand was so positive that a building programme was soon embarked upon. Given the class name Waveney, the design was the first of the modern generation of 'fast' lifeboats.

The British-built Waveneys entered service in 1967, the first at Dun Laoghaire to cover Dublin Bay and the busy approaches to Dublin port, and the second at Great Yarmouth & Gorleston in Norfolk. The Gorleston boat *Khami* (ON.1002) had an outstanding career of more than two decades and was involved in several medal winning services. The first took place on 9 November 1969 when she was launched under the command of Coxswain/Mechanic John Bryan to the Danish motor vessel *Karen Bravo*, which was listing in gale force winds and rough seas. The lifeboat endured a very rough passage until she reached the casualty, which was pitching heavily with big seas breaking over her. In taking five people off, Coxswain Bryan placed the lifeboat's port bow alongside seven times, each time synchronising the lifeboat's movements with the heavy seas to reduce the distance the men would have to jump, while keeping clear of the ship's thrashing propellers. Once the five had been taken off, the lifeboat stood by until, about midnight, the two vessels began to make for Gorleston harbour, reaching port in the early hours of 10 November. For outstanding seamanship, Bryan was awarded the Bronze medal and the Thanks of the Institution on Vellum was accorded to the other members of the crew.

The Waveney was a highly successful design and boats of the class were well liked at the stations from where they operated. Its introduction marked a breakthrough with, for the first time, the Institution looking overseas for a design of lifeboat and showing a willingness to employ the latest technology. Previously, a more cautious approach had been made to lifeboat development, with new technology shunned in favour of equipment that was thoroughly tried, tested and proven. The Waveney, however, proved that cutting-edge technology could be beneficial and that fast boats' sea-keeping qualities were good enough to consider for sea rescue. In the interests of greater speed, the RNLI was prepared to forego the heavy iron keels and twin propeller tunnels used hitherto in motor lifeboat designs. RNLI staff began to look at a larger and faster lifeboat in the late 1960s as speedier craft became necessary to meet changing demands placed on the lifeboat service by an increasing number of services to pleasure craft. The faster the lifeboat, the quicker a casualty can be reached, reducing the chances of a situation deteriorating and making a rescue more difficult.

The result of the RNLI's planning was a new 52ft type, the Arun class, which has since proved to be one of the finest lifeboat types ever developed. Capable of between eighteen and twenty knots, the Arun represented a new direction for lifeboat design. It had a fully enclosed wheelhouse for rescuers and rescued, a flared bow to protect deck and wheelhouse from spray, a broad beam for stability and a flying bridge provided an outside steering position with good visibility. Another advance was the hull material. Although the first three boats were constructed from cold-moulded wood, the fourth boat was built in glass reinforced plastic (GRP), a material which the RNLI had considered but rejected previously, but now decided it was suitable for lifeboat work. Its advantages were its strength and economy of build, as a mould could be used to manufacture identical hulls at a time when wooden and steel-hulled boats were becoming increasingly expensive.

The Aruns, of which forty-six were built, with a fantastic boat. Many outstanding rescues were performed using them, none more so than that in December 1981 by the St Peter Port lifeboat *Sir*

44ft Waveney Khami *(ON.1002) at Great Yarmouth & Gorleston, where she was involved in several outstanding services. The steel-hulled Waveney was the first of the RNLI's fast all-weather types. See table 29/3. (John Markham)*

52ft Arun Elizabeth Ann *(ON.1058) at sea off Falmouth. The Arun was a revolutionary design when first introduced and proved to be one of the most successful lifeboat types ever built for RNLI service. (Paul Richards)*

William Arnold (ON.1025), the second Arun to be built. On 13 December, she launched to the Ecuadorian motor vessel *Bonita* which was in distress in the English Channel. St Peter Port crew had carefully checked the boat in readiness for a prolonged service in heavy weather before the moorings were slipped and she set out at full speed into storm force ten winds, gusting to hurricane force twelve. The sea was extremely rough and during the passage the lifeboat broached six times but full speed was maintained throughout. At 4.30pm, she arrived on scene with the wind still force eleven and the violent storm creating fifteen metre seas. She stood by as five people were lifted off by helicopter, but when subsequent rescue attempts failed the lifeboat took over.

Sir William Arnold, under the command of Coxswain Michael Scales, spent three and half hours making a variety of approaches through floating wreckage to rescue twenty-nine people, with one man drowning. During the approaches, the lifeboat was rising level with *Bonita's* afterdeck on each crest and falling below the bottom edge of her rudder in the troughs, a distance of fifty feet. The first three men to jump to the lifeboat fell twenty-five feet to the deck and one was badly injured. In confused seas at the stern of the casualty, and despite the risk of severe damage, the lifeboat then rescued survivors using a heaving line. During one violent astern manoeuvre first one engine, then the other, failed. Although both were restarted quickly, the bow of the lifeboat was trapped under *Bonita's* transom until the lifeboat's engines pulled her clear. Out of an estimated total of fifty runs in to the casualty, ten were made to take off one man.

When no more could be done to help, Coxswain Scales set course for Brixham and the passage heading into a force ten to eleven winds and heavy seas was an extremely arduous one. Speed was reduced to make the best possible progress while preventing further injury to the survivors. The lifeboat arrived at Brixham where the crew, now completely exhausted, spent the night before returning home the following day, with only minimal damage to the lifeboat. For this outstanding service the Gold medal for conspicuous gallantry was awarded to Coxswain Scales and Bronze medals went to each of his crew. This was one of many medal-winning rescues undertaken in Arun lifeboats which proved to be such good boats that several went overseas to continue as lifeboats after their RNLI careers had come to an end.

The Inshore Lifeboat

While huge strides had been made in offshore lifeboat provision during the 1960s, a new type of lifeboat joined the RNLI's fleet at the same time. The inshore rescue boat, later designated the inshore lifeboat (ILB), was first introduced in 1963 and has since become an integral part of the lifeboat service with ever more sophisticated ILBs developed. The early ILBs were rather rudimentary inflatable boats with outboard engines. They could be launched quickly and were ideally suited for work inshore helping people cut off by the tide, stranded on rocks or adrift in small inflatables blown out to sea. They were soon improved and more equipment was added including VHF radio, flexible fuel tanks, flares, an anchor, a spare propeller and first aid kit. The ILB's advantage over the conventional lifeboat was its speed which, at twenty knots, was considerably faster than any lifeboat in service during the 1960s. Although the design has been improved considerably during the forty years ILBs have been in service, the basic tenet has remained the same and the latest ILBs are still easy to launch and ideal for inshore work.

Atlantic 75 Giles *(B-726) launching down the slipway at Porthcawl. The Atlantic design has become one of the mainstays of the modern lifeboat fleet and been used to effect some notable rescues. See table B. (Nicholas Leach)*

To supplement the 16ft inflatable inshore lifeboat, larger and more capable ILBs have been developed, including rigid-hulled craft 18ft in length and twin-engined inflatables, most notably the Atlantic 21 rigid-inflatable. The Atlantic has become one of the most successful designs of lifeboat ever and, since its development at Atlantic College in the late 1960s, has been involved in some outstanding rescues. The idea behind its development was an improvement on the basic inflatable ILB. A boat with greater speed, crew comfort and general capabilities was needed and fitting sponsons to a rigid hull provided an excellent rescue boat. A larger and faster version, the Atlantic 75, was introduced in the 1990s, and in 2005 the even larger Atlantic 85 entered the RNLI's fleet. Many fine rescues have been undertaken in Atlantic ILBs, none more so than that on 24 August 2004 involving the Porthcawl Atlantic 75 *Giles* (B-726). She launched just after 11am to the fishing vessel *Gower Pride* which, with the skipper and an injured fisherman on board, had suffered engine failure in force eight winds and rough seas.

In the atrocious sea conditions, the Atlantic was brought close enough for the crew to connect a towline and pull the casualty away from the bank. But the tow broke and the boat drifted back to the bank so a second rope was rigged and secured by a crewman who had been transferred to the fishing vessel. At one point, Gower Pride was hit by a large breaking wave on the starboard side and thrown against the lifeboat. The Atlantic was immediately manoeuvred away to avoid being damaged and began the slow tow against high seas which, at times, lifted the lifeboat's bow out of the water. By this time, Mumbles 47ft Tyne lifeboat *Ethel Anne Measures* (ON.1096) was on scene and the tow was transferred to the larger lifeboat. The two lifeboats then completed the passage back to station and safely land the skipper and his injured crewman. For her part in this fine rescue, the Porthcawl helm Aileen Jones was awarded the Bronze medal, becoming the first woman in over a century to be awarded a bravery medal and one of only nineteen other woman in the Institution's history to have received such an award.

Into the twenty-first century

The introduction of the Waveney and Arun 'fast' lifeboats in the 1960s and 1970s marked the beginning of the modernisation of the lifeboat fleet, and during the 1980s and 1990s the quest for faster and safer lifeboats continued. In the early 1980s, a large rigid-inflatable design was developed, the Medina, but never entered operational service, while a smaller 33ft type, the Brede, was conceived from a successful commercial GRP hull form. Only twelve Bredes were completed and the design, which was regarded as an intermediate type with operational limitations, was something of an anomaly in the fleet.

Following the Medina and Brede, two other new lifeboat types were developed: the 47ft Tyne for slipway launching and the 12m Mersey for carriage launching, and both have proved extremely successful. As with the Arun, both new types incorporated some notable technological advances. The Tyne, with propellers housed in partial tunnels and bilge keels, was built of steel with an aluminium alloy deck and wheelhouse. Steel had first been used in steam lifeboats in the 1890s, and again when the Clyde class cruising lifeboat was developed during the 1960s. The 44ft design acquired from the USCG, which became the Waveney, was also steel-hulled. The Tyne was built from the material because it was considered cost effective and best suited for a boat regularly enduring the stresses of slipway launching and recovery.

The most significant advance with the Mersey design was the hull material. While the first ten boats were built from aluminium, subsequent boats were moulded from fibre reinforced composite (FRC) after the material was thoroughly trialled and tested in a full size prototype boat, *Lifetime Care* (ON.1148). This boat, which subsequently served in the Relief Fleet, proved that advanced composite materials were well suited to lifeboat construction. Not only would FRC withstand the rigours of beach launching, which often involves being dragged over shingle and sand, but boats built from the material were also lighter than those of aluminium. One of the advantages of FRC was that a mould could be built from which a production series could be completed relatively quickly. As the Mersey project called for up to forty boats in service within four years, speed of construction was essential.

Both the Tyne and the Mersey designs had propellers protected by partial tunnels and extended bilge keels. Tunnels for propeller protection had been incorporated in the first motor lifeboats and used in almost every subsequent motor lifeboat design. But where the displacement-hulled boats, such as the Watsons and Barnetts, had their top speed limited by both hull form and tunnels, the Tyne and Mersey designs overcame this with a semi-planing hull and partial tunnels. The protection of propellers has been a factor in lifeboat designs since engines were first used and, although they reduced the effectiveness of the propeller, tunnels have always been seen as the best way to guard the propeller against damage.

While the demand on the RNLI's services increased considerably during the three decades of the twentieth century, the most significant development was the increase in the speed of lifeboats and the reduction in the time taken to reach casualties. In 1986, a target date of 1993 was set by when fast lifeboats would be operating from every station. In December 1993, that goal was achieved when the 12m Mersey *Freddie Cooper* (ON.1193) arrived at Aldeburgh to complete the network of fast lifeboats. As faster all-weather lifeboats became the norm, in 1990 the RNLI extended its declared area of coverage from thirty to fifty miles offshore with a lifeboat on scene within four hours of launching. The change from slow displacement to fast semi-planing lifeboats is a significant development and the ability to go to the aid of casualties fifty miles offshore would have been inconceivable to the crews of either the pulling lifeboats or the early motor craft.

But even in the 1990s, when Aruns, Tynes and Merseys made up the all-weather lifeboat fleet, the RNLI did not stand still and during the decade a new generation of even faster lifeboats was developed. The Trent and Severn types, to replace the Aruns and Waveneys which were reaching the end of their operational lives, entered service in 1992. The new types, with a speed of twenty-five knots, were built of FRC and had twin propellers protected by extended bilge keels. The Trent, at 14m in length, was the smaller of the two, while the 17m Severn was heavier and its long range made it ideal for operations at the more remote lifeboat stations, such as those on the west coast of both Scotland and Ireland.

One of the first 17m Severns to go on station was allocated to Lerwick, in Shetland. She arrived in early June 1997, was officially named *Michael and Jane Vernon* (ON.1221) on 19 July that year and four months later, on 19 November, was involved in a truly outstanding rescue. The refrigerated cargo vessel *Green Lily* was in difficulty fifteen miles south-east of the town in horrendous conditions. Tugs tried to help the crippled vessel, but in the heavy weather all tow lines parted. At 1.10pm, the lifeboat, with the crew

The first FRC lifeboat, Lifetime Care *(ON.1148), at the RNLI Depot, Poole. The hull form is clear from this photo, with the keel and bilge keels forming partial tunnels to protect the propellers. See table 36/4. (Nicholas Leach)*

47ft Tyne Phil Mead *(ON.1110) setting out from her Teesmouth station. The self-righting air-bags on the aft cabin were fitted in 2004 after doubts about the inherent righting ability of the Tyne class. See table 35/8. (Nicholas Leach)*

Guardians of Dublin Bay: 14m Trents from Howth (left) and Dun Laoghaire, Roy Barker III (ON.1258) and Anna Livia (ON.1200), exercise off the Baily lighthouse. The Trent was one of two designs developed during the 1990s for operation at stations where the lifeboat is kept afloat. See table 38/5 and 38/33. (Nicholas Leach)

strapped into their seats and Coxswain/Mechanic Hewitt Clark in command, set off into the mountainous seas to assist. Although the Coastguard helicopter reached the crippled cargo vessel, it was unable to winch anyone off due to the casualty's violent motion. When the lifeboat arrived on scene at 1.50pm, *Green Lily* was just over a mile from the shore as further attempts to tow her to safety failed and she was slowly but surely being blown ashore.

As the vessel was still rolling too violently for the helicopter to winch the crew off, and huge waves were repeatedly sweeping her, Coxswain Clark decided he had to go alongside even though the vessel was only 900 yards offshore in just 100 fathoms of water. To gain a lee, the lifeboat had to go to the vessel's port side between the ship and the rocks leaving little sea room. With Coxswain Clark and Second Coxswain Richard Simpson on the lifeboat's flying bridge and the other lifeboatmen on the open deck ready to help survivors aboard, the lifeboat was skilfully taken to within thirty feet of the casualty. Operating at the very limits of her capabilities, she was manoeuvred towards the vessel again and again so that the survivors, when the two vessels were level, could be pulled to safety. Every time the lifeboat went alongside, she was slammed hard against the vessel's side and often had to be pulled clear at the very last moment to avoid serious damage.

As *Green Lily* was getting closer to the shoreline forcing the lifeboat to operate in less and less sea room, the tug *Maersk Champion* managed to grapple her anchor-cable and tow the ship into the wind. The lifeboatmen had rescued five men but ten more were still on board. However, with the vessel now lying head-to-

Lerwick lifeboat Michael and Jane Vernon (ON.1221) approaching the cargo vessel Green Lily's port rail to save the casualty's crew. This still image was taken from a video shot by the Coastguard helicopter. See table 37/10. (RNLI)

wind, the helicopter was able to save the remaining ten men while the lifeboat stood by. Sadly, during the helicopter's rescue mission, winchman Bill Deacon, who had been lowered onto the casualty's deck, was swept overboard by an exceptionally large wave. Despite a thorough search that continued until the light faded, he was not found. *Green Lily* went aground in the appalling conditions and was eventually smashed to pieces. Coxswain Clark was unable to get the lifeboat close to her again with the mass of cargo debris, added to the already violent seas, raising safety concerns for his own crew. For this extraordinary rescue Coxswain Clark was awarded the Gold medal and Bronze medals went to the five crew. Amazingly, despite being pounded alongside the cargo ship, *Michael and Jane Vernon* suffered only superficial damage and all her equipment functioned perfectly throughout the service, testimony to the Severn's design, the fibre reinforced composite hull and the high standard of her construction.

The Severn and Trent building programmes continued until 2005 by when forty-six and thirty-eight boats respectively of each class had been completed. By then, the Tamar class, the next design of twenty-five knot lifeboat, was almost ready for service. Built to replace the 47ft Tynes and be slipway launched, the Tamar incorporated some significant technological advances including an integrated computer system to control all the boat's functions, special load-bearing seats for the crew and a small inflatable boat launched from the stern. As the Tamar build programme got underway, another new design, for a carriage-launched boat 13.7m in length, was being developed to replace the 12m Mersey. The protoype of this new design, ON.1285, was fitted out by VT Halmatic at Porchester during 2005 and fitted with two Hamilton waterjets driven by twin 510hp CAT C9 diesels to become the RNLI's first all-weather lifeboat to be powered by waterjets.

In addition to the development of new all-weather types, at the start of the twenty-first century the RNLI examined new areas of life-saving and introduced specialised rescue craft in areas never previously covered. Hovercraft were provided to work in places inaccessible by boat. RNLI rescue craft were also placed on various inland waters, while new stations were established on the Thames operating commercially developed jet-powered craft. So, a century after taking the first tentative steps to introduce motor power to the lifeboat fleet, the RNLI continues to develop new ways of saving lives at sea while at the same time refining and improving the motor lifeboat to ensure that its volunteer lifeboat crews have the best and safest tool with which to carry out rescue work.

Part 2
Motor lifeboats of the RNLI

Completed in 1922, 40ft motor self-righter V. C. S. *(ON.675) on her launching trolley on the slipway outside the lifeboat house at Appledore. This photo was taken in 1925 to mark the centenary of the Appledore lifeboat station with* V. C. S. *the first motor lifeboat to serve there. See table 4/12. (From an old postcard in the author's collection)*

47ft Watson motor Frederick Edward Crick *(ON.971) leaving Gorleston to head back to her Lowestoft station. The 47ft Watson was the culmination of more than half a century of Watson motor lifeboat design. See table 23/17. (By courtesy of K. W. Kent)*

Hayling Island inshore lifeboats Atlantic 75 Betty Battle *(B-712) and D class inflatable* Amanda, James and Ben *(D-642) on exercise. An increasing number of stations now operate two inshore lifeboats in this combination. See tables B and D. (Nicholas Leach)*

ON stands for official number, a sequential number given to all RNLI motor lifeboats. Since the 1960s, motor lifeboats have also had an operational number, made up of a prefix denoting length and the number of the boat within its class. In the engine column (p) indicates petrol and (d) indicates diesel.

1 • Self-righting motor

Introduced 1904, last built 1920, seven built including three conversions.

The first experiments with motor power took place in 1904, when the Folkestone lifeboat *J. McConnell Hussey* (ON.343) was taken out of service and fitted with a petrol engine at Guy's Yard, Cowes, IOW. The success of this conversion, and those that were subsequently carried out, pointed the way to future motor lifeboat development. The first three lifeboats converted to motor, ON.343, ON.350 and ON.407, were all self-righters, as listed below, and were basically of the same design as pulling and sailing self-righters, albeit slightly larger than the standard version used extensively throughout the nineteenth century, which was 34ft in length and had been operated since the 1850s.

While the dimensions of the early motor self-righters varied, their hull design and deck layout were based on the ideas of the nineteenth century with the design innovations focused on the engines. The challenge was to make the motor lifeboat a reality, and the problems faced by the engineers in getting a powered lifeboat to be reliable and efficient took precedence over altering or improving the basic hull design. The motor self-righters were therefore open boats, as their pulling predecessors had been, and carried sails to be used in the event of an engine failure. They had heavy keels and were also fitted with drop keels, making them in effect sailing and motor lifeboats. World War I interrupted further development of the motor lifeboat. Then, during the inter-war years, a standard motor 40ft self-righter was developed (see table 4) superseding the 38ft and 42ft boats which were essentially experimental motor lifeboats. During the trials of the converted boats, all self-righted as intended after the fitting of an engine, and this ability was never in doubt, and in fact none of them ever

One of the few lifeboats built during World War I, 42ft self-righter motor Lady Rothes *(ON.641) is launched down the slipway at Fraserburgh. (From an old postcard in the author's collection)*

capsized on service. The problems almost always centred around the reliability and performance of the engine.

During the construction of the boat for Stromness, *John A. Hay* (ON.561), the first purpose-built motor self-righter, much use was made of experience gained from the screw-driven steam lifeboats. As with these craft, the propeller for the new motor lifeboat was housed in a protective shaft tunnel made from wood with a bronze frame inside. A single drop keel replaced the two which were usual in sailing lifeboats of this type. An ingenious system was devised so that the propeller would be accessible from inside the boat and could thus be easily cleared if fouled. The early self-righting motor lifeboats were all fitted with Tylor engines which gave a good power to weight ratio.

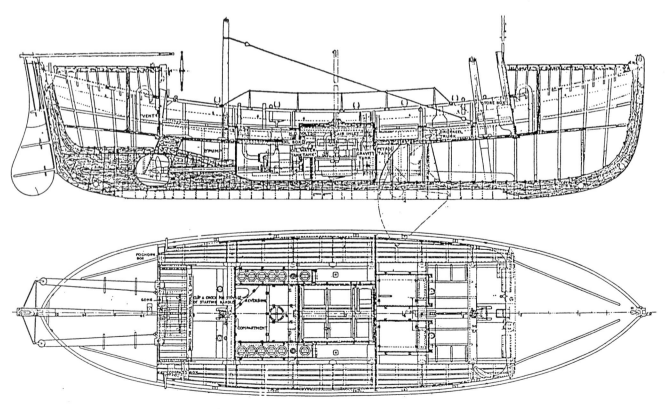

38ft motor self-righter Sir Fitzroy Clayton *(ON.628) which served at Newhaven. The high end boxes and narrow beam were typical features of the SR design.*

1 • Self-righting motor

#	Year* (Yd No) Builder Place	Length Breadth Crew	Name Donor	ON Cost Weight	Engines	Stations (launches/lives saved) Disposal
1	1893/1904 (E6) W T Ellis Lowestoft	38' 8' 14	J. McConnell Hussey/ 1905- Reserve 2a Gift Miss Curling, London.	343 £418 5t9	1x11bhp (p) Fay & Bowen 2-cyl (originally 12 oars)	Folkestone 4.12.1893-3.1903 (5/10) Newhaven 16.11.1904-4.05 (0/0) Tynemouth 1.5.1905-11 (9/8) Sunderland 1911-14 (6/3) Sold 1914
2	1893/1906 (W253) Woolfe Shadwell	42' 11' 15	Bradford/ 1905- Reserve No. 2 Bradford Lifeboat Fund.	350 £896 9t	1x40bhp Briton (p)/ 1907- 1x30bhp Tylor 4-cyl (p) (originally 12 oars)	Ramsgate 9.4.1893-1905 (121/53) Harwich 1907 (0/0) Seaton Snook 19.9.1907-09 (0/0) Seaham Harbour No.2 1909-11 (1/0) Teesmouth 16.6.1911-17 (10/12) Sold 1918
3	1897/1906 (TI15) Thames IW Blackwall	37' 9'3" 9	Michael Henry/ Reserve 2b Jewish Scholars Lifeboat Fund.	407 £728 5t19	1x24bhp 4-cyl (p) Thornycroft/ 1913- 1x20hp Gardner (originally 12 oars)	Newhaven 7.12.1897-1905 (16/16) Newhaven 1.1908-30.11.12 (23/89) Dunmore East 12.2.1914-12.19 (3/4) Sold 1919
4	1908 (TK99) Thames IW Blackwall	42' 11'6" 12	John A. Hay Legacy Mr John A. Hay, Cheltenham.	561 £2,995 11t5	1x30bhp (p) Tylor 4-cyl model A	Stromness 15.4.1909-15.2.28 (32/90) Fenit 4.7.1928-8.9.32 (3/0) Sold 1932
5	1912 (TL77) Thames IW Blackwall	38' 9'9" 11/8	Sir Fitzroy Clayton RNLI Funds.	628 £3,081 8t15	1x35bhp (p) Tylor 4-cyl model B	Newhaven 11.1912-5.18 and 14.1.1919-31.8.30 (66/108) Lizard 4.5.1918-1.1919 (2/0) Fleetwood 1.1933-35 (4/4) Sold 23.8.1935
6	1915 (TL92) Thames IW/ Saunders (S6)	42' 11'6" 12/9	Lady Rothes Gift of T. Dyer Edwardes, London.	641 £3,715 11t5	1x40bhp (p) Tylor 4-cyl model C1	Fraserburgh 13.7.1915-9.3.37 (66/65) Sold 22.2.1937
7	1920 (SP72C) Summers & Payne/ Saunders (S31)	38' 9'9" 8	Frederick H. Pilley Gift of Frederick Hounslow Pilley, Upper Norwood, London.	657 £5,592 9t11	1x45bhp (p) Tylor 4-cyl model JB4	Lizard 12.11.1920-2.34 (19/130) Port Askaig 21.3.1934-6.35 (2/0) Fleetwood 8.1935-16.2.39 (12/19) Sold 11.3.1939

* The second date, where applicable, indicates the year the boat was converted to motor.

Fleetwood lifeboat Frederick H. Pilley (ON.657), the last 38ft motor self-righter to be built. Completed in 1920 by Saunders at Cowes, during trials she reached a maximum speed of 7.49 knots and consumed thirty-five pints of petrol an hour. (From an old postcard in the author's collection)

2 · Norfolk & Suffolk motor

Introduced 1906, last built 1925, four built including one conversion.

The non-self-righting Norfolk & Suffolk type was first developed during the early nineteenth century and was similar in many respects to the sailing yawls operated throughout East Anglia. As a sailing lifeboat with a long range, it was intended for service in and around the extensive sandbanks off the coasts of Norfolk and Suffolk, many of which were some distance from the shore. The heavily-built type, with an almost flat bottom, was regarded as ideal for the conditions in the North Sea and was well suited to working in shallow waters close to the outlying sandbanks.

Of the four lifeboats selected to be converted for motor operation during the early experiments with motor power, three were self-righting types of various sizes and one, ON.432, was of the Norfolk & Suffolk type. This first boat was fitted with an early design of engine at Thames Ironworks, Blackwall, and served the Walton & Frinton station with distinction, often going to the Longsand and Kentish Knock sandbanks, proving that a motor was well suited to powering large lifeboats, adding to their effectiveness, although the sails were retained as auxiliary.

The other three Norfolk & Suffolk types were purpose-built as motor lifeboats, and intended for specific stations for which no other motor type was deemed suitable. In none was the propeller housed in a tunnel, a feature regarded as necessary by the RNLI's pioneering motor lifeboat designers, but it was protected by the deadwood at the stern. Fitted with standard engine designs, the boats' maximum speed was in excess of eight knots. The last of the type, ON.691, had a range of 117 miles at her 7.3-knot cruising speed, much greater than the similar-sized Watson types.

The type was something of an anomaly in terms of lifeboat design, and as a result only three were built. They were built as open boats, very similar to their sailing predecessors, but in the course of their careers, rudimentary shelters were added as crew comfort became an issue when the boats were used on services which lasted far longer than those performed by sailing lifeboats.

The second Norfolk & Suffolk motor lifeboat, H. F. Bailey *(ON.670), built for Cromer but stationed at Great Yarmouth & Gorleston for most of her career.*

John and Mary Meiklam of Gladswood *(ON.670) leaving the harbour at Gorleston. This photograph shows the lack of protection for the crew while the small cover for the motor can just be seen amidships. A large number of crew was needed to operate the sails, which were carried as auxiliary to the single engine. A canvas canopy was fitted in about 1927.*

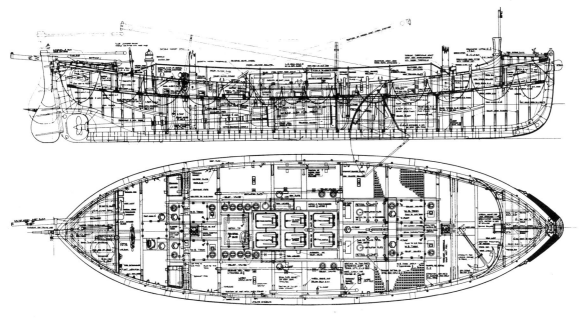

General deck arrangement and profile of 46ft 6in Norfolk & Suffolk motor lifeboat John and Mary Meiklam of Gladswood *(ON.670) which served at Gorleston for most of her career. The N&S design was basically an open boat fitted with an engine, similar in almost every respect to the sailing Norfolk & Suffolk lifeboats used extensively in the counties after which the type was named.*

2 • Norfolk & Suffolk motor

Year (Yd No) Builder Place	Length Breadth Crew	Name Donor	ON Cost Weight	Engines	Stations (launches/lives saved) Disposal
1	1900/1906* (TI32) Thames IW Blackwall	43' 12'6" 13	James Stevens No.14 Legacy of James Stevens, Birmingham.	432 £1,420 10t16	1906- 1x32bhp Blake 4SA 4-cylinder (Originally 12 oars)	Walton-on-the-Naze 5.7.1900-4.7.28 (126/227) Sold 6.1928- £180
2	1921 (S26) S E Saunders Cowes	46'6" 12'9" 15	John and Mary Meiklam of Gladswood/ 1921- Agnes Cross Legacies Miss J. A. Meiklam, Mrs May, and gift of Mrs Moysey/ 1921- Gift of Miss Agnes Cross.	663 £8,620 14t2	1x60hp 4-cyl Tylor D.1 No tunnel	Gorleston 9.2-21.3.1921 (0/0) Lowestoft 31.3.1921-19.10.39 (124/209) Dover 24.10.1940-41 (11/65) Reserve 1939-52 (28/62) Sold 10.1952- £900
3	1923 (W1566) J S White Cowes	46'6" 12'9" 13	H. F. Bailey/ 1924- John and Mary Meiklam of Gladswood Legacy of H. F. Bailey/ 1924- Legacies Miss J. A. Meiklam, Mrs May, and gift Mrs Moysey.	670 £10,993 14t10	1x80bhp 6-cyl Weyburn DE6 No tunnel	Cromer No.1 5.1923-4.5.24 (3/12) Gorleston 5.5.1924-5.39 (155/211) Reserve 1939-52 (49/62) Sold 10.1952- £950
4	1925 (W1608) J S White Cowes	46'6" 12'9" 13	Mary Scott Legacy of Miss M. A. J. Scott, Wanstead.	691 £7,827 17t	1x80bhp 6-cyl White DE6 No tunnel	Southwold 19.6.1925-29.5.40 (30/23) Reserve 5.1940-53 (52/24) Sold 3.1953- £611

* The second date indicates the year the boat was converted to motor.

John and Mary Meiklam of Gladswood (ON.670) pictrued after the canopy had been fitted to improve crew protection. At the time of their construction, the Norfolk & Suffolk lifeboats were the largest motor craft in the RNLI's fleet. (RNLI)

The last Norfolk & Suffolk motor lifeboat to be built was Mary Scott (ON.691), which served at Southwold until that station was closed in 1940. Built as an open lifeboat, she was later fitted with a shelter. After the Southwold station was closed in 1940, she was used in the Reserve fleet for a number of years, covering at stations throughout the country, including Weymouth where she is pictured at moorings in the harbour. (From an old photo from David Hancox, by courtesy of Jeff Morris)

3 • Watson motor 38ft-43ft

Introduced 1908, last built 1930, 15 built.

The early lifeboat designs were based on standard pulling and sailing lifeboat hulls, and the first motorised Watsons were no different. The basic hull shape first laid down by George Lennox Watson at the end of the nineteenth century remained more or less the same in the motor lifeboats which took his name, although the hulls became larger and larger as motive power could of course propel them more efficiently than sails or oars.

However, in the first Watson motor lifeboats efforts were concentrated on ensuring that the engine worked successfully. They therefore remained essentially open boats with the necessary alterations to incorporate a petrol engine, housed in a watertight mahogany box, and its propeller which was protected by a tunnel built into the hull. As all were single-screwed, auxiliary sails were carried, usually in the form of jib, lug and mizzen sails, and oars were also provided.

Of these early Watson motor types, the 40ft version built after 1918 became a semi-standard design of which seven were built. The first 40ft Watsons, ON.560 and ON.565, were two of the RNLI's first purpose-built motor lifeboats and as such were extensively tested. Both were powered by single 40bhp engines which gave them a maximum speed of a little over seven knots.

Elliot Galer, one of a pair of 38ft Watson motor lifeboats built in 1910, at Seaham Harbour where she served for twenty-five years. This photograph was probably taken at the boat's inauguration ceremony and at first glance it is difficult to tell that she is a motor lifeboat. (From an old postcard supplied by Brian Slee)

	Year (Yd No) Builder Place	Length Breadth Crew	Name Donor	ON Cost Weight	Engines	Stations (launches/lives saved) Disposal
1	1908 (TK98) Thames IW Blackwall	40' 11' 12/9	Maria Gift of Miss Maria Clarke, Balham, London.	560 £2,345 10t11	1x40bhp Tylor C 4-cyl (p)	Broughty Ferry 11.10.1910-7.21 (21/14) Portpatrick 8.4.1922-3.12.29 (10/6) Pwllheli 3.3.1930-4.5.31 (0/0) Shoreham Harbour 11.8-13.10.1931 (1/1) Sold 1932
2	1908 (TL.3) Thames IW Blackwall	43' 12'6" 12/9	John Ryburn Legacy of Mr William McCunn, Largs.	565 £3,183 14t2	1x40bhp Blake 4-cyl (p)/ 1914- 1x40bhp Tylor C.1	Stronsay 14.4.1909-15 (11/4) Peterhead No.2 6.10.1915-21.6.20 (21/158) Broughty Ferry 6.1921-2.35 (15/6) Sold 2.1935
3	1910 (TL.38) Thames IW Blackwall	43' 12'6" 12/9	William and Laura Legacy of Miss A. W. Clark Hall, Bournemouth.	595 £4,508 13t6	1x40bhp Blake 4-cyl (p)/ 1914- 1x40bhp Tylor C.1	Donaghadee 1.7.1910-4.6.32 (61/65) Arranmore 7.1932-17.4.35 (2/0) Sold 1935
4	1910 (TL.46) Thames IW Blackwall	38' 10' 10/8	Elliot Galer Legacy of Mr E. Galer.	602 £3,564 7t17	1x34hp Wolseley model 4 (p)	Seaham Harbour 22.4.1911-5.12.36 (26/59) Sold 1936

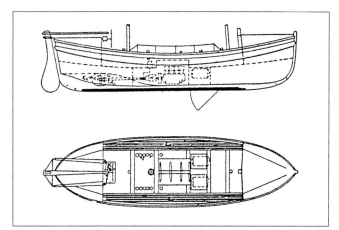

Profile and plan of the early 40ft Watson motor lifeboat from the RNLI's Annual Report showing the type without the engine shelter.

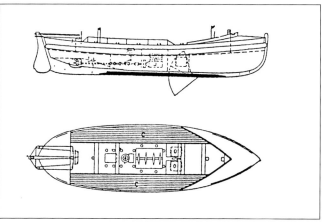

Profile and plan of the 43ft Watson motor lifeboat, of which only five were built, taken from contemporary RNLI publications.

3 · Watson motor 38ft-43ft

Year (Yd No) Builder Place	Length Breadth Crew	Name Donor	ON Cost Weight	Engines	Stations (launches/lives saved) Disposal
5 1910 (TL.47) Thames IW Blackwall	38' 10' 10/8	Helen Smitton Legacy of Mr James Hodge, Greenhays, Manchester.	603 £3,563 7t17	1x34hp Wolseley model 4 (p)	St Abbs 22.4.1911-5.12.36 (27/37) Sold 1936
6 1912 (TL.68) Thames IW Blackwall	43' 12'6" 12/9	William MacPherson Gift of Mrs William MacPherson, Helensburgh.	620 £3,423 14t5	1x60bhp Tylor 4cyl model D (p)	Campbeltown 4.7.1912-4.9.29 (12/29) Aldeburgh 10.2-23.10.1930 (0/0) Pwllheli 4.5.1931-8.40 (16/4) Sold 25.9.1940
7 1913 (TL.69) Thames IW Blackwall	43' 12'6" 12/9	Frederick Kitchen Legacy of Mr F. Kitchen, Carnarvon.	621 £3,727 14t5	1x60bhp Tylor 4cyl model D (p)	Beaumaris 9.7.1914-9.45 (38/46) Shelter fitted 1928 Reserve 1945-48 (3/0) Sold 1948
8 1912 (TL.70) Thames IW Blackwall	43' 12'6" 12/9	Alexander Tulloch Legacy of Miss J. Tulloch.	622 £3,437 14t4	1x60bhp Tylor 4cyl model D (p)	Peterhead No.2 11.12.1912-12.14 (11/28) Wrecked on service 26.12.1914, three lost
9 1918 (S16) S & Payne; S. E. Saunders	40' 11' 12/8	Samuel Oakes Legacy of Mrs E. M. Laing, Barnes.	651 £7,155 10t4	1x40bhp Tylor C2 4-cyl (p)	Spurn Point 11.11.1919-4.11.23 (33/25) Weymouth 14.5.1924-27.7.29 (16/9) Shoreham 8.10.1929-1.33 (11/7) Sold 16.1.1933
10 1922 (W1571) J. S. White Cowes	40' 11' 9	Prince David Welsh Lifeboat Fund.	677 £8,019 11t6	1x45bhp Tylor JB4 4-cyl (p)	Barry Dock 5.9.1922-9.12.37 (29/43) Sold 8.12.1937
11 1922 (W1572) J. S. White Cowes	40' 11' 9	K. B. M. Legacies of William Kirkhope, Charles Baily and Miss Charlotte McInroy.	681 £8,179 11t6	1x45bhp Tylor JB4 4-cyl (p)	Buckie 1.8.1922-25.11.49 (62/12) Reserve 1949-52 (1/0) Sold 24.9.1952
12 1929 (W1673) J. S. White Cowes	40'6" 11'8" 9/8	Lady Kylsant Gift of Royal Mail and Union Castle Steamship Company.	721 £5,865 12t	1x50bhp Weyburn CE4 4-cyl (p)	Weymouth 27.7.1929-6.11.30 (8/9) Howth 8.11.1930-17.1.37 (6/2) Wicklow 27.5.1937-7.6.56 (47/61) Sold 1956
13 1929 (W1674) J. S. White Cowes	40'6" 11'8" 9/8	J. and W. Legacies of Mrs A. Calquhoun and Mrs E. Ashton.	722 £6,052 12t10	1x50bhp Weyburn CE4 4-cyl (p)	Portpatrick 3.12.1929-20.3.37 (14/27) Reserve 1937-40 (6/2) Berwick 2.1940-9.5.57 (50/46) Sold 5.1957
14 1929 (W1675) J. S. White Cowes	40'6" 11'8" 9/8	Sir David Richmond of Glasgow Legacy of Lady Richmond, and gift from Mrs Fairlie.	723 £5,877 12t10	1x50bhp Weyburn CE4 4-cyl (p)	Troon 4.12.1929-19.2.55 (71/101) Sold 6.1956
15 1930 (W1676) J. S. White Cowes	40'6" 11'8" 9/8	G. W. Legacies of Dr T. W. Richards and Mrs E. H. Scott, and the Northampton Lifeboat Fund.	724 £5,886 12t10	1x50bhp Weyburn CE4 4-cyl (p)	Moelfre 15.1.1930-18.4.56 (71/147) Sold 5.1956

One of the four 40ft 6in Watson motor lifeboats to be built, J. and W. *(ON.722), lies at her moorings in Portpatrick harbour, where she served from 1929 to 1937. (From an old postcard supplied by Nicholas Leach)*

4 • Self-righting motor 40ft

Introduced 1908, last built 1928, 14 built

The 40ft motor self-righter, one of the earliest standard motor designs, was conceived as a medium-sized lifeboat primarily for launching down a slipway with the propeller recessed in a protective tunnel. Almost all were operated from slipways or, in one or two instances, from trolleys that ran down slipways.

The hull shape was more or less identical to the pulling and sailing self-righters, with high end boxes at bow and stern to provide the righting ability. Air cases were also fitted at the sides and in the hold area. The single engine was housed in a watertight box amidships and, because it was single-engined, auxiliary sails were carried. The mast was hinged so that it could fold flat when housed. An iron keel was fitted as was a drop keel for use when the boat was being sailed.

The first of the type, ON.563, completed in 1908, was powered by a 24bhp engine, which gave a speed of 6.79 knots and developed 650rpm. Between 1910 and 1918, a further seven boats were built but a slightly more powerful 40bhp Tylor engine was installed and this increased speed to approximately 7.5 knots. In the 1920s, the design was further modified and five 40ft boats were completed in 1922 with more powerful engines as well as a small canopy aft of the engine which contained the engine controls. The engines

The Newbons (ON.674) approaches the slipway at Sennen Cove to be rehoused. This photo shows the deck layout with the engine box, the small shelter aft of amidshps and the high end boxes typical of the SR type.

were all supplied by Tylor, apart from the last boat, but a variety of reverse gears were fitted. The last boat, ON.706, was something of an anomaly as it used the same type of engine then being fitted in the larger 45ft 6in Watsons, making it a one-off. It was built because other slipway-launched types were too large for its intended station, Swanage.

Year (Yd No) Builder Place	Length Breadth Crew	Name Donor	ON Cost Weight	Engines	Stations (launches/lives saved) Disposal
1	1908 (TL1) Thames IW Blackwall	40' 10'6" 12/9	Charterhouse Old and present Carthusians.	563 £2,946 10t17	1x24hp Tylor 4-cyl model A (p)	Fishguard 14.10.1909-8.30 (20/47) Sold 1931
2	1910 (TL54) Thames IW Blackwall	40' 10'6" 12/9	Robert Theophilus Garden Legacy of Mr R. J. Garden, London and Co Clare.	609 £4,015 10t11	1x40hp Tylor 4-cyl model C (p)	Wicklow 24.2.1911-27.5.37 (42/31) Sold 1937
3	1911 (TL58) Thames IW Blackwall	40' 10'6" 12/9	Henry Vernon Legacy of Mrs A. Vernon, Weston-super-Mare.	613 £3,664 10t18	1x40hp Tylor 4-cyl model C (p)	Tynemouth 1911-10.2.18 (26/206) Sunderland 16.2.1918-11.35 (28/64) Sold 1936
4	1911 (TL59) Thames IW Blackwall	40' 10'6" 12/9	General Farrell Legacy of Mrs C. M. Leckie, Walton-on-Thames.	614 £3,003 10t19	1x40hp Tylor 4-cyl model C (p)	St Davids 24.9.1912-3.4.36 (26/17) Sold 1936
5	1914 (TL93/S7) Thames IW/ S. E. Saunders	40' 10'6" 12/9	John Taylor Cardwell Legacy of Mr John T. Cardwell, Ilkley, Yorkshire.	642 £3,599 10t19	1x40hp Tylor 4-cyl model C.1 (p)	Arklow 2.2.1915-14.7.38 (20/20) Sold 1938

40ft SR motor Henry Frederick Swann (ON.646) on the purpose-designed launching trolley outside the lifeboat house at Tynemouth. She was one of several 40ft self-righters to be launched from a trolley on rails.

Alfred and Clara Heath (ON.672) at Salcombe. She was the first of a group of five similar 40ft self-righters built in 1922 and all fitted with 45hp engines. (From an old photo loaned by Jeff Morris).

4 · Self-righting motor 40ft

	Year (Yd No) Builder Place	Length Breadth Crew	Name Donor	ON Cost Weight	Engines	Stations (launches/lives saved) Disposal
6	1917 (S11) S. E. Saunders Cowes	40' 10'6" 12/9	Henry Federick Swann Gift of Mrs Lowe, Bath.	646 £6,901 10t18	1x40hp Tylor 4-cyl model C.2 (p)	Tynemouth 10.2.1918-24.10.39 (28/8) Reserve 1939-41 (0/0) Tynemouth 22.10.1941-11.47 (4/0) Sold 1947
7	1917 (S12) S. E. Saunders Cowes	40' 10'6" 12/9	Ethel Day Cardwell Legacy of Mr John T. Cardwell, Ilkley, Yorkshire.	647 £4,746 10t18	1x40hp Tylor 4-cyl model C.2 (p)	Teesmouth 22.11.1917-13.12.24 (8/29) Port Erin 12.8.1925-17.10.39 (19/4) Reserve 1939-42 (7/0) Sold 1942
8	1918 (S23) S. E. Saunders Cowes	40' 10'6" 12/9	Margaret Harker-Smith Legacy of Miss M. Harker Smith.	667 £5,023 10t18	1x40hp Tylor 4-cyl model C.2 (p)	Whitby 31.5.1919-12.4.38 (117/86) Sold 4.1938
9	1922 (W1574) J. S. White Cowes	40' 10'6" 12/9	Alfred and Clara Heath Legacy of Mr Alfred J. Heath, Putney, London.	672 £8,302 11t6	1x45hp Tylor 4-cyl model JB (p)	Torbay 18.3.1922-23.9.30 (39/37) Salcombe 6.12.1930-5.38 (22/73) Reserve 1938-45 (6/20) Guernsey 6.4.1940-29.8.45 (taken by enemy forces while on reserve duty at St Peter Port) Sold 2.10.1945
10	1922 (W1575) J. S. White Cowes	40' 10'6" 12/9	Jane Holland Legacy of Mr W. H. Clarke, London.	673 £8,202 11t14	1x45hp Tylor 4-cyl model JB (p)	Selsey 20.5.1922-29 (15/11) Eastbourne 27.7.1929-25.6.49 (55/65) Reserve 1949-53 (11/14) Sold 3.1953
11	1922 (W1576) J. S. White Cowes	40' 10'6" 12/9	The Newbons Legacy of Mr R. A. Newbon, Islington, London.	674 £8,622 11t16	1x45hp Tylor 4-cyl model JB (p)	Sennen Cove 1.5.1922-25.7.48 (54/36) Port St Mary 11.11.1949-19.9.50 (1/0) Sold 7.3.1951
12	1922 (W1577) J. S. White Cowes	40' 10'6" 12/9	V. C. S. Legacies of H. J. Vagg, Alfred Sleemin, and Miss L. A. Marshall.	675 £8,162 11t13	1x45hp Tylor 4-cyl model JB (p)	Appledore 2.5.1922-14.8.38 (40/41) Reserve 1938-45 (3/3) Sold 16.9.1945
13	1922 (W1573) J. S. White Cowes	40' 10'6" 12/9	Langham Legacy of Mr T. G. Langham, Maida Vale; gift from his executors.	676 £7,781 11t13	1x45hp Tylor 4-cyl model JB (p)	Bembridge 4.9.1922-24.5.39 (61/62) Reserve 5.1939-11.50 (35/38) Sold 11.1950
14	1928 (S46) S. E. Saunders Cowes	40' 10'6" 12/9	Thomas Markby Legacy of Mrs Gertrude H. Markby, Willesden.	706 £6,559 11t14	1x40hp Weyburn 4-cyl model CE.4 (p)	Swanage 14.6.1928-26.2.49 (67/27) Whitehills 22.5.1949-9.3.52 (5/0) Reserve 3.1952-57 (16/14) Sold 5.1957

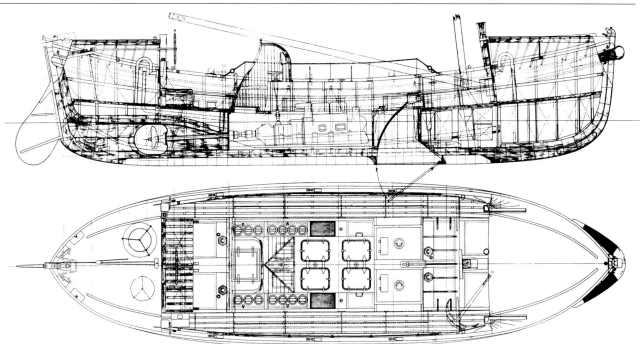

Deck plan and profile of Thomas Markby *(ON.706), from Swanage, which was the last 40ft SRM lifeboat to be built and the only one fitted with a Weyburn engine.*

5 • Watson motor 45ft

Introduced 1912, last built 1925, 22 built.

A non-self-righting design, with a similar hull shape to the Watson sailing and pulling lifeboat, the 45ft Watsons were the largest motor lifeboats built during the 1920s with the exception of the 60ft Barnetts. The early boats in the class were ordered just before the outbreak of war in 1914 and because of the difficulty of obtaining materials during the war period the boats were not completed until 1919. The original 45ft Watsons were open boats with an endbox at each end and a self-draining deck which had little freeboard. A total of eleven boats were built to the open deck design, all of which were single-engined, carried a full sail plan and were fitted with a drop keel. Although good sea boats, they gained a reputation for being very wet and so rudimentary deck shelters were fitted during 1928-9 to provide some shelter.

In 1923, the design was modified and the boats from ON.684 onwards were built with a self-draining cockpit aft and a small cabin forward of the engine room. A total of ten boats were built as part of this cabin series, which was the first class of lifeboat with a shelter to protect crew and survivors. The RNLI recognised the need for shelter on board motor lifeboats as they were able to remain at sea for much longer than sailing lifeboats. The forward cabin was equipped with bench type seats and was capable of accommodating twenty survivors. The 45ft cabin class was fitted with a single type DE engine housed in a watertight compartment, giving a speed of just over eight knots and a range of about 125 miles. The engines were designed by the RNLI: those fitted to ON.685, ON.686, ON.687, ON.694 and ON.695 were built by

Joseph Adlam *(ON.654)* with her mast down. This photo clearly shows the layout of the early 45ft Watson cabin motor lifeboats, with no forward cockpit. The hull shape and design were almost identical to the Watson sailing lifeboats developed during the 1890s. *(RNLI, by courtesy of Jeff Morris)*

J. S. White, and the others were built by Weyburn Engineering Company. A full set of sails was carried and the dropkeel was fitted at the after end of the cabin. Buoyancy was provided by ninety-one air cases which would keep the boat afloat even if every compartment was flooded.

ON.684 was re-engined in 1934 with an 85hp Ferry diesel engine and became the first RNLI lifeboat fitted with a diesel engine. ON.688 and ON.695 were named *Grace Darling* in 1924 and 1925 respectively for the Wembley Exhibition.

	Year (Yd No) Builder Place	Length Breadth Crew	Name Donor	ON Cost Weight	Engines	Stations (launches/lives saved) Disposal
1	1902/1912 (TI70) Thames IW Blackwall	45' 12'6" 12/9	Albert Edward Grand Lodge of Freemasons.	463 £1,890 14t3	(Originally 12 oars) 1x40bhp Tylor 4-cyl C (p)	Clacton 13.12.1901-3.29 (160/277) Arranmore 19.6.1929-7.32 (1/0) Sold 10.1932- £100
2	1919 (S13) S. E. Saunders Cowes	45' 12'6" 12/9	Elsie Gift of Rt Hon Arnold Morley, London.	648 £6,295 15t	1x60bhp Tylor 4-cyl D.1 (p)	St Mary's 16.10.1919-27.3.30 (24/88) Helvick Head 31.3.1930-1.7.46 (16/9) Reserve 1946-51 (12/5) Sold 1.1.1951- £425
3	1919 (S14) S. E. Saunders Cowes	45' 12'6" 12/9	Duke of Connaught/ 1920- Shamrock RNLI Funds.	649 £6,013 15t	1x60bhp Tylor 4-cyl D.1 (p)	Baltimore 20.8.1919-14.5.50 (43/34) Reserve 5.1950-2.52 (1/0) Sold 2.1952
4	1921 (S30) Smrs & Payne/ S. E. Saunders	45' 12'6" 12/9	William Evans Legacy of Mr William Evans, Wolverhampton.	653 £7,730 15t	1x60bhp Tylor 4-cyl D.1 (p)	Wexford 14.8.1921-1.25 (1921-27: 33/80) Rosslare Harbour 1.1925-25.6.27 Galway Bay 2.7.1927-3.39 (24/29) Sold 11.1940- £90
5	1921 (S27) S. E. Saunders Cowes	45' 12'6" 12/9	Joseph Adlam Legacy of Mr Joseph Adlam, Worcester.	654 £7,020 15t	1x60bhp Tylor 4-cyl D.1 (p)	Blyth 4.10.1921-16.3.48 (82/74) Reserve 1948-51 (8/0) Sold 2.1952- £400
6	1919 (S17) S. E. Saunders Cowes	45' 12'6" 12/9	Dunleary (Civil Service No.7) Civil Service Lifeboat Fund.	658 £6,074 15t	1x60bhp Tylor 4-cyl D.1 (p)	Dun Laoghaire 22.12.1919-21.7.38 (23/55) Lytham 1.1939-19.4.51 (58/30) Sold 5.1951- £500
7	1921 (S25) S. E. Saunders Cowes	45' 12'6" 12/9	Frederick and Emma Legacy of Miss E. M. Beer, Selly Park, Birmingham.	659 £7,141 15t	1x60bhp Tylor 4-cyl D.1 (p)	Wick 22.6.1921-4.10.38 (19/37) Amble 13.1.1939-8.6.50 (34/57) Sold 8.1950- £750
8	1921 (S24) S. E. Saunders Cowes	45' 12'6" 12/9	Duke of Connaught Gift of United Grand Lodge of Freemasons, England.	668 £6,889 15t	1x60bhp Tylor 4-cyl D.1 (p)	Peterhead No.2 21.6.1921-15.6.39 (45/107) Reserve 6.1939-51 (30/97) Sold 10.1951- £750

5 · Watson motor 45ft

Year (Yd No) Builder Place	Length Breadth Crew	Name Donor	ON Cost Weight	Engines	Stations (launches/lives saved) Disposal
9 1922 (W1567) J. S. White Cowes	45' 12'6" 8	The Brothers Gift of the Misses H. A. A. and C. M. Eddy.	671 £13,214 16t15	1x80bhp Weyburn 6-cyl DE.6 (p)	Penlee 6.12.1922-22.6.31 (19/12) Falmouth 14.4.1931-3.11.34 (2/0) Reserve 1934-48 (45/27) Selsey 18.6.1937-26.8.38 (2/0) Workington 9.11.1948-3.2.52 (7/0) Sold 8.1952- £800
10 1924 (W1568) J. S. White Cowes	45' 12'6" 8	Edward, Prince of Wales The Welsh Lifeboat Fund.	678 £12,811 16t18	1x80bhp Weyburn 6-cyl DE.6 (p)	Mumbles 18.5.1924-23.4.47 (64/129) Capsized on service 23.4.1947, eight lost, later burnt
11 1923 (W1569) J. S. White Cowes	45' 12'6" 8	Elizabeth Newton Legacy of Mr R. Newton.	679 £12,724 16t19	1x80bhp Weyburn 6-cyl DE.6 (p)	Hartlepool 10.1.1924-19.10.39 (23/16) Reserve 10.1939-53 (23/11) Sold 5.1953- £400
12 1923 (W1570) J. S. White Cowes	45' 12'6" 8	City of Bradford/ 1929- City of Bradford I City of Bradford Lifeboat Fund.	680 £12,758 16t19	1x80bhp Weyburn 6-cyl DE.6 (p)	Humber 14.11.1923-11.3.29 (29/37) Humber Emergency 9.1.1930-21.2.32 (7/0) Reserve 1932-52 (43/55) Sold 10.1952
13 1923 (W1594) J. S. White Cowes	45' 12'6" 8	John R. Webb/ 1931- 684 RM/ 1934- Hearts of Oak Legacy of J. Russell Webb, Leicester/ 1934- Hearts of Oak Benefit Society.	684 £8,747 17t8	1x80bhp Weyburn 6-cyl DE.6 (p) (cabin series)	Tenby 11.8.1923-11.4.30 (16/32) Barra Island 2.9.1931-28.7.32 (1/0) Yarmouth 7.1.1934-8.36 (15/7) and 18.6.1937-4.38 (3/2) Reserve 1938-55 (46/13) Sold 2.1955- £753
14 1924 (W1601) J. S. White Cowes	45' 12'6" 8	J. W. Archer Gift of J. W. Archer.	685 £7,515 17t9	1x80bhp White 6-cyl DE.6 (p) (cabin series)	Teesmouth 13.12.1924-22.2.50 (37/120) Amble 8.6.1950-9.54 (8/0) Reserve 1954-56 (6/0) Sold 7.1956
15 1924 (W1602) J. S. White Cowes	45' 12'6" 8	T. B. B. H. Legacies of Mrs Thornton, Mr Bartlett, Miss Boustred and Miss Hooper.	686 £7,435 17t6	1x80bhp White 6-cyl DE.6 (p) (cabin series)	Portrush 16.7.1924-18.7.49 (75/17) Reserve 1949-53 (10/0) Sold 1.1953- £305
16 1924 (W1610) J. S. White Cowes	45' 12'6" 8	B. A. S. P. Legacies of Mr Blackburn, Mrs Armstrong, Mrs Smart and Mrs Price.	687 £7,519 17t17	1x80bhp White 6-cyl DE.6 (p) (cabin series)	Yarmouth 31.10.1924-7.11.34 (42/30) Falmouth 3.11.1934-7.1.1940 (8/0) Reserve 1.1940-47 (12/5) Valentia 17.5.1947-2.5.51 (14/2) Reserve 1951-55 (5/0) Sold 2.1955
17 1924 (S36) S. E. Saunders Cowes	45' 12'6" 8	The Lord Southborough (Civil Service No.1) Civil Service Lifeboat Fund.	688 £8,997 17t2	1x80bhp Weyburn 6-cyl DE.6 (p) (cabin series)	Margate 27.3.1925-18.3.51 (278/269) Reserve 3.1951-55 (14/17) Sold 1.1955

The 1923-built City of Bradford I (ON.680) at Southend; her steering shelter was fitted retrospectively. (From an old photo loaned by Jeff Morris).

John R. Webb (ON.684) was the first 45ft Watson to be built with a cabin; she was destined for service initially at Tenby. (RNLI)

Year (Yd No) Builder Place	Length Breadth Crew	Name Donor	ON Cost Weight	Engines	Stations (launches/lives saved) Disposal
18	1924 (S37) S. E. Saunders Cowes	45' 12'6" 8	Manchester and Salford Manchester and Salford Lifeboat Fund.	689 £8,456 17t10	1x80bhp Weyburn 6-cyl DE.6 (p) (cabin series)	Douglas 20.11.1924-18.7.46 (27/8) Reserve 7.1946-54 (13/5) Sold 10.1954- £750
19	1925 (S38) S. E. Saunders Cowes	45' 12'6" 8	C. and S. Legacy of Miss Emily Smart, Dublin; gift from executors of Peter Coates.	690 £8,424 17t6	1x80bhp Weyburn 6-cyl DE.6 (p) (cabin series)	Dunmore East 24.3.1925-19.3.40 (12/31) Pwllheli 26.4.1940-5.11.43 (12/7) Reserve 1943-46 (6/0) Valentia 18.11.1946-17.5.47 (2/0) Sold 11.1947- £250
20	1925 (S39) S. E. Saunders Cowes	45' 12'6" 8	Milburn Legacy of Sir Charles Stamp Milburn, gift of Frederick Milburn, Newcastle.	692 £8,449 17t8	1x80bhp Weyburn 6-cyl DE.6 (p) (cabin series)	Holy Island 1.6.1925-4.11.46 (57/81) Reserve 1946-55 (32/13) Sold 9.1955- £350
21	1924 (W1603) J. S. White Cowes	45' 12'6" 8	H. F. Bailey/ 1936- J. B. Proudfoot Legacy of Henry F. Bailey/ 1936- Legacy of Miss F. Proudfoot.	694 £7,530 17t9	1x80bhp White 6-cyl DE.6 (p) (cabin series)	Cromer No.1 15.8.1924-5.12.28 and 14.5.1929-12.12.35 (67/160) Reserve 1935-47 and 1949-56 (107/190) Southend-on-Sea 2.12.1941-2.45 (23/136) Dover 28.5.1947-11.3.49 (19/6) Sold 9.1956- £350
22	1925 (W1611) J. S. White Cowes	45' 12'6" 8	M. O. Y. E. Legacies of Miss Manby, the Misses J. L. and J. C. Owen, Mr Yates and Mr Lloyd.	695 £7,614 18t15	1x80bhp White 6-cyl DE.6 (p) (cabin series)	Porthdinllaen 24.2.1926-11.3.49 (56/16) Reserve 1949-56 (17/7) Sold 4.1956- £350

The Lord Southborough (Civil Service No.1) (ON.688) at moorings as a reserve lifeboat. (From an old postcard in the author's collection)

The last 45ft Watson cabin motor lifeboat to be built, M. O. Y. E. (ON.695), on the slipway outside the lifeboat house at Porthdinllaen. (From an old postcard supplied by a Shoreline member)

6 • Self-righting motor 35ft

Introduced 1921, last built 1927, 3 built.

Most early motor lifeboats were built for stations where they would be launched either down a slipway or from a mooring. But a motor lifeboat was also needed which could be launched by carriage off an open beach. In 1921, a light experimental prototype, built specially for carriage launching, was sent for trials at Eastbourne, followed two years later by another experimental boat at Scarborough. The main problem in designing a carriage-launched motor lifeboat was that of keeping it light enough so that it could be manhandled across a beach at a time when motor tractors were not yet in widespread use. It also of course had to be strong enough to withstand heavy seas.

The 35ft motor self-righters were essentially based on a standard pulling self-righting hull fitted with a single engine which was housed in a tunnel. All carried a set of sails and the RNLI emphasised that the motor was regarded as auxiliary to the sails and oars. In the event of the engine not working, the boats would be almost as effective under oars or sails as an ordinary pulling lifeboat without an engine. Although a third 35ft self-righting motor lifeboat was built in 1927, not until 1929, when the slightly larger 35ft 6in self-righting type was introduced, did the Institution's engineers believe they had found a satisfactory design for stations where launching off a beach was practised.

The last of the small 35ft self-righting motor lifeboats, L. P. and St Helen (ON.703), under sail. The engine casing is the only thing that indicates she is a motor lifeboat. (From an old photo loaned by W. R. Wright, courtesy of Jeff Morris)

Year (Yd No) Builder Place	Length Breadth Crew	Name Donor	ON Cost Weight	Engines	Stations (launches/lives saved) Disposal
1	1921 (W1578) J. S. White Cowes	35' 8'6" 10/7	Priscilla Macbean Legacy of Mr Edward Macbean, Hastings.	655 £6,623 6t7	1x15hp Miller E4 4-cyl (p)	Eastbourne 29.7.1921-4.11.27 (11/6) Kirkcudbright 3.3.1928-8.4.31 (5/1) Maryport 19.4.1931-28.8.34 (5/18) Sold 5.9.1934
2	1923 (S35) S. E. Saunders Cowes	35' 8'10" 10/7	Herbert Joy Gift of Mr Alexander O. Joy, London, in memory of his brother.	683 £3,691 5t4	1x35hp Sage 6A 4-cyl (p)	Scarborough 28.5.1923-4.6.31 (49/9) Reserve 1931-37 (0/0) Sold 4.3.1937
3	1927 (S45) S. E. Saunders, Cowes	35' 8'10" 10/7	L. P. and St Helen Legacies of Miss A Lovelock, Mr A. H. Pett and Miss H. M. Turner.	703 £4,961 5t16	1x35hp Halford (p)/ 1930- 1x35hp Weyburn AE6 (p)	Eastbourne 4.11.1927-14.1.29 (2/0) Boulmer 28.2.1931-11.2.37 (17/3) Newcastle 6.9.1937-17.7.49 (26/63) Sold 11.11.1949

Launch of Herbert Joy (ON.683) at Scarborough, with the propeller tunnel visible at the stern housing the single screw. The manpower required to launch a lifeboat across a beach placed restrictions on the weight of such a lifeboat. (RNLI, by courtesy of Jeff Morris)

Herbert Joy (ON.683) at Scarborough, the station she served for eight years. Her double fender was unusual and not repeated on any other British-built motor lifeboat. (RNLI, by courtesy of Jeff Morris)

7 • Barnett 60ft

Introduced 1923, last built 1929, 4 built.

The 60ft Barnett was the first twin-engined and twin-screw motor lifeboat built by the RNLI. Designed by and named after James Barnett, the Consulting Naval Architect of the RNLI, the design was ground-breaking in many ways and, when the prototype *William and Kate Johnston* was launched in 1923, she was the largest lifeboat ever built in Britain. The hull, built of teak, was double-skinned, and had eleven transverse and three longitudinal steel bulkheads, forming fifteen main watertight compartments. The twin engines were housed in completely separate watertight engine room compartments so that, even if the compartments became flooded, the engines would continue to operate as long as the air intakes remained above the water. The engines themselves were designed by the RNLI and built by Weyburn Engineering Co, Godalming, or J. S. White, Cowes. The twin propellers were arranged in protective tunnels on each side of the after end of the boat, minimising the risk of damage should the boat come into contact with another vessel or be grounded on a sandbank.

With two engines, only a jury rig, consisting of a small triangular fore-lug and jib which could be set on a single mast, was provided. A searchlight, sited by the boat's mast, was fitted and a life-saving net was suspended by four corner stanchions amidships over the engine room casing, although this was removed while the boats were in service. A line-throwing gun was provided to assist in getting a line on board wrecked ships, and a rudimentary windscreen was fitted to protect the man at the helm. The class had flush decks, without sunken well or cockpits, with the shelters for the crew and mechanics also protecting the entrance to the engine room hatches which were mounted at deck level. For the first time in a lifeboat, two cabins were provided, one fore and one aft, to hold about fifty people in total. The boat could take 130 persons on board in rough weather and 200 in fine weather.

In October 1924, after the first had become operational, two more lifeboats to the 60ft design were ordered and on these second and third boats modifications were incorporated in the light of experience. The engine rooms were enlarged, as were the two cabins so that between fifty and sixty people could be accommodated. Fuel capacity was increased by 100 gallons, so the boats had a radius of action of 250 miles at a cruising speed of eight knots, approximately 100 miles more than that of the first boat. Two funnels were added amidships for the exhaust so that, instead of having exhaust outlets on the side of the boat, as with the prototype, they were now located above deck. This was beneficial because the side outlet occasionally allowed water into the engines. The fourth and last of the large Barnetts, ON.715, was completed in 1929 and at 61ft was longer than her three sister vessels due to her bow being raked forward. In other respects she was similar to the second and third boats of the class. The boats had a draught of 4ft 6in, were manned by a crew of eight, and were kept moored afloat.

Although their size was of great benefit when operating in severe weather, it limited the stations from which they could be operated. They had to be kept permanently afloat at a relatively deep-water and sheltered mooring which the crew could reach in a boarding boat. At the time, the RNLI favoured keeping lifeboats out

The prototype 60ft Barnett lifeboat William and Kate Johnston *at New Brighton. The jumping net was later removed and the twin funnels, located aft of the mast, were additions for the exhaust.*

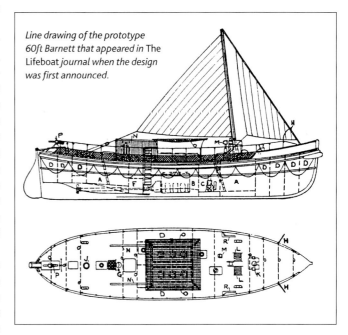

Line drawing of the prototype 60ft Barnett that appeared in The Lifeboat *journal when the design was first announced.*

of the water, in lifeboat houses, from which they would be launched via a slipway or, with the lighter lifeboats, from a carriage. Berths able to accommodate a lifeboat of such size were not widespread. The limitation imposed by the design's size therefore meant that only four of the class were built. Following the introduction of the 60ft Barnetts in the 1920s, several other lifeboat designs were developed by Barnett utilising the ideas first seen in the 60ft boats. A smaller 51ft version, known as the 'Stromness' class after the station at which the first one served, was built, incorporating twin engines and twin screws. Being smaller and lighter than the 60ft Barnett, it was suited for operation at a wider range of stations as it could be slipway launched.

Although only four lifeboats were built to Barnett's 60ft design, they embodied ideas and technology that pointed the way ahead for motor lifeboat design. As a result, twin engines, twin screws, cabins, shelters and other equipment which could only be accommodated in a motor lifeboat became the norm in all new lifeboat designs.

7 • Barnett 60ft

Year (Yd No) Builder Place	Length Breadth Crew	Name Donor	ON Cost Weight	Engines	Stations (launches/lives saved) Disposal
1	1923 (W1586) J. S. White Cowes	60' 15'	William and Kate Johnston Gifts of W. S. Johnston and his sister, W. H. Kendall; Liverpool Lifeboat Fund.	682 £16,084 41t5	2x80bhp Weyburn DE 6-cyl (p)	New Brighton 13.8.1923-23.9.50 (94/248) Sold 12.12.1950
2	1926 (S40) S. E. Saunders Cowes	60' 15'	Emma Constance Legacy of Mr John Mackie, York.	693 £15,821 41t18	2x80bhp Weyburn DE 6-cyl (p)	Aberdeen No.1 27.10.1926-30.8.51 (92/95) Sold 11.1951
3	1926 (W1626) J. S. White Cowes	60' 15'	Robert and Marcella Beck Legacy Mr R. A. Beck, Worthing.	696 £14,536 41t18	2x80bhp White DE 6-cyl (p)	Plymouth 1.7.1926-3.43 (36/70) and 2.1947-30.3.52 (14/2) Used by Navy 21.3.1943-4.46 Sold 6.1952
4	1929 (S50) S. E. Saunders Cowes	61' 15'	Princess Mary Gift of the P&O Group of Shipping Companies.	715 £14,602 43t10	2x80bhp Weyburn DE 6-cyl (p)	Padstow 25.5.1929-1.12.52 (63/48) Sold 6.1952

The third 61ft Barnett, Robert and Marcella Beck (ON.696), was stationed at Plymouth where moorings for her were easily found in the port's large harbour. (From the files of Grahame Farr)

61ft Barnett Princess Mary (ON.715), the last of the large Barnetts to be built and the only one 61ft in length, at Padstow quayside. (From an old postcard supplied by a Shoreline member)

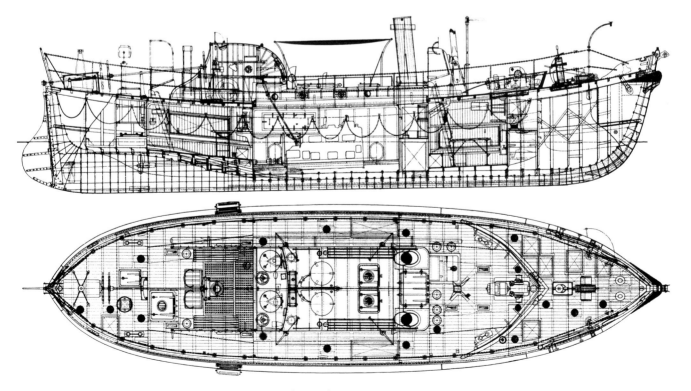

Line drawing showing 61ft Barnett Princess Mary (ON.715), the last of the large Barnetts to be built and the only one 61ft in length.

8 • Ramsgate motor

Introduced 1925, last built 1928, 3 built.

In the early 1920s, the RNLI turned its attention to the development of a motor lifeboat which could operate in shallow waters, and this culminated in the introduction of a new type in 1925. Designed for the special conditions of the Goodwin Sands, the new type was known as the Ramsgate class after the station at which the first was operated. The RNLI designers tried to combine the best elements of the Watson lifeboat with those of the Norfolk & Suffolk type, and the result was a boat that had features of both, was large for its time, at 48ft 6in in length, and could operate effectively in the comparatively sheltered waters of estuaries.

The boats were of a low, squat, open design, with no cockpits and long low end boxes, with a long straight iron keel weighing 2.6 tons. The wooden hull was subdivided into nine watertight compartments and 217 air cases. In addition to the engines, six oars were carried as were sails. ON.697 carried standing lug, mizzen and jib sails, to be used as auxiliary to the engine.

The second of three Ramsgate type lifeboats, Greater London (Civil Service No.3) *(ON.704), served for most of her career at Southend-on-Sea. (From an old postcard supplied by Nicholas Leach)*

	Year (Yd No) Builder Place	Length Breadth Crew	Name Donor	ON Cost Weight	Engines	Stations (launches/lives saved) Disposal
1	1925 (S41) S. E. Saunders Cowes	48' 13' 9	Prudential Gift from the Prudential Assurance Company, London.	697 £8,417 20t16	1x80bhp (ss) Weyburn 6-cyl DE6 (p)	Ramsgate 30.12.1925-25.9.53 (276/330) Sold 11.1953
2	1928 (W1648) J. S. White Cowes	48'6" 13' 9	Greater London (Civil Service No.3) Civil Service Lifeboat Fund.	704 £8,668 22t10	2x40bhp (ts) Weyburn 4-cyl CE4 (p)	Southend-on-Sea 5.1928-12.41 & 2.1945-4.55 (253/218) Reserve 1941-45 & 1955-57 (22/22) Sold 9.1957
3	1928 (W1649) J. S. White Cowes	48'6" 13' 9	E. M. E. D. Legacies of Mr I. Dewhirst, Miss H. Yates, Mr R. Barnes and Miss J. E. Watkins.	705 £8,700 22t10	2x40bhp (ts) Weyburn 4-cyl CE4 (p)	Walton & Frinton 4.7.1928-2.11.53 (177/217) Reserve 1953-55 (8/26) Sold 1.1956

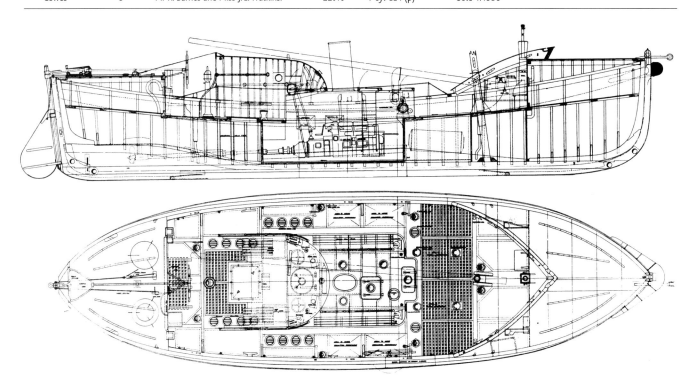

General deck arrangement of the last Ramsgate type lifeboat, E. M. E. D. (ON.705), which served at the Walton & Frinton station in Essex, to cover the northern waters of the Thames Estuary.

9 • Watson cabin motor 45ft 6in

Introduced 1926, last built 1935, 23 built.

The 45ft 6in Watson, a non-self-righting type designed by James Barnett around the traditional Watson hull shape, was a development of the 45ft Watson. It was 6in longer as a result of a more raked bow, while the end box layout was replaced by a through deck, flush with the gunwales. The steering position was located aft, while a turtle-shell shaped shelter was introduced incorporating an aft cockpit with a one-piece central windscreen. At the forward end of the aft shelter was the engine room access hatch. The exhaust funnel was positioned forward of this shelter, while towards the bow was a small shelter. In rough weather, ninety-five people could be taken on board. The hull was divided into seven watertight compartments and fitted with 142 air cases and ten relieving scuppers.

The first two boats were single-engined and had a similar speed and range to the 45ft Watsons. The fourth, ON.701, was built as a twin-engined, single-screwed craft, the only lifeboat completed with such an arrangement. In this boat, the two engines were coupled to a gearbox through which the single propeller was driven. The third boat was fitted with twin engines driving twin screws, and trials proved this to be the optimum arrangement. All the remaining boats of this class were therefore twin-screwed.

The 45ft 6in Watson motor as exemplified by Elizabeth Elson *(ON.713), pictured on reserve duties at Lowestoft, with the funnel amidships and aft steering position.* Elizabeth Elson *spent more than ten years as a Reserve lifeboat and when sold by the RNLI in 1968 she had given almost forty years of service. (Jeff Morris)*

On the twin-engined boats, the drop keel was dispensed with, and a reduced sail plan was carried. Once the reliability of the twin engines had been proved in service conditions, the sails were also dispensed with altogether.

	Year (Yd No) Builder Place	Length Breadth Crew	Name Donor	ON Cost Weight	Engines	Stations (launches/lives saved) Disposal
1	1926 (S42) S. E. Saunders Cowes	45'6" 12'6" 8	K. T. J. S. Legacies of William G. King, J. Turnbull, M. Jesset and Mrs S. H. Sandford.	698 £8,330 18t13	1x80bhp (ss) Weyburn DE.6 (p)	Longhope 1.9.1926-4.1.33 (24/25) Aith 2.5.1933-12.5.35 (3/0) Arranmore 17.8.1935-9.5.50 (37/29) Reserve 1950-52 (7/2) Sold 5.1952
2	1926 (S43) S. E. Saunders Cowes	45'6" 12'6" 8	John Russell Legacy of Miss Ann Russell.	699 £8,272 18t14	1x80bhp (ss) Weyburn DE.6 (p)	Montrose No.1 1.9.1926-9.10.39 (32/26) Reserve 1939-55 (30/49) Sold 7.1956
3	1927 (W1630) J. S. White Cowes	45'6" 12'6" 8	K. E. C. F. Legacies of Mrs E. Kirby, Mrs E. Dudley, Mr E. Kleeman and Miss M. Potton.	700 £11,116 19t5	2x40bhp (ts) Weyburn CE.4 (p)	Rosslare Harbour 7.4.1927-2.3.39 (63/127) Galway Bay 16.3.1939-22.3.52 (37/48) Reserve 1952-56 (11/8) Sold 12.1956
4	1927 (W1629) J. S. White Cowes	45'6" 12'6" 8	N. T. Legacy of Mrs Maria C. Myers and gift from Mr StephenThompson, B'ham.	701 £10,826 19t6	2x40bhp (ss) Weyburn CE.4 (p)	Barrow 19.8.1927-11.1951 (68/64) Workington 2.3.1952-3.53 (10/11) Reserve 1953-56 (8/0) Sold 12.1956
5	1929 (S47) S. E. Saunders Cowes	45'6" 12'6" 8	Edward Z. Dresden Legacy of Edward Dresden, London.	707 £8,496 20t7	2x40bhp (ts) Weyburn CE.4 (p)	Clacton-on-Sea 20.3.1929-14.1.52 (181/112) Stronsay 23.10.1952-27.2.55 (8/0) Reserve 1955-68 (49/37) Sold 12.1968
6	1928 (W1656) J. S. White Cowes	45'6" 12'6" 8	H. C. J. Legacies of H. T. Richardson, S. Stephens, and gift from John A. Fielden.	708 £8,390 18t5	2x40bhp (ts) Weyburn CE.4 (p)	Fowey 11.8-6.12.1928 (0/0) Holyhead 7.12.1928-17.5.29 (3/0) Thurso 25.6.1929-29.1.56 (102/138) Reserve 1956-62 (11/8) Sold 1962
7	1929 (S48) S. E. Saunders Cowes	45'6" 12'6" 8	City of Bradford II City of Bradford Lifeboat Fund and legacy of Mr J. M. Howson, Harrogate.	709 £8,662 18t10	2x40bhp (ts) Weyburn CE.4 (p)	Humber 13.2.1929-27.1.54 (228/305) Amble 9.1954-1.57 (7/0) Broughty Ferry 23.12.1959-17.11.60 (6/0) Reserve 1956-68 (30/4) Sold 12.1968
8	1930 (W1657) J. S. White Cowes	45'6" 12'6" 8	White Star Oceanic Steam Navigation Company (White Star Line).	710 £7,878 18t14	2x40bhp (ts) Weyburn CE.4 (p)	Fishguard 28.5.1930-20.2.56 (56/66) Reserve 1956-68 (52/13) Sold 10.6.1968

9 · Watson cabin motor 45ft 6in

Year (Yd No) Builder Place	Length Breadth Crew	Name Donor	ON Cost Weight	Engines	Stations (launches/lives saved) Disposal
9 1929 (W1662) J. S. White Cowes	45'6" 12'6" 8	James Macfee Legacy of Dr J. Macfee, Auchterarder.	711 £8,205 18t10	2x40bhp (ts) Weyburn CE.4 (p)	Cromarty 20.10.1928-2.9.55 (51/17) Thurso 11.12.1956-7.12.57 (1/0) Reserve 1955-59 (7/3) Sold 1959
10 1928 (W1663) J. S. White Cowes	45'6" 12'6" 8	C. D. E. C. Legacies C. C. Nottage, Miss G. Moss, Mrs J. Liddell and Mrs A. S. Picking.	712 £8,309 18t10	2x40bhp (ts) Weyburn CE.4 (p)	Fowey 6.12.1928-21.11.54 (65/49) Reserve 1954-59 (19/2) Sold 1959
11 1929 (W1664) J. S. White Cowes	45'6" 12'6" 8	Elizabeth Elson Legacy of Mr B. Elson.	713 £8,253 18t14	2x40bhp (ts) Weyburn CE.4 (p)	Angle 10.1.1929-19.2.57 (58/144) Reserve 1957-68 (108/67) Sold 12.1968
12 1928 (S49) S. E. Saunders Cowes	45'6" 12'6" 8	H. F. Bailey II/ 1929- Canadian Pacific Legacy of Henry F. Bailey, Brokenhurst/ 1929-Canadian Pacific Steamship Co.	714 £8,470 18t4	2x40bhp (ts) Weyburn CE.4 (p)	Cromer No.1 1928-14.5.29 (3/5) Selsey 29.7.1929-6.37 (35/30) Burnt in fire at Groves & Guttridge, 18.6.1937
13 1929 (W1666) J. S. White Cowes	45'6" 12'6" 8	Sarah Ward and William David Crossweller Legacy of William T. Crossweller, Sidcup.	716 £8,454 18t14	2x40bhp (ts) Weyburn CE.4 (p)	Courtmacsherry Harbour 3.3.1929-58 (47/63) Reserve 1958-59 (11/0) Whitehills 11.1959-61 (1/0) Sold 1961
14 1930 (S53) Saunders-Roe Cowes	45'6" 12'6" 8	Cunard Gift of Cunard Steamship Company.	728 £8,324 18t14	2x40bhp (ts) Weyburn CE.4 (p)	St Mary's 27.5.1930-12.12.55 (71/104) Reserve 1955-69 (70/26) Sold 1969
15 1930 (S54) Saunders-Roe Cowes	45'6" 12'6" 8	John R. Webb Legacy of Mr J. R. Webb, Belgrave, London.	729 £8,318 18t14	2x40bhp (ts) Weyburn CE.4 (p)	Tenby 11.4.1930-20.9.55 (91/53) Reserve 1955-69 (76/49) Sold 9.1969
16 1930 (W1694) J. S. White Cowes	45'6" 12'6" 8	Cecil and Lilian Philpott Gift of Mrs L. Philpott, London.	730 £7,982 18t14	2x40bhp (ts) Weyburn CE.4 (p)	Newhaven 8.1.1930-11.7.59 (156/99) Reserve 1959-69 (48/56) Sold 10.1969
17 1930 (W1696) J. S. White Cowes	45'6" 12'6" 8	Catherine —	732 — 18t14	2x40bhp (ts) Weyburn CE.4 (p)	Built for Bombay Port Trust in 1930 Sold 1935
18 1931 (W1705) J. S. White Cowes	45'6" 12'6" 8	W. and S. Legacies of Miss E. Young and Miss W. A. Coode.	736 £7,684 18t10	2x40bhp (ts) Weyburn CE.4 (p)	Penlee 26.6.1931-4.7.60 (94/83) Buckie 9.1960-6.61 Reserve 1960-69 (15/10) Sold 1970

The first 45ft 6in Watson class to be built, K. T. J. S. (ON.698), with her sails set during her time on station at Longhope, in Orkney. She was one of only two 45ft 6in Watsons built with a single engine. (RNLI)

Typical of the standard 45ft 6in Watson class was C. D. E. C. (ON.712), which served at Fowey for more than twenty-five years. She is pictured after her cabin had been extended aft. (RNLI)

9 · Watson cabin motor 45ft 6in

Year (Yd No) Builder Place	Length Breadth Crew	Name Donor	ON Cost Weight	Engines	Stations (launches/lives saved) Disposal
19	1931 (W1718) J. S. White Cowes	45'6" 12'6" 8	George and Sarah Strachan Legacy of George Strachan, Glasgow.	749 £7,680 18t10	2x40bhp (ts) Weyburn CE.4 (p)	Dunbar 28.6.1931-4.2.59 (74/16) Exmouth 29.2.1961-1.11.63 (2/0) Reserve 1959-61 & 1964-69 (20/9) Sold 3.1969
20	1932 (W1732) J. S. White Cowes	45'6" 12'6" 8	Civil Service No.5 Civil Service Lifeboat Fund.	753 £7,293 19t10	2x40bhp (ts) Weyburn CE.4 (p)	Donaghadee 4.6.1932-1.6.50 (80/56) Port St Mary 19.9.1950-5.7.56 (7/0) Reserve 1956-58 (7/2) Sold 2.1958
21	1933 (182) Groves & Guttridge Cowes	45'6" 12'6" 8	Thomas McCunn Legacy of Mr William McCunn, Largs.	759 £7,120 18t16	2x40bhp (ts) Weyburn CE.4 (p)	Longhope 4.1.1933-4.62 (101/308) Reserve 1962-72 (26/12) Sold 8.1972, later returned to Longhope for display
22	1935 (201) Alexr. Robertson Sandbank	45'6" 12'6" 8	Charlotte Elizabeth Gift of Miss E. Sinclair.	774 £8,380 18t16	2x40bhp (ts) Weyburn CE.4 (p) [Internal rudder]	Islay 26.6.1935-11.7.59 (101/162) Reserve 1959-61 (8/7) Sold 1961
23	1935 (196) Groves & Guttridge Cowes	45'6" 12'6" 8	Mona Gift from an anonymous lady in the west of Scotland.	775 £6,802 18t16	2x40bhp (ts) Weyburn CE.4 (p)	Broughty Ferry 6.5.1935-12.59 (72/118) Capsized on service 8.12.1959, later burnt on beach

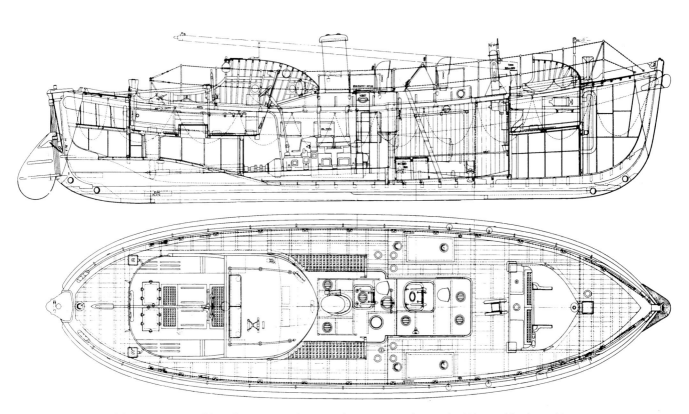

General deck arrangement of the 45ft 6in Watson cabin motor Thomas McCunn *(ON.759), which served for almost thirty years at Longhope and was one of many Watsons operated from slipways.*

10 • Barnett 'Stromness' 51ft

Introduced 1928, last built 1949, 13 built.

The 51ft Barnett was developed from the earlier and larger 60-61ft type and, designed by James Barnett, had a hull shape similar to its larger sister.   But the 51ft version, with a draft of 4ft 1in, was smaller and lighter – 26.5 tons as opposed to 44 – and thus more practical. It could be launched from a slipway, unlike the 60ft Barnett, or kept afloat at moorings. The design became known as the 'Stromness' class after the station where the first was stationed as the crew there had specifically requested a large lifeboat that could be slipway launched.

The hull, divided into eight watertight compartments and fitted with 180 air cases, was constructed from mahogany with a keel of teak and ribs of Canadian rock-elm and stem and stern post of English oak. The heavy keel gave her a greater range of stability than the 60ft Barnett. The layout incorporated a single cabin, with a single funnel amidships for the exhaust, and an aft cockpit.

The two 60hp petrol engines were housed in a watertight compartment with the air-intakes well above the waterline so the engines would continue to operate even if the engine room was flooded. At the maximum speed of nine knots, the petrol-engined versions had a range of approximately 120 miles. Two of the boats, ON.754 and ON.755, built for the Barra Island and Fenit

52ft Barnett George Shee *(ON.734) which was named after the Secretary of the RNLI and served for almost thirty years at Torbay before being sold out of service to Guatemala, where she continued in her role as a life-saver. (RNLI)*

stations, had enlarged fuel tanks to increase their cruising range to 184 miles, while ON.755 and ON.860 were re-engined with 75hp Parsons Barracuda diesels during their service careers. Amongst the equipment carried were a line-throwing gun, a searchlight, a mechanical capstan and a powered fire-fighting system.

Year (Yd No) Builder Place	Length Breadth Crew	Name Donor	ON Cost Weight	Engines	Stations (launches/lives saved) Disposal
1 1928 (S44) S. E. Saunders Cowes	51' 13'6" 8	J. J. K. S. W. Legacies of Miss J. Moody, J. P. Traill, W. Aitken, E. J. Hanson and W. Notting.	702 £13,643 25t18	2x60bhp Weyburn 6-cyl CE6 (p)	Stromness 15.2.1928-21.5.55 (92/139) Reserve 1955-64 (24/19) Sold 1965
2 1929 (W1669) J. S. White Cowes	51' 13'6" 8	A. E. D. Legacy of Captain W. A. Dobie, and gift of G. W. Hayer.	717 £10,119 27t	2x60bhp Weyburn 6-cyl CE6 (p)	Holyhead 17.5.1929-21.9.50 (84/156) Valentia 2.1951-18.9.57 (57/83) Sold 1957

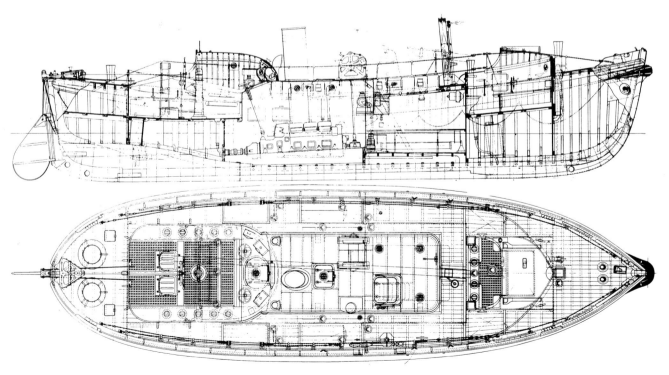

General profile and deck arrangement of the 51ft Barnett Mary Stanford *(ON.733).*

	Year (Yd No) Builder Place	Length Breadth Crew	Name Donor	ON Cost Weight	Engines	Stations (launches/lives saved) Disposal
3	1929 (W1670) J. S. White Cowes	51' 13'6" 8	William and Harriot Legacy of Mrs H. Richardson.	718 £10,469 27t2	2x60bhp Weyburn 6-cyl CE6 (p)	Stornoway 12.7.1929-27.9.54 (77/130) Reserve 1954-59 (8/2) Sold 1959
4	1929 (W1671) J. S. White Cowes	51' 13'6" 8	Queen Victoria RNLI Funds.	719 £10,481 27t	2x60bhp Weyburn 6-cyl CE6 (p)	St Peter Port 27.10.1929-6.40 (45/53) Killybegs 24.8.1941-8.45 (14/4) St Peter Port 29.8.1945-31.5.54 (78/71) Reserve 1954-58 (24/2) Sold 5.1958
5	1929 (W1672) J. S. White Cowes	51' 13'6" 8	City of Glasgow RNLI Funds.	720 £10,198 26t18	2x60bhp Weyburn 6-cyl CE6 (p)	Campbeltown 4.9.1929-24.6.53 (91/173) Reserve 1953-58 (10/12) Sold 1959
6	1930 (W1695) J. S. White Cowes	51' 13'6" 8	Lady Jane and Martha Ryland Legacy of Mr William Ryland.	731 £10,414 26t10	2x60bhp Weyburn 6-cyl CE6 (p)	Lerwick 9.7.1930-2.8.58 (79/80) Reserve 1958-69 (29/10) Sold 1969
7	1930 (S55) Saunders-Roe Cowes	51' 13'6" 8	Mary Stanford Legacy of Mr J. F. Stanford, London.	733 £9403 26t6	2x60bhp Weyburn 6-cyl CE6 (p)	Ballycotton 4.9.1930-27.7.59 (83/101) Reserve 1959-68 (47/22) Sold 2.1968
8	1930 (S56) Saunders-Roe Cowes	51' 13'6" 8	George Shee RNLI Funds.	734 £9614 27t	2x60bhp Weyburn 6-cyl CE6 (p)	Torbay 23.9.1930-19.7.58 (245/190) Reserve 1958 (1/1) Sold 12.1958
9	1930 (S57) Saunders-Roe Cowes	51' 13'6" 8	William and Clara Ryland Legacy of Mr William Ryland.	735 £9413 26t13	2x60bhp Weyburn 6-cyl CE6 (p)	Weymouth 6.11.1930-30.10.57 (156/135) Sold 1958
10	1932 (180) Groves & Guttridge Cowes	51' 13'6" 8	Lloyd's Gift of Members of Lloyd's.	754 £9443 26t2	2x60bhp Weyburn 6-cyl CE6 (p)	Barra Island 28.7.1932-27.7.57 (110/270) Reserve 1957-69 (101/80) Sold 1.1970
11	1932 (W1732) J. S. White Cowes	51' 13'6" 8	Peter and Sarah Blake Legacy of Miss S. B. Blake.	755 £8978 26t4	2x60bhp Weyburn 6-cyl CE6 (p)/1965- 2x65hp Parsons Barracuda	Fenit 8.9.1932-12.58 (38/12) Reserve 12.1958-72 (93/66) Sold 10.1972
12	1935 (197) Groves & Guttridge Cowes	51' 13'6" 8	The Rankin Gift of Miss M. D. Rankin.	776 £9122 26t2	2x60bhp Weyburn 6-cyl CE6 (p)	Aith 12.5.1935-28.1.61 (52/61) Reserve 1961-69 (47/22) Sold 1970
13	1949 (S681) Rowhedge IW Rowhedge	51' 13'6" 8	Southern Africa Southern Africa Branch of the RNLI.	860 £20,592 26t10	2x60bhp Ferry VE 6-cyl/ 1976- 2x65hp Parsons Barracuda	Dover 18.6.1949-7.1967 (263/186) Reserve 1967-81 (39/10) Sold 7.1981

51ft Barnett Lady Jane and Martha Ryland *(ON.731) on Reserve duty at Campbeltown having completed station duty at Lerwick. (MPL)*

Peter and Sarah Blake *(ON.755) under sail. Despite being fitted with twin engines, the 51ft Barnetts still carried auxiliary sails. (RNLI)*

11 • Fast lifeboat 64ft

Introduced 1929, last built 1929, 1 built

In 1929, a special 64ft high-speed lifeboat was built for Dover, designed 'for the special conditions of the Straits, across which there is not only the heavy passenger steamer traffic but a considerable daily traffic of aeroplanes', according to The Lifeboat journal. With the primary aim of rescuing airmen ditched in the English Channel, speed was crucial. So, to achieve the desired speed, a unique lifeboat was constructed to specifications different from any other contemporary motor lifeboat.

The hull was built of lighter timber and the beam was smaller in proportion to her length, thus sacrificing some stability. It was divided into eight watertight compartments with steel bulkheads, and fitted with eighty-two air cases. Whereas engines installed in most motor lifeboats of the inter-war era were between 60bhp and 80bhp, this fast lifeboat had two 375hp units. The RNLI deemed that 'the only well-tried engine suitable' was the Thornycroft Y.12 engine, mainly used in naval launches during the war, and subsequently adopted by the Royal Air Force for its fast launches. The twin 375hp engines driving twin screws gave the boat a maximum speed of 17.5 knots. Her radius of action, at seventy-eight miles, was less than that of conventional lifeboats. Operated by a crew of seven, of whom four were full-time employees of the RNLI, she was kept afloat at moorings in Dover harbour.

Naming ceremony of Sir William Hillary *(ON.725), the only 64ft fast lifeboat to be built, at Wellington Docks, Dover, on 10 July 1930. (RNLI)*

The only lifeboat built to this design served the RNLI for just a decade. When war broke out, the Admiralty had the Dover station closed but, because of the boat's design, she was of limited use elsewhere. The problem was solved in October 1940 when the Admiralty requisitioned her for air-sea rescue work and she was sold outright to the Navy a year later.

Year (Yd No) Builder Place	Length Breadth Crew	Name Donor	ON Cost Weight	Engines	Stations (launches/lives saved) Disposal
1. 1929 (T2126) J. I. Thornycroft Hampton	64' 14' 7	Sir William Hillary RNLI Funds.	725 £18,446 26t	2x375hp Thornycroft Y.12 12-cyl (p)	Dover 21.1.1930-24.10.40 (43/29) Requisitioned by Admiralty 10.1940 Sold to Navy 11.1941

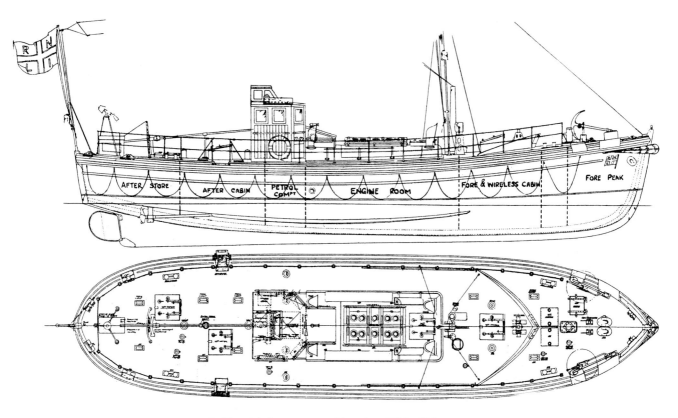

Profile and deck arrangement of the unique 64ft fast lifeboat.

12 • Self-righting motor 35ft 6in

Introduced 1929, last built 1951, 27 built.

Experiments to design a motor lifeboat that could be carriage launched took place during the 1920s until in 1929 the 35ft self-righting type, three of which had been built, was modified so that it reached the desired performance. At 35ft 6in in length and 8ft 1in broad, the new design was larger than the experimental boats and became the first production motor lifeboat specifically designed for launching off a carriage. Its introduction was an important step forward as the RNLI now had a design suitable for stations where large motor lifeboats could not be operated.

The first boat, with crew and gear on board, weighed only 6 tons 14 cwt and was thus well suited to being manhandled on a carriage for launching. It was fitted with vertical scuppers, instead of valves in the deck, and became the first motor lifeboat to be so equipped. The beam on later boats was increased so that the stability of the design was better.

The engine fitted to ON.726 was a newly-designed type intended specifically for the small motor self-righter. It had been developed from the Halford engine of the same size used in ON.703, the 35ft experimental boat that was the forerunner of the 35ft 6in self-righter. The small shelter in the self-righters provided only enough space for the mechanic, who operated the engine controls while the boat was at sea. Access to the engine itself was through large doors set at an angle to the deck.

Cyril and Lilian Bishop (ON.740) on the beach with her crew. The 35ft 6in SR motor was intended for carriage launching and was light enough to be manhandled across a beach before launching tractors had been introduced. (From an old postcard in the author's collection)

The hull incorporated large end boxes, which were kept to the minimum height required to provide the self-righting capability, and was divided into six watertight compartments with 110 air cases. A water ballast tank was incorporated, the waterline length was 32ft 1in and the draft was 2ft 8in. After World War II, the design was improved and five boats were built with twin engines and twin screws. They also had the shelter enlarged making them similar in appearance to the Liverpool class.

Year (Yd No) Builder Place	Length Breadth Crew	Name Donor	ON Cost Weight	Engines	Stations (launches/lives saved) Disposal
1. 1929 (S51) Saunders-Roe Cowes	35'6" 8'10" 7/8	City of Nottingham City of Nottingham Lifeboat Fund.	726 £4596 5t9	1x35hp (ss) Weyburn 6-cyl AE.6 (p)	Hythe 17.1.1930-24.2.36 (17/16) Clovelly 6.1936-7.9.49 (46/27) Sold 1950
2. 1930 (S52) Saunders-Roe Cowes	35'6" 8'10" 7/8	Westmorland Westmorland Lifeboat Fund.	727 £4597 5t10	1x35hp (ss) Weyburn 6-cyl AE.6 (p)	Berwick-upon-Tweed 21.2.1930-2.40 (16/10) Cullercoats 21.2.1940-15.3.51 (26/101) Sold 14.6.1951
3. 1931 (S58) Saunders-Roe Cowes	35'6" 8'10" 7/8	Louisa Polden Gift of Mr J. J. Polden, Grove Park, Kent augmented by his family.	737 £3758 5t4	1x35hp (ss) Weyburn 6-cyl AE.6 (p)	Redcar 13.5.1931-12.5.51 (36/76) Sold 1951
4. 1931 (W1708) J. S. White Cowes	35'6" 8'10" 7/8	J. H. W. Legacies of C. May, G. H. B. Haworth, S. Sackville and W. Johnson.	738 £3821 5t13	1x35hp (ss) Weyburn 6-cyl AE.6 (p)	Lytham St Annes 4.4.1931-1.39 (11/1) Padstow No.2 25.1.1939-31.11.47 (4/0) Sold 6.4.1948
5. 1931 (S59) Saunders-Roe Cowes	35'6" 8'10" 7/8	Lily Glen – Glasgow Gift of Mrs Laurence Glen, Glasgow.	739 £3742 5t9	1x35hp (ss) Weyburn 6-cyl AE.6 (p)	Girvan 11.3.1931-2.4.52 (50/18) Sold 5.1952
6. 1931 (W1709) J. S. White Cowes	35'6" 8'10" 7/8	Cyril and Lilian Bishop Gift of Mrs Lilian Philpott.	740 £3810 5t12	1x35hp (ss) Weyburn 6-cyl AE.6 (p)	Hastings 31.4.1931-18.3.50 (99/34) Sold 17.11.1950
7. 1931 (S60) Saunders-Roe Cowes	35'6" 8'10" 7/8	Morison Watson Legacy of Mrs E. H. Watson, Bridge of Allan.	741 £3718 5t12	1x35hp (ss) Weyburn 6-cyl AE.6 (p)	Kirkcudbright 8.4.1931-53 (30/15) Sold 1953
8. 1931 (W1710) J. S. White Cowes	35'6" 8'10" 7/8	Herbert Joy II Gift of Mr Alexander O. Joy, London.	742 £3791 5t11	1x35hp (ss) Weyburn 6-cyl AE.6 (p)	Scarborough 4.6.1931-10.1.51 (114/22) Sold 1951
9. 1931 (S61) Saunders-Roe Cowes	35'6" 8'10" 7/8	John and Sarah Eliza Stych Legacies of Mr and Mrs Stych.	743 £3754 5t10	1x35hp (ss) Weyburn 6-cyl AE.6 (p)	Padstow No.1 28.5.1931-8.2.38 (7/8) St Ives 8.2.1938-23.1.39 (2/1) Wrecked on service 23.1.1939, seven lost

12 · Self-righting motor 35ft 6in

Year (Yd No) Builder Place	Length Breadth Crew	Name Donor	ON Cost Weight	Engines	Stations (launches/lives saved) Disposal
10. 1931 (W1711) J. S. White Cowes	35'6" 8'10" 7/8	Laurana Sarah Blunt Legacy of Dr G. V. Blunt, Birmingham.	744 £3812 5t10	1x35hp (ss) Weyburn 6-cyl AE.6 (p)	Youghal 20.6.1931-2.8.52 (18/21) Sold 1952
11. 1931 (S62) Saunders-Roe Cowes	35'6" 8'10" 7/8	Lady Harrison Gift of Sir Heath Harrison, Bt.	745 £3754 5t10	1x35hp (ss) Weyburn 6-cyl AE.6 (p)	Ramsey 31.6.1931-24.9.48 (43/93) Aberystwyth 3.3.1949-25.10.51 (4/0) Sold 1952
12. 1931 (W1712) J. S. White Cowes	35'6" 8'10" 7/8	William Maynard Legacy of Rev W. S. F. Maynard, Gressingham, Lancs.	746 £3804 5t10	1x35hp (ss) Weyburn 6-cyl AE.6 (p)	Cloughey 19.1.1931-15.7.39 (13/36) Reserve 1939-41 and 1949-53 (0/0) Ferryside 12.7.1941-48 (5/2) Whitehills 2.7.1948-22.5.49 (3/0) Sold 2.1953
13. 1931 (S63) Saunders-Roe Cowes	35'6" 8'10" 7/8	Stanhope Smart Legacy of Mr Stanhope Smart, Huddersfield.	747 £3742 5t8	1x35hp (ss) Weyburn 6-cyl AE.6 (p)	Bridlington 8.6.1931-16.11.47 (60/53) Padstow No.2 31.1.1947-30.7.51 (0/0) Sold 1951
14. 1931 (W1713) J. S. White Cowes	35'6" 8'10" 7/8	Mary Ann Blunt Legacy of Dr G. V. Blunt, Birmingham.	748 £3791 5t10	1x35hp (ss) Weyburn 6-cyl AE.6 (p)	Clougher Head 4.7.1931-7.7.50 (20/9) Sold 1951
15. 1932 J. Thornycroft Chiswick	35'6" 8'10" 7/8	John and William Mudie Legacies of Miss I. and Miss E. Mudie.	752 £3233 6t15	1x35hp (ss) Weyburn 6-cyl AE.6 (p)	Arbroath 7.1.1932-12.7.50 (45/27) Sold 14.6.1951
16. 1932 (W1734) J. S. White Cowes	35'6" 8'10" 7/8	Civil Service No.4 Civil Service Lifeboat Fund.	756 £3342 6t6	1x35hp (ss) Weyburn 6-cyl AE.6 (p)	Whitehills 10.8.1932-4.48 (26/9) Damaged on service, 8.4.1948, none lost Sold 16.6.1948
17. 1932 (W1735) J. S. White Cowes	35'6" 8'10" 7/8	Frederick Angus Legacy of Mr F. Angus, Poole.	757 £3326 6t5	1x35hp (ss) Weyburn 6-cyl AE.6 (p)	Aberystwyth 23.9.1932-3.3.49 (25/25) Sold 17.8.1949
18. 1933 (W1745) J. S. White Cowes	35'6" 9'3" 7/8	Caroline Parsons Legacies of Miss Caroline Parsons and Mrs E. Noy.	763 £3213 6t	1x35hp (ss) Weyburn 6-cyl AE.6 (p)	St Ives 18.3.1933-1.38 (7/73) Wrecked on service 31.1.1938, none lost

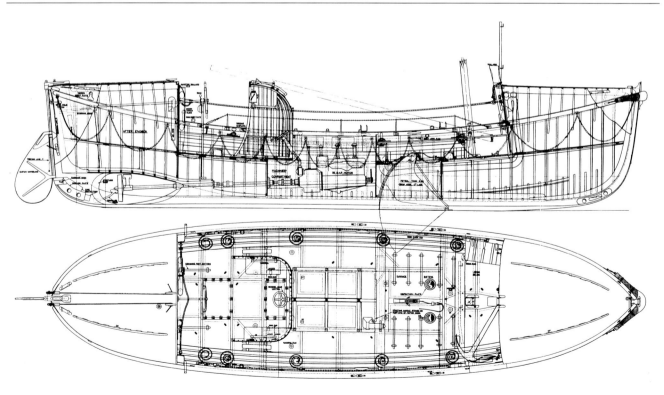

General profile and deck arrangement of the 35ft 6in SR motor Caroline Parsons *(ON.763) with a small shelter for the engine and a tunnel to protect the single screw. This lifeboat served at St Ives until she was wrecked on service in March 1938.*

12 · Self-righting motor 35ft 6in

Year (Yd No) Builder Place	Length Breadth Crew	Name Donor	ON Cost Weight	Engines	Stations (launches/lives saved) Disposal
19.	1933 (W1749) J. S. White Cowes	35'6" 9'3" 7/8	Catherine Harriet Eaton Legacy of Rev Charles P. Eaton, Milford Haven.	767 £3009 6t	1x35hp (ss) Weyburn 6-cyl AE.6 (p)	Exmouth 18.8.1933-9.10.53 (34/31) Sold 1953
20.	1933 (W1750) J. S. White Cowes	35'6" 9'3" 7/8	Thomas and Annie Wade Richards Legacy of Dr Thomas Richards, Llangadoch, augmented by Miss Sarah Lewis, Aberystwyth.	768 £3010 5t16	1x35hp (ss) Weyburn 6-cyl AE.6 (p)	Llandudno 15.9.1933-6.53 (57/38) Sold 1953
21.	1936 (W1810) J. S. White Cowes	35'6" 9'6" 7/8	Sir Heath Harrison Gift of Mary, Lady Harrison, Le Court, Liss, Hampshire.	785 £3279 6t1	1x35hp (ss) Weyburn 6-cyl AE.6 (p)	Port St Mary 18.4.1936-11.11.49 (36/31) Reserve 1949-55 (0/0) Sold 1.1956
22.	1940 (S570) Rowhedge IW Rowhedge	35'6" 9'10" 7/8	Guide of Dunkirk Girl Guides of the Empire.	826 £5523 6t8	1x35hp (ss) Weyburn 6-cyl AE.6 (p)	[Stemmed for St Ives] Cadgwith 10.5.1941-31.5.1963 (15/17) Sold 1963
23.	1947 (W5381) J. S. White Cowes	35'6" 10' 7/8	Tillie Morrison, Sheffield Gift from James and David Morrison, of Sheffield	851 £10,573 7t15	2x18hp (ts) Weyburn 4-cyl AE.4 (p)	Bridlington 16.11.1947-53 (23/0) Capsized on service 19.8.1952, one lost Llandudno 1953-59 (17/8) Sold 11.1959
24.	1950 (506) Groves & Guttridge Cowes	35'6" 10' 7/8	M. T. C. Trained Women Drivers' Association.	878 £11,283 8t12	2x18hp (ts) Weyburn 4-cyl AE.4 (p)	Hastings 18.3.1950-11.63 (107/28) Sold 1964
25.	1950 (507) Groves & Guttridge Cowes	35'6" 10' 7/8	E. C. J. R. Legacies of Mrs A. E. Wildish, Mr R. Mundy, Mr L. Chrichton and Mrs P. E. Wood.	879 £12,095 8t8	2x20hp (ts) Ferry FKR.3 3-cyl (d)	Scarborough 10.1.1951-10.56 (31/15) Capsized on service 8.12.1954, three lost Reserve 1956-63 (1/0) Sold 3.1963
26.	1950 (508) Groves & Guttridge Cowes	35'6" 10' 7/8	Isaac and Mary Bolton Legacy pf Miss Bolton and Northumberland War Distress Relief Fund.	880 £12,548 8t15	2x20hp (ts) Ferry FKR.3 3-cyl (d)	Cullercoats 15.3.1951-21.11.63 (29/31) Sold 1964
27.	1950 (510) Groves & Guttridge Cowes	35'6" 10' 7/8	City of Leeds City of Leeds Lifeboat Fund.	881 £13,939 8t16	2x20hp (ts) Ferry FKR.3 3-cyl (d)	Redcar 15.5.1951-2.65 (52/31) Sold 3.1965

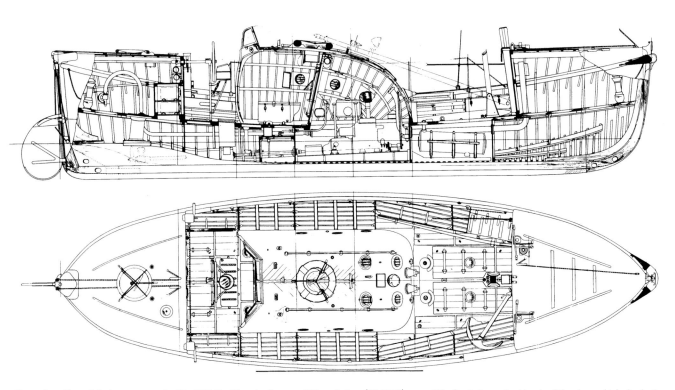

General profile and deck arrangement of the 35ft 6in SR motor Isaac and Mary Bolton *(ON.880), one of the five twin-engined boats of the class, which also had an engine shelter that gave them an appearance similar to the non-self-righting Liverpool motor lifeboats.*

13 • Liverpool single-engined motor 35ft 6in

Introduced 1931, last built 1941, 28 built.

The Liverpool motor lifeboat, designed by James Barnett, was developed from the 35ft 6in self-righting type and the two classes shared many features. The Liverpool was not self-righting, but was light enough to be suitable for carriage launching, having been designed in response to requests from crews at stations who preferred non-self-righting boats because of their greater initial stability. The protective tunnel for the propeller was formed by increasing the height of the deadwood, the external top of which formed the top of the tunnel with the propeller shaft running through the reinforced deadwood.

The hull was divided into six watertight compartments, with 149 air cases fitted into the hold, wing compartments and end boxes. End boxes were incorporated, but these were much less tall than those of the self-righting type. The single-screw versions of the class, in accordance with RNLI policy, carried auxiliary sails, consisting of jib, fore-lug and jib-headed mizzen and could be accurately described as motor sailers. A drop keel was housed in a casing beneath the well deck, just forward of the engine-room canopy and the rudder could be triced up as required.

Power came from an RNLI-designed six-cylinder Weyburn AE6 petrol engine, which developed 35bhp at 3,300 rpm and drove a shrouded single screw through a four to one reduction gear.

The 35ft 6in Liverpool motor Anne Allen *(ON.760) during trials. She served at Skegness for more than twenty years.*

The engine was watertight and able to continue running even if submerged, provided the air intake remained above water level. The fuel capacity of forty-eight gallons gave the boat a range of fifty nautical miles at her maximum speed of 7.25 knots, increasing to seventy nautical miles at a cruising speed of 6.5 knots. With a displacement of 6.75 tons and a stability range of 93 degrees, these boats could accommodate forty-five survivors, in addition to a crew of between seven and ten, in rough weather.

| Year (Yd No) | Length | Name | ON | Engines | Stations (launches/lives saved) |
| Builder | Breadth | Donor | Cost | | |
Place	Crew		Weight		Disposal
1. 1931 (175)	35′6″	Oldham	750	1x35hp	Hoylake 1.10.1931-14.2.52 (43/20)
Groves & Guttridge	10′	Gift from the inhabitants of the	£3995	Weyburn	
Cowes	8/7	town of Oldham.	5t16	6-cyl AE6	Sold 1952

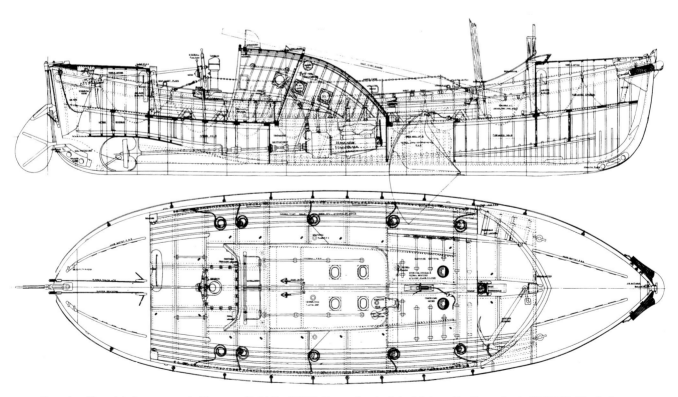

General profile and deck arrangement of the non-self-righting 35ft 6in Liverpool motor Robert Paton – The Always Ready *(ON.766). The single propeller was protected by the keel making the boat ideal for launching and recovering over a beach.*

13 • Liverpool single-engined motor 35ft 6in

Year (Yd No) Builder Place	Length Breadth Crew	Name Donor	ON Cost Weight	Engines	Stations (launches/lives saved) Disposal
2. 1932 (T2255) Thornycroft Chiswick	35'6" 10' 8/7	Anne Allen Legacy of Mrs Anne Allen, Spalding, Lincs.	760 £3340 6t8	1x35hp Weyburn 6-cyl AE6	Skegness 10.12.1932-8.12.53 (120/43) Sold 1953
3. 1933 (W1746) J. S. White Cowes	35'6" 10' 8/7	Nellie and Charlie Legacy of Mr Neil Robinson, Pitlochry.	764 £3416 6t	1x35hp Weyburn 6-cyl AE6	Anstruther 18.3.1933-18.6.50 (54/72) Sold 4.1951
4. 1933 (W1747) J. S. White Cowes	35'6" 10' 8/7	Fifi and Charles Legacy of Mr Charles C. Ashley, Mentone, France.	765 £3297 6t	1x35hp Weyburn 6-cyl AE6	Weston-super-Mare 7.9.1933-17.3.62 (68/83) Sold 10.1962
5. 1933 (W1748) J. S. White Cowes	35'6" 10' 8/7	The Always Ready/ 1934- Robert Paton – The Always Ready Legacy of Mrs E. B. Browne, but renamed after Runswick Coxswain.	766 £3187 6t	1x35hp Weyburn 6-cyl AE6	Runswick 1.10.1933-14.1.54 (51/17) Sold 5.1954
6. 1934 (194) Groves & Guttridge Cowes	35'6" 10'3" 8/7	Harriot Dixon Legacy of Mr W. E. Dixon.	770 £3317 6t	1x35hp Weyburn 6-cyl AE6	Cromer No.2 8.1934-28.10.64 (55/20) Sold 12.1964
7. 1934 (W1771) J. S. White Cowes	35'6" 10' 8/7	The Three Sisters Legacy of Miss Margaret Quiller Couch.	771 £3248 6t	1x35hp Weyburn 6-cyl AE6	Coverack 14.8.1934-24.7.54 (26/61) Sold 1954
8. 1934 (195) Groves & Guttridge Cowes	35'6" 10' 8/7	Elizabeth and Albina Whitley Legacy of Mr Whitley.	772 £3295 6t	1x35hp Weyburn 6-cyl AE6	Flamborough 31.8.1934-7.12.48 (56/63) Reserve 1948-52 (0/0) Sold 1.1953
9. 1934 (W1772) J. S. White Cowes	35'6" 10' 8/7	Joseph Braithwaite Legacy of Mr Joseph Braithwaite.	773 £3210 6t	1x35hp Weyburn 6-cyl AE6	Maryport 28.8.1934-31.12.49 (35/30) Reserve 1950-52 (1/0) Sold 12.1952
10. 1936 (W1803) J. S. White Cowes	35'6" 10'3" 8/7	W. R. A. Legacies of Mr A. Gardiner, Miss M. B. Savage, and Miss A. Matthews.	781 £3447 6t1	1x35hp Weyburn 6-cyl AE6	North Sunderland 30.1.1936-8.4.54 (56/44) Reserve 1954-58 (6/0) Sold 1958
11. 1936 (W1804) J. S. White Cowes	35'6" 10'3" 8/7	Margaret Dawson Legacy of Mrs M. Dawson.	782 £3437 6t1	1x35hp Weyburn 6-cyl AE6	Gourdon 20.1.1936-26.4.52 (37/13) Reserve 1952-5 (0/0) Sold 1956
12. 1936 (210) Groves & Guttridge Cowes	35'6" 10'3" 8/7	Foresters' Centenary Ancient Order of Foresters.	786 £3569 6t1	1x35hp Weyburn 6-cyl AE6	Sheringham 25.6.1936-10.7.61 (129/82) Sold 1961
13. 1936 (W1817) J. S. White Cowes	35'6" 10'3" 8/7	Elizabeth Wills Allen Executors of the late Miss E. W. Allen, Northam, Devon.	791 £3776 6t4	1x35hp Weyburn 6-cyl AE6	Seaham Harbour 5.12.1936-12.1.50 (18/17) Reserve 1950-53 (0/0) Sold 2.1953
14. 1936 (W1818) J. S. White Cowes	35'6" 10'3" 8/7	Annie Ronald And Isabella Forrest Gift from Miss A. Ronald, Paisley; and legacy of Mrs I. Forrest, Glasgow.	792 £3771 6t4	1x35hp Weyburn 6-cyl AE6	St Abbs 5.12.1936-20.10.49 (28/73) Reserve 1949-56 (17/7) Bridlington 22.8.1952-17.6.53 Scarborough 3.1956-21.10.58 (9/0) Llandudno 10.1959-31.1.64 (36/21) Sold 3.1965
15. 1937 (W1822) J. S. White Cowes	35'6" 10'3" 8/7	Clarissa Langdon Legacy of Mr Walter Langdon.	793 £3669 6t1	1x35hp Weyburn 6-cyl AE6	Boulmer 11.2.1937-9.10.62 (68/24) Seaham Harbour 13.2-10.9.1963 (1/0) Reserve 1963-65 (2/0) Sold 3.1965
16. 1937 (W1823) J. S. White Cowes	35'6" 10'3" 8/7	Richard Silver Oliver Legacy of Mrs I. A. Oliver, Tadcaster.	794 £3684 6t1	1x35hp Weyburn 6-cyl AE6	Cullercoats 11.2.1937-22.4.39 (3/0) Capsized on exercise 22.4.1939, six crew lost Newquay 22.3.1940-4.6.45 (21/11) Ilfracombe 10.1945-9.10.52 (15/23) Criccieth 1953-61 (13/0) Sold 1963
17. 1937 (218) Groves & Guttridge Cowes	35'6" 10'3" 8/7	Frank and William Oates Legacy of Mr C. G. Oates.	795 £3835 6t1	1x35hp Weyburn 6-cyl AE6	Eyemouth 11.3.1937-12.12.51 (17/9) Girvan 2.4.1952-2.9.56 (17/0) Reserve 1956-64 (21/8) Sold 1964

Year (Yd No) Builder Place	Length Breadth Crew	Name Donor	ON Cost Weight	Engines	Stations (launches/lives saved) Disposal
18.	1937 (219) Groves & Guttridge Cowes	35'6" 10'3" 8/7	[Herbert John] -	796 £3838 6t1	1x35hp Weyburn 6-cyl AE6	[Stemmed for Cloughey] Destroyed by fire at Groves & Guttridge boatyard, 18.6.1937
19.	1937 (S64) Saunders-Roe Cowes	35'6" 10'3" 8/7	Howard D Gift of Mr T. B. Davis, Jersey.	797 £3623 6t1	1x35hp Weyburn 6-cyl AE6	St Helier 12.8.1937-14.10.48 (23/46)* Flamborough 7.12.1948-20.6.53 (25/16) Arbroath 7.10.1953-26.6.56 (9/1) Reserve 1956-64 (13/3) Seaham Harbour 29.11.1962-13.2.63 (0/0) Sold 1964
20.	1937 (220) Groves & Guttridge Cowes	35'6" 10'3" 8/7	Ann Isabella Pyemont Gift of Mr John Pyemont, Epsom, Surrey.	798 £3908 6t1	1x35hp Weyburn 6-cyl AE6	Kilmore Quay 12.8.1937-10.65 (76/44) Sold 1966
21.	1937 (S65) Saunders-Roe Cowes	35'6" 10'3" 8/7	Helen Sutton Executors of the late Mrs Sutton.	799 £3637 6t1	1x35hp Weyburn 6-cyl AE6	Peel 17.7.1937-29.7.52 (38/14) Reserve 1952-58 (4/2) Sold 1958
22.	1937 (221) Groves & Guttridge Cowes	35'6" 10'3" 8/7	Sarah Ann Austin Legacy of Mrs Sarah Ann Walker, Leeds; Governors of the Skelton Bounty.	800 £3895 6t1	1x35hp Weyburn 6-cyl AE6	Blackpool 12.6.1937-12.61 (47/30) Reserve 1962-65 (6/0) Sold 8.1965
23.	1939 (257) Groves & Guttridge Cowes	35'6" 10'3" 8/7	Herbert John Legacies of Miss B. A. Athill and Mr S. M. Poland.	825 £4054 6t15	1x35hp Weyburn 6-cyl AE6	Cloughey 15.7.1939-17.6.52 (46/67) Youghal 2.8.1952-19.10.66 (14/30) Sold 1966
24.	1939 Morgan Giles Teignmouth	35'6" 10'3" 8/7	George and Elizabeth Gow Legacy of Mrs E. L. Gow, London.	827 £4709 6t17	1x35hp Weyburn 6-cyl AE6	Aberdeen No.2 19.10.1939-16.10.43 & 14.4.1947-62 (2/0) Taken over by RAF 1943, used for rescue work in the Azores Reserve 1962-64 (15/0) Sold 1965
25.	1939 (262) Groves & Guttridge Cowes	35'6" 10'3" 8/7	Caroline Oates Aver and William Maine Legacies of Mrs C. Aver and Miss C. L. Maine.	831 £4289 6t14	1x35hp Weyburn 6-cyl AE6	St Ives 13.1.1940-11.4.48 (50/34) Ferryside 4.1948-6.60 (4/0) Sold 7.1960
26.	1939 (263) Groves & Guttridge Cowes	35'6" 10'3" 8/7	W. & .B/ 1940- Lucy Lavers 1940- Legacy of Mr Lavers and estate of Mr E. J. Williams.	832 £4455 6t18	1x35hp Weyburn 6-cyl AE6/1963- 1x47hp Parsons Porbeagle (d)	[Stemmed- Porthoustock] Aldeburgh 2 5.1940-10.2.59 (30/7) Reserve 1959-68 (52/37) Sold 1968
27.	1940 (264) G & Guttridge Cowes	35'6" 10'3" 8/7	The Cuttle Legacy of Miss F. L. Cuttle, Rotherham.	833 £4444 6t13	1x35hp Weyburn 6-cyl AE6	Filey 22.5.1940-21.10.53 (77/28) Skegness 8.12.1953-20.4.64 (48/11) Reserve 1964-66 (0/0) Sold 8.1966
28.	1941 (265) Groves & Guttridge Cowes	35'6" 10'3" 8/7	Jose Neville Legacy of Mrs E. Neville, Barnes, Surrey.	834 £4474 6t11	1x35hp Weyburn 6-cyl AE6	Caister 15.5.1941-22.1.64 (107/75) Reserve 1964-66 (1/0) Sold 8.1966

* Under enemy control at Jersey 1.7.1940-9.5.45.

Sarah Ann Austin (ON.800) returns to the beach at Blackpool (From an old postcard supplied by Nicholas Leach)

George and Elizabeth Gow (ON.795) with sails stowed. The auxiliary sails were important for the single-engined Liverpool lifeboats. (RNLI)

14 • Beach 'Aldeburgh' motor 41ft

Introduced 1931, last built 1949, 5 built.

The 41ft Beach motor was designed for stations which employed beach launching, but where the smaller 35ft 6in types were deemed too lightweight for the local conditions. The 41ft boat was seen as a development of the Norfolk & Suffolk type and became known as the 'Aldeburgh' type after the station at which the first boat served. It was in many respects similar to the 41ft Watson motor, but had a strengthened hull to withstand the extra stresses of being dragged over a beach, as well as greater breadth, good freeboard, a flat floor, stout bilge keels and a heavy iron keel weighing one and a half tons. The type was non-self-righting, with no end boxes and flush decks fore and aft, carried no water ballast, and the hull was divided into seven watertight compartments and 135 air cases. A large after cockpit provided shelter for crew and engine controls, and 110 gallons of fuel was carried. The boats were all powered by twin petrol engines, and two of the five were re-engined with more powerful diesels while in service.

The Viscountess Wakefield *(ON.783) beaches at Hythe. The hull of the 41ft Beach type was strengthened so that it would withstand the potentially damaging beach launch and recover procedure. (RNLI)*

Year (Yd No) Builder Place	Length Breadth Crew	Name Donor	ON Cost Weight	Engines	Stations (launches/lives saved) Disposal
1. 1931 (W1726) J. S. White Cowes	41' 12'3" 10	Abdy Beauclerk Legacy of Mrs Jane E. King, St Leonards-on-Sea.	751 £6,384 15t12	2x35bhp (ts) Weyburn AE.6 6-cyl (p)	Aldeburgh No.1 11.12.1931-31.12.58 (118/139) Sold 1959
2. 1933 (183) Groves & Guttridge Cowes	41' 12'3" 10	Charles Cooper Henderson Legacy of H. Cooper Henderson.	761 £5,704 15t9	2x35bhp (ts) Weyburn AE.6 6-cyl (p)/1963- 2x47hp Parsons Porbeagle (d)	Dungeness 18.7.1933-31.8.57 (170/63) Reserve 1957-74 (126/93) Sold 1.1976
3. 1933 (184) Groves & Guttridge Cowes	41' 12'3" 10	Charles Dibdin (Civil Service No.2) Civil Service Lifeboat Fund.	762 £5,664 15t	2x35bhp (ts) Weyburn AE.6 6-cyl (p)	Walmer 28.7.1933-18.3.59 (241/412) Sold 1961
4. 1936 (207) Groves & Guttridge Cowes	41' 12'3" 10	The Viscountess Wakefield Gift of Rt Hon The Lord Wakefield of Hythe, CBE.	783 £6,089 14t8	2x35bhp (ts) Weyburn AE.6 6-cyl (p)	Hythe 24.2.1936-5.40 (17/9) Lost on beaches of Dunkirk, 31.5.1940
5. 1949 Sussex Yacht Co Shoreham	41' 12'3" 8	Beryl Tollemache Gift of Sir Lionel and Lady Tollemache, Richmond.	859 £15,012 15t2	2x35bhp (ts) Weyburn AE.6 6-cyl (p)/1963- 2x47hp Parsons Porbeagle (d)	Eastbourne 25.6.1949-21.5.77 (176/154) Reserve 1977-79 (5/7) Sold 9.1979

Plans of the second 41ft Beach motor lifeboat, Charles Cooper Henderson *(ON.761). The type was very similar to the 41ft Watson but was broader and had a strengthened hull to withstand the stresses of launch and recovery across shingle beaches, such as that at Dungeness where this lifeboat was stationed for more than twenty years.*

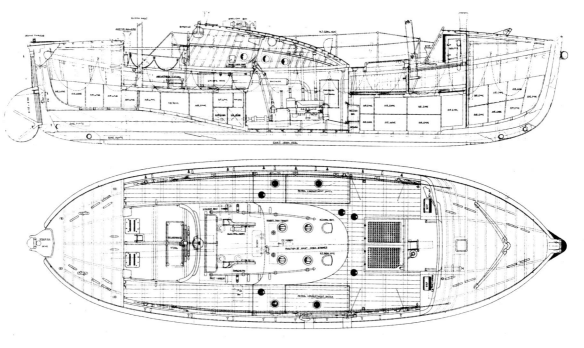

15 • Watson motor 41ft

Introduced 1933, last built 1952, 13 built

The 41ft Watson was designed for stations at which a powerful lifeboat was deemed necessary but where the larger Barnett or Watson motor lifeboats were not suitable. It was intended primarily for launching down permanent slipways. The non-self-righting hull was divided into seven watertight compartments fitted with 135 air cases, and had sixteen relieving scuppers which could free the boat of water in less than half a minute. It had two cockpits, one forward and the other aft, with room for sixteen people. The larger aft cockpit provided shelter for the crew of eight and housed the engine controls. The waterline length was 39ft 6in, the draft was 3ft 8in and the type was fitted with twin engines giving a maximum speed for 7.5 knots. The boats also carried two sails for use either as a steadying sail or in the event of engine failure. The last four boats, built between 1948 and 1952, were a modified cabin version. Many 41ft Watsons were re-engined with twin 47hp Parsons Porbeagle four-cylinder diesels, more powerful than the original engines.

The Whitby lifeboat Mary Ann Hepworth *(ON.808) bursts through a wave at the entrance to the harbour. She was one of many 41ft Watsons to be kept in a boathouse and slipway launched.*

Year (Yd No) Builder Place	Len Bre Crew	Name Donor	ON Cost Weight	Engines	Stations (launches/lives saved) Disposal
1. 1933 (181) Groves & Guttridge Cowes	41' 11'8" 8	Rosa Woodd and Phyllis Lunn Legacy Mrs Rose Lord and collections by Mr W. Lunn and Mrs Perowne.	758 £6,132 14t10	2x35bhp Weyburn AE.6 6-cyl (p)/1963- 2x47hp Parsons Porbeagle (d)	Shoreham Harbour 4.1.1933-17.1.63 (244/143) Reserve 1963-73 (53/19) Sold 1973
2. 1933 (185) Groves & Guttridge Cowes	41' 11'8" 8	Duke of York King George's Fund for Sailors.	769 £5,635 14t10	2x35bhp Weyburn AE.6 6-cyl (p)	Lizard 14.2.1934-61 (58/82) Sold 1961
3. 1936 (226) Groves & Guttridge Cowes	41' 11'8" 8	Rachel and Mary Evans Legacy of Mr T. D. Evans, Malpas, Monmouthshire.	806 £6,458 12t4	2x35bhp Weyburn AE.6 6-cyl (p)	Barry Dock 9.12.1937-3.68 (96/80) Reserve 1968-4.69 (1/0) Broke moorings at Weston, wrecked 12.4.1969
4. 1938 (227) Groves & Guttridge Cowes	41' 11'8" 8	Inbhear Mor RNLI Funds.	807 £6,506 13t18	2x35bhp Weyburn AE.6 6-cyl (d)/1963- 2x47hp Parsons Porbeagle (p)	Arklow 14.7.1938-68 (87/98) Reserve 1968-73 (23/42) Sold 1974

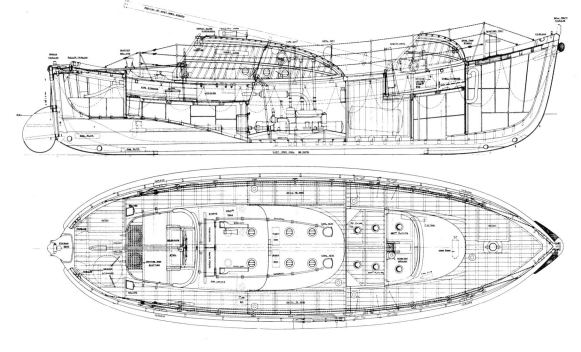

General arrangement drawing of the first 41ft Watson constructed, Rosa Woodd and Phyllis Lunn (ON.758), for Shoreham Harbour.

15 · Watson motor 41ft

Year (Yd No) Builder Place	Length Breadth Crew	Name Donor	ON Cost Weight	Engines	Stations (launches/lives saved) Disposal
5. 1938 (228) Groves & Guttridge Cowes	41' 11'8" 8	Mary Ann Hepworth Gift of Mr Hepworth.	808 £6,575 14t2	2x35bhp Weyburn AE.6 6-cyl (p)/1963 2x47hp Parsons Porbeagle (d)	Whitby 12.4.1938-11.74 (372/201) Sold 1975
6. 1938 (237) Groves & Guttridge Cowes	41' 11'8" 8	Edmund and Mary Robinson Gift of Mrs Mary Robinson, Liverpool.	812 £6,533 14t3	2x35bhp Weyburn AE.6 6-cyl (p)	New Brighton No.2 15.12.1938-23.9.50 (69/80) Reserve 9.1950-64 (45/41) Sold 3.1964
7. 1938 (238) Groves & Guttridge Cowes	41' 11'8" 8	Ann Letitia Russell Legacy of Miss A. L. Russell, Manchester.	813 £6,634 13t10	2x35bhp Weyburn AE.6 6-cyl (p)/1963- 2x47hp Parsons Porbeagle (d)	Fleetwood 16.2.1939-24.1.76 (205/158) Sold 4.1977
8. 1939 (255) Groves & Guttridge Cowes	41' 11'8" 8	Matthew Simpson Legacy of Miss C. F. Simpson, Lancaster.	823 £7,206 13t10	2x35bhp Weyburn AE.6 6-cyl (p)/1963- 2x47hp Parsons Porbeagle (d)	Port Erin 17.10.1939-1.4.72 (72/24) Reserve 1972-76 (21/14) Sold 1976
9. 1939 (256) Groves & Guttridge Cowes	41' 11'8" 8	John Pyemont Legacy of Mr John Pyemont, Epsom.	824 £7,357 13t10	2x35bhp Weyburn AE.6 6-cyl (p)	Tynemouth 24.10.1939-4.41 (20/59) Destroyed through enemy action, 9.4.1941
10. 1948 (481) Groves & Guttridge Cowes	41' 11'8" 8	Susan Ashley Legacy of Charles Carr Ashley, Mentone, France.	856 £13,357 14t16	2x35bhp Weyburn AE.6 6-cyl (p)/1963- 2x47hp Parsons Porbeagle (d)	Sennen Cove 25.7.1948-72 (87/64) Barry Dock No.2 1973-7.79 (7/3) Tynemouth (BB) 1979-80 (0/0) Display at Chatham
11. 1949 Morgan Giles Teignmouth	41' 11'8" 8	Glencoe, Glasgow Legacy of Mrs L. Glen, Glasgow.	857 £11,885 14t	2x35bhp Weyburn AE.6 6-cyl (d)/1963- 2x47hp Parsons Porbeagle (d)	Buckie 25.11.1949-8.60 (27/9) Reserve 1960-65 (9/7) Portavogie 26.10.1965-78 (39/27) Sold 1979
12. 1949 Sussex Yacht Co Shoreham	41' 11'8" 8	R. L. P. Legacy of Mrs Alice Pugh, Kensington.	859 £15,584 14t12	2x35bhp Weyburn AE.6 6-cyl (p)	Swanage 26.2.1949-10.75 (341/242) Reserve 1975-81 (13/2) Sold 8.1981
13. 1952 (897) William Osborne Littlehampton	41' 11'8" 8	St Andrew (Civil Service No.10) Civil Service Lifeboat Fund.	897 £20,700 14t5	2x35bhp Weyburn AE.6 6-cyl (p)/1963- 2x47hp Parsons Porbeagle (d)	Whitehills 9.3.1952-11.59 (9/0) Girvan 1961-68 (18/8) Arklow 1968-2.1973 (24/6) Reserve 1959-61 (5/0) and 1973-82 (25/7) Sold 1982

Ann Letitia Russell (ON.813), a 41ft Watson motor that served at Fleetwood for well over thirty years. She was one of several 41ft Watsons that was launched down a slipway. (From an old postcard supplied by Nicholas Leach)

16 • Surf light motor 32ft

Introduced 1935, last built 1941, 9 built.

The 32ft Surf non-self-righting type, designed by James Barnett, was a light boat which could be launched from a carriage and work in very shallow water. Intended for stations where launching a heavier type was difficult, the introduction of the Surf type enabled the RNLI to realise its main goal at the time of providing motor lifeboats at the few remaining statioins which operated pulling and sailing lifeboats and filled a gap in motor lifeboat cover at stations where a light boat was required. The first two boats, with crew and gear on board, weighed only 4.25 tons, 2.5 tons lighter than the 35ft 6in self-righting type. Their size and weight, however, while beneficial when launching, limited them to inshore work in moderate conditions. They were fitted with two engines and, when introduced, were the only twin-engined lifeboats capable of being carriage launched.

The most noteworthy aspect of the design was the means of propulsion that was employed. While the first boat (ON.779) was powered by screw propellers, the second (ON.780) was fitted with an innovative new means of propulsion, the Hotchkiss Internal Cone, and later boats had Gill Water Jets. The Hotchkiss Cones were seen as particularly advantageous for boats operating in shallow water, such as ON.780 from her station of Wells-next-the-Sea, as they were set inside the hull and the propeller was protected from damage.

The Surf boats had twin engines and carried two oars, but no auxiliary sails. Although three different forms of propulsion were used, the engines were all based on the same F.2 model, a special light horizontal design with twin cylinders built by Weyburn Engineering to an RNLI design for full load operation of 3,000rpm but rated down to 2,400rpm. As the normal arrangment for Hotch-kiss Cones was for a pair to be fitted, this dictated the need for twin engines. The performance of the boats differed, with the screw-powered boat having a slight edge over those powered by

The first 32ft Surf motor lifeboat Rosabella *(ON.779) at Ilfracombe. The only Surf lifeboat to be powered by conventional screw propellers, she was a completely open boat with the engine housed in a wooden box amidships. (From an old photo supplied by Jeff Morris)*

the Cones. ON.779 achieved a top speed of 7.5 knots and was able to travel fifty-six miles without refuelling while ON.780, fitted with Hotchkiss Cones, managed 6.82 knots in calm weather, 6.66 knots in rough conditions, and 4.25 knots on one engine with a radius at cruising speed of forty-three miles.

The non-self-righting hull, made of double-skin mahogany, was essentially open with small end boxes fore and aft. The bulkheads surrounding the engines and fuel tanks were also of double mahogany. Between 80 and 100 air cases were fitted to the boats throughout the hull. Because they were not intended to be at sea for more than a few hours, they were initially open lifeboats, although small shelters became a feature from the third of the class onwards. Unusually for motor lifeboats, they were steered by tiller, the position of which changed in some of the class. It was placed further forward on some of the boats by the utilisation of relieving ropes.

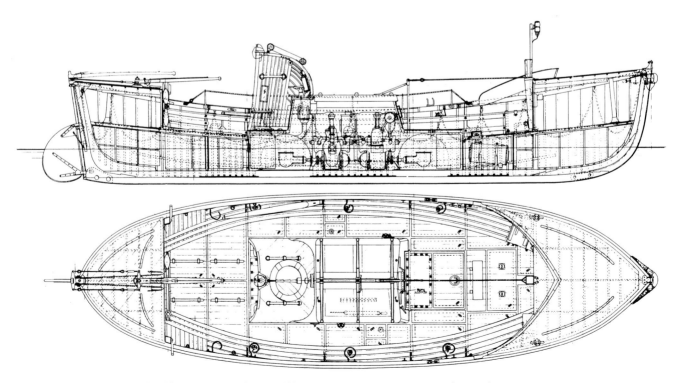

General arrangement and profile drawings of the fourth Surf lifeboat to be built, Thomas Kirk Wright *(ON.811), fitted with Hotchkiss Cone impellers.*

16 · Surf light motor 32ft

Year (Yd No) Builder Place	Length Breadth Crew	Name Donor	ON Cost Weight	Engines	Stations (launches/lives saved) Disposal
1. 1935 (W1790) J. S. White Cowes	32' 9' 7	Rosabella Legacy of John Hogg, Boscombe.	779 £3,264 3t17	2x12hp Weyburn F2 Twin screw	Ilfracombe 9.3.1936-4.6.45 (24/12) Sold to KNZHRM 6.1946 (Terschelling 1946-55) Sold 1955
2. 1935 (206) Groves & Guttridge Cowes	32' 9' 7	Royal Silver Jubilee 1910-1935 Gift of Mrs E. W. Montford, JP.	780 £2,918 3t17	2x12hp Weyburn F2 Hotchkiss cone	Wells 6.2.1936-4.6.45 (43/23) Sold to KNZHRM 6.1946 (ren. Rosilee, Vlieland 1946-59) Sold 1959
3. 1938 (235) Groves & Guttridge Cowes	32' 9'3" 7	Augustus and Laura Legacy Miss E. A. Northey, London.	810 £3,355 4t16	2x12hp Weyburn F2 Hotchkiss cone	Newbiggin 21.10.1938-3.8.50 (28/17) Sold 2.10.1950
4. 1938 (236) Groves & Guttridge Cowes	32' 9'3" 7	Thomas Kirk Wright Legacy Mr T. Kirk Wright, Bournemouth.	811 £3,337 4t19	2x12hp Weyburn F2 Hotchkiss cone	Poole 12.1.1939-18.7.62 (64/15) Sold 1963 Display at Poole from 1975
5. 1939 (250) Groves & Guttridge Cowes	32' 9'3" 7	Kate Greatorex Legacy Mrs K. Greatorex, Mytton Hall, Shrewsbury.	816 £3,478 5t6	2x12hp Weyburn F2 Gill Jet Units	Minehead 30.5.1939-10.12.51 (20/7) Sold 27.3.1952
6. 1939 (251) Groves & Guttridge Cowes	32' 9'3" 7	Laurence Ardern, Stockport Legacy Mrs M. A. Ardern, Prestbury.	817 £3,492 5t6	2x12hp Weyburn F2 Hotchkiss cone	Barmouth 22.5.1939-11.3.49 (35/1) Reserve 1949-51 (0/0) Sold 27.12.1951
7. 1939 (W5007) J. S. White Cowes	32' 9'3" 7	The Gordon Warren Legacy of Mr H. B. G. Warren, Liverpool.	835 £3,701 4t14	2x12hp Weyburn F2 Hotchkiss cone	Rhyl 3.11.1939-15.9.49 (35/5) Reserve 1949-51 (0/0) Sold 10.1.1952
8. 1940 (R225) Alexr. Robertson Sandbank	32' 9'3" 7	Norman Nasmyth Legacy of the late Norman J. Nasmyth, Glenfarg.	836 £3,690 4t10	2x12hp Weyburn F2 Hotchkiss cone	Montrose No.2 30.6.1940-18.5.50 (0/0) Reserve 1950-65 (0/0) Sold 1966
9. 1941 (R224) Alexr. Robertson Sandbank	32' 9'3" 7	John Ryburn Legacy of Mr William McCunn, Largs.	837 £3,791 4t14	2x12hp Weyburn F2 Hotchkiss cone	Newburgh 6.1941-30.9.65 (11/19) Capsized 26.1.1942 on service, two lost Sold 1966

32ft Surf motor The Gordon Warren *(ON.835) was one of the Surf type to be fitted with Hotchkiss cone propulsion units. She served at Rhyl for ten years from where she was launched across a flat, shallow beach. (From an old photo supplied by Jeff Morris)*

32ft Surf motor Laurence Ardern, Stockport *(ON.817), fitted with Hotchkiss cone propulsion units, served at Barmouth for ten years. Her shallow draft made her ideally suited to crossing the bar of the Mawddach estuary. (From an old photo supplied by Jeff Morris)*

17 • Harbour 28ft

Introduced 1938, 1 built.

The 28ft Harbour class was a small motor lifeboat, only one of which was built. Specially designed for the Poolbeg station by Richard Oakley, the RNLI's Surveyor and later Consulting Naval Architect, she was 28ft long and weighed just over three tons. A series of small self-righting lifeboats served at Poolbeg until the early years of the twentieth century when whale-boats were purpose-built for the station. When a motor lifeboat was to be sent for service, as no comparable class of motor lifeboat existed with which to replace the small 30ft pulling boat, the Harbour class was designed. The boat operated from her base at Poolbeg in Dublin Docks and covered the comparatively sheltered waters of the Liffey river and estuary.

The boat's hull was divided into eight watertight compartments and fitted with twenty-nine air cases; unusually for a lifeboat, she had a transom stern. Her crew numbered five and she could take eighteen people in rough weather. The 20hp engine, built in a watertight compartment, powered a single screw and at her maximum speed of 7.5 knots she had a range of forty miles. This design foreshadowed the need at certain stations for a smaller type of rescue boat that could be used close inshore and could be regarded as the forerunner of the inshore lifeboat. A class of ten

The unique 28ft Harbour lifeboat Helen Blake *(ON.809) served at Poolbeg and covered the Liffey estuary and the inland waters of Dublin Bay.*

Harbour lifeboats was planned and, had the war not broken out soon afterwards, more boats of the class would almost certainly have been built. The sole example of the Harbour class has been on display as part of the Lifeboat Collection in Chatham Historic Dockyard since the mid-1990s.

Year (Yd No) Builder Place	Length Breadth Crew	Name Donor	ON Cost Weight	Engines	Stations (launches/lives saved) Disposal
1 1938 (G&G 234) Groves & Guttridge Cowes	28' 8' 5	Helen Blake Legacy Mrs Helen Blake, Handcross.	809 £1,893 3t4	1x20hp Hyland XL 4-cyl (p)	Poolbeg 4.1938-31.10.59 (13/5) Sold 11.1959

The 28ft Harbour lifeboat Helen Blake *(ON.809) on the river Liffey in the centre of Dublin, probably on a fund-raising trip.*

18 • Liverpool twin-engined 35ft 6in

Introduced 1940, last built 1954, 31 (32) built.

For stations that employed carriage launching, the RNLI built two types of motor lifeboat – the self-righter and the non-self-righting Liverpool class. Advances in one type mirrored the developments with the other and so, with the introduction of twin engines and twin screws in the post-1945 motor self-righters, the Liverpool class was developed with twin engines and twin screws. The introduction of the motor tractor to assist beach launching and recovery meant heavier boats could be used for carriage launching as weight was not such a great consideration, so having twin engines and carrying more equipment was possible. The Liverpool class weighed approximately 8.5 tons, more than two tons heavier than the original light self-righting motor types of the late 1920s.

The 35ft 6in Liverpool was built with a ballast tank which filled with half a ton of water when the boats went afloat. The hull was divided into six watertight compartments and fitted with 120 air cases. The engine room formed one of the watertight compartments and the engines would continue to run even if the engine room was flooded. Clearing the decks of water took about twelve seconds. The diesel-engined version, from ON.869 onwards, had a top speed of 7.5 knots and carried enough fuel to travel 120 miles

Launch of William and Laura *(ON.870) at Newcastle (Down), a station this lifeboat served for more than thirty years. (Colin Watson)*

at full speed. In the 1960s, nearly all of the original twin-screw Liverpools built with petrol engines were re-engined with more powerful diesel engines, which gave the boats a greater range and were more economical to run. The Liverpool class was phased out when the 37ft Oakley was introduced at many carriage stations and was replaced at some by Atlantic 21 rigid-inflatables.

Year (Yd No) Builder Place	Length Breadth Crew	Name Donor	ON Cost Weight	Engines	Stations (launches/lives saved) Disposal
1. 1940 (275) Groves & Guttridge Cowes	35'6" 10'8" 7	[W. and B.] — —	839 — —	2x18hp Weyburn 6-cyl AE4 (p)	[Prototype - not stemmed] Blitzed at Yard 4.5.1942
2. 1945 (418) Groves & Guttridge Cowes	35'6" 10'8" 7	Cecil Paine Legacy of Mr A. C. Paine.	850 £7,462 7t15	2x18hp Weyburn AE4 6-cyl (p)/ 1964- 2x32hp Parsons Penguin (d)	Wells 25.7.1945-1.6.65 (47/20) Kilmore Quay 10.1965-2.72 (22/0) Reserve 1972-73 (0/0) Sold 1973
3. 1945 (485) Groves & Guttridge Cowes	35'6" 10'8" 7	Edgar, George, Orlando and Eva Child Legacies of Mr R. B. Pol, Mr O. F. Child, and others.	861 £9,751 8t14	2x18hp Weyburn AE4 6-cyl (p)/ 1965- 2x32hp Parsons Penguin (d)	St Ives 11.4.1948-4.68 (116/61) Reserve 7.1968-70 (3/0) Blackpool 6.1970-5.6.75 (16/3) Relief 1975-82 (0/0) Sold 1983
4. 1948 (486) Groves & Guttridge Cowes	35'6" 10'8" 7	Thomas Corbett Gift from the Thomas Corbett Charity, London.	862 £9,581 8t10	2x18hp Weyburn AE4 6-cyl (p)/ 1964- 2x32hp Parsons Penguin (d)	Ramsey 24.9.1948-20.2.70 (60/10) Hoylake 26.9.1970-18.5.74 (12/6) Clogher Head 11.1974-81 (12/0) Sold 1982
5. 1948 (487) Groves & Guttridge Cowes	35'6" 10'8" 7	St Albans St Albans Lifeboat Fund.	863 £9,836 7t17	2x18hp Weyburn AE4 6-cyl (p)/ 1964- 2x32hp- Parsons Penguin (d)	New Quay 12.12.1948-7.70 (66/78) Sold 12.1970
6. 1948 (488) Groves & Guttridge Cowes	35'6" 10'8" 7	The Chieftain Legacy of P. C. Peak, Branksome, Dorset.	864 £9,943 7t19	2x18hp Weyburn AE4 6-cyl (p)/ 1964- 2x32hp Parsons Penguin (d)	Barmouth 11.3..1949-27.2.82 (113/132) Sold 14.4.82
7. 1949 (500) Groves & Guttridge Cowes	35'6" 10'8" 7	Anthony Robert Marshall Legacy of A. R. Marshall, Liverpool.	869 £11,763 8t4	2x20hp Ferry Kadenacy FKR3 3-cyl (d)/ 1965- 2x32hp Parsons Penguin (d)	Rhyl 15.9.1949-26.9.68 (102/51) Reserve 1968-72 (3/0) Pwllheli 7.1972-18.5.79 (20/6) Sold 1980
8. 1949 (501) Groves & Guttridge Cowes	35'6" 10'8" 7	William and Laura Legacy of Miss A. W. Clarke Hall, Bournemouth.	870 £10,843 8t	2x18hp Weyburn AE4 6-cyl (p)/ 1964- 2x32hp Parsons Penguin (d)	Newcastle 17.7.1949-5.80 (58/54) Sold 9.1980
9. 1949 (502) Groves & Guttridge Cowes	35'6" 10'8" 7	William Cantrell Ashley Legacy of Charles Carr Ashley, Mentone, France.	871 £10,964 8t13	2x18hp Weyburn AE4 6-cyl (p)/ 1964- 2x32hp Parsons Penguin (d)	Clovelly 7.9.1949-3.67 (38/24) Sold 1968

18 · Liverpool twin-engined 35ft 6in

Year (Yd No) Builder Place	Length Breadth Crew	Name Donor	ON Cost Weight	Engines	Stations (launches/lives saved) Disposal
10. 1949 (503) Groves & Guttridge Cowes	35'6" 10'8" 7	J. B. Couper of Glasgow Legacy of James B. Couper, Argyllshire.	872 £10,899 8t3	2x18hp Weyburn AE4 6-cyl (p)/ 1965- 2x32hp Parsons Penguin (d)	St -Abbs 20.10.1949-7.2.53 (4/1) Kirkcudbright 4.1953-2.5.65 (35/17) Youghal 1966-71 (10/3) Poole 1972-17.1.74 (31/19) Reserve 1974-75 (2/0) Sold 2.1976
11. 1950 (504) Groves & Guttridge Cowes	35'6" 10'8" 7	George Elmy Legacy of Miss E. Elmy, Stoke Newington.	873 £10,983 8t1	2x18hp Weyburn AE4 6-cyl (p)/ 1963- 2x32hp Parsons Penguin (d)	Seaham Harbour 12.1.1950-11.62 (26/20) Capsized on service 17.11.1962, nine crew lost Reserve 1963-69 (9/2) Poole 11.1969-72 (12/3) Sold 9.1972
12. 1950 (505) Groves & Guttridge Cowes	35'6" 10'8" 7	Robert Lindsay Legacy of Mr R. Lindsay, jnr, Carnoustie.	874 £11,857 8t6	2x20hp Ferry Kadenacy FKR3 3-cyl (d)	Arbroath 12.7.1950-10.53 (4/0) Capsized on service 27.10.1953, six crew lost Girvan 2.9.1955-60 (13/2) Criccieth 16.11.1961-6.4.68 (12/0) Sold 1968
13. 1950 (511) Groves & Guttridge Cowes	35'6" 10'8" 7	Richard Ashley Legacy of Mr Charles Carr Ashley, Mentone, France.	875 £13,154 8t8	2x20hp Ferry Kadenacy FKR3 3-cyl (d)	Newbiggin 3.8.1950-5.9.66 (44/11) Sold 1967
14. 1950-(512) Groves & Guttridge Cowes	35'6" 10'8" 7	James and Ruby Jackson Legacy of Mr J. Jackson.	876 £13,231 8t7	2x20hp Ferry Kadenacy FKR3 3-cyl (d)	Anstruther 3.8.1950-5.65 (63/45) Reserve 1965-67 (0/0) Sold 1969
15. 1950 (W5416) J S White Cowes	35'6" 10'8" 7	George and Caroline Ermen Legacy of Mr G. H. Ermen, Chester.	877 £14,596 8t8	2x20hp Ferry Kadenacy FKR3 3-cyl (d)	Clogher Head 7.7.1950-11.74 (50/24) Sold 7.1974
16. 1951 (RIW721) Rowhedge IW Rowhedge	35'6" 10'8" 7	B. H. M. H. Legacies of Mr C. H. Bailey and Mrs L. Hall, plus gift of Mr F. H. Heys and anonymous.	882 £13,913 8t8	2x18hp Weyburn AE4 6-cyl (p)/ 1964- 2x32hp Parsons Penguin (d)	Minehead 10.12.1951-5.73 (46/11) Relief 1973-81 (16/9) Clogher Head 1981-26.8.84 (3/0) Sold 1985
17. 1951 (515) Groves & Guttridge Cowes	35'6" 10'8" 7	Bassett-Green Gift of Mr W. H. Bassett Green, Winchcombe.	891 £14,038 8t3	2x20hp Ferry Kadenacy FKR3 3-cyl (d)	Padstow No.2 30.7.1951-3.62 (13/6) Poole 18.7.1962-11.69 (17/9) Sold 1969
18. 1951 (516) Groves & Guttridge Cowes	35'6" 10'8" 7	Aguila Wren Aguila Wren Memorial Fund and legacy of Mr Moorhouse.	892 £14,172 7t19	2x20hp Ferry Kadenacy FKR3 3-cyl (d)	Aberystwyth 10.1951-64 (21/14) Redcar 2.1965-11.1972 (32/24) Sold 12.1972
19. 1951 (517) Groves & Guttridge Cowes	35'6" 10'8" 7	Clara and Emily Barwell Legacies of the Misses C. and E. H. Barwell.	893 £14,008 8t9	2x20hp Ferry Kadenacy FKR3 3-cyl (d)	Eyemouth 12.12.1951-63 (14/6) Reserve 1963-68 (11/2) Sold 2.1969
20. 1952 (518) Groves & Guttridge Cowes	35'6" 10'8" 7	Oldham IV RNLI General Funds.	894 £14,162 8t4	2x20hp Ferry Kadenacy FKR3 3-cyl (d)	Hoylake 14.2.1952-26.9.70 (62/45) Sold 9.10.1970

Launch of Anthony Robert Marshall *(ON.869) at Rhyl, with the crew standing by ready to release the holding chains. (Jeff Morris)*

One of five twin-screw Liverpool motor lifeboats completed in 1950, Richard Ashley *(ON.875) on trials before serving at Newbiggin. (RNLI)*

18 • Liverpool twin-engined 35ft 6in

Year (Yd No) Builder Place	Length Breadth Crew	Name Donor	ON Cost Weight	Engines	Stations (launches/lives saved) Disposal
21. 1952 (519) Groves & Guttridge Cowes	35'6" 10'8" 7	Edith Clauson-Thue Legacies of Miss E. M. M. Clauson Thue, Sir Lockhart, Miss Anderson.	895 £14,436 8t18	2x20hp Ferry Kadenacy FKR3 3-cyl (d)	Gourdon 26.4.1952-4.5.69 (14/0) Sold 1969
22. 1952 (520) Groves & Guttridge Cowes	35'6" 10'8" 7	Constance Calverley Legacy of Miss C. Calverley.	902 £14,337 8t15	2x20hp Ferry Kadenacy FKR3 3-cyl (d)	Cloughey 17.6.1952-26.10.65 (22/21) Reserve 1965-70 (2/0) Sold 1970
23. 1952 (521) Groves & Guttridge Cowes	35'6" 10'8" 7	Helena Harris – Manchester & District XXXI Legacy of Miss Harris, and Manchester & District Branch.	903 £13,764 8t5	2x20hp Ferry Kadenacy FKR3 3-cyl (d)	Peel 29.5.1952-5.72 (32/15) Sold 1972
24. 1952 (522) Groves & Guttridge Cowes	35'6" 10'8" 7	Robert and Phemia Brown Legacy of Captain Robert Brown, Anstruther.	904 £14,200 8t4	2x20hp Ferry Kadenacy FKR3 3-cyl (d)	Ilfracombe 6.10.1952-7.66 (46/24) Sold 1967
25. 1952 (523) Groves & Guttridge Cowes	35'6" 10'8" 7	Katherine and Virgoe Buckland Legacies of Cdr. Buckland, Mr H. Woodhead, and British Services Charities.	905 £14,395 8t7	2x20hp Ferry Kadenacy FKR3 3-cyl (d)	Pwllheli 21.1.1953-7.72 (44/11) Sold 1972
26. 1952 (524) Groves & Guttridge Cowes	35'6" 10'8" 7	W. Ross MacArthur of Glasgow Legacy of Mr W. Ross MacArthur, Glasgow.	906 £14,398 8t10	2x20hp Ferry Kadenacy FKR3 3-cyl (d)	St Abbs 7.2.1953-11.64 (32/13) Reserve 1964-68 (4/0) Sold 1968
27. 1953 (525) Groves & Guttridge Cowes	35'6" 10'8" 7	Tillie Morrison, Sheffield II Legacy of Mr Whitaker and RNLI Funds.	914 £14,482 8t6	2x20hp Ferry Kadenacy FKR3 3-cyl (d)	Bridlington 17.6.1953-9.67 (106/36) Reserve 1967-68 (0/0) Sold 1969
28. 1953 (526) Groves & Guttridge Cowes	35'6" 10'8" 7	Friendly Forester Ancient Order of Foresters.	915 £15,738 8t1	2x20hp Ferry Kadenacy FKR3 3-cyl (d)/ 1969- 2x32hp P'sons Penguin (d)	Flamborough 20.5.1953-18.1.83 (186/89) Sold 1984
29. 1953 (527) Groves & Guttridge Cowes	35'6" 10'8" 7	Maria Noble Legacies of Mr H. Noble, Mr West, Mrs Andrews and Mr Williams.	916 £14,594 8t6	2x20hp Ferry Kadenacy FKR3 3-cyl (d)	Exmouth 9.10.1953-2.60 (30/35) Blackpool 12.1961-6.70 (25/3) Reserve 1970-73 (0/0) Sold 1974
30. 1954 (528) Groves & Guttridge Cowes	35'6" 10'8" 7	Isa and Penryn Milsted Legacy of Mrs A. P. Milsted, London.	917 £14,881 8t4	2x20hp Ferry Kadenacy FKR3 3-cyl (d)	Filey 21.10.1953-18.5.68 (87/12) Sold 1969
31. 1954 (529) Groves & Guttridge Cowes	35'6" 10'8" 7	Elliott Gill Legacy of Miss E. M. Gill, Leicester.	918 £15,254 8t15	2x20hp Ferry Kadenacy FKR3 3-cyl (d)	Runswick 14.1.1954-9.70 (39/24) Reserve 1970-74 (1/0) Sold 8.1974
32. 1954 (530) Groves & Guttridge Cowes	35'6" 10'8" 7	Grace Darling RNLI General Funds.	927 £15,040 8t10	2x20hp Ferry Kadenacy FKR3 3-cyl (d)/ 1971- 2x32hp Parsons Penguin (d)	North Sunderland 8.4.1954-7.67 (69/16) Reserve 1967-71 (6/1) Youghal 1971-23.5.84 (31/17) Display from 1985 at Bristol, later Chatham Dockyard

Helena Harris – Manchester & District *(ON.903) at Peel where she was launched down a steep slipway without the aid of a motor tractor. (RNLI)*

Friendly Forester *(ON.915) at sea off Flamborough Head. (From an old postcard in the author's collection)*

19 • Watson cabin motor 46ft

Introduced 1936, last built 1946, 28 built, 2 not finished.

Following a conference held at Clacton in 1933 to consider what alterations should be incorporated into a new design of Watson cabin lifeboat, the 46ft version was produced by James Barnett. Although slightly longer and wider than the 45ft 6in design it replaced, the first few 46ft lifeboats were similar in many respects to the predecessor. However, on later boats, while the layout of the after end of the boat and engine room remained much the same, the fore shelter was dispensed with to give a clear fore-deck and the anchor cable was stowed in a well at the after end of the cabin. Many variations of the 46ft design were built as it was gradually improved during the decade it was in production and became the mainstay of the RNLI's fleet in the immediate post-1945 era.

The rudder installation on the 46ft Watsons varied with some of the early boats fitted with inside rudders and stern frames, while in others the stern frames were omitted. After crews at two stations complained about the handling of their boats with inside rudders and stern frames, these boats were converted to outside rudders in an attempt to improve matters. In some of the later boats, the cable well was omitted and a return made to the stowage of the cable on deck in trays. The rudder arrangements on 46ft Watson cabin lifeboats were as follows: internal rudders were fitted in ON.777, ON.788, ON.789, ON.801, ON.802, ON.803, ON.804, ON.805, ON.814, ON.815, ON.818, ON.830, ON.840, ON.846, ON.847, ON.848; external rudders were fitted to ON.778, ON.784, ON.790, ON.819, ON.820, ON.821, ON.822, ON.828, ON.829, ON.838 and ON.841.

The deck layouts were also modified to suit local conditions with ON.805 and ON.815 designed for the conditions experienced at their respective stations where dangerous bars had to be

The first 46ft Watson motor to be built, H. F. Bailey (ON.777), was sent to Cromer in Norfolk. Under the command of Coxswain Henry Blogg, she was involved during World War II in some of the most famous rescues in the history of the RNLI. (MPL)

crossed. ON.820 and ON.838, built for Gorleston and Lowestoft respectively, did not follow the conventional layout. The coxswains at these two stations would not accept the standard Watson type which they considered unsuitable for working on the sandbanks of the Norfolk and Suffolk Coast. Further layout modifications were made to ON.840 and ON.846 with the steering position moved amidships, forward of the engine room.

The boats were originally powered by twin Weyburn petrol engines but, with the development of diesel engines, later boats were fitted with twin Ferry four-cylinder diesels, driving twin screws through a two-to-one reduction gear. The hull was divided into eight watertight compartments and fitted with 190 air cases.

Year (Yd No) Builder Place	Length Breadth Crew	Name Donor	ON Cost Weight	Engines	Stations (launches/lives saved) Disposal
1. 1935 (204) Groves & Guttridge Cowes	46' 12'9" 8	H. F. Bailey Legacy of Henry Francis Bailey, Brockenhurst.	777 £7,308 20t	2x40hp Weyburn CE4 4-cyl (p)	Cromer No.1 15.12.1935-45 (154/448) Helvick Head 15.8.1946-7.60 (24/12) Reserve 1960-72 (21/15) Sold 1972
2. 1935 (205) Groves & Guttridge Cowes	46' 12'9" 8	Edward and Isabella Irwin Legacy of Mrs I. Irwin, Morpeth, Northumberland.	778 £7,378 20t	2x40hp Weyburn CE4 4-cyl (p)	Sunderland 8.11.1935-5.63 (89/88) Reserve 1963-69 (64/29) Sold 1971
3. 1935 (208) Groves & Guttridge Cowes	46' 12'9" 8	Civil Service No.6/ 1956- Swn-Y-Mor (Civil Service No.6) Civil Service Lifeboat Fund.	784 £7,618 19t9	2x40hp Weyburn CE4 4-cyl (p)	St Davids 3.4.1936-8.63 (90/108) Eyemouth 17.11.1964-12.67 (3/0) Reserve 1967-72 (21/7) Sold 2.1973
4. 1936 (213) Groves & Guttridge Cowes	46' 12'9" 8	S. G. E. Legacies of Mr D. H. Altschul, Mrs J. E. C. Edmunds and Miss H. E. G. Gartside.	787 £8,505 19t13	2x40hp Ferry VE4 4-cyl (d) [first LB built with diesel engines]	Yarmouth 22.8.1936-6.37 (2/31) Destroyed by fire at Groves & Guttridge, 18.6.1937
5. 1937 (R211) Alexr. Robertson Sandbank	46' 12'9" 8	Jeanie Speirs Gift of Mrs E. S. Paterson, Paisley.	788 £8,434 21t5	2x40hp Weyburn CE4 4-cyl (p)	Portpatrick 20.3.1937-18.7.61 (66/18) Sold 4.1961
6. 1936 (215) Groves & Guttridge Cowes	46' 12'9" 8	R. P. L. Legacies of Miss M. A. Butterworth, Mr L. W. Rignal, and Miss M. S. Phillips.	789 £8,191 21t2	2x40hp Ferry VE4 4-cyl (d)	Howth 7.5.1937-18.7.62 (95/62) Sold 7.9.1962
7. 1936 (216) Groves & Guttridge Cowes	46' 12'9" 8	John and Charles Kennedy Legacy of Mrs M. Kennedy, Steyning, Sussex.	790 £8,178 21t	2x40hp Ferry VE4 4-cyl (d)	Fraserburgh 9.3.1937-2.53 (99/199) Capsized on service 9.2.1953, six lost later broken up

Year (Yd No) Builder Place	Length Breadth Crew	Name Donor	ON Cost Weight	Engines	Stations (launches/lives saved) Disposal
8. 1938 (R219) Alexr. Robertson Sandbank	46' 12'0" 8	Sir Arthur Rose Gift of Miss Margaret Lithgow, Tobermory.	801 £8,358 22t	2x40hp Ferry VE4 4-cyl (d)	Tobermory 15.11.1938-13.11.47 (28/20) Mallaig 15.1.1948-27.10.57 (43/76) Courtmacsherry 1958-69 (22/9) Reserve 1969-72 (7/4) Sold 2.1973
9. 1938 (R218) Alexr. Robertson Sandbank	46' 12'9" 8	City of Edinburgh RNLI Funds, in appreciation of Scottish Branches.	802 £8,155 20t18	2x40hp Ferry VE4 4-cyl (d)/ 1966- 2x65hp Parsons Barracuda (d)	Wick 4.10.1938-68 (133/204) Reserve 2.1969-76 (39/27) Sold 7.1976
10. 1938 (R217) Alexr. Robertson Sandbank	46' 12'9" 8	Canadian Pacific Gift of Canadian Pacific Steamship Company.	803 £8,314 20t5	2x40hp Ferry VE4 4-cyl (d/ 1961- 2x47hp Parsons Marlin/ 1963- 2x65hp Parsons Barracuda	Selsey 26.8.1938-22.1.69 (286/157) Reserve 1969-77 (44/35) Sold 3.2.1978
11. 1938 (W1831) J. S. White Cowes	46' 12'9" 8	S. G. E. Legacies of Mr D. Altshul, Mrs J. E. C. Edmunds and Miss H. E. Gartside.	804 £8,266 20t5	2x40hp Ferry VE4 4-cyl (d)	Yarmouth 12.4.1938-31.5.43 and 22.2.1945-9.63 (139/164) Reserve 5.1943-5 (2/0) Sold 4.1964
12. 1938 (W1832) J. S. White Cowes	46' 12'9" 8	Samuel and Marie Parkhouse Legacy of Mrs Marie Parkhouse, Cricklewood.	805 £8,451 20t5	2x40hp Ferry VE4 4-cyl (d)	Salcombe 12.5.1938-6.62 (100/126) Sold 9.1963
13. 1938 (W1839) J. S. White Cowes	46' 12'9" 8	Dunleary II RNLI Funds.	814 £8,258 20t2	2x40hp Ferry VE4 4-cyl (d)	Dun Laoghaire 21.7.1938-67 (104/136) Lochinver 25.7.1967-69 (9/0) Reserve 1969-72 (19/11) Dunmore East 6.1972-6.73 (8/4) Sold 7.8.1974
14. 1938 (W1840) J. S. White Cowes	46' 12'9" 8	Violet Armstrong Gift of Gordon Armstrong, Beverley, Yorkshire.	815 £8,833 21t19	2x40hp Ferry VE4 4-cyl (d)	Appledore 14.8.1938-5.62 (69/62) Sold 10.1962
15. 1939 (W1871) J. S. White Cowes	46' 12'9" 8	Mabel Marion Thompson Legacy of Miss M. M. Thompson, Bognor Regis.	818 £9,649 21t1	2x40hp Ferry VE4 4-cyl (d)	Rosslare Harbour 2.3.1939-1.52 (59/54) Galway Bay 22.3.1952-10.68 (177/72) Arranmore 10.1968-8.70 (9/4) Reserve 1970-74 (11/10) Sold 4.1975
16. 1939 (R222) Alexr. Robertson Sandbank	46' 12'9" 8	Julia Park Barry, of Glasgow Gift of Mrs Park Barry, Glasgow.	819 £9,055 20t6	2x40hp Ferry VE4 4-cyl (d)/ 1964- 2x65hp Parsons Barracuda	Peterhead 15.6.1939-10.69 (162/496) Reserve 10.1969-2.79 (64/26) Sold 3.1979
17. 1939 (W1872) J. S. White Cowes	46' 12'9" 8	Louise Stephens Legacy of Mrs L. Stephens, Ewhurst, Surrey.	820 £9,351 20t19	2x40hp Ferry VE4 4-cyl (d)	Gt Yarmouth & Gorleston 4.5.1939-19.8.67 (305/177) Eyemouth 10.1967-7.2.74 (6/0) Sold 8.1974

Gorleston's 46ft Watson Louise Stephens *(ON.820) was specially adapted for the conditions encountered at that station. (From an old postcard in the author's collection)*

Jesse Lumb *(ON.822), stationed at Bembridge, was a typical 46ft Watson with the main cockpit aft and a small shelter forward. She is pictured after the aft cockpit had been covered. (From an old postcard in the author's collection)*

19 • Watson cabin motor 46ft

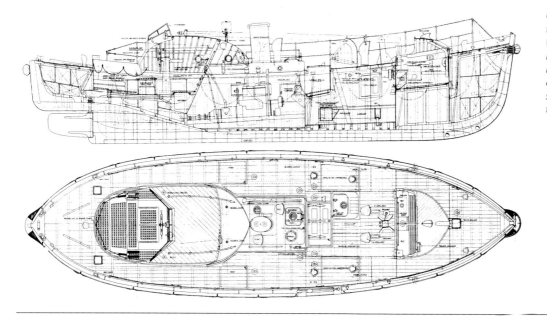

General arrangement of the 1938-built 46ft Watson Dunleary II *(ON.814), for Dun Laoghaire, with an internal rudder and deck layout typical of most 46ft Watsons. She was slipway launched during her time in service.*

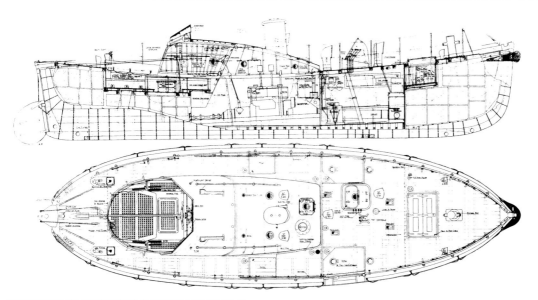

General arrangement of the Great Yarmouth & Gorleston Watson Louise Stephens *(ON.820), one of several 46ft Watsons built to the requirements of a specific station. Both this boat and ON.838, which served at Lowestoft, were of the 'Gorleston' sub-type with features such as a shallower draft than standard Watsons making them well suited for services on the outlying sandbanks and shallow water found in the North Sea off the Norfolk and Suffolk coasts.*

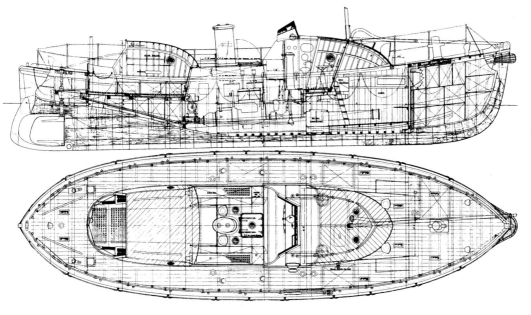

General arrangement of Henry Blogg *(ON.840) which, with ON.846, was one of only two 46ft Watsons with a midship steering position. The boats' deck layout incorporated two shelters of similar design but different size with the exhaust funnel positioned amidships. ON.840 was originally allocated to Douglas but was diverted to Cromer where she was liked so much by the much-respected Coxswain Henry Blogg and his crew that she remained on station there and was renamed in the Coxswain's honour.*

19 · Watson cabin motor 46ft

Year (Yd No) Builder Place	Length Breadth Crew	Name Donor	ON Cost Weight	Engines	Stations (launches/lives saved) Disposal
18. 1939 (R223) Alexr. Robertson Sandbank	46' 12'9" 8	The Good Hope An anonymous gift.	821 £9,070 20t10	2x40hp Ferry VE4 4-cyl (d)/ 1966- 2x65hp Parsons Barracuda	Montrose No.1 9.10.1939-72 (77/32) Reserve 1972-80 (35/26) Sold 1981
19. 1939 (W1873) J. S. White Cowes	46' 12'9" 8	Jesse Lumb Legacy of Miss Annie Lumb, Huddersfield.	822 £9,455 20t10	2x40hp Ferry VE4 4-cyl (d)/ 1965- 2x65hp Parsons Barracuda	Bembridge 24.5.1939-17.1.70 (294/280) Reserve 1970-80 (59/19) Sold 6.7.1981
20. 1939 (W5004) J. S. White Cowes	46' 12'9" 8	The Princess Royal (Civil Service No.7) Civil Service Lifeboat Fund.	828 £10,145 20t8	2x40hp Ferry VE4 (d)/ 1965- 2x65hp Parsons Barracuda (d)	Hartlepool 19.10.1939-22.6.68 (152/94) Reserve 1968-76 (41/24) Sold 1976
21. 1939 (W5005) J. S. White Cowes	46' 12'9" 8	Crawford and Constance Conybeare Gift of Mrs Constance Conybeare, London.	829 £10,268 20t14	2x40hp Ferry VE4 4-cyl (d)	Falmouth 17.1.1940-9.68 (122/126) Reserve 1968-74 (32/30) Sold 8.1974
22. 1939 (W5006) J. S. White Cowes	46' 12'9" 8	Annie Blanche Smith Legacies Mrs Smith, Mrs Lucas, plus the executors of the late Mr Stephens.	830 £10,279 20t14	2x40hp Ferry VE4 4-cyl (d)	Dunmore East 19.3.1940-9.70 (88/88) Reserve 10.1970-71 (0/0) Sold 7.1971
23. 1939 (W5015) J. S. White Cowes	46' 12'9" 8	Michael Stephens Legacy of Mrs Louise Stephens, Ewhurst, Surrey.	838 £10,104 20t2	2x40hp Ferry VE4 4-cyl (d)	Lowestoft 19.10.1939-7.63 (134/73) Exmouth 1.11.1963-13.8.68 (25/11) Reserve 1968-76 (21/9) Sold 1.1976
24. 1945 Sussex Yacht Co Shoreham	46' 12'9" 8	Millie Walton/ 1947- Henry Blogg Legacy of Mrs M. E. Walton, Derby/ 1947- RNLI Funds.	840 £15,242 21t2	2x40hp Ferry VE4 4-cyl (d)	[Stemmed for Douglas] Cromer No.1 20.12.1945-3.4.66 (99/149) Reserve 1966-76 (58/65) Sold 4.1977
25. 1943 (W5111) J. S. White Cowes	46' 12'9" 8	Manchester and Salford XXIX Manchester and Salford Lifeboat Fund.	841 £11,912 20t12	2x40hp Ferry VE4 4-cyl (d)	Pwllheli 5.11.1943-21.1.53 (21/4) Workington 3.1953-72 (116/67) Reserve 1972-74 (7/0) Sold 8.1974
26. 1940 (309) Groves & Guttridge Cowes	46' 12'9" 8	[Millie Walton] —	842 — —	2x40hp Ferry VE4 4-cyl (d)	[Stemmed for Douglas] Destroyed in air raid on builder's yard, 4.5.1942
27. 1940 (310) Groves & Guttridge Cowes	46' 12'9" 8	[Charles Henry Ashley] —	843 — —	2x40hp Ferry VE4 4-cyl (d)	[Stemmed for Porthdinllaen] Destroyed in air raid on builder's yard, 4.5.1942
28. 1945 (MG456) Morgan Giles Teignmouth	46' 12'9" 8	Field Marshall and Mrs Smuts Southern African Branch of the RNLI.	846 £13,865 20t4	2x40hp Ferry VE4 4-cyl (d)	Beaumaris 25.9.1945-2.2.77 (136/119) Reserve 1977-79 (0/0) Sold 21.8.1979
29. 1946 (R622) Rowhedge IW Rowhedge	46' 12'9" 8	Gertrude Legacy of Lady Struthers.	847 £17,048 21t	2x40hp Ferry VE4 4-cyl (d)/ 1965- 2x65hp Parsons Barracuda (d)	Holy Island 4.11.1946-31.3.68 (37/9) Exmouth 13.8.1968-11.2.70 (11/0) Sheerness 22.4.1971-4.4.74 (91/61) Fowey 1.5.1980-25.11.81 (8/2) Reserve 5.1974-1.82 (42/29) Sold 2.1982
30. 1946 (390) Groves & Guttridge Cowes	46' 12'9" 8	Millie Walton Legacy of Mrs Walton.	848 £14,462 20t5	2x40hp Ferry VE4 4-cyl (d)	Douglas 18.7.1946-29.3.56 (25/17) Amble 4.1.1956-74 (67/12) Reserve 1974-77 (4/10) Sold 24.10.1977

20 • Watson cabin motor 46ft 9in

Introduced 1947, last built 1956, 28 built.
Specifications • length 46ft 9in, beam 12ft 9in, crew 7/8.

The 46ft 9in Watson was the next development of the Watson motor, and although the first five boats were 9in longer than the 46ft version which the type superseded, they had an almost identical deck layout, with turtle-shaped shelters, funnel exhausts and a stern cockpit. Of the first five boats, three were re-engined, having the funnels removed, and the aft cockpit was fitted with a wheelhouse to give improved crew protection.

In 1948, the deck layout was comprehensively redesigned after experience had shown that, with twin screws, auxiliary sails were no longer needed and an aft steering position from where the coxswain could watch the sails was unnecessary. In the redesigned version, the wooden turtle shelter was replaced by an aluminium structure which incorporated three sections – a midship steering position in an open cockpit; a small shelter forward of the cockpit housing the access hatch to the engine room along with the engine controls and gauges; and a large deck cabin behind the cockpit reached via a sliding door and housing the wireless and other electronic aids that were subsequently fitted. The midship steering position enabled the coxswain to communicate with the mechanic at the engine controls in front of him and the radio operator in the cabin behind him.

North Foreland (Civil Service No.11) (ON.888) at the top of the slipway at Margate. The deck layout of the 46ft 9in Watson as built with an open cockpit is clearly shown in this photo. (From an old postcard in the author's collection)

The hull was constructed of wood, with the superstructure of aluminium alloy to reduce top weight. At the aft end of the cabin was a second aft cockpit which featured a sliding door into the cabin through which stretchers could be passed. This cockpit also incorporated a second helm position for use in emergencies. The new design also featured an ingenious exhaust system. Instead of passing through a funnel sited amidships, the fumes were carried up pipes inside the main mast and released well above the crew.

Although when built the boats had an open cockpit, this was enclosed or partially enclosed from the early 1960s onwards. All were fitted with air-bags to give a once-only self-righting ability, except those with stern cockpit, ON.849, ON.852 to ON.855, and ON.908. The rudder positions varied; the first nine had internal rudders, with external rudders fitted from about 1952 as attempts were made to improve the boats' manoeuvrability. Many were also fitted with more powerful engines during their careers.

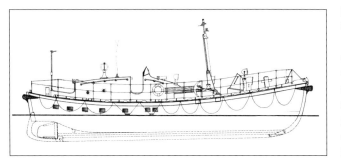

Year (Yd No) Builder Place	Name Donor	ON Cost Weight	Engines (all twin screw)	Stations (launches/lives saved) Disposal
1. 1947 (391) Groves & Guttridge Cowes	William Gammon - Manchester and District XXX Manchester & Salford Lifeboat Fund.	849 £16,962 20t	2x40hp Ferry VE4 (d)/ 1968- 2x65hp Parsons Barracuda (d)	Mumbles 19.7.1947-27.8.74 (134/74) Relief 1974-82 (41/10) Sold 3.1983
2. 1947 (W5395) J. S. White Cowes	Tynesider Tyneside Blitzed Lifeboat Fund.	852 £16,367 21t15	2x40hp Ferry VE4 (d)/ 1965- 2x65hp Parsons Barracuda (d)	Tynemouth 11.1947-4.79 (153/140) Relief 7.1980-83 (8/0) Sold 2.1984
3. 1947 (W5399) J. S. White Cowes	Winston Churchill (Civil Service No.8) Civil Service Lifeboat Fund.	853 £16,535 21t4	2x40hp Ferry VE4 (d)/ 1966- 2x65hp Parsons Barracuda (d)	Blyth 2.2.1948-18.9.79 (68/39) Relief 1.1980-11.82 (22/6) Sold 7.1983
4. 1949 (AR255) Alexr. Robertson Sandbank	Sarah Tilson Legacy of W. M. Tilson, Richmond, Surrey.	854 £17,790 20t2	2x40hp Ferry VE4 (d)	Baltimore 15.5.1950-5.78 (70/21) Sold 12.1979
5. 1949 (AR256) Alexr. Robertson Sandbank	W. M. Tilson Legacy of W. M. Tilson, Richmond, Surrey.	855 £18,057 19t18	2x40hp Ferry VE4 (d)	Arranmore 9.5.1950-31.10.68 (55/20) Sold 8.1970
6. 1948 (W5405) J. S. White Cowes	Elizabeth Rippon Legacy of Mrs Elizabeth Rippon, Hull.	865 £19,094 22t8	2x40hp Ferry VE4 (d)/ 1966- 2x65hp Barracuda (d)	St Helier 14.10.1948-28.2.75 (141/58) Relief 1975-77 (5/0) Sold 10.1977
7. 1949 (W5406) J. S. White Cowes	Charles Henry Ashley Legacy of Charles Carr Ashley, Mentone, France.	866 £19,040 22t	2x40hp Ferry VE4 (d)/ 1969- 2x70hp Watermota Sea Lion	Porthdinllaen 11.3.1949-28.4.79 (151/89) Relief 5.1979-86 (35/14) Sold 3.1987

20 · Watson cabin motor 46ft 9in

Year (Yd No) Builder Place	Name Donor	ON Cost Weight	Engines (all twin screw)	Stations (launches/lives saved) Disposal
8. 1949 (W5407) J. S. White Cowes	Lady Scott (Civil Service No.4) Civil Service Lifeboat Fund.	867 £18,972 22t	2x40hp Ferry VE4 (d)/ 1972- 2x70hp Thornycroft 380 (d)	Portrush 18.7.1949-11.3.81 (148/73) Relief 9.1981-86 (31/0) Sold 7.1987
9. 1950 Sussex Yacht Co Shoreham	John and Lucy Cordingley Legacy of Mrs L. J. Cordingley, Bournemouth.	868 £19,816 22t4	2x40hp Ferry VE4 (d)	Teesmouth 22.2.1950-60 (33/18) Helvick Head 7.1960-25.3.69 (19/12) Relief 3.1969-81 (44/13) Sold 11.1981
10. 1950 (W5420) J. S. White Cowes	Sir Samuel Kelly Gift of Lady Kelly.	885 £25,073 22t6	2x40hp Ferry VE4 (d)/ 1972- 2x70hp Ford Mermaid 595	Donaghadee 27.5.1950-12.76 (134/79) Relief 12.1976-12.79 (14/20) Sold 1980
11. 1951 (105) Sussex Yacht Co Shoreham	Sarah Townsend Porritt Legacy of Miss Kate Porritt, Rossendale, Lancashire.	886 £24,427 22t17	2x40hp Ferry VE4 (d)/ 1971- 2x70hp Thornycroft 380	Lytham St Annes 19.4.1951-3.78 (78/35) Relief 10.1978-82 (16/8) Sold 10.1982
12. 1951 (W5423) J. S. White Cowes	Sir Godfrey Baring RNLI Funds.	887 £24,628 21t17	2x40hp Ferry VE4 (d)/ 1972- 2x70hp Ford Mermaid 595	Clacton-on-Sea 14.1.1952-19.1.68 (226/106) Wick 2.1968-12.70 (16/25) Workington 6.9.1972-4.2.82 (53/4) Relief 5.1982-7.86 (30/8) Sold 7.1986
13. 1951 (W5424) J. S. White Cowes	North Foreland (Civil Service No.11) Civil Service Lifeboat Fund.	888 £24,846 22t	2x40hp Ferry VE4 (d)	Margate 18.3.1951-2.12.78 (389/216) Relief 1978-81 (6/0) Displayed at Bristol, then Chatham Historic Dockyard
14. 1952 Camper & Nicholson Gosport	Douglas Hyde RNLI Funds.	896 £33,196 22t19	2x40hp Ferry VE4 (d)/ 1970- 2x70hp Watermota Sea Lion	Rosslare Harbour 1.1952-17.6.69 (75/47) Dunmore East 10.1970-7.72 (11/5) Sold 2.1973
15. 1951 (W5429) J. S. White Cowes	Herbert Leigh Gift of Mr Leigh.	900 £25,855 21t13	2x40hp Ferry VE4 (d)/ 1977- 2x70hp Thornycroft 380	Barrow 15.11.1951-9.82 (136/71) Relief 1983-88 (33/17) Sold 1990
16. 1953 (W5430) J. S. White Cowes	Michael and Lily Davis Legacies of Mrs L. Davis, Mr Fox, Mrs Halfon and Mr Graystone.	901 £28,811 21t15	2x40hp Ferry VE4 (d)	Ramsgate 25.9.1953-17.6.76 (318/309) Reserve 1976-79 (10/4) Sold 1979
17. 1954 (549) Groves & Guttridge Cowes	Duchess of Kent RNLI Funds.	908 £31,773 21t5	2x40hp Ferry VE4 (d)/ 1965- 2x65hp Parsons Barracuda	Fraserburgh 4.6.1954-27.1.70 (46/11) Capsized on service 21.1.1970, five lost, broken up 10.1970
18. 1953 (W5431) J. S. White Cowes	Edian Courtauld Gift of Mr Augustine Courtauld.	910 £29,687 22t	2x40hp Ferry VE4 (d)/ 1967- 2x65hp Parsons Barracuda	Walton-on-the-Naze 2.11.1953-23.7.77 (224/143) Reserve 9.1977-8.81 (24/1) Sold 8.1981

46ft 9in Watson John and Lucy Cordingley *(ON.868) was initially built for service at Teesmouth, but later moved to Helvick Head, by which time the cockpit had been enclosed as in this photograph. (From an old postcard in the author's collection)*

Launch of Duchess of Kent *(ON.908) down the slipway at Fraserburgh. This midship-steering version of the 46ft 9in Watson was built in 1954 and tragically capsized on service in 1970 with the loss of five crewmembers. (From an old postcard in the author's collection)*

20 · Watson cabin motor 46ft 9in

Year (Yd No) Builder Place	Name Donor	ON Cost Weight	Engines (all twin screw)	Stations (launches/lives saved) Disposal
19. 1954 (W5432) J. S. White Cowes	City of Bradford III City of Bradford Lifeboat Fund.	911 £29,593 21t15	2x40hp Ferry VE4 (d)/ 1968- 2x65hp Parsons Barracuda (d)	Humber 27.1.1954-77 (351/107) Lytham St Annes 4.2.1978-16.3.85 (26/6) Sold 8.1985
20. 1954 (550) Groves & Guttridge Cowes	Deneys Reitz Southern African Branch of the RNLI.	919 £31,922 21t17	2x40hp Ferry VE4 (d)/ 1970- 2x70hp Watermota Sea Lion (d)	Fowey 21.11.1954-5.80 (155/36) Sold 9.1980
21. 1955 (551) Groves & Guttridge Cowes	Greater London II (Civil Service No.30) Civil Service Lifeboat Fund.	921 £32,163 21t7	2x40hp Ferry VE4 (d)/ 1969- 2x70hp Watermota Sea Lion (d)	Southend-on-Sea 3.4.1955-28.3.76 (253/139) Beaumaris 2.2.1977-11.4.89 (38/21) Sold 1991
22. 1955 (W5437) J. S. White Cowes	Henry Comber Brown Legacies of Mr H. Comber Brown and Miss A. E. Haldane.	925 £31,674 21t10	2x40hp Ferry VE4 (d)/ 1969- 2x70hp Watermota Sea Lion (d)	Tenby 20.9.1955-6.9.86 (373/178) Sold 1987
23. 1955 (W5438) J. S. White Cowes	Guy and Clare Hunter Legacies of Mrs C. Hunter, Mrs Brown, Mrs Widdrington, and others.	926 £32,103 21t3	2x40hp Ferry VE4 (d)/ 1972- 2x70hp Ford Mermaid 595 (d)	St Mary's 12.1955-7.81 (177/110) Fowey 11.1981-1.82 (0/0), Penlee 9.1.1982-8.5.83 (12/4) Padstow 9.9.1983-2.8.84 (13/3) Cromer 4.9.1984-12.85 (9/2) Reserve 8.1984-6.88 (28/9) Sold 6.1988
24. 1955 (552) Groves & Guttridge Cowes	Lilla Marras, Douglas and Will Legacies of Mrs J. L. Marras, London; Mr J. Douglas, Langbank; and Mrs W. Kennedy of Glenbarr; also gift of Miss Robb and RNLI funds.	928 £33,723 21t4	2x40hp Ferry VE4 (d)/ 1978- 2x70hp Thornycroft 380 (d)	Cromarty 2.9.1955-4.68 (24/10) Falmouth 9.1968-7.71 and 25.11.1972-10.74 (46/16) Reserve 10.1974-6.82 (30/11) Donaghadee 7.9.1978-23.8.79 (4/0) Sold 10.1982
25. 1956 (W5439) J. S. White Cowes	R. A. Colby Cubbin No.1 Legacy of Mrs Ellen Mary Marsh Gordon Cubbin, Onchan, Douglas, Isle of Man.	929 £32,000 21t15	2x40hp Ferry VE4 (d)/ 1979- 2x70hp Thornycroft 380 (d)	Douglas 29.3.1956-25.11.88 (113/95) Sold 1989
26. 1956 (W5440) J. S. White Cowes	R. A. Colby Cubbin No.2 Legacy of Mrs Ellen Mary Marsh Gordon Cubbin, Onchan, Douglas, Isle of Man.	930 £32,829 21t3	2x40hp Ferry VE4 (d)	Port St Mary 5.7.1956-9.76 (47/39) Reserve 9.1976-10.77 (0/0) Sold 10.1977
27. 1956 (W5441) J. S. White Cowes	Richard Vernon and Mary Garforth of Leeds Legacies of Richard Vernon & Isaac Garforth, Leeds, plus RNLI funds.	931 £33,587 21t11	2x40hp Ferry VE4 (d)/ 1980- 2x70hp Thornycroft 380 (d)	Angle 19.2.1957-29.6.87 (153/71) Wicklow 15.9.1987-10.10.88 (6/0) Sold 1989
28. 1956 (W5442) J. S. White Cowes	Howard Marryat Legacy of Mr H. Marryat and gift from Mr R. Marryat.	932 £33,863 21t11	2x40hp Ferry VE4 (d)/ 1982- 2x70hp Thornycroft 380 (d)	Fishguard 4.9.1957-28.5.81 (130/73) Barrow 20.9.1982-4.9.86 (20/11) Moelfre 4.4.1987-22.1.88 (4/4) Relief 4-12.1988 (0/0) Sold 9.1989

46ft 9in Watson Sir Samuel Kelly (ON.885) in the latter days of her service life, with an enclosed wheelhouse amidships, radar fitted to the wheelhouse roof, and an air-bag for self-righting mounted on the after cabin. (RNLI)

21 • Barnett 52ft

Introduced 1950, last built 1960, 20 built.
Specifications • length 52ft, length (waterline) 49ft 6in, beam 13ft 6in and draft 4ft 6in (up to ON.924); beam 14ft and draft 4ft 7in (from ON.935); crew 8.

The 52ft Barnett can be regarded as the culmination of James Barnett's ideas about lifeboat design and development. The class, which was a development of the 51ft version, which it replaced, had the distinctive deck feature of a midship steering position, as well as twin engines, twin screws and shelter for rescued and rescuers, advances that had been intro-duced into lifeboat design under Barnett's supervision. The deck arrangements were similar to the post-war Watson cabin types, also designed by Barnett, with midship steering and deck cabin.

The first boats of the class were designed with a simple open cockpit at the steering position but, from ON.935 onwards, a fully enclosed wheelhouse was incorporated, with all-round windows which could be hinged down if required. Kent clear-view screens were fitted to the front windows. The first ten boats had enclosed wheelhouses fitted over the steering position while in service. The last ten all had raised bulwarks at bow and stern.

The hull was subdivided into ten watertight compartments, the engine room had a double bottom and a total of 324 air cases were installed. Twin 72hp Gardner 6LW diesels, which gave the boats a maximum speed of nine knots, were installed, while sufficient fuel was carried to give a range of 180 nautical miles at full speed. In addition to the crew, the 52ft Barnett could carry 100 people in rough weather. All 52ft Barnetts were fitted with air-bags in the 1970s to give a once-only self-righting capability.

From the small cockpit aft, emergency steering could be rigged, and access to the midship cabin was from either this cockpit or the wheelhouse itself so the crew could get to the after cockpit

52ft Barnett James and Margaret Boyd (ON.913) shortly after her completion in 1954 with an open cockpit position and cabin painted light grey. (From an old postcard in the author's collection)

through the cabin without having to go on deck. The door from the cockpit provided stretcher access and the cabin was equipped with settee/lockers and heaters, as well as doubling as a chartroom with a small alcove set aside for the radio operator. As external doors were not watertight, scuppers were fitted in the side of the boat at cabin-floor level, so that water entering the cabin or wheelhouse flowed under the lockers and overboard.

A Coventry Victor generating set in the engine room supplied electrical power, and the deck winch, a feature of most Barnett boats, was mounted on the engine-room casing and driven off the port engine. Instead of the more usual anchor rope, the 52ft Barnetts had wire cables which passed from the winch through a wire-cutter, provided in case the wire had to be cut quickly in an emergency, to a stopper on the foredeck.

Year (Yd No) Builder Place	Name Donor	ON Cost Weight	Engines	Stations (launches/lives saved) Disposal
1. 1950 (W5418) J. S. White Cowes	Norman B. Corlett Gift of Mr W. E. Corlett and members of his family.	883 £29,265 27t18	2x60bhp Ferry VE6 (d)/ 1968- 78hp Ford Thornycroft 360	New Brighton 23.9.1950-16.4.73 (215/116) Relief 1973-81 (72/21) Sold 2.1982
2. 1950 (W5419) J. S. White Cowes	St Cybi (Civil Service No.9) Civil Service Lifeboat Fund.	884 £28,906 27t18	2x60bhp Ferry VE6 (d)/ 1966- 75hp Parsons Barracuda I (d)	Holyhead 21.9.1950-30.6.80 (243/152) Relief 1980-85 (14/9) Sold 1986
3. 1951 (W5425) J. S. White Cowes	Hilton Briggs Legacy of Mrs A. Briggs, Birkdale, Southport.	889 £29,928 27t19	2x60bhp Ferry VE6 6-cyl (d)	Aberdeen No.1 30.8.1951-25.9.58 (21/20) Fenit 10.1959- 30.4.69 (18/11) Longhope 22.5-15.12.70 (6/0) Relief 1969-74 (30/17) Invergordon 12.8.1974-11.75 (0/0) Sold 7.1976
4. 1952 (W5426) J. S. White Cowes	Thomas Forehead and Mary Rowse Gift of Miss A. Charlton Rowse, Birmingham.	890 £30,875 27t5	2x60bhp Ferry VE6 (d)/ 1972- 78hp Ford Thornycroft 360 (d)	Plymouth 30.3.1952 -22.5.74 (169/63) Relief 1974-79 (32/20) Sold 4.12.1982
5. 1952 (W5427) J. S. White Cowes	Joseph Hiram Chadwick Legacy of Miss E. E. Chadwick, Rochdale.	898 £31,584 27t9	2x60bhp Ferry VE6 (d)/ 1968- 78hp Ford Thornycroft 360 (d)	Padstow No.1 12.1952-11.67 (91/15) Galway Bay 1968-77 (194/7) Reserve 1977-79 (21/9) Sold 4.1980
6. 1953 (W5428) J. S. White Cowes	City of Glasgow II City of Glasgow Lifeboat Fund.	899 £31,629 27t3	2x60bhp Ferry VE6 (d)/ 1969- 78hp Ford Thornycroft 360 (d)	Campbeltown 24.6.1953-14.10.79 (110/50) Sold 4.1980

21 • Barnett 52ft

Year (Yd No) Builder Place	Name Donor	ON Cost Weight	Engines	Stations (launches/lives saved) Disposal
7. 1954 (W5433) J. S. White Cowes	Euphrosyne Kendal Legacy of Mrs E. Kendal.	912 £34,916 27t10	2x60bhp Ferry VE6 (d)/ 1972- 70hp Ford Mermaid 595 (d)	St Peter Port 31.5.1954-12.10.72 (158/115) Dunmore East 6.1973-19.3.75 (10/7) Reserve 1975-83 (67/48) Sold 18.5.1983
8. 1954 (W5434) J. S. White Cowes	James and Margaret Boyd Legacy of Miss C. Boyd, Mrs C. Grant, Dr J. Tennant.	913 £35,294 27t5	2x60bhp Ferry VE6 (d)/ 1969- 78hp Ford Thornycroft 360 (d)	Stornoway 27.9.1954-7.73 (143/36) Relief 1973-74 (8/0) Macduff 1974-5 (8/6) Invergordon 1975- 16.7.84 (10/2) Sold 11.1.1985
9. 1955 (W5435) J. S. White Cowes	John Gellatly Hyndman Legacy of Miss Elsie Amelia Hyndman, Greenock.	923 £35,616 27t12	2x60bhp Ferry VE6 (d)/ 1969- 78hp Ford Thornycroft 360 (d)	Stronsay 27.2.1955-30.5.72 (116/47) Relief 1972-84 (51/45) Sold 23.8.1985
10. 1957 (W5436) J. S. White Cowes	Archibald and Alexandra M. Paterson Gift of Miss Margaret M. Paterson, Florida, USA.	924 £36,919 27t6	2x60bhp Ferry VE6 (d)/ 1970- 78hp Ford Thornycroft 360 (d)	Stromness 21.5.1955-12.10.84 (123/52) Arranmore 1.3.1985-5.4.86 (10/1) Lowestoft 19.10.1986-16.11.87 (19/0) Sold 5.1989
11. 1957 (W5466) J. S. White Cowes	R. A. Colby Cubbin No.3 Legacy of Mrs Ellen Mary Marsh Gordon Cubbin, Onchan, Douglas, Isle of Man.	935 £38,500 28t6	2x72bhp Gardner 6LW 6-cyl (d)	Barra Island 27.7.1957-16.6.84 (129/19) Capsized on service 18.11.1979, none lost Sold 11.1984
12. 1957 (W5467) J. S. White Cowes	E. M. M. Gordon Cubbin Legacy of Mrs Ellen Mary Marsh Gordon Cubbin, Onchan, Douglas, Isle of Man.	936 £38,500 27t8	2x72bhp Gardner 6LW 6-cyl (d)	Mallaig 27.10.1957-16.7.82 (142/52) Relief 1982-85 (5/0) Sold 1985
13. 1957 (568) Groves & Guttridge Cowes	Rowland Watts Legacy of Mr R. Watts, Essex.	938 £38,500 28t3	2x72bhp Gardner 6LW 6-cyl (d)	Valentia 18.9.1957-14.3.83 (158/132) Relief 1983-85 (20/6) Sold 1985
14. 1958 (569) Groves & Guttridge Cowes	Frank Spiller Locke Legacy of Dr Frank Spiller Locke.	939 £38,500 27t19	2x72bhp Gardner 6LW 6-cyl (d)	Weymouth 30.10.1957-15.3.76 (249/126) Galway Bay 1977-18.12.85 (140/8) Sold 10.10.1986

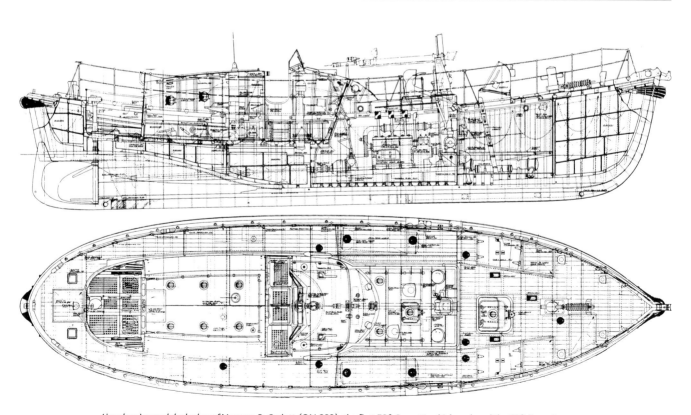

Line drawing and deck plan of Norman B. Corlett *(ON.883), the first 52ft Barnett, which replaced the 60ft Barnett* William and Kate Johnston *(ON.682) at the New Brighton station.*

21 • Barnett 52ft

Year (Yd No) Builder Place	Name Donor	ON Cost Weight	Engines	Stations (launches/lives saved) Disposal	
15. 1958 (570) Groves & Guttridge Cowes	Claude Cecil Staniforth Legacy of Mr C. C. Staniforth.	943 £38,500 27t12	2x72bhp Gardner 6LW 6-cyl	Lerwick 21.8.1958-8.6.78 (94/32) Arranmore 28.10.1978-1.3.85 (88/10) Sold 11.1985	
16. 1959 (591) Groves & Guttridge Cowes	Ramsay-Dyce Legacy of Mr William Ramsay, Dyce.	944 £38,232 27t19	2x72bhp Gardner 6LW 6-cyl	Aberdeen 25.9.1958-3.6.76 (59/30) Reserve 1976-78 (7/0) Lochinver 3.8.1978-13.2.85 (21/0)	Sold 8.1985
17. 1960 (W5469) J. S. White Cowes	Princess Alexandra of Kent RNLI Funds.	945 £38,500 28t7	2x72bhp Gardner 6LW 6-cyl	Torbay 19.7.1958-10.4.75 (157/69) Reserve 1975-83 (41/19) Tynemouth 12.1979-28.2.80	Sold 1984
18. 1960 (578) Groves & Guttridge Cowes	Ethel Mary Trustees of the late Mrs Brereton.	949 £39,900 28t3	2x72bhp Gardner 6LW 6-cyl	Ballycotton 27.7.1959-27.4.85 (121/70) Reserve 1985-87 (0/0) Baltimore 3.6.1987-88 (11/5)	Sold 1989
19. 1960 (583) Groves & Guttridge Cowes	The Duke of Cornwall (Civil Service No.33) Civil Service Lifeboat Fund.	952 £40,500 27t11	2x72bhp Gardner 6LW 6-cyl	Lizard-Cadgwith 31.10.1960-17.7.84 (99/85) Padstow 31.7-28.12.1984 (5/6) Reserve 1984-89 (22/8)	Sold 1989
20. 1960 (W5495) J. S. White Cowes	John and Frances Macfarlane Gift of Mr J. Macfarlane and Mrs A. Macfarlane.	956 £40,000 27t15	2x72bhp Gardner 6LW 6-cyl	Aith 28.1.1961-19.7.86 (57/28) Sold 10.1986	

52ft Barnett Norman B. Corlett *as built, with an open cockpit. The forward cabin arrangement on the first ten 52ft Barnetts was similar to that of the 46ft 9in Watsons and was more rounded than on the latter ten boats of the class. (From an old photo in the author's collection)*

The last 52ft Barnett to be built, John and Frances Macfarlane *(ON.956), off Shetland, after being fitted with a self-righting air-bag. The deck layout and shape of the superstructure of the last ten 52ft Barnetts was similar to that of the 47ft Watsons. (RNLI)*

22 • Watson motor 42ft

Introduced 1954, last built 1962, 10 built including three Beach versions.
Specifications • length 42ft, beam 12ft (12ft 3in Beach version), draft 3ft 7in, crew 7.

The requirement for a medium-sized motor lifeboat, intended primarily for slipway launching but also to be kept afloat, was fulfilled initially by the 40ft Watson design of the 1920s, the 41ft Watson of the 1930s and in the post-1945 era by the 42ft version. Although the largest and most advanced of any of the mid-sized Watson designs, in fact it differed very little from its predecessors in terms of the hull shape with the propellers in protective tunnels and the design not self-righting.

Perhaps the most significant aspect of the design was its powerplant – for the first time commercially-built diesel engines, in the shape of 48hp Gardner 4LW marine diesels, in a watertight engine room, were used, making ON.907 the first lifeboat to be powered by such engines. Installing diesel engines that were widely used commercially meant savings in both running and upkeep. The engine controls were initially positioned so that they were operated by the mechanic but, as the boats were updated with new equipment during their service careers, more sophisticated controls were introduced enabling the coxswain or person at the helm to work the engines directly. The first boat had a top speed of 8.38 knots and she carried enough fuel to travel 238 miles at full speed without refuelling.

The 42ft Watson had an aluminium superstructure while the wooden hull was divided into nineteen watertight compartments and fitted with 150 air cases. A watertight double bottom below the engine room floor, with watertight fore and after bulkheads, provided a box within the hull that was virtually watertight. Other modifications introduced for the first time included a combined mast exhaust, a Kent clear-view screen, a twin R/T aerial which gave a better range than previous aerials, and wooden bulwarks forward and aft for greater protection from the sea. A cabin was sited forward of the engine room and the boat was fitted with radio telephony and a loudhailer, while a line-throwing pistol and electric searchlight were also carried. In rough weather, seventy people could be taken on board.

During their service careers, most 42ft Watsons were fitted with fixed shelters over the aft cockpit to improve crew protection, exemplified in this photograph of the prototype William Taylor of Oldham (ON.907). (Jeff Morris)

In May 1954, the prototype was taken on a lengthy sea trial up the east coast of Britain to Inverness, through the Caledonian Canal and down the west coast back to Littlehampton visiting lifeboat stations on the way. This not only gave many crews the chance to handle the boat at first hand, but also thoroughly tested the new design as the extended passage was the equivalent of about five years of service. In 1957, a Beach version was developed. This was constructed with a specially widened and strengthened hull to withstand grounding during the launch and recovery procedure at the few stations where beach launching was employed. The Beach lifeboats were in other respects similar to their Watson counterparts with the hull divided into nineteen watertight compartments and the superstructure of aluminium.

ON.946 was fitted with a mizzen mast at the request of her crew, for steadying in rough weather. ON.967 was the only boat built with an enclosed steering position but enclosed wheelhouses were later fitted to all but one of the 42ft Watsons to improve crew protection. In the table, WH indicates the year in which the cockpit was enclosed by a fixed wheelhouse to improve crew protection.

	Year (Yd No) Builder Place	Name Donor	ON Cost Weight	Engines (WH added)	Stations (launches/lives saved) Notes Disposal
1.	1954 (907) William Osborne Littlehampton	William Taylor of Oldham Legacy of Miss Clare S.Taylor, Oldham.	907 £29,688 16t5	2x48bhp Gardner 4LW (d) (1965)	Coverack 24.7.1954-31.5.72 (49/32) Reserve 1972-73 (11/10) Arklow 2.1973-7.3.1986 (54/30) Sold 8.1986
2.	1955 (909) William Osborne Littlehampton	James and Barbara Aitken Legacies of Miss A. Aitchison and Mrs A. Aitken, and gift of Dr and Mrs Aitken.	909 £25,859 15t18	2x48bhp Gardner 4LW (d) (1971)	Troon 19.2.1955-68 (91/32) Girvan 1968-15.10.76 (29/26) Damaged on service 15.10.1976 and sold 1977
3.	1956 (922) William Osborne Littlehampton	Watkin Williams Legacy of Miss Mary Eames Williams, Deganwy, Carnarvonshire.	922 £27,801 16t18	2x48bhp Gardner 4LW (d) (1972)	Moelfre 18.4.1956-9.77 (131/143) Oban 1978-11.1981 (20/0) Reserve 1981-83 (0/0) Sold 5.1983
4.	1956 (933) William Osborne Littlehampton	J. W. Archer Gift of Mr J. W. Archer.	933 £27,871 16t5	2x48bhp Gardner 4LW (d) (1971)	Wicklow 7.6.1956-18.9.87 (166/69) Sold 31.3.1989
5.	1956 (563) Groves & Guttridge Cowes	The Duke of Montrose RNLI Funds.	934 £28,500 16t9	2x48bhp Gardner 4LW (d) (1971)	Arbroath 26.6.1956-17.12.1982 (64/30) Reserve 1982-84 (7/0) Sold 1984

22 • Watson motor 42ft

Year (Yd No) Builder Place	Name Donor	ON Cost Weight	Engines (WH added)	Stations (launches/lives saved) Notes Disposal	
6. 1957 (937) William Osborne Littlehampton	Mabel E. Holland Gift of Miss Maud E. Holland.	937 £30,000 16t17	2x48hp Gardner 4LW (d) (7.1967)	Dungeness 31.8.1957-7.9.78 (220/74) Reserve 1979-83 (10/0) Sold 1983	[Beach version]
7. 1957 (941) William Osborne Littlehampton	William and Mary Durham Legacies of Mrs M. E. Durham and Mrs M. G. Davenport.	941 £29,500 16t16	2x48bhp Gardner 4LW (d) (1971)	Berwick 9.5.1957-17.9.1976 (55/18) Girvan 1977-16.2.1983 (21/7) Sold 10.1983	
8. 1958 (W5470) J. S. White Cowes	Alfred and Patience Gottwald Legacy of Mrs P. A. Gottwald.	946 £30,000 17t1	2x48hp Gardner 4LW (d) (not fitted)	Aldeburgh 9.2.1959-4.8.79 (84/31) Reserve 1979-80 (0/0) Sold 1980	[Beach version]
9. 1958 (948) William Osborne Littlehampton	Charles Dibdin (Civil Service No.32) Civil Service Lifeboat Fund.	948 £30,000 17t7	2x48hp Gardner 4LW (d) (1972)	Walmer 18.3.1959-3.2.75 (143/115) Eastbourne 21.5.1977-26.4.79 (11/13) Aldeburgh 4.8.1979-7.6.82 (13/5) Reserve 1975-77 and 1982-88 (total 28/4) Sold 1988	[Beach version]
10. 1962 (600) Groves & Guttridge Cowes	Dorothy and Philip Constant Gift of Mr and Mrs Philip Constant, Bexhill-on-Sea.	967 £36,000 16t10	2x48bhp Gardner 4LW (d)	Shoreham Harbour 17.1.1963-21.8.81 (187/122) Oban 8.11.1981-10.6.1982 (7/1) Reserve 1982-87 (9/15) Sold 4.1988	

The first 42ft Beach lifeboat to be built, Mabel E. Holland *(ON.937), is beached at Dungeness. This photograph, which shows the lines and cabin arrangement of the 42ft Beach lifeboats, dates from the 1960s before the aft cockpit had been enclosed by a shelter. (From an old postcard supplied by Paul Russell)*

Charles Dibdin (Civil Service No.32) *(ON.948) on the launching cradle at the head of the beach at Walmer. All three of the 42ft Beach lifeboats were launched on skids across open beaches at their respective stations and were kept on some kind of cradle. (Phil Weeks)*

23 • Watson cabin motor 47ft

Introduced 1955, last built 1963, 18 built.
Specifications • length 47ft, beam 13ft, draft 4ft 5in.

The 47ft Watson cabin class represented a major revision of the basic Watson design and proved to be the last Watson type built. It was the result of a design review that came to fruition in 1955 which resulted in the main features of all three lifeboat types then in production, namely the 46ft 9in Watson, 52ft Barnett and 42ft Watson, being altered. The new 47ft Watson began the process with deck features copied to the other types. The main aluminium superstructure was extended forward and the forward shelter, which housed the engine controls, was more spacious than on other Watsons. The midship steering position was fully enclosed from the outset and the wheelhouse roof was extended aft so sliding doors could be fitted port and starboard. Power came from twin 60hp Gardner diesels with the exhaust carried up the main mast. The hull was more bulky than on previous Watsons and substantial bulwarks were fitted above the fenders fore and aft. With a displacement of 23 tons, the boats' maximum speed was 8.9 knots and the range was 280 nautical miles.

From 1973 onwards, the 47ft Watsons were modified to become self-righting. Most were fitted with an air-bag to give a once-only righting ability, while six were rebuilt to become inherently self-righting. The modifications on these six involved considerable structural changes including the replacement of the superstructure

47ft Watson motor Kathleen Mary *(ON.950) was built in 1959 and served at Newhaven as that station's last slipway launched lifeboat. (From an old postcard in the author's collection)*

forward of the wheelhouse with a longer and higher structure, an extension of the after cabin to include the original after cockpit, and the fitting of polyurethane foam blocks covered with glass reinforced plastic to the after cabin top; the top buoyancy provided by these three modifications gave the boat a self-righting capability. Those boats that were converted also had their engines uprated to 70hp. All conversions were undertaken at William Osborne's Arun Shipyard, Littlehampton.

Year (Yd No) Builder Place	Name Donor	ON Cost Weight	Engines (SR method)	Stations (launches/lives saved) Notes Disposal
1. 1955 (920) William Osborne Littlehampton	Dunnet Head (Civil Service No.31) Civil Service Lifeboat Fund.	920 £35,000 22t9	2x60bhp Gardner 5LW	Thurso 29.1-10.12.1956 (1/4) Destroyed by fire in boathouse, 10.12.1956
2. 1957 (W5468) J. S. White Cowes	Pentland (Civil Service No.31) Civil Service Lifeboat Fund (RNLI Funds to replace ON.920).	940 £34,346 22t9	2x60bhp Gardner 5LW/ uprated to 70bhp (CM 1974-5)	Thurso 15.12.1957-15.12.70 (49/15) Reserve 1970-8.74 (8/0) Mumbles 27.8.1974-3.7.85 (50/21) Workington 21.2.1986-23.9.90 (29/4) Sold 3.1991
3. 1958 (576) Groves & Guttridge Cowes	Margaret Legacies of Mr A. Black and Mr J. H. Taylor.	947 £35,000 22t7	2x60bhp Gardner 5LW (Air-bag)	Dunbar 4.2.1959-24.6.1986 (72/34) Sold 1987
4. 1959 (950) William Osborne Littlehampton	Kathleen Mary An anonymous gift, in memory of Kathleen Mary Haddock.	950 £34,500 22t11	2x60bhp Gardner 5LW (CM 1978-9)	Newhaven 22.7.1959-5.5.77 (234/123) Porthdinllaen 27.4.1979-27.4.87 (53/28) Appledore 18.6.1987-7.6.88 (4/1) Relief 1988-90 (0/0) Sold 4.1990
5. 1959 (951) William Osborne Littlehampton	Francis W. Wotherspoon of Paisley Legacy of Mr F. W. Wotherspoon.	951 £35,000 22t7	2x60bhp Gardner 5LW (Air-bag)	Islay 11.7.1959-2.5.79 (93/60) Relief 1979-2.82 (3/0) Fishguard 2.4-9.1981 (3/1) Workington 2.1982-21.2.86 (22/3) Sold 10.1986
6. 1960 (584) Groves & Guttridge Cowes	Sarah Jane and James Season Legacy of Mr Arthur Season, Ilkley, and others.	953 £35,000 22t11	2x60bhp Gardner 5LW (Air-bag)	Teesmouth 3.5.1960-22.1.86 (101/28) Shoreham Harbour 16.7.1986-9.8.88 (39/27) Sold 1989
7. 1960 (954) William Osborne Littlehampton	Solomon Browne Legacies of Miss L. Browne and others.	954 £35,500 22t14	2x60bhp Gardner 5LW (Air-bag)	Penlee 4.7.1960-12.81 (238/91) Wrecked on service 19.12.1981, eight lost
8. 1960 (955) William Osborne Littlehampton	The Robert An anonymous gift.	955 £35,500 22t17	2x60bhp Gardner 5LW/ 1977- uprated to 70bhp (Air-bag,-CM 1976-7)	Broughty Ferry 17.11.1960-6.5.78 (29/3) Baltimore 5.1978-17.7.84 (44/31) Lytham St Annes 9.3.1985-1.12.88 (25/11) Beaumaris 11.4.1989-4.7.91 (2/1) Sold 2.1992

Year (Yd No) Builder Place	Name Donor	ON Cost Weight	Engines (SR method)	Stations (launches/lives saved) Notes Disposal
9. 1961 (587) Groves & Guttridge Cowes	The Jeanie An anonymous gift.	957 £35,500 22t13	2x60bhp Gardner 5LW (Air bag)	Portpatrick 1.3.1961-3.86 (89/46) Sold 1987
10. 1961 (588) Groves & Guttridge Cowes	Laura Moncur Legacy of Miss L. Moncur, gift from Miss J. B. Moncur, plus RNLI funds.	958 £35,500 22t12	2x60bhp Gardner 5LW/ 1974- uprated to 70bhp (CM 1972-3)	Buckie 6.1961-5.4.1984 (66/39) Relief 1984-88 (12/8) Appledore 19.10.1986-18.6.87 Sold 11.1988
11. 1961 (589) Groves & Guttridge Cowes	Helen Wycherley Legacy of Mr H. Wycherley, gift from Miss Jane W. Robb, plus RNLI funds.	959 £35,500 22t5	2x60bhp Gardner 5LW (Air-bag)	Whitehills 6.1961-69 (11/1) Courtmacsherry Harbour 23.8.1969-2.12.87 (67/4) Sold 12.1988
12. 1962 (W5520) J. S. White Cowes	T. G. B. An anonymous gift.	962 £35,500 23t16	2x60bhp Gardner 5LW (Air-bag)	Longhope 4.1962-3.69 (34/24) Capsized on service 17.3.1969, eight lost Arranmore 29.9.1970-28.10.78 (41/31) Relief 1979-85 (58/24) Sold 1986
13. 1962 (W5521) J. S. White Cowes	A. M. T. Legacies of E. A. Austin, New Barnet; Miss J. Mulhauser, Carshalton; A. Toon, Shilton.	963 £37,000 23t10	2x60bhp Gardner 5LW (Air-bag)	Howth 18.7.1962-23.8.1986 (197/83) Relief 1987-89 (15/4) Sold 6.1989
14. 1962 (W5522) J. S. White Cowes	The Baltic Exchange Contributions from members of The Baltic Exchange.	964 £36,500 23t10	2x60bhp Gardner 5LW (Air-bag)	Salcombe 6.1962-30.8.88 (258/76) Capsized on service 10.4.1983, none lost Sold 1989
15. 1962 (594) Groves & Guttridge Cowes	Louisa Anne Hawker Gift of Mr G. P. D. Hawker, Exeter.	965 £40,000 23t11	2x60bhp Gardner 5LW (Air-bag)	Appledore 5.1962-19.10.86 (149/52) Sold 4.8.1987
16. 1963 (W5531) J. S. White Cowes	William Myers and Sarah Jane Myers Legacy of Miss E. Myers, Saltburn-on-Sea, and RNLI funds.	969 £40,500 23t3	2x60bhp Gardner 5LW (CM 1975-6)	Sunderland 5.1963-17.4.90 (201/36) Relief 1990-1.2.92 (0/0) Sold 1992
17. 1963 (W5532) J. S. White Cowes	Frederick Edward Crick Legacy of Mrs Florence May Crick, Longfield, Kent.	970 £40,500 24t3	2x60bhp Gardner 5LW (Air-bag)	Lowestoft 7.1963-19.10.86 (247/109) Sold 10.1986
18. 1963 (W5533) J. S. White Cowes	Joseph Soar (Civil Service No.34) Civil Service Lifeboat Fund.	971 £40,500 23t1	2x60bhp Gardner 5LW (CM 1976-7)	St Davids 9.1963-11.12.85 (99/45) Dunbar 24.6.1986-8.88 (6/0) Shoreham Harbour 8.9.1988-30.9.90 (29/8) Sold 3.8.1992

CM – Cabin modified for self-righting

47ft Watson motor The Baltic Exchange (ON.964) moored in the middle of the estuary at Salcombe. The casing which houses the self-righting air-bag is fitted to the aft cabin and this inflated successfully when the boat was capsized on service on 10 April 1983. (Paul Russell)

47ft Watson motor William Myers and Sarah Jane Myers (ON.969) at Sunderland, where she was the last slipway-launched lifeboat. The extended superstructure in front of the wheelhouse was added in the mid-1970s to make the boat inherently self-righting. (H. V. J. Cutter)

24 • Oakley self-righter 37ft

Introduced 1957, last built 1971, 26 built.
Specifications • length 37ft, beam 11ft 6in, draft 3ft 4in, crew 7/8.

The 37ft Oakley class was designed by and named after Richard Oakley, the RNLI's Consulting Naval Architect. Developed during the mid-1950s, it was the first lifeboat design to have a high degree of inherent stability and also be self-righting in the event of a capsize. Righting was achieved by the use of an ingenious water ballast system which involved the transfer of 1.54 tons of water ballast into a righting tank on the port side if the boat turned over. During trials, righting took about six seconds from the overturned position to the boat being upright.

The 37ft Oakley was built of wood and, with a displacement of 12.5 tons, was suitable for handling ashore and carriage launching over a beach. The water ballast taken on once afloat provided good sea-keeping qualities and a solid working platform. The hull was subdivided into eleven watertight compartments and contained 222 air cases. PVC was used to provide buoyancy and blocks were used instead of smaller air cases.

Only once was the self-righting ability called upon on service when ON.997 was capsized twice off Kilmore Quay on 24 December 1977. On both occasions, she righted herself successfully and the engines were restarted, but of four crew members washed overboard during the second capsize, one was never recovered. Without the self-righting system, however, it is unlikely if any would have survived.

The first five Oakleys were fitted with twin Perkins P4M four-cylinder diesel engines giving a maximum speed of approximately eight knots. The remaining boats of the class were fitted with slightly more powerful Ford Parsons Porbeagle four-cylinder diesels of 52bhp. Two of the Perkins-engined boats were re-engined with the Porbeagle engine during their service career. ON.972 was rebuilt in 1982-3 for the unique launching conditions at

Launch of the first 37ft Oakley J. G. Graves of Sheffield (ON.942) from the beach at Scarborough where she served for twenty years. The Oakley was designed specifically for carriage launching and many saw service on the east coast of England where a number of stations employ this method of launching.

Flamborough. Between 1982 and 1986, a wheelhouse to enclose the cockpit was fitted to all the Oakleys. As boathouse height was a prime consideration for carriage-launched boats, the wheelhouse was folding as no fixed structure could be added above the casing top. Radar was installed during the 1970s and fitted on a tripod mast at the forward end of the engine casing.

During the mid-1980s several of the Oakleys suffered serious problems of hull deterioration, and as a result a number had to be virtually rebuilt. When taken out of service, the boats were deemed unsuitable for private sale and the RNLI adopted a policy whereby a sale would only be agreed if the boat in question was going on static display and not afloat. Where a suitable buyer could not be found, the boats were broken up and a number of boats were dismantled as a result.

Cutaway drawing of the 37ft Oakley as built, with open cockpit and before radar was fitted.
Key: (1) Steering gear box, (2) Drogue, (3) Non-skid deck covering, (4) Emergency tiller, (5) Air cases, (6) Drogue cable tray, (7) Line-throwing gun locker, (8) Coxswain's platform, (9) Compass binnacle, (10) Hatch to batteries, (11) Fire extinguishers, (12) Radio telephone, (13) Engine controls, (14) Echo sounder, (15) Breeches Buoy, (16) Engine exhaust silencer, (17) Exhaust outlet, (18) Air supply to engine room, (19) Air escape from water ballast tank, (20) Top of water ballast tank, (21) Deck lights, (22) Socket for searchlight, (23) Deck floodlight, (24) Navigation lights, (25) Watertight hatch, (26) Cockpit drain trunk, (27) Stowage locker, (28) Bollard, (29) Socket for loudhailer, (30) Breakwater, (31) Stem fairlead, (32) Bow pudding.

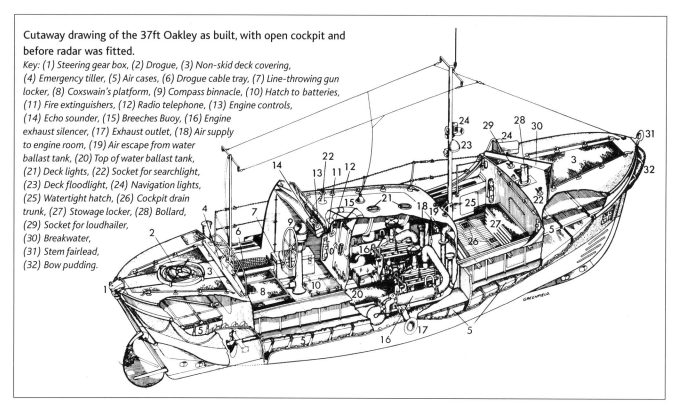

24 • Oakley self-righter 37ft

Year (Yd No) Builder Place	Name Donor	ON (Op No) Cost Weight	Engines (all twin-screw diesels)	Stations (launches/lives saved) Disposal
1. 1957 (WO942) William Osborne Littlehampton	J. G. Graves of Sheffield Gift of the J. G. Graves Charitable Trust.	942 (37-01) £26,700 11t4	2x43hp Perkins P4M	Scarborough 21.10.1958-8.11.78 (105/9) Relief 1979-88 (31/9) Clogher Head 9.1988-3.91 (9/3) Newcastle 1992-93 (2/0) Display at Chatham Historic Dockyard
2. 1961 (WO960) William Osborne Littlehampton	The Manchester Unity of Oddfellows Gift Independent Order of Odd Fellows, Manchester Unity Friendly Society.	960 (37-02) £28,500 11t17	2x43hp Perkins P4M/ 1982- 2x52hp Ford Thornycroft	Sheringham 10.7.1961-10.8.90 (126/74) Sold 4.1991 for display
3. 1961 (W5496) J. S. White Cowes	Calouste Gulbenkian Gift of the Calouste Gulbenkian Foundation.	961 (37-03) £34,000 11t17	2x43hp Perkins P4M	Weston-super-Mare 17.3.1961-1.3.69 (33/6) Relief 4.1970-11.90 (107/15) New Quay 28.1.1990-17.1.91 (6/6) Sold 11.1991
4. 1962 (595) G & Guttridge Cowes	Robert and Dorothy Hardcastle Legacy of Hugh Robert Hardcastle, Boston Spa, Yorkshire.	966 (37-04) £33,000 11t16	2x43hp Perkins P4M	Boulmer 10.1962-31.3.68 (30/9) Filey 18.5.1968-2.6.91 (180/221) Relief 1992-93 (1/0) Sold 4.1993
5. 1963 (WO972) William Osborne Littlehampton	The Will and Fanny Kirby The Mr and Mrs W. L. Kirby Benevolent Fund.	972 (37-05) £33,000 12t1	2x43hp Perkins P4M/ 1982- 2x52hp Ford Thornycroft	Seaham Harbour 10.9.1963-24.2.79 (46/66) Relief 2.1979-82 (9/7) Flamborough 18.1.1983-16.8.93 (142/43) Display at Chatham Historic Dockyard
6. 1964 (WO973) William Osborne Littlehampton	Fairlight Legacies of Mrs K. E. Wood and Mrs F. M. Dudman.	973 (37-06) £33,000 12t8	2x52hp Parsons Porbeagle 4-cyl	Hastings 29.8.1964-15.5.88 (207/144) Relief 5.1988-9.89 (5/0) St Ives 9.1989-23.10.90 (19/11) New Quay 27.1.1991-8.4.92 (3/0) Sold 10.1994
7. 1964 (WO974) William Osborne Littlehampton	Jane Hay Legacies of Mrs M. Erskine, Miss A. Smith, and gift from Miss Gillespie.	974 (37-07) £31,848 12t4	2x52hp Parsons Porbeagle 4-cyl	St Abbs 3.11.1964-12.7.74 (20/8) Relief 7.1974-5.80 (30/12) Newcastle 11.5.1980-3.8.92 (70/13) Broken up 1995 at Arklow
8. 1964 (G&G604) G & Guttridge Cowes	Sir James Knott Sir James Knott Trust, and RNLI General Funds.	975 (37-08) £33,000 12t4	2x52hp Parsons Porbeagle 4-cyl	Cullercoats 21.11.1963-4.5.69 (15/14) Relief 5.1969-11.72 (5/4) Redcar 28.11.1972-13.7.85 (78/63) Relief 1985-5.89 (28/0) Sold 1990 for display
9. 1964 (G&G605) G & Guttridge Cowes	Lilly Wainwright Legacy of Mr J. H. Wainwright, gift of Arthur Jowett Fund, plus RNLI funds.	976 (37-09) £33,000 12t8	2x52hp Parsons Porbeagle 4-cyl	Llandudno 30.1.1964-7.8.90 (124/58) Kilmore Quay 26.1.1991-1.12.92 (11/2) Sold 9.1993
10. 1964 (G&G606) G & Guttridge Cowes	Charles Fred Grantham Legacies of Mrs E. W. Montford and Miss E. M. Dearden.	977 (37-10) £33,000 12t4	2x52hp Parsons Porbeagle 4-cyl	Skegness 20.4.1964-7.8.90 (148/96) Scarborough 10.1990-91 (5/4) Relief 1.1991-7.92 (1/0) Broken up 8.1993 at Ridge, Dorset

37ft Oakley Jane Hay *(ON.974) as built, with an open after cockpit and no radar. She served at St Abbs and Newcastle during her career. (RNLI)*

37ft Oakley Charles Fred Grantham *(ON.977), built for Skegness, with her after cockpit open. (From an old postcard in the author's collection)*

24 • Oakley self-righter 37ft

Year (Yd No) Builder Place	Name Donor	ON (Op No) Cost Weight	Engines (all twin-screw diesels)	Stations (launches/lives saved) Disposal
11. 1964 (W5542) J. S. White Cowes	The Royal Thames Legacy of Mr D. A. Forster, various gifts and RNLI funds.	978 (37-11) £31,749 12t5	2x52hp Parsons Porbeagle 4 cyl	Caister 21.2.1964-17.10.69 (30/15) Runswick 20.9.1970-30.6.78 (37/30) Pwllheli 18.5.1979-25.1.91 (32/7) Clogher Head 29.3.1991-3.3.93 (5/0) Scrapped and sold 10.1994
12. 1964 (W5543) J. S. White Cowes	James and Catherine Macfarlane/ 1967- Amelia Legacy of Mr R. F. Macfarlane/ 1967- legacy of Mrs A. Borland, RNLI funds.	979 (37-12) £33,000 12t8	2x52hp Parsons Porbeagle 4-cyl	Relief 23.5.1964-8.11.78 (43/12) Scarborough 8.11.1978-27.9.91 (116/18) Sold 2.1992, display at Charlestown
13. 1964 (W5544) J. S. White Cowes	William Henry and Mary King Legacy of Miss J. G. King and RNLI General Funds.	980 (37-13) £33,000 12t8	2x52hp Parsons Porbeagle 4-cyl	Cromer No.2 28.10.1964-22.6.67 (12/1) Bridlington 2.9.1967-15.12.88 (278/83) North Sunderland 30.3.1989-7.8.90 (8/0) Display at Drayton Park School, London
14. 1965 (WO 981) William Osborne Littlehampton	Mary Pullman Gift from the late Sir Derek Wheeler, Bt.	981 (37-14) £33,000 12t6	2x52hp Parsons Porbeagle 4-cyl	Kirkcudbright 2.5.1965-26.4.89 (89/34) Display at Baytree Garden Centre, Spalding
15. 1965 (WO 982) William Osborne Littlehampton	Ernest Tom Neathercoat Legacy Mr E. T. Neathercoat, CBE, and RNLI Funds.	982 (37-15) £34,000 12t3	2x52hp Parsons Porbeagle 4-cyl	Wells 1.6.1965-3.7.90 (85/16) North Sunderland 14.8.1990-7.91 (16/0) Display at Oulton Broad and Wells
16. 1965 (WO 983) William Osborne Littlehampton	The Doctors Gift of Dr Nora Allan.	983 (37-16) £34,000 12t5	2x52hp Parsons Porbeagle 4-cyl	Anstruther 26.5.1965-18.3.91 (78/22) Relief 1991-93 (0/0) Sold 1993 for display at Buckie Drifter Centre
17. 1964 Herd & McKenzie Buckie	Mary Joicey Donation from the trustees of the late Mrs Mary Joicey, Sunningdale, Berks.	984 (37-17) £37,000 12t18	2x52hp Parsons Porbeagle 4-cyl	Newbiggin 5.9.1966-28.2.81 (52/24) Relief 1981-89 (52/12) [inc Redcar 13.7.1985- Hastings 15.5.1988-15.3.89 (9/3) 22.7.86 (2/0)] St Ives 29.3-21.9.1989 (5/0) Display at Child-Beale Trust, Reading, then Newbiggin
18. 1967 Herd & McKenzie Buckie	Valentine Wyndham-Quin Legacy of Mr H. P. Harris and an anonymous gift.	985 (37-18) £37,000 12t6	2x52hp Parsons Porbeagle 4-cyl	Clacton-on-Sea 19.1.1967-7.83 (179/61) Clogher Head 26.8.1984-9.9.88 (9/5) Display at Cromer, then Harwich Maritime Museum
19. 1966 Morris & Lorimer Sandbank	Lloyd's II Gift from the Corporation of Lloyd's and Lloyd's Brokers.	986 (37-19) £34,000 12t10	2x52hp Parsons Porbeagle 4-cyl	Ilfracombe 8.7.1966-20.7.90 (136/116) Sheringham 8.10.1990-18.4.92 (12/0) Broken up 1992 at Otterham, Kent
20. 1967 (WO 991) William Osborne Littlehampton	Edward and Mary Lester Gift and legacy of Mrs Mary Lester.	991 (37-20) £37,500 11t6	2x52hp Parsons Porbeagle 4-cyl	North Sunderland 18.7.1967-30.3.89 (109/27) Broken up 1989 at Southampton
21. 1968 (WO 992) William Osborne Littlehampton	Frank Penfold Marshall Gift of Mrs Dagmar Marshall.	992 (37-21) £37,000 12t	2x52hp Parsons Porbeagle 4-cyl	St Ives 7.1968-29.3.89 (226/85) Broken up 1989 at Southampton
22. 1968 (WO 993) William Osborne Littlehampton	Har-Lil Legacy of Miss Jeanie B. Watt, Renfrewshire.	993 (37-22) £37,000 12t	2x52hp Parsons Porbeagle 4-cyl	Rhyl 26.9.1968-23.12.1990 (109/28) Sold 12.1991
23. 1968 (WO 994) William Osborne Littlehampton	Vincent Nesfield Mrs J Giddens' Fund, legacy of Mr Cowls and Mr Ringer.	994 (37-23) £38,000 12t8	2x52hp Parsons Porbeagle 4-cyl	Relief 1969-93 (98/39) Port Erin 4.1.1972-1.7.73 (1/0) Kilmore Quay 25.9.1989-26.1.91 (12/3) Broken up 1995 at Dumbarton
24. 1970 (WO 995) William Osborne Littlehampton	James Ball Ritchie Gift of Mrs A. A. Ritchie.	995 (37-24) £38,500 12t2	2x52hp Parsons Porbeagle 4-cyl	Ramsey 20.2.1970-12.7.91 (144/77) Broken up 1992 at Arklow
25. 1970 (WO 996) William Osborne Littlehampton	Birds Eye Birds Eye Foods.	996 (37-25) £38,500 12t3	2x52hp Parsons Porbeagle 4-cyl	New Quay 16.7.1970-28.1.90 (90/42) Display at Sea Watch Centre, Moelfre
26. 1971 (WO 18) William Osborne Littlehampton	Lady Murphy Legacy of Lady Frances Murphy.	997 (37-26) £38,360 12t1	2x52hp Parsons Porbeagle 4-cyl	Kilmore Quay 7.2.1972-25.9.88 (49/5) Capsized on service 24.12.1977 Broken up 1995 at Arklow

*Launch of the second 37ft Oakley
Manchester Unity of Oddfellows
(ON.960) from the steeply inclined
beach at Sheringham. The boat was
in the latter stages of her career with
radar fitted and enclosed aft cockpit.
(Paul Russell)*

*37ft Oakley Valentine Wyndham-
Quin (ON.985) being recovered up
the slipway at Clacton-on-Sea in the
early days of her career with an open
aft cockpit and no radar. She was one
of a handful of 37ft Oakleys which
were slipway launched. (RNLI)*

*37ft Oakley James Ball Ritchie
(ON.995) on the beach at Ramsey,
Isle of Man, during the latter stages
of her service career. After leaving
Ramsey, she was broken up, a fate
that befell many of the Oakley
lifeboats as they were deemed
unsuitable for private sale because of
the complicated self-righting system
using ballast tanks and pipework.
(Phil Weeks)*

25 • Rother 37ft 6in

Introduced 1972, last built 1982, 14 built.
Specifications • length 37ft 6in, beam 11ft 6in, draft 3ft 6in, crew 7/8.

The 37ft 6in Rother was a development of the 37ft Oakley, and named after the river Rother, a tributary of the river Arun which flows through Littlehampton, where the first of the class was built. The shape of the hull was basically the same as that of the Oakley but, as the RNLI wanted to incorporate radar in new lifeboats built after 1972, the design was modified using experience gained through operating the Oakleys. The hull and layout were redesigned so that the self-righting potential was derived from the hull form itself, thus removing the need for the water ballast transfer system. The superstructure, enlarged to give enough buoyancy for inherent self-righting, was extended forward to meet the fore endbox to form a cabin, and an enclosed wheelhouse was incorporated which supported the radar.

The enclosed forecabin, with access through the engine room and an escape hatch through the roof, provided for the first time in a small boat a watertight cabin for survivors. The space originally given to the water ballast tank in the Oakleys was taken up by a double-bottom void ensuring that the engine room would not be flooded if the hull was holed. The radar scanner was fitted at the aft end of the wheelhouse roof and hinged to swing down into a stowed position beneath the roofline to conform to the restricted headroom of boathouses at stations where they served. The radar control unit and screen, together with other radio equipment, was mounted in a recess built into the after engine room bulkhead.

The 37ft 6in Rother was fitted with twin 52bhp Ford Thornycroft type 250 four-stroke marine diesel engines, driving twin propellers though two-to-one reduction gearboxes at 2,000rpm. The boats had a maximum speed of approximately eight knots and a range at full speed of 180 nautical miles. Two of the Rothers, ON.1024 and ON.1068, were built with strengthened hulls to withstand the rigours of launching over a beach on skids.

The Hampshire Rose *(ON.1024) on the slipway at the head of the beach at Walmer. (Phil Weeks)*

The RNLI's carriage-launch rig as typified by Harold Salvesen *(ON.1022) entering the water at Rhyl prior to launching. (Nicholas Leach)*

	Year (Yd No) Builder Place	Name Donor	ON (Op No) Cost Weight	Engines (all twin-screw diesels)	Stations (launches/lives saved) Disposal
1.	1972 (WO19) William Osborne Littlehampton	Osman Gabriel Gift of Major Osman B. Gabriel, Hove, Sussex.	998 (37-27) £60,000 12t10	2x52hp Ford Thornycroft 250	Port Erin 1.7.1973-22.6.92 (70/55) Sold 3.1993
2.	1973 (WO20) William Osborne Littlehampton	Diana White An anonymous gift, part of the Cornish Lifeboat Appeal.	999 (37-28) £89,000 12t12	2x52hp Ford Thornycroft 250	Sennen Cove 11.1973-12.10.91 (80/63) Sold 1992
3.	1974 (WO21) William Osborne Littlehampton	Mary Gabriel Gift of Major Osman B. Gabriel, Hove, Sussex.	1000 (37-29) £90,000 13t8	2x52hp Ford Thornycroft 250	Hoylake 18.5.1974-12.10.90 (99/44) Rhyl 23.12.1990-3.4.92 (6/0) Sold 10.1992
4.	1974 (656) Groves & Guttridge, Cowes	Harold Salvesen Gift of the Salvesen Trust.	1022 (37-30) £95,000 13t2	2x52hp Ford Thornycroft 250	Amble 6.1974-6.86 (61/6) Relief 6.1986-92 (34/3) Rhyl 3.4-23.6.1992 (1/0) Sold 10.1992
5.	1974 (657) Groves & Guttridge, Cowes	J. Reginald Corah Gift of the J. Reginald Corah Foundation.	1023 (37-31) £95,000 13t4	2x52hp Ford Thornycroft 250	Swanage 10.1975-12.6.92 (411/240) Sold 6.1995
6.	1974 (WO141) William Osborne Littlehampton	The Hampshire Rose The Hampshire Rose Appeal.	1024 (37-32) £95,000 12t11	2x52hp Ford Thornycroft 250	Walmer 3.2.1975-5.5.90 (132/57) Relief 1990-92 (6/2) Anstruther 18.3-16.10.1991 (8/0) Sold 10.1992

Year (Yd No) Builder Place	Name Donor	ON (Op No) Cost Weight	Engines (all twin-screw diesels)	Stations (launches/lives saved) Disposal
7. 1977 (WO1117) William Osborne Littlehampton	Silver Jubilee (Civil Service No.38) Civil Service and Post Office Lifeboat Fund.	1046 (37-33) £105,000 13t7	2x52hp Ford Mermaid 397 4-cyl (d)	Margate 4.10.1977-19.12.91 (163/76) Relief 1991-1.7.93 (1/0) Sold 3.1994
8. 1977 (WO1118) William Osborne Littlehampton	Horace Clarkson H. Clarkson & Co Ltd.	1047 (37-34) £107,000 12t17	2x52hp Ford Mermaid 397 4-cyl (d)	Moelfre 10.1977-3.11.86 (55/22) Relief 1987-93 (49/37) Sold 5.1993
9. 1977 (WO1119) William Osborne Littlehampton	Alice Upjohn Gift of Miss U. M. Upjohn.	1048 (37-35) £130,000 12t18	2x52hp Ford Mermaid 397 4-cyl (d)	Dungeness 23.9.1977-24.9.92 (147/45) Relief 1992-93 Sold 1995
10. 1979 (WO1666) William Osborne Littlehampton	Shoreline Shoreline Appeal.	1054 (37-36) £210,000 13t6	2x52hp Ford Mermaid 397 4-cyl (d)	Blyth 18.10.1979-26.10.82 (9/1) Arbroath 17.12.1982-26.8.93 (42/5) Sold 2.1994
11. 1979 (WO1667) William Osborne Littlehampton	Duke of Kent Eastbourne Lifeboat Appeal.	1055 (37-37) £210,000 12t10	2x52hp Ford Mermaid 397 4-cyl (d)	Eastbourne 26.4.1979-1.8.93 (353/86) Sold 6.1995
12. 1981 (WO2091) William Osborne Littlehampton	Princess of Wales Welsh Lifeboat Appeal, and other sources.	1063 (37-38) £239,197 13t6	2x52hp Ford Mermaid Melody (d)	Barmouth 27.3.1982-7.10.92 (36/8) Relief 1992-93 (0/0) Sold 15.5.1993
13. 1981 (WO2092) William Osborne Littlehampton	The Davys Family Gift of Mrs A. E. Mason.	1064 (37-39) £240,000 12t18	2x52hp Ford Mermaid Melody (d)	Shoreham Harbour 21.8.1982-16.7.86 (58/16) Relief 7.1986-93 (27/6) Sold 7.1995
14. 1982 (WO2222) William Osborne Littlehampton	James Cable Aldeburgh Lifeboat Appeal, and other sources.	1068 (37-40) £246,000 13t5	2x52hp Ford Mermaid Melody (d)	Aldeburgh 7.6.1982-19.12.93 (53/24) Sold 8.1994

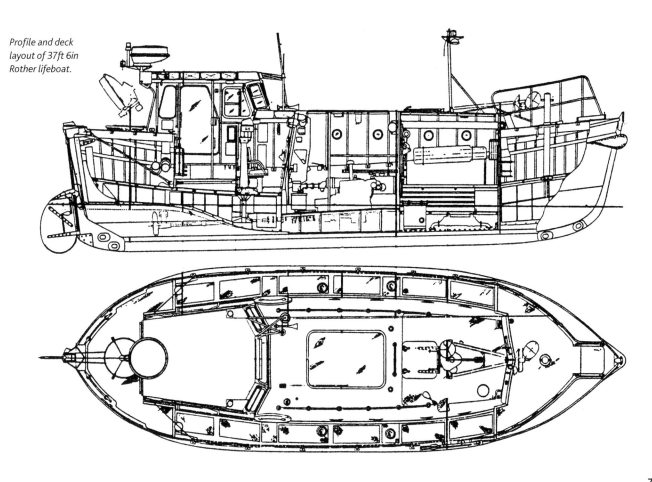

Profile and deck layout of 37ft 6in Rother lifeboat.

26 • Oakley self-righting 48ft 6in

Introduced 1963, last built 1970, 5 built.
Specifications • length 48ft 6in, length (waterline) 45ft 9in, beam 14ft, draft 4ft 8in, crew 7/8.

The 48ft 6in Oakley, designed by Richard Oakley, was a larger version of the 37ft Oakley, providing cabin accommodation for survivors, and was intended for stations with a slipway or permanent moorings afloat. The design employed the transfer of 2.75 tons of water ballast for self-righting in a system similar to that used in the smaller 37ft Oakley. The first version had an aft cockpit which was open towards the stern, while the deck layout of the other four consisted of an enclosed steering position positioned amidships. In these latter four boats, the after cockpit was dispensed with and a cabin formed in its place, extending to the after end of the wheelhouse. This aft cabin accommodated a loaded stretcher as well as serving as the chartroom.

All 48ft 6in Oakleys were fitted with twin Gardner 6LX diesel engines developing 110bhp at 1,200rpm and driving through a 2:1 reduction gearbox. The first of the class, ON.968, was fitted with a Decca Type 202 radar set, provided as a memorial to Joseph Conrad, which together with other standard electronic equipment was housed in a console built into the port side of the wheelhouse at the fore end of the shelter. In the late 1980s, the Oakleys were prone to serious hull deterioration caused by electrolysis resulting from the water ballast system combining with the aluminium

The prototype 48ft 6in Oakley The Earl and Countess Howe *(ON.968) on display at the RNLI Depot, Poole. The only boat of the class built with an open stern cockpit, she was displayed in Poole for many years until being broken up in 2004 after being deemed beyond economic repair. (Nicholas Leach)*

alloy construction of the inner bottom. As a result, some were withdrawn from service prematurely and deemed beyond repair. The boats, deemed unsuitable for private sale, were initially put on display at various locations. However, two were later broken up and another became a private pleasure boat.

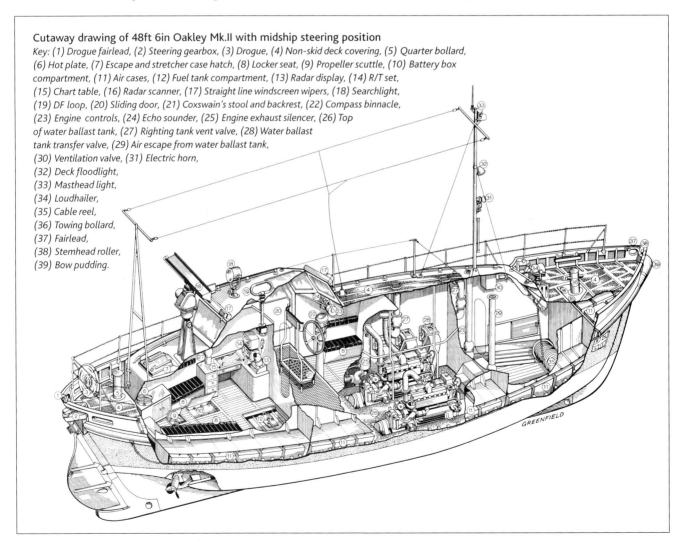

Cutaway drawing of 48ft 6in Oakley Mk.II with midship steering position
Key: (1) Drogue fairlead, (2) Steering gearbox, (3) Drogue, (4) Non-skid deck covering, (5) Quarter bollard, (6) Hot plate, (7) Escape and stretcher case hatch, (8) Locker seat, (9) Propeller scuttle, (10) Battery box compartment, (11) Air cases, (12) Fuel tank compartment, (13) Radar display, (14) R/T set, (15) Chart table, (16) Radar scanner, (17) Straight line windscreen wipers, (18) Searchlight, (19) DF loop, (20) Sliding door, (21) Coxswain's stool and backrest, (22) Compass binnacle, (23) Engine controls, (24) Echo sounder, (25) Engine exhaust silencer, (26) Top of water ballast tank, (27) Righting tank vent valve, (28) Water ballast tank transfer valve, (29) Air escape from water ballast tank, (30) Ventilation valve, (31) Electric horn, (32) Deck floodlight, (33) Masthead light, (34) Loudhailer, (35) Cable reel, (36) Towing bollard, (37) Fairlead, (38) Stemhead roller, (39) Bow pudding.

26 • Oakley self-righting 48ft 6in

Year (Yd No) Builder Place	Name Donor	ON (Op No) Cost Weight	Engines (all twin-screw diesels)	Stations (launches/lives saved) Disposal
1. 1963 (WO968) William Osborne Littlehampton	The Earl and Countess Howe RNLI General Funds.	968 (48-01) £40,348 29t2	2x110hp Gardner 6LX	Yarmouth 2.1963-19.2.77 (168/92) Walton and Frinton 12.7.1977-15.1.84 (64/21) Display at RNLI Depot, Poole, 1983 to 2004, broken up 2004 at Portishead
2. 1967 (944) Berthon Bt Co Lymington	James and Catherine MacFarlane Gift of Mr Robert E. MacFarlane, Glasgow.	989 (48- 02) £53,000 31t14	2x110hp Gardner 6LX	Padstow 19.7.1967-9.10.83 (109/63) The Lizard 17.7.1984-20.12.87 (22/6) Sold 1988, diusplay at Land's End complex
3. 1966 (WO990) William Osborne Littlehampton	Ruby and Arthur Reed Gift of Mrs R. M. Reed, Eastbourne.	990 (48- 03) £60,000 30t2	2x110hp Gardner 6LX	Cromer 3.1967-9.84 (125/58) St Davids 12.1985-5.88 (10/0) Sold 9.1988, display at Hythe Marina, Southampton
4. 1968 (WO1015) William Osborne Littlehampton	Charles Henry Legacy of Mr Charles Henry, Teddington, Middlesex.	1015 (48-12) £72,000 30t	2x110hp Gardner 6LX	Selsey 22.1.1969-21.11.83 (176/80) Baltimore 17.7.1984-3.6.87 (35/33) Sold 1987, display at Merry Hill, nr Dudley, to 2000
5. 1970 (WO1016) William Osborne Littlehampton	Princess Marina Gift of H. M. Thomson Trust and legacy of Mrs D. H. Napier, Dumbarton.	1016 (48-13) £72,000 30t8	2x110hp Gardner 6LX	Wick 7.1970-16.9.88 (70/31) Display at National Motor Boat Museum , Pitsea, 1989 to 2003, broken up 2004 at Portishead

The penultimate 48ft 6in Oakley Charles Henry (ON.1015) at Selsey in July 1982 with D class inflatable D-277. After leaving service, she was placed on display at Merry Hill Shopping Centre in Dudley until sold and converted for use at sea as a private pleasure boat. (Tony Denton)

The last 48ft 6in Oakley to be built, Princess Marina (ON.1016), served at Wick for her whole career. She was one of four Oakleys built with a midship steering position. (RNLI, by courtesy of Jeff Morris)

27 • Solent 48ft 6in

Introduced 1969, last built 1973, 11 built.
Specifications • length 48ft 6in, length (waterline) 45ft 9in, beam 14ft, draft 4ft 8in, crew 7/8.

The 48ft 6in Solent design was based on the 48ft 6in Oakley Mark II and was almost identical in external appearance and internal layout. However, the Solent was constructed with an all-welded steel hull and aluminium alloy upperworks, with the intention of reducing building costs, and was fitted with an iron ballast keel weighing 4.25 tons. The design was inherently self-righting and this capability was achieved by the large watertight wheelhouse, so the somewhat complicated system of water ballast transfer used in the 48ft 6in Oakley was eliminated.

In place of the water ballast tank, a double bottom was formed below the engine room and this, the forepeak, the void under the after cabin and the wing compartments were all filled with rigid foam polyurethane to increase buoyancy and obviate the need for air cases. The hull was divided by four main watertight bulkheads and twenty-five watertight compartments. Cabin arrangements differed with the first eight boats fitted with sliding doors and a vertical steering wheel, while the last three had hinged wheelhouse doors and seated steering positions.

Power came from twin Gardner 6LX diesel engines, each of 110hp at 1,300rpm, with Gardner 2UC reverse and 2:1 reduction gearboxes. The two fuel tanks each had a capacity of 120 gallons. Twin spade rudders gave improved manoeuvrability over the Oakley and Watson designs. The design was designated the Solent class in July 1969 after the river close to the yard where the first of the boats was built.

The much-travelled 48ft 6in Solent R. Hope Roberts (ON.1011) at Courtmacsherry Harbour. (Phil Weeks)

Hugh William, Viscount Gough (ON.1020) leaving Dunbar where she served during the last years of her lifeboat career. (Phil Weeks)

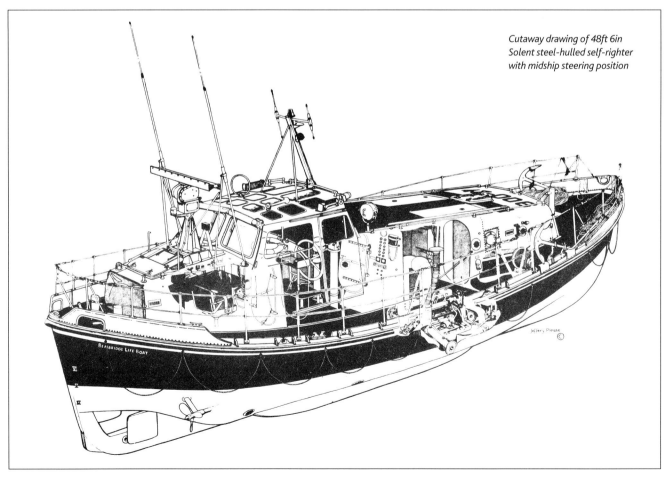

Cutaway drawing of 48ft 6in Solent steel-hulled self-righter with midship steering position

Year (Yd No) Builder Place	Name Donor	ON (Op No) Cost Weight	Engines (All twin screw diesels)	Stations (launches/lives saved) Disposal
1. 1969 (625) G & Guttridge Cowes	George Urie Scott Gift of Mrs Elizabeth Scott, Glasgow, in memory of her late husband.	1007 (48-004) £70,000 27t0	2x110hp Gardner 6LX	Lochinver 27.5.1969-3.8.78 (25/2) Rosslare Harbour 3.11.1979-1.6.84 (26/4) Lochinver 13.2.1985-20.7.89 (27/0) Sold 1990
2. 1969 (626) G & Guttridge Cowes	James and Mariska Joicey Legacy of Mrs Mariska Joicey, Richmond, Surrey.	1008 (48-005) £65,000 27t10	2x110hp Gardner 6LX	Peterhead 10.1969-7.12.86 (72/41) Lizard 20.12.1987-17.8.88 (3/0) Relief 8.1988-4.89 (10/0) Sold 1990
3. 1969 (627) G & Guttridge Cowes	Jack Shayler and the Lees Legacies of Miss A. Shayler and Mr A. Lees, and RNLI Funds.	1009 (48-006) £59,323 27t15	2x110hp Gardner 6LX	Bembridge 17.1.1970-24.8.87 (150/109) Relief 8.1988-5.93 (15/7) Sold 6.1994
4. 1970 (628) G & Guttridge Cowes	David and Elizabeth King and E. B. Legacy of Miss C. A. King, plus an anonymous gift.	1010 (48-007) £58,936 27t9	2x110hp Gardner 6LX	Longhope 15.12.1970-26.3.88 (77/32) Invergordon 7.1988-4.89 (3/0) Sold 1990
5. 1969 (930) C & Nicholson Gosport	R. Hope Roberts Legacies of Mrs A. Ronald, Mrs R. Hope and Mrs Roberts, and an anonymous gift.	1011 (48-008) £70,000 27t17	2x110hp Gardner 6LX	Rosslare Harbour 16.7.1969-3.11.79 (49/28) Fraserburgh 11.1979-5.85 (28/12) Galway Bay 12.1985-7.87 (37/5) Courtmacsherry Harbour 12.1987-5.93 (47/34) Sold 1993
6. 1970 (931) C & Nicholson Gosport	City of Birmingham City of Birmingham Lifeboat Appeal.	1012 (48-009) £72,000 27t17	2x110hp Gardner 6LX	Exmouth 11.2.1970-4.8.83 (58/19) Walton & Frinton 15.1.1984-1.8.93 (186/40) Sold 7.1995
7. 1971 (932) C & Nicholson Gosport	The Royal British Legion Jubilee The Royal British Legion.	1013 (48-010) £72,000 27t11	2x110hp Gardner 6LX	Relief 9.1971-11.89 (56/50) Fraserburgh 29.4-3.11.1979 (3/11) Peterhead 7.12.1986-14.1.88 (11/0) Sold 2.4.1990
8. 1970 (933) C & Nicholson Gosport	The Three Sisters An anonymous gift.	1014 (48-011) £65,000 27t7	2x110hp Gardner 6LX	Thurso 12.1970-3.88 (97/23) Wicklow 10.10.1988-9.2.89 (2/0) Sold 2.4.1990
9. 1972 (653) G & Guttridge Cowes	Lady MacRobert The MacRobert Trust.	1019 (48-014) £73,000 26t12	2x110hp Gardner 6LX	Montrose 12.1972-28.5.89 (61/17) Relief 10.1989-12.93 (38/35) Sold 3.1994
10. 1973 (654) G & Guttridge Cowes	Hugh William, Viscount Gough Gift of The Viscount Gough and Dowager Viscountess Gough.	1020 (48-015) £73,000 27t4	2x110hp Gardner 6LX	Stornoway 7.1973-6.3.84 (75/49) Barra Island 16.6.1984-22.7.88 (18/29) Dunbar 28.10.1988-1.8.93 (33/8) Sold 9.1993
11. 1973 (655) G & Guttridge Cowes	Douglas Currie Douglas Currie Trust and legacy of Mr Davidson.	1021 (48-016) £65,113 27t5	2x110hp Gardner 6LX	Relief 10.1973-4.74 (5/0) Kirkwall 6.1974-8.75 (8/12) Macduff 9.1975-9.84 (22/6) Fraserburgh 5-11.1985 (3/4) Portpatrick 1.3.1986-3.89 (22/17) Workington 23.9.1990-8.6.92 (15/0) Sold 1992

Full names of builders: G & Guttridge – Groves & Guttridge, of Cowes; C & Nicholson – Camper & Nicholson, of Gosport

28 • Clyde cruising 70ft

Introduced 1965, last built 1974, 3 built.
Specifications • ON.987 and ON.1030 – length 71ft
(21.64m), beam 18ft (5.49m); ON.988 length 70ft (21.44m),
beam 17ft (5.18m); length (waterline) (ON.987) 66ft.

The 70ft Clyde class, the largest rescue vessel ever built by the RNLI, originated in the early 1960s after members of the Institution's Management Committee visited the lifeboat societies of Holland and Germany where cruising lifeboats were successfully employed. In 1961, following a review of this visit, the decision was taken to commission the building of two long-range lifeboats. The result was the Clyde class, named after the river on which the first two boats were built and designed as a cruising rescue craft with a full-time crew living on board.

The class was not only the RNLI's largest lifeboat but was also the first to be constructed of steel. The hull design of the first and third boats, ON.987 and ON.1030, was produced by the RNLI's Naval Architect Richard Oakley and that of ON.988 by John Tyrrell, FRINA, of Arklow, Ireland. These first two boats were similar in appearance, although dimensions, underwater lines and layout were slightly different. Further alterations were made to the layout during annual surveys, particularly in the case of the survivors' cabin. The third boat had a modified superstructure, larger than on the first two boats, giving the boat a completely different appearance, but none was self-righting.

Unlike other lifeboat types, the Clyde had facilities for the crew to sleep on board and the crew's quarters, arranged aft below deck, included four berths, lockers and a lavatory. At the after end of the wheelhouse was a small messroom and galley with an electric cooker and refrigerator. In the forward cabin was stowage for six stretchers, and some of the seats could be converted into berths. Two additional rescue craft were carried on board: the duty inflatable inshore rescue boat, stowed on the engine casing forward of the wheelhouse, was powered by a 33hp outboard motor and launched by derricks; a smaller boat of similar type, with an 18hp engine, was stowed in the forward cabin. The vessel's hull was divided by six watertight bulkheads and each engine room was separated from the other by a longitudinal centre line bulkhead which was also watertight.

Power was provided by twin Gardner 8L3B diesel engines, each developing 230bhp at 1,150rpm. At the maximum speed of 11.14 knots, the Clyde had a range of 650 nautical miles, while at the cruising speed of 10.4 knots, at 1,000rpm, the range increased to 860 nautical miles. A flying bridge steering position with dupli-cated controls was incorporated into the superstructure's design. Three anchors were carried: standard RNLI pattern anchors in recesses to port and starboard, and a stockless anchor housed in the hawsepipe at the stemhead which can be raised using a hydraulic windlass on the foredeck. The last boat, ON.1030, was built as a relief for the first two, but in fact served at Clovelly while ON.987 became the relief vessel.

ON.987 went into service in 1965 at Clovelly, North Devon, from where she covered St George's Channel, the southern end of the Irish Sea and the mouth of the Bristol Channel; ON.988 performed a similar duty from a base at Kirkwall, in Orkney, covering the

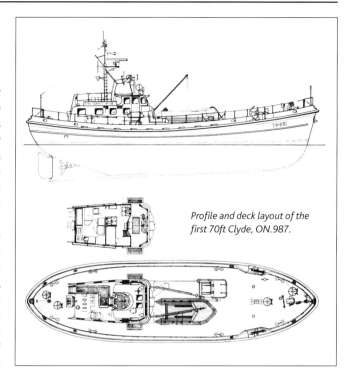

Profile and deck layout of the first 70ft Clyde, ON.987.

The first 70ft Clyde, Charles H. Barrett (Civil Service No.35) *(ON.987), was funded by the long-established Civil Service Lifeboat Fund and served at Clovelly and in the Orkney area before being allocated to the Relief Fleet. (By courtesy of Tony Denton)*

treacherous Pentland Firth and surrounding area. With such a large range, and as they were fully equipped with crew quarters, the Clydes were capable of remaining at sea for prolonged periods as a completely self-contained unit. However, despite having relatively large sea areas to cover from their respective operational bases, cruising operations were not appropriate to the kinds of rescues typically performed by the RNLI's lifeboats. In addition, the Clyde's draught was often too great for many rescue situations, and the boats proved too costly to maintain and operate with full-time crews. In the end, the stations at which they were based used them as though they were ordinary lifeboats.

28 · Clyde cruising 70ft

Year (Yd No) Builder Place	Name Donor	ON (Op No) Cost Weight	Engines (All twin screw diesels)	Stations (launches/lives saved) Disposal
1. 1965 (2271) Yarrow & Co Scotstoun	Charles H. Barrett (Civil Service No.35) Civil Service Lifeboat Fund.	987 (70-001) £63,907 82t0	2x230hp Gardner 8L3B 8-cylinder	Trials 2.1966-3.68 (at Ullapool 1966-67) Clovelly 3.1968-9.75 (179/38) Relief 1975-27.5.88 (107/58) Sold 12.1988
2. 1966 (2272) Yarrow & Co Scotstoun	Grace Paterson Ritchie Legacy of Miss Grace P. Ritchie.	988 (70-002) £65,113 78t14	2x230hp Gardner 8L3B 8-cylinder	Relief 1966-75 (54/12) Kirkwall 3.1968-6.74 (57/43) Kirkwall 8.1975-7.88 (73/29) Sold 1.1989
3. 1974 (Y44) Bideford Ship Yd North Devon	City of Bristol Special Appeal in Bristol, and legacies of Mrs Q. Rimer, Dr S. M. Riddick, Mr S. V. Shrosbree, and Mr H. J. Vagg.	1030 (70-003) £196,000 85t4	2x230hp Gardner 8L3B 8-cylinder	Clovelly 9.1975-8.88 (191/84) Sold 12.1988

The second of the three Clyde cruising lifeboats, Grace Paterson Ritchie *(ON.988), served in Orkney and Kirkwall for most of her RNLI career. After RNLI service, she was sold to the National Lifesaving Association of Iceland and renamed* Henry H. Halfdanssen. *In 2001, she was replaced by a newer lifeboat in Iceland and sold again, this time to a private buyer who brought her to the west coast of Scotland and renamed her* Grace Ritchie.

The last of the Clyde cruising lifeboats to be built was City of Bristol *(ON.1030), which served at Clovelly, covering the Bristol Channel between 1975 and 1988. She was noticeably different to the other two boats, with a much enlarged superstructure. (Tony Denton)*

29 • Waveney fast afloat 44ft

Introduced 1966, last built 1982, 22 built.
Specifications • length 44ft 10in, beam 12ft 8in, waterline length 40ft, draft 3ft 11in, maximum speed 13-15 knots.

The 44ft Waveney was based on the United States Coast Guard design for a 44ft steel-hulled lifeboat. The USCG delegation at the International Lifeboat Conference in Edinburgh in 1963 described the 44ft design as the product of the most comprehensive design, construction and evaluation project ever undertaken for a Coast Guard rescue craft.

The RNLI then acquired one of these boats from the USCG. It arrived in London in May 1964 and, as the prototype vessel numbered 44-001, was taken on a tour of lifeboat stations in Britain and Ireland to assess its suitability. It was the first design of 'fast' lifeboat, and as such represented a radical departure from the traditional designs of lifeboat then used by the RNLI, but received very favourable comments from lifeboat crews during the tour and subsequent trials. Once these were complete, the RNLI ordered six boats incorporating some additions and modifications. The success of these first six boats resulted in a programme of construction which went on for over two decades.

The design was self-righting by virtue of the inherent buoyancy, and was designated the Waveney class after the river close to the boatyard where the RNLI's first six boats were built. The hull was constructed from welded Corten steel, and the bulkheads, hull framing, raised decks and cockpit deck were all constructed of mild steel. To protect the vessel against damage should it be grounded, a double bottom was provided in the forward half-length of the

The prototype Waveney 44-001 was built in the USA and came to the UK in 1964. She served the majority of her career as a Relief lifeboat. (RNLI)

boat, and a strong keel extended aft. The hull was further divided into seven watertight compartments, framed by a combination of transverse and longitudinal bulkheads. The compartments consisted of cable locker, forward cabin, crew's cabin, engine room, void compartment, after cabin and steering gear compartment.

Not only were more than 100 boats of the 44ft design built by the USCG, but the design also saw service with the Canadian Coastguard, the Norwegian lifeboat service, the Iranian Navy and the lifeboat service in Portugal. A number of the RNLI's Waveneys were sold out of service to foreign lifeboat societies and continued life-saving duties in Australia, New Zealand and Namibia.

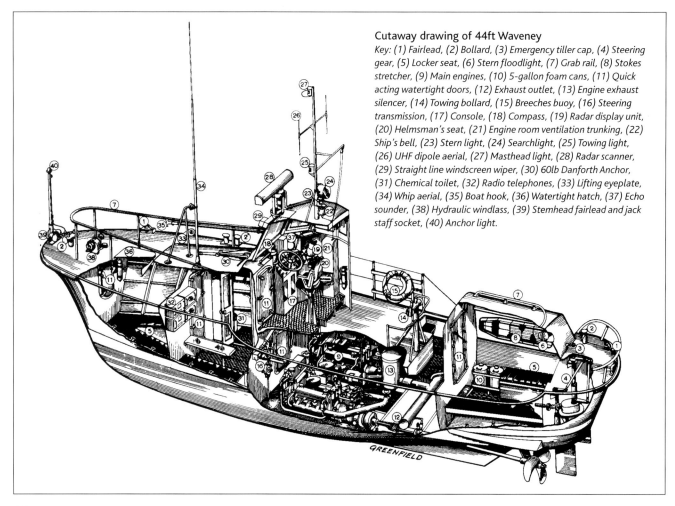

Cutaway drawing of 44ft Waveney
Key: (1) Fairlead, (2) Bollard, (3) Emergency tiller cap, (4) Steering gear, (5) Locker seat, (6) Stern floodlight, (7) Grab rail, (8) Stokes stretcher, (9) Main engines, (10) 5-gallon foam cans, (11) Quick acting watertight doors, (12) Exhaust outlet, (13) Engine exhaust silencer, (14) Towing bollard, (15) Breeches buoy, (16) Steering transmission, (17) Console, (18) Compass, (19) Radar display unit, (20) Helmsman's seat, (21) Engine room ventilation trunking, (22) Ship's bell, (23) Stern light, (24) Searchlight, (25) Towing light, (26) UHF dipole aerial, (27) Masthead light, (28) Radar scanner, (29) Straight line windscreen wiper, (30) 60lb Danforth Anchor, (31) Chemical toilet, (32) Radio telephones, (33) Lifting eyeplate, (34) Whip aerial, (35) Boat hook, (36) Watertight hatch, (37) Echo sounder, (38) Hydraulic windlass, (39) Stemhead fairlead and jack staff socket, (40) Anchor light.

Year (Yd No) Builder Place	Name Donor	ON (Op No) Cost Weight	Engines (all twin-screw diesels)	Stations (launches/lives saved) Disposal
1. 1964 USCG Yard, Curtis Bay	[Not named] USCG Boat No.44328 RNLI General Funds.	— (44-001) — 16t14	2x200hp Cummins V6/1973- 2x250hp Mermaid 595/ 1982- 2x203hp Cat D3208	Trials round Britain 1964-67 Relief 1.2.1967-6.3.97 (291/100) Falmouth 8.1978-19.6.79 Display at Chatham Historic Dockyard, Kent
2. 1966 (B348) Brooke Marine Lowestoft	John F. Kennedy Legacy of Miss Charlotte M. H. Gibson, Wellington, Somerset, and RNLI Funds.	1001 (44-002) £33,000 17t15	2x215hp Cummins V6/1983- 2x203hp Caterpillar D3208	Dun Laoghaire 5.1967-29.3.90 (228/155) Relief 29.3.1990-22.8.96 (72/10) Sold 1997
3. 1967 (B349) Brooke Marine Lowestoft	Khami Gift of Mr and Mrs T. G. Bedwell.	1002 (44-003) £33,361 17t9	2x215hp Cummins V6/1982- 2x203hp Caterpillar D3208	Gt Yarmouth & Gorleston 19.8.1967-5.80 (234/71) Relief 6.1980-11.5.97 (240/90) Sold 5.1999
4. 1967 (B350) Brooke Marine Lowestoft	Faithful Forester Ancient Order of Foresters.	1003 (44-004) £35,000 17t18	2x215hp Cummins V6/1982- 2x203hp Caterpillar D3208	Dover 7.1967-10.1979 (199/138) Holyhead 6.1984-20.9.85 (22/22) Relief 10.1979-27.6.97 (112/40) Sold 5.1999
5. 1967 (B351) Brooke Marine Lowestoft	Margaret Graham An anonymous gift.	1004 (44-005) £37,838 17t13	2x215hp Cummins V6/1982- 2x203hp Caterpillar D3208	Harwich 27.9.1967-3.1980 (173/77) Relief 5.1980-6.86 (50/14) Amble 9.6.1986-7.99 (164/6) Sold 4.8.1999
6. 1968 (B352) Brooke Marine Lowestoft	Arthur and Blanche Harris Legacy of Mrs B. A. L. Harris, London.	1005 (44-006) £35,000 17t5	2x215hp Cummins V6/1979- 2x203hp Caterpillar D3208	Barry Dock 14.3.1968-74 (108/44) Relief 1974-8.79 (33/7) Donaghadee 23.8.1979-17.12.85 (78/43) Relief 1985-93 (55/18) and 1995-14.6.96 (9/5) Courtmacsherry Harbour 28.5.1993-9.95 (17/7) Sold 5.1999
7. 1968 (B353) Brooke Marine Lowestoft	Connel Elizabeth Cargill W. A. Cargill CharitableTrust.	1006 (44-007) £34,386 17t18	2x215hp Cummins V6/1982- 2x203hp Caterpillar D3208	Troon 8.1968-25.8.85 (238/137) Arklow 7.3.1986-6.6.90 (29/19) Relief 1990-27.9.97 (33/3) Sold 5.1999
8. 1974 (G&G658) G & Guttridge Cowes	Eric Seal (Civil Service No.36) Civil Service Lifeboat Fund.	1026 (44-008) £100,000 17t18	2x260hp General Motors 8V-53	Eyemouth 2.1974-3.96 (153/45) Sold 2000
9. 1974 (G&G659) G & Guttridge Cowes	Helen Turnbull Legacy of Mr J. B. Turnbull, and Medway Lifeboat Appeal.	1027 (44-009) £100,000 17t12	2x260hp General Motors 8V-53	Sheerness 4.4.1974-3.96 (649/297) Achill 28.8.1996-10.10.97 (9/0) Relief 1997-98 (25/7) Sold 28.11.1998
10. 1974 (G&G660) G & Guttridge Cowes	Thomas Forehead & Mary Rowse II Legacy of Mr T. Field.	1028 (44-010) £100,000 18t2	2x260hp General Motors 8V-53	Plymouth 22.5.1974-31.10.87 (178/90) Fowey 26.1.1988-10.96 (169/35) Relief 10.1996-3.12.97 (4/0) Sold 1999
11. 1974 (G&G661) G & Guttridge Cowes	Augustine Courtauld Gift of Mr W. P. Courtauld, and Mayor of Poole's Appeal.	1029 (44-011) £81,000 18t1	2x260hp General Motors 8V-53	Poole 11.1974-10.83 (106/32) Relief 10.1983-85 (8/5) and 10.1987-6.90 (9/0) Troon 8.1985-10.87 (53/38) Arklow 5.6.1990-2.97 (78/26) Sold 21.5.1999

Margaret Graham *(ON.1004)* outside the Brooke Marine boatyard at Lowestoft where she and five other Waveneys were built. *(Jeff Morris)*

Helen Turnbull *(ON.1027)* on relief duty in February 1998 at Fleetwood, where she served for almost a year. *(Nicholas Leach)*

Year (Yd No) Builder Place	Name Donor	ON (Op No) Cost Weight	Engines	Stations (launches/lives saved) Disposal
12. 1974 (663) Gr & Guttridge Cowes	The White Rose of Yorkshire Gift of Miss Gwynaeth Milburn, Harrogate.	1033 (44-012) £81,000 19t2	2x260hp General Motors 8V-53	Whitby 11.1974-12.88 (239/51) Invergordon 4.1989-5.96 (66/10) Relief 5.1996-22.3.97 (7/0) Sold 11.6.1999
13. 1974 (664) G & Guttridge Cowes	Thomas James King Proceeds of Jersey Lifeboat Appeal.	1034 (44-013) £100,000 18t2	2x260hp General Motors 8V-53	St Helier 8.2.1975-12.89 (288/155) Relief 1989-93 (20/11) and 1.1996-6.1.97 (0/0) Dunbar 1.8.1993-1.96 (21/0) Sold 8.1998
14. 1974 (665) G & Guttridge Cowes	St Patrick Proceeds of Irish Lifeboat Appeal.	1035 (44-014) £100,000 18t10	2x260hp General Motors 8V-53	Dunmore East 3.1975-96 (252/83) Sold 21.5.1999
15. 1975 (666) G & Guttridge Cowes	Lady of Lancashire An anonymous gift.	1036 (44-015) £130,000 18t4	2x260hp General Motors 8V-53	Fleetwood 1.1976-10.89 (168/94) Dun Laoghaire 3.1990-95 (80/4) Relief 1995-5.96 (0/0) Sold 1996
16. 1976 (Y59) Bideford Ship Yd North Devon	Ralph and Joy Swann Legacy Mrs A. G. Crathorne, and RNLI funds.	1042 (44-016) £130,000 19t0	2x250hp Mermaid 595T/ 1981- 2x250hp Caterpillar D3208T	Ramsgate 14.7.1976-2.90 (292/199) Tobermory 6.8.1990-2.91 (14/2) Portree 2.5.1991-6.96 (60/4) Relief 1996-97 (13/1) Achill 10.10.1997-26.1.98 Sold 1998
17. 1976 (Y60) Bideford Ship Yd North Devon	The Nelsons of Donaghadee/ 1979- Wavy Line Wavy Line Grocers Association.	1043 (44-017) £174,688 18t10	2x250hp Mermaid 595T/ 1978- 2x250hp Caterpillar D3208T	Donaghadee 10.1976-78 (1/0) Relief 1978-90 (111/51) and 1997-98 (0/0) Sunderland 4.1990-97 (113/20) Sold 1998
18. 1977 (Y61) Bideford Ship Yd North Devon	The Scout The Scout Association.	1044 (44-018) £122,000 18t18	2x250hp Mermaid 595T/ 1982- 2x250hp Caterpillar D3208T	Hartlepool 2.1977-7.97 (250/20) Capsized on service, 28.2.1993, none lost Sold 1997
19. 1977 (Y62) Bideford Ship Yd North Devon	Louis Marchesi of Round Table National Association of Round Tables, Great Britain.	1045 (44-019) £150,000 18t14	2x250hp Mermaid 595T/ 1981- 2x250hp Caterpillar D3208T	Newhaven 5.1977-85 (289/134) Alderney 10.1986-94 (170/123) Exmouth 8.7.1994-7.96 (39/5) Relief 12.1996-4.97 (0/0) Sold 12.2.1999
20. 1980 (FM687) Fairey Marine Cowes	John Fison Gift of Mrs D. E. Fison and Mrs Knowles-Franks, legacy of Mrs Sutcliffe.	1060 (44-020) £260,000 18t16	2x250hp Caterpillar D3208T	Harwich 11.3.1980-10.96 (232/97) Relief 1996-22.7.99 (52/5) Sold 24.8.1999
21. 1980 (FM694) Fairey Marine Cowes	Barham Legacies of Mr C. A. S. Stringer, Walton-on-Thames, and Mrs A. G. Miles, Southbourne.	1065 (44-021) £260,000 18t9	2x250hp Caterpillar D3208T	Gt Yarmouth & Gorleston 5.1980-3.96 (254/71) Relief 4.1996-99 (26/11) Sold 1.11.1999
22. 1982 (FM710) Fairey Marine Cowes	The William and Jane Legacies of Miss Hewson, Mrs Grey, Mr Dunn and others.	1079 (44-022) £319,940 18t1	2x250hp Caterpillar D3208T	Blyth 26.10.1982-12.95 (136/43) Larne 19.3.1996-11.96 (23/11) Sold 7.1999

Ralph and Joy Swann (ON.1042) putting out from Ramsgate, the station she served until 1990. (Nicholas Leach)

The penultimate Waveney, Barham (ON.1065), returning to harbour at Gorleston in 1995, just before she left service. (Nicholas Leach)

30 • Keith Nelson intermediate 40ft

Introduced 1968, 1 built.
Specifications • length 41ft 2in, beam 12ft, speed 19 knots.

The unique 40ft Keith Nelson was introduced in the late 1960s as an experimental lifeboat at a time when the RNLI was examining new design ideas and looking to build faster lifeboats. Designed by TT Boat Designs Ltd, of Bembridge, IOW, and moulded of glass reinforced plastic (GRP) by Halmatic Ltd, Havant, for Keith Nelson, Bembridge, the 40ft boat was used to test whether a standard GRP hull could withstand severe weather conditions and to enable the RNLI to assess its possibilities for future lifeboat construction. It became the first RNLI lifeboat to be built of GRP and underwent lengthy sea trials before being sent to selected stations for operational evaluation. The intention was to find a lifeboat as seaworthy as conventional lifeboats but faster and, by using GRP in the construction, produced at substantially lower cost.

The internal and deck layout was designed by the RNLI, in conjunction with Keith Nelson, using a combination of chopped strand and woven rovings. About 440 cubic feet of polyurethane foam in blocks was incorporated to provide reserve buoyancy. The layout from forward consisted of the forepeak, forecabin, wheelhouse, engine room, aft shelter and after peak with the forecabin fitted with two seats and stowage for equipment. The forepeak was filled with foam and enclosed by a watertight bulkhead. The wheelhouse chart room contained the engine control panels and the electronic equipment. The radar scanner and VHF and UHF antennae were mounted above the wheelhouse. An RFD six-man life raft was mounted on the aft deck and a towing post was fitted at the after end off the bridge deck.

The bulkheads and fuel tanks were moulded in the hull, with fuel carried in four tanks. The deck was a separate GRP moulding bonded onto the hull. Fitted with twin Thornycroft six-cylinder four-stroke turbo-charged diesel engines developing 155hp at 2,400rpm, the boat had a maximum speed of nineteen knots and a cruising speed of seventeen knots. The two-to-one reduction

Ernest William and Elizabeth Ellen Hinde *(ON.1017), the only 40ft Keith Nelson lifeboat used by the RNLI, at Calshot. (RNLI)*

gearboxes were supplied by the Self Changing Gear Co and were of the MRF 500 hydraulic type. With a fuel capacity of 320 gallons, at her cruising speed, she had a range of 440 nautical miles.

The new boat was numbered 40-001 when introduced and, as part of her trials, was sent to Sheerness on evaluation with a view to Sheerness becoming a new lifeboat station. She remained at Sheerness from April to November 1969, then went to Calshot where she was used to establish a new station at the mouth of the Solent and gained a distinguished service career. Although 40-001 was successful and she proved that GRP was a suitable material for lifeboat design, one of the drawbacks of the Keith Nelson design was that it was not self-righting. So, by the 1980s, with the RNLI looking to operate a fleet entirely of self-righting lifeboats, it was taken out of service as soon as a suitable replacement – in the form of the 33ft Brede – was available.

Year (Yd No) Builder Place	Name Donor	ON (Op No) Cost Weight	Engines (twin-screw diesels)	Stations (launches/lives saved) Disposal
1. 1968 (1017) Keith Nelson Bembridge	Ernest William and Elizabeth Ellen Hinde Legacy of Mrs E. E. Hinde.	1017 (40-001) £24,559 11t15	2x125hp Thornycroft T.400	Sheerness 4.1969-20.11.69 (32/4) Calshot 25.7.1970-3.85 (199/88) Sold 9.1985

Out of the water at RNLI Depot, Poole, Ernest William and Elizabeth Ellen Hinde *at the end of her life-saving career and about to be sold out of service. (Nicholas Leach)*

31 • Thames fast afloat 50ft

Introduced 1973, last built 1974, 2 built.
Specifications • length 50ft, beam 14ft 6in, crew 5/6.

The 50ft Thames was one of two designs for a fast lifeboat produced in the early 1970s (the Arun was the other) when the RNLI's Committee of Management realised that, after the successful introduction of the Waveney, a slightly larger and faster boat was needed. RNLI staff undertook the initial design, a detailed design study was carried out by Brooke Marine Ltd of Lowestoft, and a model was tank-tested by the British Hovercraft Corporation. The success of the tests resulted in an order for two boats with Brooke Marine, builder of the first Waveneys.

The design was based on that of the Waveney but was 6ft longer, with the additional length absorbed by an enclosed wheelhouse/chartroom with a flying bridge above and an increase in the size of the engineroom below. The hull plating was of Corten steel and the boat was subdivided by watertight bulkheads into seven compartments: forepeak, anchor cable locker, forecabin, midships cabin, engine-room, after cabin and tiller flat. A double bottom extended from the forepeak to the after engine-room bulkhead and the boat was self-righting through inherent buoyancy, provided that the two watertight doors were closed.

During their early years of service, the boats were fitted with Decca Navigation Mk.21 equipment and a Kelvin Hughes Type 17 W radar, together with other standard electronic equipment. The main engines were twin General Motors 8V-71 diesels, each developing 390bhp at 2,300rpm, fitted with Allison hydraulically operated reverse reduction gearboxes. These gave a cruising speed of seventeen knots and a maximum speed of nineteen knots. The

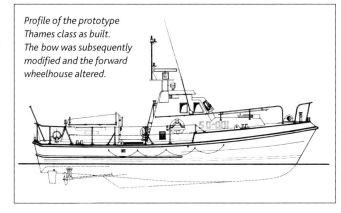

Profile of the prototype Thames class as built. The bow was subsequently modified and the forward wheelhouse altered.

fuel capacity of 400 gallons meant that, at full speed, the range was almost 200 nautical miles, which increased to 229 nautical miles at cruising speed.

During trials, the original bow on both boats proved unsuitable so a new temporary GRP bow was built for ON.1032 and tested. The new bow reduced wetness and enabled a better wheelhouse layout to be found for the crew and so, after the trials, new steel bows were built for both boats which then entered service. The design was designated the Thames class because most of the design work was carried out at the RNLI's London Offices by the Thames. Four further boats were ordered during 1974: ON.1038-ON.1041, 50-003 to 50-006; the first two from Brooke Marine, and the others from Richard Dunston, Hessle, near Hull. However, these were cancelled, never having been allocated stations, as the Arun class being developed at the same time was deemed more suitable.

	Year (Yd No) Builder Place	Name Donor	ON (Op No) Cost Weight	Engines	Stations (launches/lives saved) Disposal
1.	1973 (B394) Brooke Marine Lowestoft	Rotary Service Gift of Rotary International of Gt Britain and Ireland, legacies of Mr Craig, Miss Redgate and Miss Fowkes.	1031 (50-001) £199,041 24t15	2x390hp General Motors 8V71T	Falmouth 1974-78 (45/17) Dover 3.10.1979-97 (454/200) Sold 1997
2.	1974 (B395) Brooke Marine Lowestoft	Elizabeth Ann/ 1979- Helmut Schroder of Dunlossit Various gifts and legacies/1979- gift of Bruno Schroder and Mrs Mallinckrodt.	1032 (50-002) £200,000 27t4	2x390hp General Motors 8V71T	Relief 1975-79 (trials only) Islay 2.5.1979-97 (210/60) Crew training (Poole) 1997-98 Capsized on service 18.11.1979, none lost Sold 1998

The two Thames lifeboats together at the RNLI Depot, Poole, after having been withdrawn from service at Dover and Islay. The second, ON.1032, was sold to New Zealand and renamed P&O Nedlloyd Rescue. (Tony Denton)

Helmut Schroder of Dunlossit (ON.1032) on engine trials off Islay. The cradle and launch ramps for a Y class inflatable can be seen above the aft cabin. She capsized and righted on service on 18 November 1979. (Nicholas Leach)

32 • Arun fast afloat 52-54ft

Introduced 1971, last built 1990, 46 built.
Specifications • length 52ft and 54ft (15.86m and 16.50m),
breadth 17ft (5.20m), draft 5ft (1.50m); speed 18.2
knots, range 220 nautical miles at full speed; crew 6 or 7;
displacement 25.25 tons (prototype), 32.25 tons (steel),
31 tons (GRP).

During the 1960s the RNLI Committee of Management was
looking to continue introducing faster offshore lifeboats into the
RNLI fleet, which had started with the Waveney class in 1966. In
1969, the Committee decided to proceed with the design of a fast
52ft lifeboat with a speed of between 18 and 20 knots. The hull
was designed by Alan McLachlan, of Messrs G. L. Watson, Glasgow,
and the general arrangement and superstructure layout was by the
RNLI's technical staff. The design was designated the class name
Arun after the river at Littlehampton, where the first boat was built,
and the first of the new class was launched in 1971.

The Arun, which could reach speeds in excess of eighteen knots,
was twice as fast as earlier classes of lifeboats due to her semi-
planing hull form. The hull shape and watertight wheelhouse
pro-vided the buoyancy necessary for an inherent self-righting
capability, and the flying bridge incorporated an upper steering
position. The hull of the prototype was of cold moulded timber
construction on laminated timber frames, with a double bottom
extending practically the full length of the hull. An inner skin
was formed to the sides of the boat and the resultant void,
together with the double bottom, was filled with expanded foam
polyurethane. The decking, longitudinal and transverse bulkheads,
inner skin, and bottom were all made from mahogany plywood
and transverse bulkheads subdivided the boat into six watertight
compartments: forepeak, anchor cable locker, forecabin, engine-
room, after cabin and steerage flat.

The prototype Arun had the flying bridge at the rear of the
superstructure and a straight sheerline. The second boat also had
the flying bridge at the rear of the superstructure but, as with
all subsequent boats, had a cutaway freeboard to enable easier
recovery of people in the water. The third boat was modified so
that the flying bridge was forward and the Y class inflatable was
placed behind it at the rear of the superstructure. The boat was
steered from either inside the wheelhouse or from the flying bridge
on top of the superstructure. Inside the wheelhouse were seats,
with safety belts and arm rests, for each member of the crew,
with special positions for the coxswain, navigator, radio operator,
mechanic and crew members, as well as provision for a doctor.
The hull was divided into 26 watertight compartments. The two
survivors' cabins below deck contained rescue equipment including
first aid gear, stretchers, emergency rations and blankets. A small Y
class inflatable was carried on the wheelhouse roof for work close
inshore. The Y boat was originally launched by means of a manual
davit, but this was later replaced by a ramp system down which the
inflatable was launched over the stern.

The first three boats, ON.1018, ON.1025 and ON.1037, were
all constructed in cold-moulded timber but later boats, with the
exception of ON.1100, which was the only steel-hulled Arun, were
constructed from glass reinforced plastic. Various other changes
were made during the build programme: from 1978, ON.1058
(52-11), an aluminium alloy wheelhouse was reintroduced; from
1979, the wheelhouse layout was redesigned and an open plan
introduced; and from 1988, ON.1149 (52-43), the hull laminate

The prototype Arun lifeboat Arun *(ON.1018) off Barry Dock. (Nicholas Leach)*

The second 52ft Arun, Sir William Arnold *(ON.1025) at St Peter Port, Guernsey.
Like ON.1018, she had a unique superstructure arrangement that was not
repeated on any of the later Aruns. (Brian Green)*

was changed to epacryn resin. The length of the boats varied
slightly, with the five boats 54-03, 54-04, 54-05, 54-06, and 54-07
built 2ft longer at 54ft in length through having a rounded transom,
indicated by the operational number '54'. Subsequent boats had
a square transom and were 52ft in length. All GRP-hulled boats
were moulded by Halmatic Ltd, Havant, and fitted out by the
builder listed. The wooden and steel-hulled Aruns were assembled
complete by the builder as listed.

The original main engines were twin Caterpillar TA 0336 diesels
but the second boat, 52-02, was fitted with twin Caterpillar TA 343
diesels, each developing 460bhp at 2,000 rpm through two to one
reduction gearboxes and each fitted with two 90 amp alternators.
In addition to standard radio and other electronic equipment, these
boats were fitted with Decca Mk.101 Super Radar, Decca Navigator
Mk.21, and Decca Automatic Pilot Type 350. The last boat of the
class was built in 1990 after a number of modifications had been
made throughout the build programme.

The Arun was one of the most successful classes of lifeboat
ever built and in 1982 the RNLI received a Design Council Award,
presented by HRH Duke of Edinburgh, for the hull shape and overall
design of the boat, the first lifeboat to achieve such recognition.
Such was the success of the design that other lifeboat societies
have used it. In 1988, a steel-hulled 52ft Arun was built by the
Canadian Coast Guard, the success of which led to the building of
further Aruns in aluminium for service in Canada. The type is also
used in Greek waters, with ten moulded by Halmatic for the Greek
Coastguard, while the RNLI has sold Aruns to lifeboat societies and
rescue services in Iceland, Finland, Chile and Australia.

32 • Arun fast afloat 52-54ft

Year (Yd No) Builder Place	Name Donor	ON (Op No) Cost Weight	Engines	Stations (launches/lives saved) Notes/disposal
1. 1971 (22) William Osborne Littlehampton	Arun Birds Eye Foods, Miss Alice Johnston, and various other legacies.	1018 (52-01) £128,000 25t5	2x375hp Caterpillar D336/ 1992- Caterpillar 3208TA (wood)	St Peter Port 1.10.1972-6.11.73 (25/13) Barry Dock 7.6.1974-5.97 (331/75) Sold 1997
2. 1973 (93) William Osborne Littlehampton	Sir William Arnold Special Local Appeal.	1025 (52-02) £135,000 28t13	2x460hp Caterpillar D343 (wood hull)	St Peter Port 6.11.1973-6.97 (503/224) Sold 1998
3. 1975 (700) William Osborne Littlehampton	Edward Bridges (Civil Service and Post Office No.37) Civil Service and Post Office LB Fund.	1037 (54-03) £150,000 30t8	2x460hp Caterpillar D343 (wood hull)	Torbay 4.1975-16.4.94 (456/285) Display at Chatham Historic Dockyard
4. 1976 (1250) Halmatic Ltd/ William Osborne	Tony Vandervell The Vandervell Foundation.	1049 (54-04) £200,000 31t16	2x460hp Caterpillar D343 (GRP hull)	Weymouth 3.1976-11.6.99 (598/359) Sold 1999
5. 1976 (WR4665) Halmatic Ltd Havant	B. P. Forties British Petroleum Co Ltd and students of Aberdeen University.	1050 (54-05) £170,000 31t16	2x460hp Caterpillar D343 (GRP hull)	Aberdeen 6.1976-28.8.98 (112/11) Sold 1998
6. 1976 (1255) Halmatic Ltd/ William Osborne	The Gough-Ritchie Gift of Mrs A. A. Ritchie, Baldine, Isle of Man.	1051 (54-06) £210,000 31t12	2x460hp Caterpillar D343 (GRP hull)	Port St Mary 9.1976-5.98 (162/63) Sold 10.1998
7. 1977 (WR4908) Halmatic Ltd Havant	City of Bradford IV City of Bradford Lord Mayor Appeal, and other funds.	1052 (54-07) £163,453 32t8	2x460hp Caterpillar D343 (GRP hull)	Humber 3.1977-8.87 (416/106) Thurso 26.3.1988-3.89 (12/2) Ballyglass 17.10.1989-8.90 (9/0) Tobermory 7.2.1991-7.98 (186/24) Sold 1999
8. 1977 (1565) Halmatic Ltd/ William Osborne	Joy and John Wade The Wade Foundation and the Yarmouth IOW Lifeboat Appeal.	1053 (52-08) £187,000 32t14	2x460hp Caterpillar D343 (GRP hull)	Yarmouth 19.7.1977-24.1.2001 (677/258) Relief 1-8.2001 (3/0) Sold 3.2002

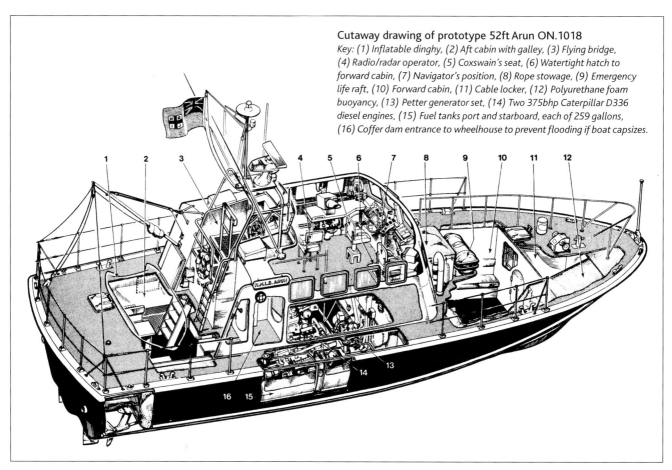

Cutaway drawing of prototype 52ft Arun ON.1018
Key: (1) Inflatable dinghy, (2) Aft cabin with galley, (3) Flying bridge, (4) Radio/radar operator, (5) Coxswain's seat, (6) Watertight hatch to forward cabin, (7) Navigator's position, (8) Rope stowage, (9) Emergency life raft, (10) Forward cabin, (11) Cable locker, (12) Polyurethane foam buoyancy, (13) Petter generator set, (14) Two 375bhp Caterpillar D336 diesel engines, (15) Fuel tanks port and starboard, each of 259 gallons, (16) Coffer dam entrance to wheelhouse to prevent flooding if boat capsizes.

Year (Yd No) Builder Place	Name Donor	ON (Op No) Cost Weight	Engines	Stations (launches/lives saved) Notes/disposal
9. 1978 (WR5172) Halmatic Ltd Havant	Spirit of Tayside Broughty Ferry Lifeboat Appeal.	1056 (52-09) £250,000 34t0	2x460hp Caterpillar D343 (GRP hull)	Broughty Ferry 6.5.1978-2.99 (123/1) Sold 1999
10. 1978 (1850) Halmatic Ltd/ William Osborne	Soldian Lerwick Lifeboat Appeal and various legacies.	1057 (52-10) £250,000 32t2	2x460hp Caterpillar D343 (GRP hull)	Lerwick 8.1978-6.97 (245/260) Relief 1997-98 (1/0) and 1999-12.2001 Achill 26.1.1998-4.99 (6/3) Sold 6.2002
11. 1979 (1945) Halmatic Ltd/ William Osborne	Elizabeth Ann John Slater Foundation, Sir Kirby Laing Foundation, and Cornish Lifeboat Appeal.	1058 (52-11) £299,737 32t1	2x460hp Caterpillar D343 (GRP hull)	Falmouth 6.1979-97 (249/52) Relief 2.1997-12.2001 (67/3) Sold 6.2002
12. 1979 (WR5845) Halmatic Ltd Havant	Walter and Margaret Couper Legacy of Miss Margaret G. Couper.	1059 (52-12) £302,748 32t0	2x460hp Caterpillar D343 (GRP hull)	Campbeltown 9.1979-5.99 (274/130) Relief 1999-19.5.2001 (13/1) Sold 19.5.2001
13. 1979 (2020) Halmatic Ltd/ William Osborne	George and Olive Turner Legacy Mrs O. B. Turner, the Sir James Knott Trust, and Tyneside Lifeboat Appeal.	1061 (52-13) £300,000 31t16	2x460hp Caterpillar D343 (GRP hull)	Tynemouth 2.1980-10.99 (286/58) Relief 21.10.1999-18.9.2000 (1/0) Sold 25.9.2000
14. 1980 Halmatic Ltd/ W. A. Souter	Edith Emile Gift of Mrs Edith E. Currie, Brentwood, Essex.	1062 (52-14) £350,000 31t16	2x460hp Caterpillar D343 (GRP hull)	Relief 1980-98 (249/36) Sold 2000
15. 1980 (2150) Halmatic Ltd/ William Osborne	Hyman Winstone Gift of Mrs Marie Winstone, Sheffield.	1067 (52-15) £350,000 31t3	2x485hp Caterpillar 3408TA (GRP hull)	Holyhead 7.1980-12.10.83 (44/30) Ballycotton 4.1985-98 (216/62) Relief 3-11.1998 (0/0) Larne 11.1998-8.2000 (13/0) Relief 2000-6.7.02 (43/4) Sold 2003
16. 1981 (2250) Halmatic Ltd/ William Osborne	Richard Evans (Civil Service No.38) Civil Service and Post Office Lifeboat Fund.	1070 (52-16) £350,000 30t17	2x485hp Caterpillar 3408TA (GRP hull)	Portrush 1.3.1981-4.2000 (316/69) Relief 2000-6.03 Sold 2003, wrecked on passage to Iceland, 12.2003
17. 1981 (FM707) Halmatic Ltd/ Fairey Marine	Sir Max Aitken The Beaverbrook Foundation.	1071 (52-17) £350,000 31t0	2x485hp Caterpillar 3408TA (GRP hull)	Relief 1981-27.11.2002 (359/117) Sold 2002
18. 1981 (2305) Halmatic Ltd/ William Osborne	Robert Edgar Gift of Mrs Esme S. Edgar and Mr Anthony Edgar.	1073 (52-18) £350,000 32t12	2x485hp Caterpillar 3408TA (GRP hull)	St Mary's 6.1981-12.97 (121/84) Relief 12.1997-26.8.99 (14/0) Weymouth 9.1999-7.2002 (70/1) Sold 2002
19. 1981 Halmatic Ltd/ W. A. Souter	Marie Winstone Gift of Mrs Marie Winstone.	1076 (52-19) £300,000 32t0	2x485hp Caterpillar 3408TA (GRP hull)	Fishguard 25.8.1981-94 (138/33) Torbay 3.2.1995-2001 (280/63) Relief 2001-6.02 (3/0) Sold 2002

The last of three wooden-hulled Aruns, Edward Bridges (Civil Service and Post Office No.37) (ON.1037), on trials. She was also the first of five Aruns that were 54ft in length due to a rounded transom. (Brian Green)

The 54ft Arun B. P. Forties (ON.1050) departing Aberdeen where she was stationed for twenty-two years. She was only the third GRP-hulled lifeboat the RNLI had ever built. (Tony Denton)

Year (Yd No) Builder Place	Name Donor	ON (Op No) Cost Weight	Engines	Stations (launches/lives saved) Notes/disposal
20. 1982 (2400) Halmatic Ltd/ William Osborne	Duchess of Kent United Grand Lodge of Freemasons.	1077 (52-20) £350,000 31t16	2x485hp Caterpillar 3408TA (GRP hull)	Relief 27.4.1982-10.2002 (215/71) Sold 2003
21. 1981 (2450) Halmatic Ltd/ William Osborne	Davina and Charles Matthews Hunter Legacy of Miss Lilian Ferguson Hunter, in memory of her parents.	1078 (52-21) £350,000 31t1	2x485hp Caterpillar 3408TA (GRP hull)	Mallaig 16.7.1981-1.2001 (309/44) Relief 2001-6.03 (36/2) Sold 8.2003
22. 1981 Halmatic Ltd/ W. A. Souter	Ralph and Bonella Farrant RNLI General Funds.	1081 (52-22) £330,000 30t14	2x485hp Caterpillar 3408TA (GRP hull)	Relief 26.7.1982-8.94 (226/106) Fenit 18.8.1994-2.99 (91/49) Relief 1999-8.2003 (116/24) Sold 2004
23. 1982 (2510) Halmatic Ltd/ William Osborne	Margaret Frances Love Legacies of Mr Frank Love and Lady Frances Murphy.	1082 (52-23) £356,000 30t12	2x485hp Caterpillar 3408TA (GRP hull)	Valentia 14.3.1982-11.96 (192/73) Barry Dock 11.5.1997-8.2003 (129/10) Sold 2005
24. 1983 (FM715) Halmatic Ltd/ Fairey Marine	Mabel Alice Gift of Mr David Robinson, in memory of his wife.	1085 (52-24) £350,000 30t12	2x485hp Caterpillar 3408TA (GRP hull)	Penlee 8.5.1983-2.2003 (275/83) Sold 2004
25. 1983 (2590) Halmatic Ltd/ William Osborne	A. J. R. and L. G. Uridge Lionel G. Uridge Will Trust and gift of Mrs A. A. Burnley.	1086 (52-25) £350,000 30t15	2x485hp Caterpillar 3408TA (GRP hull)	Relief 15.9.1983-2003 (345/111) Torbay 4.1994-2.95 (43/26) Sold 2003
26. 1984 (2620) Halmatic Ltd/ William Osborne	St Brendan RNLI General Funds.	1092 (52-26) £370,000 30t8	2x485hp Caterpillar 3408TA (GRP hull)	Rosslare Harbour 1.6.1984-9.2001 (147/28) Written off after damaged in collision when hit at moorings by ferry, 9.9.2001, sold 2003
27. 1984 (2650) Halmatic Ltd/ William Osborne	Charles Brown Gift of Mr David Robinson.	1093 (52-27) £370,000 31t11	2x485hp Caterpillar 3408TA (GRP hull)	Buckie 5.4.1984-5.2003 (270/172) Relief 5.2003-04 (13/0) Sold 2004
28. 1984 Halmatic Ltd/ W. A. Souter	Sir Max Aitken II Gift of the Beaverbrook Foundation.	1098 (52-28) £377,974 31t0	2x485hp Caterpillar 3408TA (GRP hull)	Stornoway 6.3.1984-2.99 (238/67) Relief 3.2-6.8.99 (2/0) and 2004- Longhope 12.8.1999-6.2004 (20/0)
29. 1984 (2700) Halmatic Ltd/ William Osborne	Joseph Rothwell Sykes and Hilda M. Legacies of Mr J. Sykes, Mrs N. Sykes, and other gifts.	1099 (52-29) £370,000 31t0	2x485hp Caterpillar 3408TA (GRP hull)	Stromness 12.10.1984-10.98 (89/8) Broughty Ferry 20.1.1999-4.2001 (52/0) Relief 2001-6.02 (2/0) Sold 2002
30. 1986 (FM722) Fairey Marine Cowes	Snolda Various oil companies, Local Appeal, and the Miss I. F. Harvey Trust.	1100 (52-030) £391,021 32t5	2x485hp Caterpillar 3408TA (steel hull)	Aith 19.7.1986-5.98 (79/29) Training 1998- (Numbered TL-01)
31. 1984 Halmatic Ltd/ W. A. Souter	Newsbuoy Special Appeal by the Newspaper Society.	1103 (52-31) £400,000 31t5	2x485hp Caterpillar 3408TA (GRP hull)	Relief 23.10.1984-2004 Plymouth 1.11.2002-15.2.03 Sold 2005

Charles Brown (ON.1093) on exercise off Buckie in her original livery with the operational number on the superstructure. (Nicholas Leach)

The only Arun to be built from steel, Snolda (ON.1100), in her role as training lifeboat TL-01 at the RNLI Depot, Poole. (Peter Edey)

The unusual sight of two 52ft Aruns together. The Queen Mother *(ON.1149, on left) and* Sir Max Aitken II *(ON.1098) exercise off Longhope pier after the former had replaced the latter at the station, June 2004. (Nicholas Leach)*

52ft Arun City of Glasgow III *(ON.1134) on exercise off Troon harbour in 1995. She was one of many Aruns to be operated from stations throughout Scotland. (Nicholas Leach)*

52ft Arun Mabel Williams *(ON.1159) at Calshot. Built for Ballyglass, she served at Calshot for less than three years and was the last Arun on station duty. (Nicholas Leach)*

Year (Yd No) Builder Place	Name Donor	ON (Op No) Cost Weight	Engines	Stations (launches/lives saved) Disposal
32. 1985 (2790) Halmatic Ltd/ William Osborne	Keith Anderson Gift of Mrs Esme Anderson, London.	1106 (52-32) £390,000 30t15	2x485hp Caterpillar 3408TA (GRP hull)	Newhaven 9.8.1985-10.99 (521/119) Relief 15.11.1999-10.2000 (0/0) Hartlepool 25.10.2000-8.03 (56/2) Sold 2004
33. 1985 (2830) Halmatic Ltd/ William Osborne	City of Belfast The City of Belfast Appeal.	1107 (52-33) £415,000 31t5	2x485hp Caterpillar 3408TA (GRP hull)	Donaghadee 7.12.1985-17.4.2003 (322/58) Relief 2003-04 (14/0) Sold 2004
34. 1986 Halmatic Ltd/ W. A. Souter	Margaret Russell Fraser Bequest Margaret Fraser, Glasgow, and various other gifts and legacies.	1108 (52-34) £415,000 31t5	2x485hp Caterpillar 3408TA (GRP hull)	Relief 14.6.1986-2001 (293/152) Calshot 4.4.2002-8.04 (118/15) Sold 2005
35. 1986 (1013) Halmatic Ltd/ Berthon Bt Co	City of Dublin The City of Dublin Appeal.	1113 (52-35) £415,000 31t86	2x485hp Caterpillar 3408TA (GRP hull)	Howth 22.8.1986-3.2002 (260/63) Relief 3.2002-03 (25/0) Sold 5.2004
36. 1987 (3010) Halmatic Ltd/ William Osborne	Roy and Barbara Harding RNLI General Funds.	1118 (52-36) £415,000 30t3	2x485hp Caterpillar 3408TA (GRP hull)	Aran Islands 4.7.1987-6.97 (315/43) Castletownbere 7.4.1998-30.1.2004 (83/26) Sold 9.2004
37. 1987 (1014) Halmatic Ltd/ Berthon Bt Co	Kenneth Thelwall Bequest of Mr K. Thelwall, Walkington, Yorkshire.	1123 (52-37) £415,000 30t6	2x485hp Caterpillar 3408TA (GRP hull)	Humber 13.8.1987-3.97 (383/68) Relief 1997-98 (28/10) Holyhead 17.9.1998-12.2003 (101/15) Sold 2005
38. 1987 (0002) Halmatic Ltd/ W. A. Souter	City of Glasgow III The City of Glasgow Appeal, and other gifts and legacies.	1134 (52-38) £415,000 30t9	2x485hp Caterpillar 3408TA (GRP hull)	Troon 25.10.1987-25.2.2004 (432/139) Relief 25.2.2004-04 Sold 2004
39. 1988 (WR8722) Halmatic Ltd Havant	Mickie Salvesen Legacy of Mrs Mary Salvesen.	1135 (52-39) £490,000 31t0	2x485hp Caterpillar 3408TA (GRP hull)	Kirkwall 5.7.1988-3.98 (89/35) Relief 3-8.1998 (1/0) and 7.2000-8.03 (29/9) Aberdeen 28.8.1998-7.2000 (25/0) Barry Dock 8.8.2003-
40. 1988 (0007) Halmatic Ltd/ W A Souter	City of Plymouth City of Plymouth Appeal, and other gifts and legacies.	1136 (52-40) £490,000 29t3	2x485hp Caterpillar 3408TA (GRP hull)	Plymouth 26.1.1988-1.11.2002 (579/115) Relief 11.2002-9.2004 (4/0) Sold 2005
41. 1988 (1015) Halmatic Ltd/ Berthon Bt Co	Ann Lewis Fraser The Fraser of Allander Foundation.	1143 (52-41) £552,162 30t	2x485hp Caterpillar 3408TA (GRP hull)	Barra Island 7.1988-6.98 (103/44) Tobermory 5.7.1998-2003 (103/4) Relief 2003-04 (8/0) Sold 2004
42. 1989 Halmatic Ltd/ Robson	Murray Lornie Trustees of the Ben Vorlich Trust, Jersey.	1144 (52-42) £553,417 32t	2x500hp Caterpillar 3408TA (GRP hull)	Lochinver 20.7.1989-2004 (144/64) Castletownbere 1-8.2004 (18/0) Relief 8.2004-04 Sold 2004
43. 1989 (WO3170) Halmatic Ltd/ William Osborne	The Queen Mother Bequest of Miss Sarah Sinclair Gray, Dunoon, and RNLI funds.	1149 (52-43) £580,514 31t4	2x500hp Caterpillar 3408TA (GRP hull)	Thurso 24.3.1989-2004 (168/59) Longhope 6.2004-10.06 Relief 2006-07
44. 1989 (WO3200) Halmatic Ltd/ William Osborne	Hibernia The Irish Government through the Irish Sailors Act 1988.	1150 (52-44) £580,000 29t18	2x500hp Caterpillar 3408TA (GRP hull)	Relief 1989-2007
45. 1990 Halmatic Ltd/ Robson	Mabel Williams Bequest of Mabel Williams.	1159 (52-45) £640,000	2x500hp Caterpillar 3408TA (GRP hull)	Ballyglass 29.8.1990-8.98 (52/19) Relief 8.1998-9.2001 Rosslare Harbour 10.9.2001-7.2.04 (28/19) Calshot 8.2004-2.07
46. 1990 (WO3269) Halmatic Ltd/ William Osborne	Duke of Atholl Bequest of Sir David Robinson.	1160 (52-46) £640,000 29.6 tonnes	2x500hp Caterpillar 3408TA (GRP hull)	Relief 1990-2003 and 2004- Hartlepool 17.8.2003-27.9.04 (27/0)

33 • Brede intermediate 33ft

Introduced 1979, last built 1985, 12 built.
Specifications • length 33ft (10.06m), beam 12ft (3.66m), waterline length 27ft 6in (8.38m), draft 4ft 3in (1.30m), displacement 8.5 tons.

The 33ft Brede was based on the Lochin 33 commercial angling boat which had been developed and built by Lochin Marine, of Rye, Sussex. The Brede, named after the river which flows through Rye where all the boats were built by Lochin Marine, was intended to replace a small number of offshore lifeboats where the cost of providing a new offshore lifeboat could not be justified on operational grounds. A new type was required which could fill a gap in capability between the largest inshore lifeboat, the Atlantic 21, and the smallest offshore lifeboat. The RNLI therefore turned to a commercial company, Lochin Marine, whose 33ft GRP-hulled design fitted the requirements.

The first Brede was fitted out by Lochin, numbered 33–01 by the RNLI, and was fitted with a large buoyancy block aft to give a self-righting capability. After trials with this first boat, a second boat was ordered incorporating a series of modifications including an enlarged wheelhouse providing the self-righting capability with increased headroom and rearward sloping forward windows. This improved design provided the basis for the subsequent boats and, during the next three years, a further ten were constructed which were sent to selected lifeboat stations in England and Scotland. All were fitted with twin Caterpillar 3208 NA naturally-aspirated

The prototype Brede lifeboat 33-01 during her trials. The large foam block at her stern provided a self-righting capability. This boat was used for trials only after which it was sold by the RNLI. (RNLI)

diesel engines developing 203bhp at 2,800rpm enabling a speed of approximately twenty knots to be attained. With a fuel capacity of 182 gallons, at the maximum speed of twenty knots, the Brede had a range of 140 nautical miles. The boat was manned by five crew and the hull was divided into five main watertight compartments.

Although they proved to be capable life-saving craft, the Bredes did not have long operational careers and were replaced by larger all-weather lifeboats which the RNLI had not been able to justify financially when the Brede design was first developed.

Year (Yd No) Builder Place	Name Donor	ON (Op No) Cost Weight	Engines	Stations (launches/lives saved) Disposal
1. 1979 (1066) Lochin Marine Rye, Sussex	[Not named] RNLI General Funds.	1066 (33-01) – –	2x203hp Caterpillar 3208 NA	Trials only 1980-82 (with well deck aft) Sold 1982
2. 1982 (1080) Lochin Marine Rye, Sussex	Ann Ritchie Gift of Mrs A. A. Ritchie, Isle of Man.	1080 (33-02) £110,000 9t6	2x203hp Caterpillar 3208 NA	Oban 25.10.1982-19.9.87 (186/20) Scrapped 1.1988
3. 1982 (1083) Lochin Marine Rye, Sussex	Leonore Chilcott Gift of Mr Paul Chilcott, Guernsey.	1083 (33-03) £153,475 8t10	2x203hp Caterpillar 3208 NA	Fowey 16.10.1982-1.88 (56/19) Sold 1990
4. 1982 (1084) Lochin Marine Rye, Sussex	Philip Vaux Bequest of Mrs Elizabeth Felicity Vaux.	1084 (33-04) £150,000 8t10	2x203hp Caterpillar 3208 NA	Girvan 16.2.1983-4.89 (57/17) Sold 1989
5. 1983 (1087) Lochin Marine Rye, Sussex	Merchant Navy Merchant Navy Appeal.	1087 (33-05) £150,000 8t10	2x203hp Caterpillar 3208 NA	Relief 18.4.1983-9.87 (34/10) Oban 19.9.1987-28.3.89 (73/11) Sold 1990

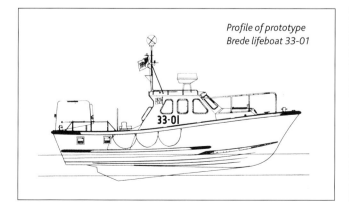

Profile of prototype Brede lifeboat 33-01

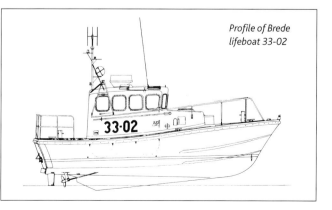

Profile of Brede lifeboat 33-02

33 · Brede intermediate 33ft

Year (Yd No) Builder Place	Name Donor	ON (Op No) Cost Weight	Engines	Stations (launches/lives saved) Disposal
6. 1983 (1088) Lochin Marine Rye, Sussex	Caroline Finch Legacies of Mr W. H. Finch, Mr H. E. Rohll, Mrs M. G. Shaw and Mr W. J. Orley.	1088 (33-06) £150,000 8t12	2x203hp Caterpillar 3208 NA	Exmouth 4.8.1983-8.7.94 (178/64) Sold 1994
7. 1983 (1089) Lochin Marine Rye, Sussex	Inner Wheel Inner Wheel Clubs of Great Britain and Ireland.	1089 (33-07) £155,000 8t11	2x203hp Caterpillar 3208 NA	Poole 16.10.1983-5.9.2001 (812/176) Calshot 12.2001-4.4.02 (3/0) Sold 2002
8. 1984 (1090) Lochin Marine Rye, Sussex	Foresters Future Ancient Order of Foresters, plus other gifts and legacies.	1090 (33-08) £145,000 8t13	2x203hp Caterpillar 3208 NA	Alderney 10.3.1984-86 (70/74) Relief 10.1986-2.9.2002 (210/35) Sold 2002
9. 1984 (1101) Lochin Marine Rye, Sussex	Enid of Yorkshire Gift of Mr Arnold T. Sanderson, North Ferriby, North Humberside.	1101 (33-09) £150,000 9t6	2x203hp Caterpillar 3208 NA	Relief 22.6.1984-8.9.97 (113/12) Sold 1997
10. 1984 (1102) Lochin Marine Rye, Sussex	Nottinghamshire The Nottinghamshire Lifeboat Appeal.	1102 (33-10) £145,000 8t11	2x203hp Caterpillar 3208 NA	Invergordon 16.7.1984-7.88 (21/6) Oban 26.3.1989-7.97 (502/30) Sold 1997
11. 1985 (1104) Lochin Marine Rye, Sussex	Safeway Safeway Food Stores Appeal.	1104 (33-11) £155,000 8t11	2x203hp Caterpillar 3208 NA	Calshot 24.3.1985-12.2001 (259/40) Sold 2002
12. 1985 (1105) Lochin Marine Rye, Sussex	Amateur Swimming Associations Amateur Swimming Associations of England, Scotland and Wales.	1105 (33-12) £160,000 8t11	2x203hp Caterpillar 3208 NA	Relief 30.5.1985-89 (48/20) Girvan 11.4.1989-29.8.93 (60/5) Sold 9.1993

The second 33ft Brede, Ann Ritchie (ON. 1080), incorporated a larger wheelhouse than the prototype to make her self-righting. (RNLI)

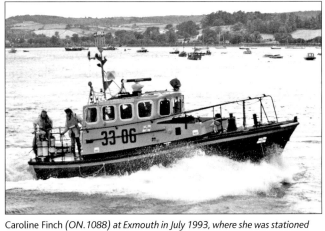

Caroline Finch (ON. 1088) at Exmouth in July 1993, where she was stationed for just over a decade. (Tony Denton)

Relief 33ft Brede Enid of Yorkshire (ON. 1101) on duty at Oban, one of the stations that operated Bredes. (Nicholas Leach)

One of the longest-serving 33ft Bredes was Safeway (ON. 1104), which operated from Calshot for more than fifteen years. (Nicholas Leach)

34 • Medina rigid-inflatable

Introduced 1980, last built 1982, 3 built.
Specifications • overall length 39ft 6in (12.12m), beam 14ft (4.27m), rigid-hull length 34ft 6in (10.56m), rigid-hull beam 11ft 4in (3.45m), crew 4.

The Medina class was an experimental rigid-inflatable design, nearly 40ft in length, based on the concept of the smaller Atlantic 21 rigid-inflatable. The first two boats were funded by an appeal, launched in 1979, supported by Lord Louis Mountbatten. Within a few days of the appeal launch, however, Lord Mountbatten was assassinated and as a result this appeal attracted considerable support, enabling two lifeboats to be funded. The prototype was an open boat with self-righting capability provided by an inflatable air-bag. The second and third boats were built with enclosed wheelhouses, which gave inherent self-righting. Although the hull shape and basic design concept showed initial promise, problems were experienced with finding engines of a suitable power-to-weight ratio, although several different units were tried, coupled to both propellers and waterjets. Further problems occurred when the hull was damaged after beach launching and recovery.

After bottom damage to the hull of ON.1069, William Osborne's boatyard designed a stronger hull structure which was used for the hull of ON.1091 and this proved more successful. Fitting an

The prototype Medina ON.1069 during her initial trials. (RNLI)

effective wheelhouse was also not straightforward and ON.1072 had two different wheelhouse structures. The boats' rigid-hulls and deck were built from marine ply with an aluminium wheelhouse and inflatable sponsons, of ten tons displacement. Despite exhaustive trials and numerous modifications over eight years, the RNLI decided that the design would not meet the Institution's standards and the project was abandoned. By the end of the 1980s, all boats had been sold having never been used in service and spent long periods in storage.

Year (Yd No) Builder Place	Name Donor	ON Cost Weight	Engines	Notes Disposal
1. 1980 W. A. Souter Cowes	Mountbatten of Burma Appeal by Romsey Branch, in honour of Lord Mountbatten.	1069 – –	2x212hp Sabre with twin Sternpower Type 83 outdrives/ 1983-3x203hp Seadrive outboards (p)	Trials at Brighton 6.1983, Littlehampton (stored) Open boat with steering console, SR via air-bag Sold 1.10.1989
2. 1981 W. A. Souter Cowes	Countess Mountbatten of Burma Appeal by Romsey Branch, in honour of Lord Mountbatten.	1072 – –	2x Volvo TAMD 60B and Volvo Type 750 outdrives/ 2x350hp Caterpillar 3208TA & Parker PP140 Jet Unit	Visited Dungeness 7.1985, Redcar 11.1985, Blackpool 5.1986, Dunbar, Appledore Watertight wheelhouse, SR in four secs; larger wheelhouse fitted by William Osborne 1984 Sold 11.8.1989
3. 1982 (WO2576) William Osborne Littlehampton	[Not named] RNLI funds.	1091 – –	2x285hp Caterpillar with Castoldi type 06 3208 water jets	Trials, RNLI Depot, Poole (stored) Enclosed wheelhouse Sold 30.4.1989

The second Medina was built with an enclosed wheelhouse to provide both crew protection and an inherent self-righting capability. This wheelhouse proved unsatisfactory and on the later boat, ON.1091, it was enlarged. (RNLI)

35 • Tyne fast slipway 47ft

Introduced 1982, last built 1990, 40 built.
Specifications • length 47ft (14.3m), beam 15ft (4.6m),
draught 4ft 2in (1.27m), crew 6.

The Tyne was designed in the late 1970s to replace the nine-knot Watson and Barnett displacement-hulled lifeboats at stations which employed slipway launching. Faster lifeboats had already been introduced into the RNLI's fleet but these could only be kept afloat. A new 'fast' lifeboat was required, but formulating such a design involved working within certain parameters so that the boat could fit into existing lifeboat houses. The parameters stipulated an overall length not exceeding 47ft 3in, a maximum beam of 15ft and a height from the underside of the keel to the top of the wheelhouse of 13ft. The weight could not exceed 24 tons, ensuring that most boathouses in service could take the new design.

The basic lines plan for the hull of the fast slipway lifeboat (FSB), as it was first designated, was provided by the National Maritime Institute. The hull was semi-planing with a shallow draught of 4ft 2in (1.27m), a long straight keel with a shallow conventional sheerline and a flared bow above the waterline. Protection for the propellers was given by partial tunnels, substantial bilge keels, and a straight wide keel extending to the transom and ending in a hauling shoe, all necessary for slipway launching and working in shoal waters. The wheelhouse had a low profile to fit into existing boathouses, with a flying bridge midships, and there was a separate cabin aft of the upper steering position. The hull plating and internal structure was built from corrosion-resistant steel, with aluminium alloy for the deck and superstructures. Other materials, notably wood and glass reinforced plastic, were considered but rejected on grounds of wear resistance and cost.

The class name Tyne was chosen to reflect the close connection of P. Denham Christie, chairman of the Boat Committee, with the FSB project. Mr Denham Christie came from Newcastle and served as coxswain of the Tynemouth lifeboat from 1953 to 1963.

The first two Tynes, ON.1074 and ON.1075, served as pre-production prototypes and were subjected to a period of evaluation as changes were made to improve and refine the design. The changes were then incorporated into the production boats. The hull shapes of all the boats are essentially the same, but on the first two boats the deck has a step in the sheerline. Aft of this step, the deck has a very heavy camber which is covered by a lightweight false side deck. This was deemed an unnecessary complication and so with the third boat, ON.1094, the turtle side decks were changed to flush decks. In addition, the after engine room bulkhead was moved to increase the size of the after cabin from this boat onwards.

The first two Tynes were fitted with General Motors 8V-71 diesel engines, similar to those installed in the 50ft Thames lifeboats. With engineroom space severely limited, engines with a high power-to-size and power-to-weight ratio were needed, something the GM diesels offered. After the 8V-71 model had been installed in the two pre-production prototypes, a newer model, the GM 6V-92, had been developed and this was used in the boats from ON.1094. Further changes were made as more Tynes were built, and from ON.1114 onwards the main deck was constructed from aluminium rather than steel. This boat was also fitted with a ZF

The prototype 47ft Tyne City of London (ON.1074) during her trials prior to going on station at Selsey. The flying bridge windscreen did not extend across the width of the wheelhouse when she was built. (RNLI)

160 BW gearbox rather than the standard GM gearbox, the Allison Type M20 used in the first ten boats, as it was slightly lighter and offered an improved reduction ratio.

Twin rudders were fitted and these were power assisted with hand hydraulic controls. Two main fuel tanks, holding 510 gallons of diesel between them, were supplemented by a reserve tank of 102 gallons. This gave the boats a range of 238 nautical miles. Trim planes were incorporated into the stern to enable the running trim to be altered to suit the sea conditions.

During the 1990s, a number of the boats were re-engined with twin 565bhp six-cylinder Detroit Diesel Series 92 DDEC diesels in an attempt to overcome the problems with the original engines which caused them to stall and backdrive. The backdriving caused the fuel lift pump seals to blow out resulting in the engines being disabled. The first set of the electronically controlled DDEC engines was fitted to the Relief Tyne ON.1142 and the extensive trials carried out to prove the system showed that the new engines completely eliminated the tendency to stall and backdrive, while also providing improved fuel management and a slightly greater speed. Problems with the new engine system were experienced in the late 1990s and many of the re-engined boats had to be withdrawn from service while the faults were rectified.

The continual modifications made as the boats were in production resulted in an increase in weight and so the self-righting ability was reviewed with the result that an increase in superstructure volume was required. From boat number thirty, ON.1145, the aft cabin height was increased by 125mm. All boats subsequently had this modification carried out while undergoing survey. In 2004, during the development of the Tyne's replacement (see table 39), further questions were raised about the boat's self-righting ability and consequently the decision was made to fit air-bags to the aft cabin.

Although most Tynes were operated from slipway stations, a number were kept afloat as the design's protected propellers made it ideal for shallow water. Tynes were built for stations, such as Salcombe, Lowestoft and St Helier, where the lifeboat lies afloat but has to operate over sandbars or rocks.

35 · Tyne fast slipway 47ft

Year (Yd No) Builder Place	Name Donor	ON (Op No) Cost Weight	Engines	Stations (launches/lives saved) Disposal
1. 1982 (FM708) Fairey Marine Cowes	City of London City of London Appeal.	1074 (47-001) £430,000 25t5	2x425hp General Motors 8V-71-TI	Selsey 21.11.1983-2.2006 (415/58) Sold 2007
2. 1982 (FM709) Fairey Marine Cowes	Sam and Joan Woods RNLI General Funds.	1075 (47-002) £430,000 24t11	2x425hp General Motors 8V-71-TI	Relief 1984-93 (59/24) and 1996-2007 Walton & Frinton 1.8.1993-5.96 (67/10) Sold 2007
3. 1984 (FM716) Fairey Marine Cowes	James Burrough Gift of Miss H. B. Allen, East Clandon, near Guildford, Surrey	1094 (47-003) £445,000 24t0	2x425hp General Motors 6V-92-TA	Padstow 28.12.1984-7.2006 Sold 2007
4. 1985 (717/2770) Fairey Marine/ William Osborne	St Cybi II (Civil Service No.40) Civil Service Lifeboat Fund.	1095 (47-004) £445,000 24t4	2x425hp General Motors 6V-92-TA	Holyhead 20.9.1985-11.12.97 (267/119) Relief 1997-2007 Sold 2007
5. 1985 (FM718) Fairey Marine Cowes	Ethel Anne Measures J. F. & E. A. Measures Charity, Mumbles Lifeboat Appeal, various other donors.	1096 (47-005) £430,000 25t5	2x425hp General Motors 6V-92-TA	Mumbles 3.7.1985-7.2006 Relief 2006-07 Sold 2007
6. 1985 (FM719) Fairey Marine Cowes	Ruby and Arthur Reed II Bequest of Mrs R. M. Reed and Cromer Lifeboat Appeal.	1097 (47-006) £430,000 25t5	2x425hp General Motors 6V-92-TA	Cromer 16.12.1985-17.11.96 (75/29) Relief 1997-98 (28/0) Cromer 4.3.1999-3.07 Sold 2007

Cutaway drawing of 47ft Tyne
Key: (1) Engine, (2) Anchor, (3) Watertight door, (4) Propeller, (5) Aerial, (6) Navigation lights, (7) Radar, (8) Steering wheel, (9) Stretcher, (10) Breeches buoy, (11) Drogue, (12) Bollard, (13) Jackstay, (14) Helmsman's seat, (15) Toilet, (16) Searchlight, (17) Loudhailer, (18) Seat belts, (19) Radio, (20) Binoculars, (21) Veering line, (22) First aid kit, (23) Fire extinguisher, (24) Mouth-to-mouth resuscitator, (25) Battery, (26) Blue flashing light, (27) Stemhead fairlead fitting, (28) Haul-up cleat, (29) Sternlight, (30) Fenders, (31) Rubber fendering, (32) Stanchion, (33) Fairleads, (34) Non-slip deck paint, (35) Lifeline, (36) Chart and magnifier.

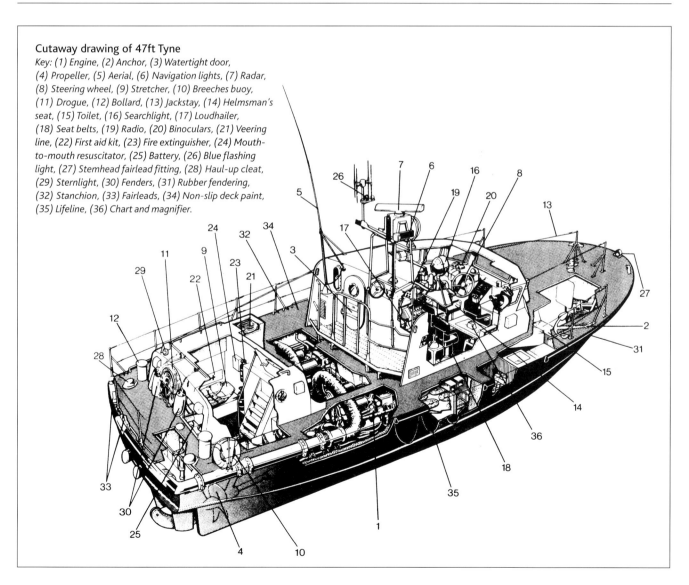

35 · Tyne fast slipway 47ft

Year (Yd No) Builder Place	Name Donor	ON (Op No) Cost Weight	Engines	Stations (launches/lives saved) Disposal
7. 1985 (FM1058) Fairey Marine Cowes	City of Edinburgh The City of Edinburgh Lifeboat Appeal.	1109 (47-007) £430,000 24t0	2x425hp General Motors 6V-92-TA	Fraserburgh 30.11.1985-8.5.2002 (180/115) Relief 5.2002-
8. 1985 (FM1059) Fairey Marine Cowes	Phil Mead Trustees of Phil Mead Trust, and proceeds of local appeal.	1110 (47-008) £450,000 25t5	2x425hp General Motors 6V-92-TA	Teesmouth 22.1.1986-29.4.2006 (352/42) Relief 4.2006-
9. 1986 (FM1060) Fairey Marine Cowes	William Luckin Bequest of Mrs Rose Mary Luckin, and RNLI Funds.	1111 (47-009) £450,000 25t5	2x425hp General Motors 6V-92-TA	Arranmore 5.4.1986-22.1.2000 (280/46) Lough Swilly 11.4.2001-
10. 1986 (2880) Wright, Derby/ William Osborne	RFA Sir Galahad Royal Fleet Aux Appeal, Shropshire LB Appeal, and Tenby Branch Appeal.	1112 (47-010) £445,000 25t5	2x425hp General Motors 6V-92-TA	Tenby 6.9.1986-4.2006 (364/254) Relief 4.2006-
11. 1987 (2970) Wright, Derby/ William Osborne	The Lady Rank The Rank Foundation.	1114 (47-011) £450,000 25t5	2x425hp General Motors 6V-92-TA	Angle 23.6.1987-
12. 1987 (2990) Wright, Derby/ William Osborne	Good Shepherd An Ecumenical Appeal to Churches, with various other gifts and legacies.	1115 (47-012) £537,000 25t66	2x425hp General Motors 6V-92-TA	Relief 14.4.1988-13.11.2000 Lough Swilly 13.11.2000-11.4.2001 (2/0) Relief 11.4.2001-
13. 1987 (1116) Wright, Derby/ Lochin Marine	Robert and Violet Anonymous gift.	1116 (47-013) £537,000 24t98	2x425hp General Motors 6V-92-TA	Moelfre 22.1.1988-
14. 1986 (FM1073) Fairey Marine Cowes	James Bibby Gift of Mr J. B. Bibby, of Liverpool.	1117 (47-014) £450,000 22t9	2x425hp General Motors 6V-92-TA	Barrow 4.9.1986-
15. 1987 (FM1106) Fairey Marine Cowes	Hetty Rampton Trustees of Miss Hetty Mabel Rampton's Charity.	1120 (47-015) £508,696 25t5	2x425hp General Motors 6V-92-TA	Porthdinllaen 27.4.1987-
16. 1987 (1121) Wright, Derby/ Harrison, Amble	Norman Salvesen Bequest of Mrs Norman Salvesen.	1121 (47-016) £537,000 25t8	2x425hp General Motors 6V-92-TA	Wick 16.9.1988-13.2.97 (120/54) Sennen Cove 5.12.1998-
17. 1987 (0012) Wright, Derby/ W. A. Souter	Owen and Anne Aisher Gift of Sir Owen Aisher, Branksome, Poole.	1122 (47-017) £537,000 26t	2x425hp General Motors 6V-92-TA	Relief Fleet 1988-
18. 1987 (FM1189) Fairey Marine Cowes	Max Aitken III The Beaverbrook Foundation.	1126 (47-018) £537,000 24t98	2x425hp General Motors 6V-92-TA	Bembridge 15.12.1987-

47ft Tyne Ethel Anne Measures *(ON.1096), one of the first batch of six Tynes to be built, at speed off Mumbles. (Nicholas Leach)*

Recovery of Ruby and Arthur Reed II *(ON.1097) at Cromer, showing the bilge keels and propeller arrangement. (Nicholas Leach)*

Year (Yd No) Builder Place	Name Donor	ON (Op No) Cost Weight	Engines	Stations (launches/lives saved) Disposal
19. 1987 (FM1190) Fairey Marine Cowes	Babs and Agnes Robertson Anonymous gift (Robertson and Baxter Ltd, Glasgow).	1127 (47-019) £537,000 25t2	2x425hp General Motors 6V-92-TA	Peterhead 14.1.1988-4.2006 Relief 4-7 2006 Mumbles 7.2006-
	1128 and 1129 (47-020 and -021) cancelled 1986			
20. 1987 (1130) Wright, Derby/ Lochin Marine	The Baltic Exchange II The Baltic Exchange with other gifts and bequests.	1130 (47-022) £584,362 25t14	2x425hp General Motors 6V-92-TA	Salcombe 30.8.1988-
21. 1987 (0027) Wright, Derby/ W. A. Souter	City of Sheffield The City of Sheffield Lifeboat Appeal.	1131 (47-023) £566,000 25t2	2x425hp General Motors 6V-92-TA	Whitby 12.12.1988-10.4.96 (239/88) Relief 4.1996-7.97 and 10.2000-9.01 Hartlepool 24.7.1997-23.10.2000 (31/8) Poole 5.9.2001-
22. 1987 (FM1191) Fairey Marine Cowes	Spirit of Lowestoft The Lowestoft Appeal with other gifts and legacies.	1132 (47-020) £520,166 25t04	2x425hp General Motors 6V-92-TA	Lowestoft 16.11.1987-
23. 1987 (FM1192) Fairey Marine Cowes	The Famous Grouse The Famous Grouse Competition Appeal.	1133 (47-021) £537,000 25t37	2x425hp General Motors 6V-92-TA	Relief 12.12.1987-4.2004 Kilmore Quay 7.4.2004-
24. 1988 (FM1193) Fairey Marine Cowes	Hilda Jarrett Legacy of Mrs H. J. Jarrett, together wth other bequests and RNLI Funds.	1137 (47-024) £560,000 25t25	2x425hp General Motors 6V-92-TA	Baltimore 3.3.1988-
25. 1988 (FM1194) Fairey Marine Cowes	Lord Saltoun Legacy of Mrs Norman Salvesen.	1138 (47-025) £537,000 25t07	2x425hp General Motors 6V-92-TA	Longhope 26.3.1988-12.8.99 (41/9) Relief 8.1999-
26. 1988 (FM1195) Fairey Marine Cowes	Garside Legacies of Thomas Harold Garside and Dorothy Garside.	1139 (47-026) £537,000 25t38	2x425hp General Motors 6V-92-TA	St Davids 25.5.1988-
27. 1988 (FM1196) Fairey Marine Cowes	George Gibson Mr G. C. Gibson, OBE, through the Gibson Charitable Trust.	1140 (47-027) £537,000 25t	2x425hp General Motors 6V-92-TA	Appledore 19.6.1988-
28. 1989 (1141) Wright, Derby/ Marshall-Branson	Sir John Fisher The Sir John Fisher Foundation.	1141 (47-028) £560,000 26t43	2x425hp General Motors 6V-92-TA	Relief 1989-92 (5/0) Workington 8.6.1992-
29. 1989 (0056) Wright, Derby/ W. A. Souter	Mariners Friend The H. B. Allen Charitable Trust.	1142 (47-029) £550,000 26t35	2x425hp General Motors 6V-92-TA	Relief 20.9.1989-

Angle lifeboat The Lady Rank *(ON.1114), one of several Tynes built for service at Welsh stations, on exercise in Milford Haven. (Nicholas Leach)*

Spirit of Lowestoft *(ON.1132) off the Suffolk coast. She was one of several Tynes operated from afloat moorings. (Nicholas Leach)*

Year (Yd No) Builder Place	Name Donor	ON (Op No) Cost Weight	Engines	Stations (launches/lives saved) Disposal
30. 1988 (FM1208) Fairey Marine Cowes	David Robinson Legacy of the late Sir David Robinson.	1145 (47-030) £537,000 25t10	2x425hp General Motors 6V-92-TA	The Lizard 17.8.1988-
31. 1988 (FM1209) Fairey Marine Cowes	Voluntary Worker The Volvo Concessionaires Ltd and Tesco Stores Ltd.	1146 (47-031) £537,000 25t12	2x425hp General Motors 6V-92-TA	Lytham St Annes 1.12.1988-1.90 (10/8) Relief 20.1.1990-2005 Selsey 2.2006-
32. 1988 (FM1210) Fairey Marine Cowes	Sir William Hillary Legacy of the late Mr A. J. Woolfenden, Gawsworth, Cheshire.	1147 (47-032) £537,000 25t9	2x425hp General Motors 6V-92-TA	Douglas 25.11.1988-
33. 1989 (FM1237) Fairey Marine Cowes	Mary Irene Millar Legacy of the late Mrs M. I. Millar, plus other gifts.	1151 (47-033) £590,000 25t5	2x425hp General Motors 6V-92-TA	Portpatrick 16.3.1989-
34. 1989 (FM1238) Fairey Marine Cowes	Moonbeam Mr and Mrs Roland Sutton, Grampian.	1152 (47-034) £590,000 25t7	2x425hp General Motors 6V-92-TA	Montrose 28.5.1989-
35. 1989 (FM1239) Fairey Marine Cowes	Annie Blaker Bequest of Annie Lydia Blaker, and RNLI general funds.	1153 (47-035) £590,000 25t77	2x425hp General Motors 6V-92-TA	Wicklow 8.10.1989-
36. 1989 (0068) Wright, Foston Derby	Kenneth Thelwall II Bequest of Kenneth Thelwall, Walkington, Yorkshire.	1154 (47-036) £590,000 26t24	2x425hp General Motors 6V-92-TA	Ramsgate 27.4.1990-24.8.94 (92/16) Walton and Frinton 15.5.1996-
37. 1989 (FM1257) FBM Marine Cowes	Sarah Emily Harrop Bequest of Sarah Emily Harrop.	1155 (47-037) £590,000 25t92	2x425hp General Motors 6V-92-TA	Lytham St Annes 14.1.1990-10.10.98 (91/17) Relief 1998-
38. 1989 (FM1258) FBM Marine Cowes	William Street The W. O. Street Foundation; bequests of Maj Percy Holley, Francis Balshaw; gift from Miss H. Richmond.	1156 (47-038) £590,000 26t58	2x425hp General Motors 6V-92-TA	Fleetwood 15.10.1989-
39. 1990 (FM1259) FBM Marine Cowes	Alexander Coutanche Jersey Lifeboat Appeal and the States of Jersey.	1157 (47-039) £590,000 25t69	2x425hp General Motors 6V-92-TA	St Helier 13.12.1989-
40. 1990 (1158) Wright, Derby/ Mshl Branson	Hermione Lady Colwyn Shoreham Lifeboat Appeal and bequest of Lady Colwyn.	1158 (47-040) £590,000	2x425hp General Motors 6V-92-TA	Shoreham Harbour 30.9.1990-

The Tyne hull shape with its long bilge keels is exemplified by relief Tyne Voluntary Worker (ON.1146) at the RNLI Depot, Poole, awaiting her next temporary duty. (Nicholas Leach)

Sir William Hillary (ON.1147) on the slipway outside her boathouse at Douglas on the Isle of Man. She is named after the founder of the RNLI who was himself originally from Douglas. (Tony Denton)

Relief 47ft Tyne Lord Saltoun *(ON.1138) on exercise at Baltimore in south-west Ireland during a stint there in 2004. Only two lifeboat stations in Ireland employed slipway launching during the Tyne era. (Nicholas Leach)*

Launch of Annie Blaker *(ON.1153) down the slipway at Wicklow where the boathouse had to be significantly converted to accommodate the 47ft Tyne. (Nicholas Leach)*

The spectacular sight of a slipway launch as Hermione Lady Colwyn *(ON.1158), the last 47ft Tyne to be built, hits the water after leaving her boathouse at Shoreham Harbour. (Nicholas Leach)*

36 • Mersey fast carriage 12m

Introduced 1986, last built 1993, 38 built.
Specifications • length 38ft (11.57m), beam 12ft 6in
(3.81m), depth 6ft (1.86m), displacement 13 tonnes.

The fast carriage lifeboat (FCB) was developed for use at stations where a carriage launch was practised, and fulfilled the RNLI's stated commitment of 1983 to have fast lifeboats at all stations by 1990. Designers of the FCB had to ensure the new boat would fit inside existing boathouses and could be launched by the same method as the Oakley and Rother lifeboats it would replace. These limitations led to the development of a boat with an overall length of 38ft and a beam of 12ft 6in and twin engines driving twin propellers which were protected by semi-tunnels.

The hull was of round bilge semi-displacement form with a soft nose stem and a tunnel stern to give protection to the propellers. The hull is subdivided by four watertight bulkheads into five compartments which comprise a forepeak cable locker, a survivors' cabin with seating for ten people, machinery space, tank space and an after peak steering gear compartment. The first FCB was a full-scale prototype which never saw service but was used for trialling the hull shape, while the second and third boats (ON.1124 and ON.1125) were production prototypes with aluminium hulls. Aluminium was chosen because of its weight-saving properties compared to steel as the weight of the boat was crucial if the design was to reach the desired speed and because it was to be launched from a carriage.

During 1987-88, a new material, fibre reinforced composite (FRC), was evaluated by the RNLI and used for a fourth hull. Both aluminium and FRC were materials new to RNLI lifeboat design. FRC was thoroughly tested in a full-scale prototype, ON.1148, which was built from an epoxy resin matrix reinforced with glass and Kevlar fibres. The decision to use FRC was taken to speed up the construction process as the aim was to have forty boats in service within four years. FRC enabled a moulded hull to be built, thus utilising pre-constructed sections and pre-assembled components, resulting in an overall shorter build time. ON.1148 was ordered in September 1987 and delivered in March 1988. The trials that followed included seakeeping and handling. She was then run on and off Dungeness beach 243 times, then dragged for almost a mile over the shingle. This represented twenty years' launching but, as inspection of the bottom revealed, caused no damage to the hull

ON.1125, one of the two production prototype 12m Merseys, launching during trials at Bridlington in the late 1980s. (Paul Arro)

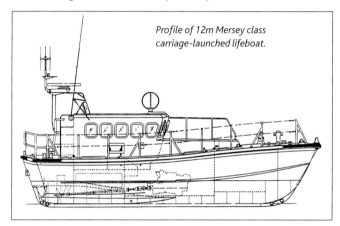

Profile of 12m Mersey class carriage-launched lifeboat.

apart from scuffing the paint. After the FRC prototype (ON.1148), the next eight hulls (ON.1161 to ON.1168) were also of aluminium but from ON.1169 onwards FRC was used and proved to be ideal in operational conditions, so much so that subsequent lifeboat designs have been built from it.

The design was given the class name Mersey in line with the RNLI's policy of naming lifeboat classes after rivers. Mersey was chosen to maintain a link with the Liverpool class, to reaffirm the Institution's links with the area and its maritime tradition, and stations on the approaches to the river received boats of the class.

Year (Yd No) Builder Place	Name Donor	ON (Op No) Cost Weight	Engines	Stations (launches/lives saved) Disposal
1. 1986 (2940) Cunningham/ William Osborne	[Not named] —	1119 — —	2x285hp Caterpillar 3208T (aluminium hull)	Experimental prototype Used for trials only Scrapped and hull sold 1989
2. 1987 (WO3130) Aluminium SB/ William Osborne	Peggy and Alex Caird Bequest of Miss M. M. Caird, Hull.	1124 (12-001) £350,000 13.85 te	2x285hp Caterpillar 3208T (aluminium hull)	Bridlington 15.12.1988-8.95 (105/19) Relief 8.1995-
3. 1987 (WO3070) Aluminium SB/ William Osborne	Sealink Endeavour Sealink British Ferries Ltd Promotion, bequests Dr W. Murphy, Mrs Dorothy M. Kellett and other gifts and legacies.	1125 (12-002) £350,000 14 te	2x285hp Caterpillar 3208T (aluminium hull)	Trials 1987-3.89 Hastings 13.3.1989-
4. 1988 (0061) Green Marine/ W. A. Souter	Lifetime Care The Volvo Concessionaires Limited promotion.	1148 (12-11) £550,000 13.67 te	2x285hp Caterpillar 3208T (FRC hull)	Relief 1989-

36 • Mersey fast carriage 12m

Year (Yd No) Builder Place	Name Donor	ON (Op No) Cost Weight	Engines	Stations (launches/lives saved) Disposal
5. 1989 (FM1266) FBM Ltd Cowes	Doris M. Mann of Ampthill Legacy of Doris M. Mann, Ampthill, Beds.	1161 (12-003) £468,209 14.91 te	2x285hp Caterpillar 3208T (aluminium hull)	Wells 3.7.1990-
6. 1990 (FM1267) FBM Ltd Cowes	Royal Shipwright The Worshipful Company of Shipwrights, and others.	1162 (12-004) £430,000 14.46 te	2x285hp Caterpillar 3208T (aluminium hull)	Relief 1990-3.2007 Cromer 3.2007-
7. 1990 (FM1268) FBM Ltd Cowes	Lady of Hilbre Mersey Lifeboat Appeal, and other gifts and legacies.	1163 (12-005) £430,556	2x285hp Caterpillar 3208T (aluminium hull)	Hoylake 12.10.1990-
8. 1990 (FM1269) FBM Ltd Cowes	Andy Pearce Bequest of Andrew Pearce, with other gifts and legacies.	1164 (12-006) £429,494	2x285hp Caterpillar 3208T (aluminium hull)	Llandudno 23.11.1990-
9. 1990 (WO3317) Aluminium SB/ William Osborne	Spirit of Derbyshire Spirit of Derbyshire and Ilfracombe Lifeboat Appeals.	1165 (12-007) £444,498 14.25 te	2x285hp Caterpillar 3208T (aluminium hull)	Ilfracombe 20.7.1990-
10. 1990 (0084) Aluminium SB/ W.A. Souter	Lincolnshire Poacher Lincolnshire Lifeboat Appeal and Van Geest Charitable Trust.	1166 (12-008) £460,212 14.16 te	2x285hp Caterpillar 3208T (aluminium hull)	Skegness 7.8.1990-
11. 1990 (WO3359) Aluminium SB/ William Osborne	The Princess Royal (Civil Service No.41) Civil Service, Post Office and British Telecom Lifeboat Fund.	1167 (12-009) £445,432	2x285hp Caterpillar 3208T (aluminium hull)	St Ives 23.10.1990-

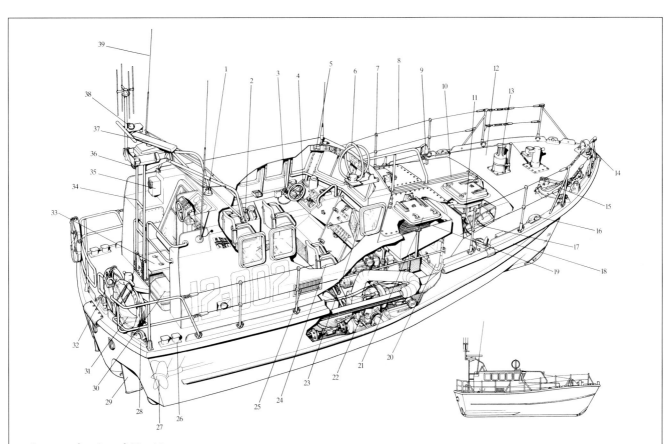

Cutaway drawing of 12m Mersey
Key: (1) Compass, (2) Torches, (3) Intercom, (4) Steering wheel, (5) Echo sounder, (6) DF loop, (7) Stanchion, (8) Guard wires, (9) Loudspeaker, (10) Boathook, (11) Fire extinguisher, (12) Non-slip deck paint, (13) Capstan, (14) Fairlead, (15) Anchor, (16) Starboard fairlead fitting, (17) Stretcher, (18) Fendering, (19) Fend-off, (20) Watertight door, (21) Watertight hatch, (22) Main engine, (23) Radar, (24) Seat, (25) Engine room air-filter, (26) Bollard, (27) Propeller, (28) Stern fairlead, (29) Rudder, (30) Liferaft, (31) Drogue, (32) Breeches buoy, (33) Access hatch, (34) Mast, (35) Capsize valve, (36) Navigation light, (37) Radar scanner, (38) Blue flashing light, (39) Whip aerial.

36 • Mersey fast carriage 12m

Year (Yd No) Builder Place	Name Donor	ON (Op No) Cost Weight	Engines	Stations (launches/lives saved) Disposal
12. 1990 (0085) Aluminium SB/ W.A. Souter	Lilly and Vincent Anthony Bequest of Miss Amy Anthony.	1168 (12-010) £552,881	2x285hp Caterpillar 3208T (aluminium hull)	Pwllheli 25.1.1991-
13. 1991 (FM1277) Green Marine/ FBM Ltd	Marine Engineer Institute of Marine Engineers, with other gifts and legacies.	1169 (12-12) £650,000	2x285hp Caterpillar 3208T (FRC hull)	Relief 25.4.1991-8.95 (22/4) Bridlington 13.8.1995-
14. 1991 (FM1278) Green Marine/ FBM Ltd	Keep Fit Association Keep Fit Association Appeal with other gifts and legacies.	1170 (12-13) £651,481	2x285hp Caterpillar 3208T (FRC hull)	Filey 2.6.1991-
15. 1991 (FM1279) Green Marine/ FBM Ltd	Ann and James Ritchie Bequest of Mrs Ann Ritchie.	1171 (12-14) £577,746	2x285hp Caterpillar 3208T (FRC hull)	Ramsey 12.7.1991-
16. 1991 (FM1280) Green Marine/ FBM Ltd	Frank and Lena Clifford of Stourbridge Legacy of Mr Frank Clifford.	1172 (12-15) £649,376	2x285hp Caterpillar 3208T (FRC hull)	New Quay 8.4.1992-
17. 1991 (FM1281) Green Marine/ FBM Ltd	Grace Darling Grace Darling Anniversary Appeal, and other gifts.	1173 (12-16) £652,978	2x285hp Caterpillar 3208T (FRC hull)	North Sunderland/Seahouses* 7.8.1991
18. 1991 (FM1282) Green Marine/ FBM Ltd	Kingdom of Fife Anstruther Lifeboat Appeal, and legacy of Dr Nora Allan.	1174 (12-17) £655,000	2x285hp Caterpillar 3208T (FRC hull)	Anstruther 16.10.1991-
19. 1991 (FM1283) Green Marine/ FBM Ltd	Fanny Victoria Wilkinson and Frank Stubbs Legacy of Mr Frank Stubbs.	1175 (12-18) £653,911	2x285hp Caterpillar 3208T (FRC hull)	Scarborough 27.9.1991-
20. 1991 (FM1284) Green Marine/ FBM Ltd	The Four Boys Land's End Lifeboat Appeal, and money raised by Stoke Poges Appeal.	1176 (12-19) £455,000	2x285hp Caterpillar 3208T (FRC hull)	Sennen Cove 5.12.1991-12.98 (90/47) Relief 12.1998-7.99 (1/0) Amble 22.7.1999-
21. 1991 (FM1285) Green Marine/ FBM Ltd	Leonard Kent Legacy of the late Mr Leonard Kent.	1177 (12-20) £629,121	2x285hp Caterpillar 3208T (FRC hull)	Margate 19.12.1991-
22. 1991 (FM1286) Green Marine/ FBM Ltd	Margaret Jean Gift of Peter and Jean Bath, Cambridgeshire.	1178 (12-21) £650,000	2x285hp Caterpillar 3208T (FRC hull)	Relief 4.2.1992-

* Station renamed Seahouses in April 1999

The prototype 12m Mersey Peggy and Alex Caird (ON.1124) during recovery at Barmouth in February 2004. This photograph shows the keel and tunnel arrangement incorporated into the hull design to protect the propellers during the recovery procedure. (Nicholas Leach)

The second prototype 12m Mersey ON.1125 during trials at Bridlington on 27 February 1988. She has no markings and was in the early stages of development. The trials were held to assess the hull suitability for beach launching and recovery. (Tony Denton)

Doris M. Mann of Ampthill
(ON.1161), the first production 12m
Mersey, crossing the bar at Wells-
next-the-Sea. She was one of only
eight aluminium-hulled Merseys.
(Nicholas Leach)

Launch of 12m Mersey Lincolnshire
Poacher (ON.1166) from the beach
at Skegness using the Talus MB-H
tractor as part of the RNLI's standard
beach launch and recovery rig.
(Nicholas Leach)

Grace Darling (ON.1172) on exercise
off Seahouses, with the Farne Islands
visible in the background.
(Nicholas Leach)

Year (Yd No) Builder Place	Name Donor	ON (Op No) Cost Weight	Engines	Stations (launches/lives saved) Disposal
23. 1992 (0101) Green Marine/ W. A. Souter	Ruby Clery Bequest of Miss Ruby Alexander Clery, London.	1181 (12-22) £662,663	2x285hp Caterpillar 3208T (FRC hull)	Peel 10.6.1992-
24. 1992 (FM1322) Green Marine/ FBM Ltd	Robert Charles Brown The J. Reginald Corah Foundation Fund, Maud Elkington Charitable Trust.	1182 (12-23) £669,043	2x285hp Caterpillar 3208T (FRC hull)	Swanage 12.6.1992-
25. 1992 (0102) Green Marine/ W. A. Souter	Lil Cunningham Gift of Miss Betty H. I. Cunningham, Derby.	1183 (12-24) £640,092	2x285hp Caterpillar 3208T (FRC hull)	Rhyl 21.6.1992-
26. 1992 (FM1323) Green Marine/ FBM Ltd	Bingo Lifeline Bingo Association of Great Britain, bequest of Mrs Anne Mills, and other gifts and legacies.	1184 (12-25) £660,000	2x285hp Caterpillar 3208T (FRC hull)	Relief 29.7.1992-
27. 1992 (WO3546) Green Marine/ William Osborne	Moira Barrie Legacy of the late Miss Barrie, Worcestershire.	1185 (12-26) £683,097	2x285hp Caterpillar 3208T (FRC hull)	Barmouth 7.10.1992-
28. 1992 (0103) Green Marine/ W. A. Souter	Pride and Spirit Gift of Mr and Mrs Eric Cass, of Virginia Water, Surrey.	1186 (12-27) £645,034	2x285hp Caterpillar 3208T (FRC hull)	Dungeness 24.9.1992-
29. 1992 (WO3555) Green Marine/ William Osborne	Mary Margaret Bequests of Denis A. S. Williams and Mary Margaret Williams.	1187 (12-28) £678,261	2x285hp Caterpillar 3208T (FRC hull)	Kilmore Quay 2.12.1992-4.2004 (211/48) Relief 4.2004-
30. 1992 (FM1324) Green Marine/ FBM Marine	Eleanor and Bryant Girling Bequest of Mrs Eleanor B. Girling.	1188 (12-29) £704,230	2x285hp Caterpillar 3208T (FRC hull)	Newcastle 8.9.1993-
31. 1992 (0104) Green Marine/ W. A. Souter	Her Majesty The Queen An Appeal to Police Constabularies in UK with other gifts and legacies.	1189 (12-30) £650,000	2x285hp Caterpillar 3208T (FRC hull)	Relief 25.1.1993-11.96 (27/11) Cromer 7.11.1996-4.3.99 (21/6) Relief 3-12.1999 (4/0) Lytham St Annes 16.12.1999-
32. 1992 (WO3560) Green Marine/ William Osborne	Doris Bleasdale Bequest of Miss Doris Bleasdale.	1190 (12-31) £671,910	2x285hp Caterpillar 3208T (FRC hull)	Clogher Head 3.3.1993-
33. 1993 (FM1325) Green Marine/ FBM Ltd	Joy and Charles Beeby Legacy of Charles Beeby, Long Itchington, Warwickshire.	1191 (12-32) £680,000	2x285hp Caterpillar 3208T (FRC hull)	Berwick-upon-Tweed 5.2.1993-
34. 1993 (0105) Green Marine/ W. A. Souter	Fisherman's Friend Promotion by Lofthouse of Fleetwood, with other gifts and legacies.	1192 (12-33) £650,000	2x285hp Caterpillar 3208T (FRC hull)	Relief 13.4.1993-
35. 1993 (FM1326) Green Marine/ FBM Ltd	Freddie Cooper Legacy of Mrs Winifred May Cooper.	1193 (12-34) £674,776	2x285hp Caterpillar 3208T (FRC hull)	Aldeburgh 19.12.1993-
36. 1993 (FM1327) Green Marine/ FBM Ltd	Inchcape Funded by local appeal, gifts and legacies; named after Inchcape Rock off Arbroath.	1194 (12-35) £680,000	2x285hp Caterpillar 3208T (FRC hull)	Arbroath 26.8.1993-
37. 1993 (WO3582) Green Marine/ William Osborne	Royal Thames Appeal by Royal Thames Yacht Club local appeal and other gifts and legacies.	1195 (12-36) £680,000	2x285hp Caterpillar 3208T (FRC hull)	Eastbourne 19.7.1993-
38. 1993 (0106) Green Marine/ W. A. Souter	Silvia Burrell Legacy of the late Miss Silvia Burrell, of Edinburgh.	1196 (12-37) £680,000	2x285hp Caterpillar 3208T (FRC hull)	Girvan 29.8.1993-

Builders: Cunningham and Sons, Ford, Sussex built the hull of the prototype under sub-contract; William Osborne Ltd, Littlehampton, fitted out the prototype and other boats as listed; Aluminium Shipbuilders, Shoreham, Sussex, built all aluminium hulls; Green Marine, Lymington, built all FRC hulls; W. A. Souter and FBM Ltd (Fairey Brooke Marine), both of Cowes, fitted out boats as listed.

Pride and Spirit *(ON.1186) at speed off Dungeness. The operational number was located on the cabin superstructure before the change of livery moved it to the bow.* (Nicholas Leach)

Joy and Charles Beeby *(ON.1191) launches down the slipway at Berwick-upon-Tweed. She was one of only three Merseys to operate from slipway stations. Of the other two, the Mersey at Sennen Cove was replaced by a 47ft Tyne leaving only Berwick and Swanage using a slipway launch.* (Nicholas Leach)

The last 12m Mersey to be built, Silvia Burrell *(ON.1196), moored at Girvan. She was one of only a handful of Merseys to operate from berths.* (Nicholas Leach)

37 • Severn fast afloat 17m

Introduced 1991, last built 2004, 46 built.
Specifications • length 17m (55ft 9in), breadth 5.5m (18ft), draught 1.68m (5ft 6in), fuel capacity 5,500 litres (1,200 gallons), displacement 37.5 tonnes (36.9 tons).

The Arun and Waveney lifeboats, designed in the 1960s and 1970s, operated from stations where they were kept afloat at moorings. Although both had been extremely successful lifeboat types, the RNLI felt that with experience, technical progress and further advances in marine design these lifeboats could be improved and new, faster all-weather lifeboats could be built which would be better equipped and able to reach 25 knots. As a result, two new designs were developed by the RNLI's in-house designers in the late 1980s and early 1990s, designated as Fast Afloat Boat (FAB) 3 and Fast Afloat Boat 4, to replace the Waveneys and Aruns.

The larger of the two, FAB3, was 17m in length and the prototype was powered by twin Caterpillar 3412TA diesel engines, each of 1,050hp at 2,150rpm, giving a speed of 25 knots. In production boats the engines were upgraded to 1,200bhp running at 2,300rpm. Unlike other lifeboat types, FAB3's engines were positioned aft, to give easier access to the machinery for maintenance, and the propellers were driven via U-drive shafts.

The hard chine hull form used for both designs was more or less identical, and incorporated propeller protection in the shape of a tunnel and bilge keels. FAB3's hull was built from fibre reinforced composite (FRC), which combines strength with relatively light weight, and was subdivided by six watertight bulkheads into seven compartments. The deck sheerline was dropped in a similar way to the Arun class, reducing the freeboard to help casualty handling. The deckhouse contained permanent seating for six crew and a doctor, with provision for two loaded stretchers. Housed in the forward console in the wheelhouse are the engine controls, the hydraulic steering unit and wheel, together with all the other controls necessary for operating the lifeboat. These controls were duplicated on the flying bridge. A bow thruster was fitted to improve manoeuvrability. A small Y class inflatable was carried on the wheelhouse roof for inshore work, and was launched and recovered by a lightweight framework and winch. This system was subsequently replaced by a small powered davit mounted on the starboard end of the superstructure. Lifting the inflatable by davit reduced the time and effort needed to launch and recover it.

The prototype 17m Severn 17-01 (ON.1179) on trials. This lifeboat was never used in service but became a trials platform and subsequently a training lifeboat number TL-02. The flying bridge on the production boats was moved slightly aft and the overall length of the superstructure was slightly shortened. (RNLI)

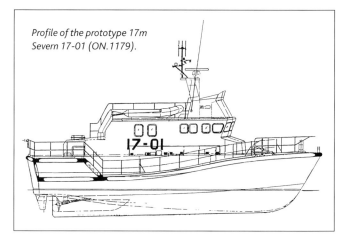

Profile of the prototype 17m Severn 17-01 (ON.1179).

Before entering service, in December 1992 FAB3 was designated the class name Severn, and FAB4 became the Trent, after the rivers that run through the heart of the country from where the RNLI receives a large amount of income. Apart from the prototype, the hull of which was built by Halmatic at Havant, all hulls and super-structures were fabricated in FRC by Green Marine, Lymington, and fitted out by various builders, as listed.

Year (Yd No) Builder Place	Name Donor	ON (Op No) Cost Weight	Engines	Stations (launches/lives saved) Disposal
1. 1991 (03444) Halmatic Ltd/ William Osborne	Maurice and Joyce Hardy/1995- un-named 1998- Peter and Marion Fulton RNLI general funds.	1179 (17-01) £1,350,000	2x1050bhp Caterpillar 3412TA	Trials 1992-98 Training 1998-9.2004 (numbered TL-02) Sold 1.2005
2. 1994 (1023) Green Marine/ Berthon Bt Co	The Will The Will Charitable Trust.	1201 (17-02) £1,692,011	2x1200bhp Caterpillar 3412TA	Relief 1996-97 Falmouth 11.3.1997-17.12.2001 (91/24) Relief 2002-
3. 1994 (1024) Green Marine/ Berthon Bt Co	Albert Brown Bequest of Victoria Maisie Brown, London, in memory of her husband.	1202 (17-03) £1,563,238	2x1200bhp Caterpillar 3412TA	Harwich 2.10.1996-
4. 1994 (MR3845) Green Marine/ Halmatic Ltd	Spirit of Guernsey Guernsey Severn Lifeboat Appeal, and various legacies and gifts.	1203 (17-04) £1,652,417	2x1200bhp Caterpillar 3412TA	St Peter Port 6.6.1997-

Note: the figures for cost are approximations.

The first production Severn, The Will (ON.1201). Originally allocated to Stornoway, she was used in the Relief Fleet before serving at Falmouth for over four years and then returning to the Relief. (RNLI)

Harwich Severn Albert Brown (ON.1202) was the first 17m Severn to go on station. This photo shows her after the fitting of the Y boat launch davit. (Nicholas Leach)

St Peter Port Severn Spirit of Guernsey (ON.1203) during the station's bicentenary celebrations in 2003. (N. Leach)

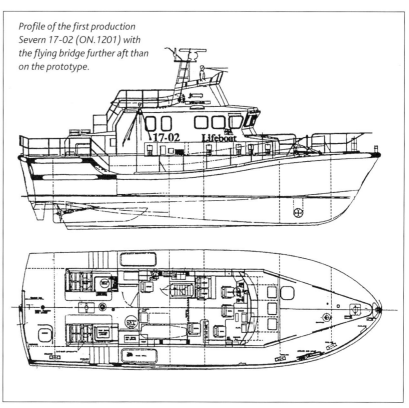

Profile of the first production Severn 17-02 (ON.1201) with the flying bridge further aft than on the prototype.

37 · Severn fast afloat 17m

Year (Yd No) Builder Place	Name Donor	ON (Op No) Cost Weight	Engines	Stations (launches/lives saved) Disposal
5. 1996 (MR3861) Green Marine/ Halmatic Ltd	Pride of the Humber Humber Lifeboat Appeal; fund-raising by volunteers of the North-East region; and various bequests.	1216 (17-05) £1,464,125	2x1200bhp Caterpillar 3412TA	Humber 8.3.1997-
6. 1996 (1025) Green Marine/ Berthon Bt Co	David Kirkaldy Mr David Kirkaldy.	1217 (17-06) £1,514,578	2x1200bhp Caterpillar 3412TA	Aran Islands 6.6.1997-
7. 1996 (1426) Green Marine/ FBM Ltd, Cowes	John and Margaret Doig Bequest of Miss Mary Doig together with other legacies.	1218 (17-07) £1,469,303	2x1200bhp Caterpillar 3412TA	Valentia 29.11.1996-
8. 1996 (1427) Green Marine/ FBM Ltd, Cowes	Helmut Schroder of Dunlossit II Mr Bruno Schroder and Mrs George Mallinckrodt.	1219 (17-08) £1,437,168	2x1200bhp Caterpillar 3412TA	Islay 9.3.1997-
9. 1996 (1026) Green Marine/ Berthon Bt Co	City of London II City of London Centenary appeal, and other gifts and legacies.	1220 (17-09) £1,595,834	2x1200bhp Caterpillar 3412TA	Dover 15.3.1997-
10. 1997 (1433) Green Marine/ FBM Ltd, Cowes	Michael and Jane Vernon The Lerwick Lifeboat Appeal and various legacies and donations.	1221 (17-10) £1,580,000	2x1200bhp Caterpillar 3412TA	Lerwick 2.6.1997-
11. 1997 (1027) Green Marine/ Berthon Bt Co	The Whiteheads Bequest of Miss Olive Elsie Whitehead, Newquay, Cornwall.	1229 (17-11) £1,725,000	2x1200bhp Caterpillar 3412TA	St Mary's (Scilly) 1.12.1997-
12. 1997 (1435) Green Marine/ FBM Ltd, Cowes	Edna Windsor Bequest from Mrs Edna Windsor.	1230 (17-12) £1,725,000	2x1200bhp Caterpillar 3412TA	Barra Island 13.6.1998-
13. 1997 (1436) Green Marine/ FBM Ltd, Cowes	Margaret Foster Legacy of Miss Margaret Ellen Foster, Emsworth, Hampshire.	1231 (17-13) £1,725,000	2x1200bhp Caterpillar 3412TA	Kirkwall 26.3.1998-
14. 1998 (1028) Green Marine/ Berthon Bt Co	Charles Lidbury Bequest of Miss Mary Lidbury, Dulverton, Somerset.	1232 (17-14) £1,725,000	2x1200bhp Caterpillar 3412TA	Aith 2.5.1998-
15. 1998 (1442) Green Marine/ FBM Ltd, Cowes	Bryan and Gordon Legacies from Bryan Clifford Griffiths and Gordon William Griffiths.	1235 (17-15) £1,725,000	2x1200bhp Caterpillar 3412TA	Ballyglass 14.8.1998-
16. 1998 (1030) Green Marine/ Berthon Bt Co	Violet, Dorothy and Kathleen Bequest of Miss Violet Jane Matton, Seaford, East Sussex.	1236 (17-16) £1,725,000	2x1200bhp Caterpillar 3412TA	Stromness 22.10.1998-
17. 1998 (1443) Green Marine/ FBM Ltd, Cowes	Fraser Flyer (Civil Service No.43) Civil Service, Post Office & BT Lifeboat Fund, the Ancient Order of Foresters and other gifts and legacies.	1237 (17-17) £1,725,000	2x1200bhp Caterpillar 3412TA	Relief 4.2.1999-
18. 1999 (1031) Green Marine/ Berthon Bt Co	Tom Sanderson Legacy of Mr Tom Sanderson, Milnthorpe, Cumbria.	1238 (17-18) £1,700,000	2x1200bhp Caterpillar 3412TA	Stornoway 1.2.1999-
19. 1999 (1448) Green Marine/ FBM Ltd, Cowes	Ernest and Mary Shaw Gift of the late Ernest J. Shaw and his widow, Mrs Mary Shaw, Glasgow.	1241 (17-19) £1,796,000	2x1200bhp Caterpillar 3412TA	Campbeltown 31.5.1999-
20. 1999 (1032) Green Marine/ Berthon Bt Co	Spirit of Northumberland The Tynemouth Lifeboat Appeal and other gifts and legacies.	1242 (17-20) £1,750,000	2x1200bhp Caterpillar 3412TA	Tynemouth 21.10.1999-
21. 1999 (1449) Green Marine/ FBM Ltd, Cowes	David and Elizabeth Acland Combination of seven legacies and a number of gifts.	1243 (17-21) £1,700,000	2x1200bhp Caterpillar 3412TA	Newhaven 8.11.1999-

Aith lifeboat Charles Lidbury *(ON.1232) serves the most northerly of the RNLI's lifeboat stations, which has a huge area to cover, including the often treacherous seas north of Shetland. (Nicholas Leach)*

Campbeltown's 17m Severn class lifeboat Ernest and Mary Shaw *(ON.1241) shows her speed off Davaar Island at the mouth of Campbeltown Loch. (Nicholas Leach)*

Newhaven lifeboat David and Elizabeth Acland *(ON.1243) on exercise off the Sussex coast, April 2007. (Nicholas Leach)*

Year (Yd No) Builder Place	Name Donor	ON (Op No) Cost Weight	Engines	Stations (launches/lives saved) Disposal
22. 1999 (1033) Green Marine/ Berthon Bt Co	Myrtle Maud Legacy of Myrtle Maud Campbell Orde.	1244 (17-22) IR£2,034,120	2x1200bhp Caterpillar 3412TA	Arranmore 27.1.2000-
23. 2000 (1455) Green Marine/ FBM Ltd, Cowes	Katie Hannan Legacy of Mrs Katrina Hannan, London, together with local appeal.	1247 (17-23) £1,700,000	2x1200bhp Caterpillar 3412TA	Portrush 15.6.2000-
24. 2000 (1035) Green Marine/ Berthon Bt Co	Bon Accord Local appeal, donations and legacies, named after City's motto.	1248 (17-24) £1,750,000	2x1200bhp Caterpillar 3412TA	Aberdeen 20.7.2000-
25. 2000 (1456) Green Marine/ FBM Ltd, Cowes	Eric and Susan Hiscock (Wanderer) Bequest of Mrs Susan Oakes Hiscock, Yarmouth, IOW.	1249 (17-25) £1,800,000	2x1200bhp Caterpillar 3412TA	Yarmouth 12.2000-
26. 2000 (1036) Green Marine/ Berthon Bt Co	Henry Alston Hewat Legacy of Miss Catherine M. Hewat, Glasgow, and Mallaig Lifeboat Appeal.	1250 (17-26) £1,800,000	2x1200bhp Caterpillar 3412TA	Mallaig 30.1.2001-
27. 2001 (0144) Green Marine/ Souter Sh Yd	Volunteer Spirit Fund-raising by branches and guilds during RNLI's 175th anniversary.	1254 (17-27) £1,800,000	2x1200bhp Caterpillar 3412TA	Relief 8.5.2001-
28. 2001 (1037) Green Marine/ Berthon Bt Co	Alec and Christina Dykes Bequest of the late Mrs Helen Christina Dykes, of Torbay.	1255 (17-28) £1,800,000	2x1200bhp Caterpillar 3412TA	Torbay 31.10.2001-
29. 2001 (0145) Green Marine/ Souter Sh Yd	Richard Cox Scott Bequest of Mrs Ruth M. Dix Scott, Cornwall, in memory of her husband.	1256 (17-29) £1,800,000	2x1200bhp Caterpillar 3412TA	Falmouth 18.12.2001-
30. 2001 (1038) Green Marine/ Berthon Bt Co	William Gordon Burr Legacy of Mrs Norah Burr, late of Lightcliffe, Halifax.	1257 (17-30) £1,800,000	2x1200bhp Caterpillar 3412TA	Relief 15.2.2002-
31. 2002 (051) Green Marine/ DML Devonport	Roger and Joy Freeman Legacy of Hilda Freeman, Solihull, with various other legacies.	1260 (17-31) £1,800,000	2x1200bhp Caterpillar 3412TA	Relief 10.9.2002-
32. 2002 (0150) Green Marine/ Souter Sh Yd	Ernest and Mabel Gift of Miss Beryl Taylor, Surrey, and other gifts and legacies.	1261 (17-32) £1,800,000	2x1200bhp Caterpillar 3412TA	Weymouth 16.7.2002-
33. 2002 (1039) Green Marine/ Berthon Bt Co	Beth Sell Legacy of Mrs Mima Elizabeth Sell, with bequests of Mrs Cyril H. Wells and others.	1262 (17-33) £1,900,000	2x1200bhp Caterpillar 3412TA	Relief 16.8.2002-

Myrtle Maud (ON.1244) at RNLI Depot, Poole. The hull shape, including the bilge keels and the bow thruster, can be seen in this photo. (Nicholas Leach)

Falmouth lifeboat Richard Cox Scott (ON.1256) on trials before going on station. She was named by HM The Queen on 1 May 2002. (Peter Edey)

Year (Yd No) Builder Place	Name Donor	ON (Op No) Cost Weight	Engines	Stations (launches/lives saved) Disposal
34. 2002 (052) Green Marine/ DML Devonport	Osier Legacy of Peter Albert George Acke.	1263 (17-34) £1,900,000	2x1200bhp Caterpillar 3412TA	Relief 11.10.2002-
35. 2002 (0151) Green Marine/ Souter Sh Yd	Sybil Mullen Glover Legacy of Mrs Daphne Sybil Glover.	1264 (17-35) £1,900,000	2x1200bhp Caterpillar 3412TA	Plymouth 15.2.2003-
36. 2002 (1040) Green Marine/ Berthon Bt Co	Ivan Ellen Legacy of Harold Ivan Leech.	1265 (17-36) £1,900,000	2x1200bhp Caterpillar 3412TA	Penlee 15.3.2003-
37. 2003 (054) Green Marine/ DML Devonport	William Blannin Legacies of Kenneth Maurice Williams, of Salisbury, with other gifts and legacies.	1268 (17-37) £1,800,000	2x1200bhp Caterpillar 3412TA	Buckie 27.5.2003-
38. 2002 (1041) Green Marine/ Berthon Bt Co	Daniel L. Gibson Legacy of John Gibson, Yorkshire.	1269 (17-38) £1,900,000	2x1200bhp Caterpillar 3412TA	Relief 2002-
39. 2002 (055) Green Marine/ DML Devonport	Elizabeth Fairllie Ramsey Bequest of Elizabeth Ramsey, of Edinburgh, and J. T. Graham.	1270 (17-39) £1,800,000	2x1200bhp Caterpillar 3412TA	Tobermory 20.8.2003-
40. 2003 (056) Green Marine/ DML Devonport	Julian and Margaret Leonard Legacy of Julian and Mrs Margaret Leonard, Saffron Walden and Brighton.	1271 (17-40) £1,800,000	2x1200bhp Caterpillar 3412TA	Lochinver 25.11.2003-
41. 2003 (1042) Green Marine/ Berthon Bt Co	Christopher Pearce Bequest of Christopher Michael Pearce.	1272 (17-41) £1,900,000	2x1200bhp Caterpillar 3412TA	Holyhead 21.12.2003-
42. 2003 (057) Green Marine/ DML Devonport	The Taylors Bequest of Mrs Vera Rita Elizabeth Taylor, Aberdeen.	1273 (17-42) £1,800,000	2x1200bhp Caterpillar 3412TA	Thurso 7.4.2004-
43. 2004 (0160) Green Marine/ Souter Sh Yd	Donald and Barbara Broadhead Bequest of Mrs Barbara Broadhead, Newark, together with other gifts.	1276 (17-43) £1,800,000	2x1200bhp Caterpillar 3412TA	Rosslare Harbour 9.7.2004-
44. 2004 (1043) Green Marine/ Berthon Bt Co	Annette Hutton Legacy of Annette A. M. Hutton, Blackrock, Co Dublin.	1277 (17-44) £1,800,000	2x1200bhp Caterpillar 3412TA	Castletownbere 12.8.2004-
45. 2004 (0161) Green Marine/ Souter/Berthon	The Duke of Kent Six different legacies combined.	1278 (17-45) £1,800,000	2x1200bhp Caterpillar 3412TA	Relief 25.2.2005-
46. 2004 (1044) Green Marine/ Berthon Bt Co	Margaret Joan and Fred Nye Legacies of Miss Joan Nye, Miss C. H. G. Willis, Mrs M. Howarth, and others.	1279 (17-46) £1,800,000	2x1200bhp Caterpillar 3412TA	Relief 17.11.2004-

William Gordon Burr *(ON.1257) on speed trials prior to entering service. She was one of several Severns built for the Relief fleet. (Peter Edey)*

Thurso lifeboat The Taylors *(ON.1273) moored alongside the purpose-built pontoon berth at Scrabster Harbour. (Nicholas Leach)*

38 • Trent fast afloat 14m

Introduced 1991, last built 2004, 38 built.
Specifications • length 14.26m (46ft 9in), breadth 4.53m (14ft 10in), depth 2.5m (8ft 4in), draught 1.295m (4ft 3in), fuel 4,100 litres (900 gallons), displacement 25.5 tonnes.

The 14m Trent class was developed as Fast Afloat Boat 4 at the same time as the 17m Severn. Both types were capable of twenty-five knots and were intended to replace the Waveney and Arun fast afloat boats dating from the 1960s and 1970s. The Trent's hull shape was essentially a scaled-down version of that of the Severn and shared many features including substantial bilge keels to protect the propellers and allow the boat to take the ground. The design was built from fibre reinforced composite (FRC) and the hull, deck and superstructure are of sandwich construction.

The sheerline sweeps down for ease of survivor recovery and the hull, subdivided by five bulkheads into six compartments, was of a hard chine design. The six compartments comprise a forepeak cable locker, fore store, forecabin/survivor cabin, tank space, machinery space and an aft peak steering compartment. The wheelhouse had permanent seating for six crew, with provision for one stretcher in the wheelhouse and another in the fore cabin. The engine controls were duplicated on the flying bridge.

The engine room configuration was a departure from previous RNLI lifeboats with the engines staggered. One powered the propeller through a U-drive shaft arrangement and the other via a conventional straight drive. This layout was adopted to provide more space and help in the ease of machinery maintenance. The prototype was fitted with twin 808bhp MAN D2840LXE marine diesels rated at 2,300rpm, coupled to twin ZF BW 195S type reverse/reduction gearboxes of 2.03:1 ratio. Approximately 4,100 litres (900 gallons) of fuel was carried, enabling ten hours of running at full speed as well as ten per cent of fuel in hand.

In December 1992, at the official press launch, the type was designated the class name Trent after the river that runs through the heart of the country from where the RNLI receives a large proportion of its income. During the previous three months, the prototype had been taken on extensive coastal evaluation trials being based, in turn, out of Newhaven, Dover, Lowestoft, Grimsby, Tynemouth, Eyemouth, Kirkwall, Portree, Campbeltown, Portrush,

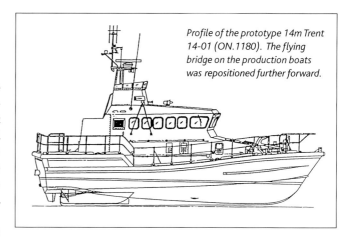

Profile of the prototype 14m Trent 14-01 (ON.1180). The flying bridge on the production boats was repositioned further forward.

Profile of the first production 14m Trent 14-02 (ON.1197) with the flying bridge repositioned and other minor changes to the internal layout.

Dun Laoghaire, Dunmore East, Fleetwood, Barry Dock and Fowey. The first production Trent was accepted in July 1994 but the initial boats were plagued by a series of teething problems, mainly to the machinery, but since these were resolved the design has given outstanding service around the coast. The entire building programme took a further ten years to complete. All hulls and superstructures were fabricated in FRC by Green Marine, at their Lymington yard, and then fitted out by the builders listed below.

The prototype 14m Trent 14-01 (ON.1180) on trials in December 1992. This lifeboat, named Earl and Countess Mountbatten of Burma (ON.1180), served at Alderney on a temporary basis and then became a Relief lifeboat. (RNLI)

38 · Trent fast afloat 14m

	Year (Yd No) Builder Place	Name Donor	ON (Op No) Cost Weight	Engines	Stations (launches/lives saved)
1.	1991 (WO3522) Green Marine/ William Osborne	Earl and Countess Mountbatten of Burma Funds donated nationwide to the Mountbatten of Burma Appeal.	1180 (14-01) £1,000,000	2x808hp MAN D2840LXE	Trials 1991-94 Alderney 7.3.1994-21.7.95 (42/27) Relief 1995-
2.	1994 (WO3612) Green Marine/ William Osborne	Esme Anderson Bequest of Mrs Esme Grace Anderson.	1197 (14-02) £1,368,399	2x808hp MAN D2840LXE	Ramsgate 24.8.1994-
3.	1994 (0107) Green Marine/ Souter Sh Yd	Blue Peter VII Proceeds of BBC TV programme Blue Peter Pieces of Eight Appeal (1993-4).	1198 (14-03) £1,182,622	2x808hp MAN D2840LXE	Fishguard 2.9.1994-
4.	1994 (WO3617) Green Marine/ William Osborne	Roy Barker I Bequest of Frederick Roy Barker, St Lawrence, Jersey, Channel Islands.	1199 (14-04) £1,224,165	2x808hp MAN D2840LXE	Alderney 21.7.1995-
5.	1994 (0108) Green Marine/ Souter Sh Yd	Anna Livia Proceeds of the Dublin Bay Lifeboat Fund, with other gifts and legacies.	1200 (14-05) £1,193,978	2x808hp MAN D2840LXE	Dun Laoghaire 29.6.1995-
6.	199 (MR3778) Green Marine/ Halmatic Ltd	Windsor Runner (Civil Service No.42) Civil Service, Post Office and British Telecom Lifeboat Fund.	1204 (14-06) £1,150,394	2x808hp MAN D2840LXE	Blyth 21.12.1995-16.7.2004 (95/15) Relief 16.7.2004-

One of the first Trents to go on station, Blue Peter VII (ON.1198), arrives at her Fishguard station for the first time in August 1994. She was the first all-weather lifeboat to be funded by the BBC Blue Peter TV programme, which had already funded several inshore lifeboats. (Nicholas Leach)

One of the first batch of 14m Trents to be built, Windsor Runner (Civil Service No.42) (ON.1204), leaves Blyth on exercise, July 1996. She served at Blyth for nine years until being withdrawn and reallocated to the Relief Fleet. (Nicholas Leach)

38 · Trent fast afloat 14m

Year (Yd No) Builder Place	Name Donor	ON (Op No) Cost Weight	Engines	Stations (launches/lives saved)
7. 1994 (WO3618) Green Marine/ William Osborne	Frederick Storey Cockburn Bequest of Frederick Storey Cockburn.	1205 (14-07) £1,103,695	2x808hp MAN D2840LXE	Courtmacsherry Harbour 18.9.1995-
8. 1995 (0109) Green Marine/ Souter Sh Yd	Douglas Aikman Smith Bequest of Mr Aikman Smith, owner of Shortridge Ltd, Dumfries.	1206 (14-08) £1,045,325	2x808hp MAN D2840LXE	Invergordon 4.5.1996-
9. 1995 (WO3614) Green Marine/ William Osborne	Sir Ronald Pechell Bt Bequest of Dora, Lady Pechell, with a local appeal in Dunbar.	1207 (14-09) £1,082,746	2x808hp MAN D2840LXE	Dunbar 17.12.1995-
10. 1995 (0110) Green Marine/ Souter Sh Yd	Samarbeta Volvo Cars UK Limited and legacies from Elizabeth Longman and Constance Rogers.	1208 (14-10) £1,034,005	2x808hp MAN D2840LXE	Great Yarmouth & Gorleston 25.2.1996-
11. 1995 (WO3656) Green Marine/ William Osborne	Barclaycard Crusader Barclaycard Profiles points holders, with other legacies and gifts.	1209 (14-11) £1,096,226	2x808hp MAN D2840LXE	Eyemouth 31.3.1996-
12. 1995 (0111) Green Marine/ Souter Sh Yd	Forward Birmingham Forward Birmingham Lifeboat Campaign, with gifts and legacies.	1210 (14-12) £1,116,298	2x808hp MAN D2840LXE	Exmouth 6.7.1996-
13. 1995 (WO3657) Green Marine/ William Osborne	George and Ivy Swanson Bequest of Mrs Ivy Ethel Swanson, together with various other bequests.	1211 (14-13) £1,149,481	2x808hp MAN D2840LXE	Sheerness 16.3.1996-
14. 1996 (0112) Green Marine/ Souter Sh Yd	George and Mary Webb The Mary Webb Trust.	1212 (14-14) £1,103,008	2x808hp MAN D2840LXE	Whitby 10.4.1996-
15. 1996 (WO3658) Green Marine/ William Osborne	Henry Heys Duckworth Gift of Mrs Lilian Duckworth, in memory of her husband.	1213 (14-15) £1,104,656	2x808hp MAN D2840LXE	Relief 23.2.1996- Barry Dock 23.1-28.7.2006
16. 1996 (0113) Green Marine/ Souter Sh Yd	Stanley Watson Barker Bequest of Stanley Watson Barker, Dagenham, Essex; and other legacies.	1214 (14-16) £1,115,189	2x808hp MAN D2840LXE	Portree 7.6.1996-
17. 1996 (WO3659) Green Marine/ William Osborne	Elizabeth and Ronald Mrs Elizabeth Mary Manners-Clarke.	1215 (14-17) £1,075,285	2x808hp MAN D2840LXE	Dunmore East 7.10.1996-
18. 1997 (0114) Green Marine/ Souter Sh Yd	Maurice and Joyce Hardy Gift and bequest from Maurice Hardy CBE CEng, Twyford, and USA.	1222 (14-18) £970,411	2x808hp MAN D2840LXE	Fowey 10.10.1996-
19. 1997 (WO3690) Green Marine/ William Osborne	Ger Tigchelaar Mr Frits Oppenheim.	1223 (14-19) £1,175,606	2x808hp MAN D2840LXE	Arklow 19.2.1997-
20. 1997 (0115) Green Marine/ Souter Sh Yd	Roy Barker II Bequest of Frederick Roy Barker, St Lawrence, Jersey, Channel Islands.	1224 (14-20) £1,127,664	2x808hp MAN D2840LXE	Wick 13.2.1997-
21. 1997 (WO3691) Green Marine/ William Osborne	MacQuarie Bequest Lt Cdr Hugh MacQuarie Stone MBE RD, bequest of Mrs Mary Noond.	1225 (14-21) £1,127,868	2x808hp MAN D2840LXE	Sunderland 28.3.1997-2.10.2004 (282/16) Relief 10.2004-
22. 1997 (0116) Green Marine/ Souter Sh Yd	Edward Duke of Windsor Bequest of late Duchess of Windsor, and other legacies.	1226 (14-22) £1,580,000	2x808hp MAN D2840LXE	Relief 15.4.1997-
23. 1997 (WO3692) Green Marine/ William Osborne	Mora Edith Macdonald Bequest of Miss Mora Edith Macdonald, Glasgow.	1227 (14-23) £1,200,000	2x808hp MAN D2840LXE	Oban 17.7.1997-

Invergordon's 14m Trent Douglas Aikman Smith *(ON.1206) is put through her paces in the Cromarty Firth. (Nicholas Leach)*

14m Trent George and Ivy Swanson *(ON.1211) from Sheerness provides all-weather lifeboat cover for the Thames Estuary. (Nicholas Leach)*

Relief 14m Trent Henry Heys Duckworth *(ON.1213) on exercise off Gorleston. (Nicholas Leach)*

38 • Trent fast afloat 14m

Year (Yd No) Builder Place	Name Donor	ON (Op No) Cost Weight	Engines	Stations (launches/lives saved)
24. 1997 (0117) Green Marine/ Souter Sh Yd	Dora Foster McDougall Bequest of Mrs Dora Foster McDougall.	1228 (14-24) £1,580,000	2x808hp MAN D2840LXE	Relief 12.10.1997-
25. 1998 (WO3735) Green Marine/ William Osborne	Austin Lidbury Bequest of Miss Mary Lidbury, Dulverton, Somerset.	1233 (14-25) £1,200,000	2x808hp MAN D2840LXE	Ballycotton 5.3.1998-
26. 1998 (WO3736) Green Marine/ William Osborne	The Gough-Ritchie II The Ritchie Charitable Trust.	1234 (14-26) £1,190,000	2x808hp MAN D2840LXE	Port St Mary 21.5.1998-
27. 1999 (WO3764) Green Marine/ William Osborne	Robert Hywel Jones Williams Legacy of Robert Hywel Jones Williams.	1239 (14-27) £1,200,000	2x808hp MAN D2840LXE	Fenit 28.2.1999-
28. 1999 (WO3765) Green Marine/ William Osborne	Sam and Ada Moody Bequest of Ada Moody.	1240 (14-28) £1,200,000	2x808hp MAN D2840LXE	Achill 28.4.1999-
29. 2000 (0138) Green Marine/ Souter Sh Yd	Inner Wheel II Inner Wheel Appeal 1997-2000 together with various legacies.	1245 (14-29) £1,200,000	2x808hp MAN D2840LXE	Relief 3.4.2000-06 Barry Dock 12.9.2006-
30. 2000 (0139) Green Marine/ Souter Sh Yd	Dr John McSparran Bequest of Miss Margaret McSparran, Co Antrim, in memory of her brother.	1246 (14-30) £1,400,000	2x808hp MAN D2840LXE	Larne 3.8.2000-
31. 2001 (0142) Green Marine/ Souter Sh Yd	Elizabeth of Glamis Broughty Ferry Lifeboat Appeal, and legacies of Dr Ian Campbell Low and Dr Ronald Bonar.	1252 (14-31) £1,200,000	2x808hp MAN D2840LXE	Broughty Ferry 14.4.2001-
32. 2001 (0143) Green Marine/ Souter Sh Yd	Corinne Whiteley Legacy of Mrs Corinne Whiteley, Mansfield.	1253 (14-32) £1,200,000	2x808hp MAN D2840LXE	Relief 9.5.2001-
33. 2002 (0148) Green Marine/ Souter Sh Yd	Roy Barker III Bequest of Frederick Roy Barker, St Lawrence, Jersey, Channel Islands.	1258 (14-33) £1,250,000	2x808hp MAN D2840LXE	Howth 16.3.2002-
34. 2002 (0149) Green Marine/ Souter Sh Yd	Willie and May Gall Bequest of Mrs May Crombie Gall.	1259 (14-34) £1,240,452	2x808hp MAN D2840LXE	Fraserburgh 8.5.2002-
35. 2003 (0154) Green Marine/ Souter Sh Yd	John Neville Taylor Bequest of John Neville Taylor, Westcliffe-on-Sea, Essex	1266 (14-35) £1,300,000	2x808hp MAN D2840LXE	Relief 17.11.2002-
36. 2003 (0155) Green Marine/ Souter Sh Yd	Saxon Bequest of Mrs Freda Berwyn Rivers, London, in memory of her husband.	1267 (14-36) £1,300,000	2x808hp MAN D2840LXE	Donaghadee 17.4.2003-
37. 2004 (0158) Green Marine/ Souter Sh Yd	Betty Huntbatch Bequest of Mrs Betty Huntbatch, Brentwood, Essex.	1274 (14-37) £1,300,000	2x808hp MAN D2840LXE	Relief 9.2003-9.04 Hartlepool 27.9.2004-
38. 2004 (0159) Green Marine/ Souter Sh Yd	Jim Moffat The Moffat Charitable Trust and Lifeboats of the Clyde Appeal.	1275 (14-38) £1,300,000	2x808hp MAN D2840LXE	Troon 25.2.2004-

Note: the figures for cost are approximations.

Relief lifeboat Inner Wheel II *(ON.1245) on exercise off Fenit in 2005. She was taken out of the Relief Fleet the following year to become station lifeboat at Barry Dock. (Nicholas Leach)*

Broughty Ferry Trent Elizabeth of Glamis *(ON.1252) at moorings in the river Tay. The berth in which she lies was specially constructed to improve boarding arrangements at the station. (Nicholas Leach)*

The last 14m Trent to go on station, Jim Moffat *(ON.1275), arrives at Troon for the first time, February 2004. (Nicholas Leach)*

39 • Tamar fast slipway 16m

Introduced 2005, in production.
Specifications • length 16m (45ft 11in), breadth 5m (14ft 10in), draught 1.35m (4ft 3in), weight 31.5 tonnes, crew 6, endurance 10 hours at 25 knots, twin 1,000hp turbo-charged diesels driving twin fixed-pitch five-bladed propellers, 4,300 litres fuel carried.

The Tamar class, developed as FSB2 (Fast Slipway Boat 2), was designed to replace the eighteen-knot Tyne (FSB1) class lifeboats in service with the RNLI since the 1980s. The RNLI's technical department began work on the concept design in 1996 and carried out many months of model testing using DERA's test tanks in Gosport with the main aim to build a lifeboat, capable of being slipway launched, that could achieve speeds up to twenty-five knots. After testing many models for manoeuvring and sea-keeping abilities the RNLI selected one on which to base the hull form of FSB2. The FSB2 programme then went out to competitive tender, resulting in a four-phase contract being placed with Plymouth-based Devonport Management Limited (DML).

The first phase of the programme was the development of the experimental boat. Having been fitted out, this boat was launched in September 2001 and used on extensive evaluation trials which resulted in this experimental boat being converted into a fully-fledged prototype lifeboat. The prototype was evaluated by operations staff, after which a second vessel was ordered. This pre-production boat was used to resolve problems in the build processes to ensure the minimum of changes during the construction of the station boats. The FSB2 had a flat rather than raked keel to enable it to be slipway launched. The propellers were raised up and, as the engines were to be started in the boathouse and be run dry for some time, particular attention was paid to engine exhaust cooling and lubrication. The propellers and rudders were protected by a central keel and smaller side keels, which support the boat on the slipway, and enable stern-first recovery.

Construction of the Tamar involved similar methods to both the Trent and Severn classes. DML employed the composite boat build-ing company Green Marine of Lymington, builder of Trent and Severn hulls, to manufacture the hull and deck structure for FSB2. With weight an important issue, the best material for the hull construction was fibre reinforced plastic (FRP), made up of a single skin, longitudinally-stiffened bottom and a sandwich construction topsides similar to the construction used for the Trents and Severns. The rest deck, bulkheads and superstructure

The prototype Tamar ON.1251 at St Peter Port in 2003, participating in the celebrations marking the station's bicentenary. (Nicholas Leach)

Self-righting trials of the first Tamar lifeboat Peter and Lesley-Jane Nicholson *(ON.1280) at DML, November 2004. (RNLI)*

were made of FRP sandwich construction. Composite hulls provide great strength yet are relatively lightweight structures, and the RNLI had undertaken much research and development work in the use of advanced composites.

The Tamar was powered by twin 1,015bhp (746bkW) Cat C18 marine diesel engines, which fitted into the hull with a sufficient power-to-weight performance to reach the intended speed. The in-line, six-cylinder, eighteen-litre engine provided good acceleration and fuel economy as well as low emissions.

A considerable amount of new technology was incorporated into the Tamar design. The boat was controlled using fly-by-wire technology with a joystick replacing the wheel. Mechanical back-up was provided in the event of system failure. An innovative systems and information management system (SIMS) was fitted to integrate electronic systems such as navigation, communications, engine management and radar, displaying details on flat screens. From an operational point of view, the crew obtained information from one screen, enabling most of the lifeboat's functions to be managed remotely reducing the need for crew to move around the boat while underway, lessening the chance of accidents. Using SIMS also allows better task-sharing between crew members, as the various functions required to operate the lifeboat can be accessed via screens at any of the six crew positions. A new seat design was introduced that reduced loadings on crew members' spines in rough weather. The two control stations were also considerably higher to enable better visibility or 'height of eye' than on a Tyne, particularly useful when searching for a casualty in the water.

Naming ceremony of the first Tamar lifeboat to go on station, Haydn Miller *(ON.1281) at Tenby's harbour, June 2006. (RNLI)*

39 • Tamar fast slipway 16m

	Year (Yd No) Builder Place	Name Donor	ON (Op No) Cost Weight	Engines	Stations (launches/lives saved)	Notes Disposal
1.	2000 (050) Green Marine/ DML Devonport	[Un-named]	1251	2x1,015bhp Caterpillar C18 6-cylinder	Trials 2000-04	Rebuilt 2003 Sold 2007
2.	2005 (062) Green Marine/ DML Devonport	Peter and Lesley-Jane Nicholson RNLI funds.	1280 (16-01)	2x1,015bhp Caterpillar C18 6-cylinder	Relief 7.12.2005-	
3.	2005 (063) Green Marine/ DML Devonport	Haydn Miller Bequest of Haydn Gustav Miller.	1281 (16-02)	2x1,015bhp Caterpillar C18 6-cylinder	Tenby 28.4.2006-	
4.	2006 (064) Green Marine/ DML Devonport	The Misses Robertson of Kintail Gift from The Robertson Trust, Glasgow.	1282 (16-03)	2x1,015bhp Caterpillar C18 6-cylinder	Peterhead 29.4.2006-	
5.	2006 (065) Green Marine/ DML Devonport	Spirit of Padstow Gift of the late Mrs Mickie Allen.	1283 (16-04) £2,500,000	2x1,015bhp Caterpillar C18 6-cylinder	Padstow 17.7.2006-	
6.	2006 (066) Green Marine/ DML Devonport	Helen Comrie Legacy of Thomas L. M. Comrie.	1284 (16-05) £2,500,000	2x1,015bhp Caterpillar C18 6-cylinder	Longhope 26.10.2006-	
7.	2007 Green Marine/ DML Devonport	Frank and Anne Wilkinson Bequest of the late Mrs Anne Mary Elizabeth Wilkinson, Huddersfield.	1286 (16-06) £2,500,000	2x1,015bhp Caterpillar C18 6-cylinder	Relief 4.2007-	
8.	2007 (068) Green Marine/ DML Devonport	Lester Bequest of Mr Derek Clifton Lethern, Southfields, London.	1287 (16-07)	2x1,015bhp Caterpillar C18 6-cylinder	Cromer	
9.	2007 (069) Green Marine/ DML Devonport	Grace Dixen	1288 (16-08)	2x1,015bhp Caterpillar C18 6-cylinder	Barrow	
10.	2008 (070) Green Marine/ DML Devonport	Baltic Exchange III	1289 (16-09)	2x1,015bhp Caterpillar C18 6-cylinder	Salcombe	
11.	2008 (071) Green Marine/ DML Devonport		1290 (16-10)	2x1,015bhp Caterpillar C18 6-cylinder	Angle	
12.	2008 (072) Green Marine/ DML Devonport		1291 (16-11)	2x1,015bhp Caterpillar C18 6-cylinder		

First launch down the newly-built slipway at Trevose Head for Padstow's 16m Tamar lifeboat Spirit of Padstow (ON.1283) on 3 July 2006, the day she arrived on station, with 47ft Tyne James Burrough behind. (Nicholas Leach)

Helen Comrie (ON.1284) on exercise off Longhope, where she operates from a specially-built mooring. The staton, situated on the island of Hoy, is one of three in Orkney and covers the treacherous Pentland Firth. (Nicholas Leach)

A class rigid-hulled inshore lifeboats

During the 1960s, the RNLI was examining various ways of improving the effectiveness of the inflatable inshore lifeboat (ILB), introduced during the early years of the decade and now well established. A number of designs for rigid-hulled ILBs were looked at, starting with the experimental Hatch boat designed by George Hatch, AMRINA, an RNLI senior draughtsman. The boat was built in wood by William Osborne Ltd at Littlehampton and was displayed at the International Boat Show at Earls Court in January 1967. The new craft was intended to serve a dual purpose, operating as both a boarding boat, to take lifeboat crews from the shore to lifeboats at moorings, and as a rescue boat. Experience had shown that boarding boats were quite often needed for rescues when speed was essential, and the Hatch boat, faster than any other lifeboat then in service, fulfilled this need.

The boat's hull form was similar to that of offshore power boats, with a moderately high freeboard and a flared bow. In calm water, speeds of up to twenty-six knots could be achieved. The boat measured 20ft 6in overall with a beam of 6ft 11in and a depth of 3ft 3in. The boat had wide flush decks fore and aft, handrails and lifelines at the deck edge and a propeller guard, while the hull was divided by bulkheads to give four watertight compartments with a large open cockpit for crew and survivors enabling at least eight people to be taken comfortably on board. Foamed polystyrene blocks were built into the hull throughout to give positive buoyancy. An inboard engine with outboard drive was chosen to utilise the advantages of outboard drives without the vulnerability of an outboard engine. The prototype was fitted with a Volvo Penta AQ110/100 petrol unit rated at 110bhp and was normally operated by two crew.

Only two wooden Hatch boats were completed as, during 1968, while the boat was being trialled, the RNLI commissioned another design of fast rigid-hulled boat for inshore rescue. Designed by J. A. McLachlan, MRINA, the first of the class was ordered in September 1969. The McLachlan was 18ft 6in overall, 16ft 4in at the waterline and had a beam of 8ft 3in. The design incorporated several notable features, including a ragged chine hull and seawater ballast stability tanks. The ragged chines were a series of steps which effectively

The prototype Hatch boat 18-01 on trials in the mid-1960s. She was subsequently renumbered A-1 and then based at Plymouth for much of her operational career. (RNLI)

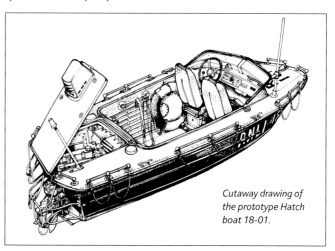

Cutaway drawing of the prototype Hatch boat 18-01.

reduced the hull surface in contact with the water and thus minimised the pounding found with normal hard-chine boats. Nine chines extended the full length of the hull, each inclined at an angle to the water to cushion the underside and deflect spray. The hull was divided into watertight compartments filled with polyurethane foam with three water stability ballast tanks, forward, centre and aft, fitted.

The steering and engine controls were positioned amidships in

---

A-1 (ex 18-01)   1966/20'6" x 7'3" Hatch
Displayed at St Malo, France, during International LB Conference, 5-9.6.1967.
Falmouth 1967-67, Shoreham 1967-67, Plymouth 7.1968-5.72

A-2 (ex 18-03)   1966/20'6" x 7'3" Hatch
Poole 1967-69, Torbay 7.1969-10.74

A-500 (ex 17-01)   1968/17'1" x 7' Dell Quay Dory
Eastney 8.1968-6.69, Ramsgate 7.1969-12.71, Poole 2.1972-12.73

A-501 Bob Abbott (ex 17-02)   1969/17'1" x 7' Dell Quay Dory
Named Bob Abbott while at Lyme Regis, in memory of Coxswain Robert W. Abbott.
Lyme Regis 6.1969-9.73, Poole 7.1974-5.75

A-502 (ex 17-003)   1969/17'1" x 7' Dell Quay Dory
Poole 6.1969-2.72, Ramsgate 2.1972-5.75, Poole 8.1975-1.85

A-503 (ex 18-02)   1967/20'6" x 8' McLachlan
Eastney 7.1967-7.70, Pill 7.1971-10.72

A-504 (ex 18-004)   1970/18'6" x 8' McLachlan
Weston-super-Mare 5.1970-12.83

A-505 (ex 18-005)   1970/18'6" x 8' McLachlan
Eastney 7.1970-9.71, Oban 5.1972-5.73, Eastney 12.1974-10.75, Humber (used as
Boarding Boat) 1977-87

A-506   1971/18'6" x 8' McLachlan
Relief 10.1972-6.76, Peel 5.1972-10.72, Poole 12.1976-8.79, Plymouth 8.1979-8.80

A-507   1971/18'6" x 8' McLachlan
Weston-super-Mare 12.1972-2.73, Peel 5.1973-8.75; Relief 8.1975-7.76, Plymouth
8.1976-10.83, Peel 7.1976-8.76

A-508   1971/18'6" x 8' McLachlan
Eastney 9.1971-12.74, Invergordon 7.1976-11.79, Falmouth 4.1980-1.88

A-509   1972/18'6" x 8' McLachlan
Plymouth 5.1972-10.76, Relief 1978-88, Brighton 5.1978-7.78, sold 1988

A-510   1973/18'6" x 8' McLachlan
Pill 3.1973-10.74, Ramsgate 6.1975-8.84, Humber (Boarding Boat) 6.1986-1.87

A-511   1973/18'6" x 8' McLachlan
Oban 6.1974-82, Relief 4.1984-9.85, Sold 9.1985

A-512   1974/18'6" x 8' McLachlan
Torbay 3.1975-6.87, Falmouth 1-5.1988, scrapped at Grimsby 5.1988

A-513 Sam and Iris Coles   1984/20' x 7'2" Boston Whaler
Funded by Mayor of Poole Charity Year and a local appeal.
Poole 1.1985-12.94, capsized on service 23 November 1986, removed from station
for repair, returned 10.6.1988.

A class rigid-hulled inshore lifeboats

a semi-enclosed, streamlined bridge structure which housed the wheel, compass, engine throttles and radio equipment. Draining was achieved by standard RNLI-pattern side scuppers. The high foredeck provided reasonable protection for at least eight survivors, whilst the crew of two were sheltered by the midships structure with its own breakwater and wind deflector. Twin 60hp inboard petrol engines with outboard drives were mounted in watertight engine compartments in the stern to give a speed of twenty-two knots. In later boats, stern drive diesel engines were installed in place of the petrol versions.

The first McLachlan, 18-02, was 20ft 6in long with a beam of 8ft and an overall depth of 7ft 3in, and was built of mahogany by W. A. Souter at Cowes. She was wooden-hulled and used for trials at a number of stations. In September 1969, the RNLI ordered further McLachlans with GRP hulls from William Osborne and fitted with twin 90bhp Evinrude inboard diesel engines coupled to outboard drives. The wooden prototype was used as the plug for the mould used for the GRP-hulled boats.

As well as the McLachlan, the RNLI also tested out a commercially designed rigid-hulled boat manufactured by Dell Quay and known as a Dory. The Dory was built of glass reinforced plastic (GRP) with the cavity between hull and deck filled under pressure by rigid polyurethane foam. The hull, strengthened to take the aluminium-built steering console, had two eighteen-gallon petrol tanks incorporated into the base with a locker above to store equipment.

Two 36hp Penta outboard engines were fitted to give a top speed of twenty-five knots. The draft with engines in use was eighteen inches and only eight inches with the engines raised.

Although only a handful of McLachlans and Dell Quay Dorys were built, they gave good service during the 1970s and 80s. At Poole, in Dorset, where the large natural harbour is part of the local lifeboat station's 'patch', the Dell Quay Dory, with its small draft, was particularly suitable to cover what is a unique area. As a result, when a new ILB was needed for the station in the 1980s, the Poole crew requested another Dory. However, as Dell Quay had gone out of business, a standard American-built Boston Whaler Outrage was acquired and fitted out as a lifeboat by the RNLI's Cowes Base to meet the unique requirements of Poole Harbour. The console and roll bar were designed to allow the boat to pass under the bridges, even at high water.

Although the Boston Whaler was a one-off, many components standard to the Atlantic 21 were incorporated in the fit-out. A towing bollard was fitted aft and the boat was equipped to operate day and night in moderate sea conditions. With an overall length of 20ft (6m), a maximum beam of 7ft 2in (2.2m) and a maximum draft (at rest) of just 2ft (0.6m), the boat was ideally suited to work in Poole harbour. Power was provided by twin 60hp Evinrude outboard motors giving a maximum speed of 30 knots. The fuel capacity of 50 gallons gave an endurance at full speed of 5.8 hours, and the boat was operated by three crew.

Dell Quay Dory 17-01, during trials, was later numbered A-500. The design proved to be particularly suitable for use at some stations. (Builder's photo)

The 18ft 6in McLachlan design as exemplified by 18-005, pictured on builder's trials. She was later renumbered A-505. (Builder's photo)

The 18ft 6in McLachlan A-512 at Torbay. She was not fitted with the steering console like the other McLachlan lifeboats.

The unique 20ft Boston Whaler Outrage lifeboat A-513 Sam and Iris Coles at Poole. (John Buckby)

B class rigid-inflatable inshore lifeboats

**Specifications • Atlantic 21: 22ft 9in x 7ft 6in, hull 19ft 4in;
Atlantic 75: 24ft x 8ft 8in; Atlantic 85: 8.3m x 2.8m.**

The Atlantic rigid-inflatable inshore lifeboat is one of the most successful designs of lifeboat ever produced in the British Isles. The type has been modified, enlarged and improved over more than three decades to become an extremely efficient and effective rescue tool, whilst being the fastest lifeboat in service with the RNLI since its inception in the late 1960s.

The Atlantic was developed during the 1960s after the introduction of the 16ft inflatable inshore lifeboat had proved to be a great success. However, while effective for daylight operation in moderate conditions, the 16ft inflatable had its limitations and a more sophisticated and capable inshore lifeboat type was needed which could operate in worse weather and at night. The RNLI experimented with the ILB during the 1960s but eventually chose one developed by Rear Admiral Desmond John Hoare at Atlantic College, based at St Donat's Castle in South Wales.

Admiral Hoare, who died in 1988, developed the new design after being dissatisfied with the standard ILB supplied by the RNLI which was not well suited to the short, steep seas of the Bristol Channel, where strong currents and a massive tidal rise and fall meant a really fast and manoeuvrable boat was needed. Under his guidance, a series of experimental boats were built which incorporated a rigid floor and deep-vee hull. The sides and bow were enclosed within a continuous buoyancy tube divided into airtight compartments while the transom, which supported the twin outboard engines, was open to allow any water shipped to escape. The rigid hull supported the weight of the boat and, without the inflatable sponsons in contact with the water, gave the boat greater sea-keeping and a speed of over thirty knots could be achieved. The sponsons gave the boat great stability while the upper surface of the rigid hull formed the floor of the boat.

The first experimental boat went to Gorleston for trials and another, with a longer and modified hull, went to Lyme Regis. The new design was further refined and developed with modifications resulting in the construction of B-1, B-2 and B-3 and these boats were adopted by the RNLI and classified as the Atlantic 21. The rigid hulls were originally built of plywood and subdivided into watertight compartments, but when full-scale production began they were moulded from glass reinforced plastic (GRP) by Halmatic of Havant. The GRP hulls were taken to Cowes where the sponson was secured to the hull and the boat fitted out by RNLI staff.

The RNLI's designers added a self-righting capability to the original boat. The engines were inversion-proofed to enable them to restart after a capsize, using a method devised by the RNLI with an inflatable air bag mounted flat on a rollbar above the engines at the stern. Should the boat be capsized, a crew member activates a gas bottle which inflates the bag and rights the boat in a few seconds. The three crew sit on the delta-shaped console in the centre of the lifeboat, the helmsman steering with one hand on the wheel while adjusting the throttles with the other hand.

The first boat of the new design went on station at Hartlepool in 1972 and the advantages of the design soon became apparent as an increasing number of stations operated them. During the 1970s and 1980s, as the pattern of casualties continued to change and faster lifeboats were required at more stations, many of the smaller offshore lifeboats were replaced by Atlantics, including at places such as Newbiggin, Clacton, Youghal, Redcar, Kirkcudbright

B-504 at Littlehampton. She was one of the very earliest Atlantic 21s to enter service, and this photo shows her in her original configuration with no roll bar at the stern and seating for three in line rather than in a triangle pattern as became standard on both the Atlantic 21 and 75. (Jeff Morris)

and Sheringham. During their first two decades of service, Atlantic 21s launched over 15,000 times, saving nearly 5,000 lives.

In the early 1990s, the boat was further improved with the development of a larger version, designated the Atlantic 75, at the RNLI's Inshore Lifeboat Centre (ILC) at Cowes. The 75 was 38cm longer overall and 20cm broader than the Atlantic 21, and her name was derived from the length of nearly 7.5m. Twin 70hp outboard motors gave a maximum speed of thirty-two knots, making her the fastest lifeboat in the RNLI fleet. The hull design was revised so that she gave a softer ride than her predecessor for the three-man crew and survivors. The hulls were built of GRP at Souters Shipyard in West Cowes, and fitted out at the ILC, while the crew seating arrangements and self-righting roll bar remained much the same as on the 21, albeit slightly enlarged.

In total, ninety-six Atlantic 21s and ninety-seven Atlantic 75s were built by the RNLI, although not all entered service in the UK with some going to foreign lifeboat societies. Production of the Atlantic 75 ended in 2003, by when the RNLI was developing its replacement, the Fast Inshore Boat 1, a larger and faster rigid-inflatable with seating for four and space for more equipment. The RNLI developed and tested the new version of the Atlantic rigid-inflatable during 2004-5, and towards the end of 2005 the first of the new type, designated the Atlantic 85, was ready for service. The Atlantic 85 which, at 8.3m in length, is almost a metre larger than the Atlantic 75 and considerably larger than the original Atlantic 21, has seating for four crew members as well as room for more equipment. Powered by twin 115hp Yamaha four-stroke engines and built from foam-cored carbon composite, it has a top speed of thirty-five knots and is equipped with radar for operations in poor visibility. At every stage of the project, experienced Atlantic helmsmen were involved while crew members from every Atlantic lifeboat station played a part in testing the new boat.

A mark of the success of the rigid-inflatable design, upon which the Atlantic is based, is its use by a number of overseas lifeboat societies. Many organisations have bought them second-hand from the RNLI, while in the Netherlands rigid-inflatables are used extensively in a wide variety of sea conditions. The design has also been used in the commercial small boat world and a plethora of derivatives is available to the private or commercial buyer, all of them with rigid hull, inflatable sponsons and outboard motors.

B class rigid-inflatable inshore lifeboats

Atlantic 21 B-523 Blue Peter I *at Littlehampton. The Blue Peter television programme has consistently raised money to buy lifeboats, and Littlehampton was the first beneficiary of this fund-raising drive. No fewer than six other lifeboat stations have inshore lifeboats funded by viewers of the programme. (Supplied by Paul Russell)*

Atlantic 21 B-549 Blenwatch *at Porthcawl. Built originally for New Brighton, this Atlantic replaced a D class inflatable at Porthcawl and was one of only a small number of Atlantics to be fitted with a windscreen which provided a limited degree of protection for helmsman and crew. (Nicholas Leach)*

Atlantic 21 B-554 American Ambassador *at Atlantic College, the place where the design originated in the 1960s. The College takes students from more than 70 countries in the world and as part of their education they undertake a service to the community, which includes the opportunity to crew and operate the inshore lifeboat. Many crew members from Atlantic College are of international origin thereby making the station unique within the British Isles. (RNLI)*

B class rigid-inflatable inshore lifeboats

B-500	1970/Atlantic 21 Mk.I

Royal Navy; Lyme Regis 1970; Mudeford 1970; Hartlepool 1970; Appledore 1972-73; Largs 7.1972-72; Relief 1973-77; Littlehampton 5.1973-73; Hartlepool 10.1973-73

B-501	1970/Atlantic 21 Mk.I

Relief 1970 77; Lyme Regis 1973-73

B-502	1971/Atlantic 21 Mk.I

Trials 1970-72

B-503	1971/Atlantic 21 Mk.I

Hartlepool 4.1972-9.75

B-504 Blue Peter I (1972-3)	1971/Atlantic 21 Mk.I

Littlehampton 6.1972-7.73; Hartlepool 1973; Relief 1974-81

B-505 Major Osman Gabriel	1972/Atlantic 21 Mk.I

Queensferry 9.1972-10.75; Relief 1975-82; Silloth 1979-80; Atlantic College 1980-82

B-506	1971/Atlantic 21 Mk.I

West Mersea 10.1972-2.76; Relief 1973-84; Staithes & Runswick 3.1978-4.78

B-507	1971/Atlantic 21 Mk.I

KZHMRS (South Holland)

B-508	1973/Atlantic 21 Mk.I

Atlantic College 7.1973-80

B-509	1973/Atlantic 21 Mk.II

New Brighton 5.1973-81; Relief 1981-85

B-510	1973/Atlantic 21 Mk.II

KZHMRS (South Holland)

B-511 Co-Operative No.1	1973/Atlantic 21 Mk.II

Co-operative Women's Guild.

Largs 8.1973-9.73; Hayling Island 3.1975-10.79; Newbiggin 3.1980-81; Hunstanton 3.1982-12.82; Relief 1983-85; Clacton-on-Sea 1985-89; Relief 1989-97

B-512 US Navy League (named 1987)	1973/Atlantic 21 Mk.II

Appropriated to the American British Lifeboat Appeal in 1987.

Lyme Regis 9.1973-7.80; Relief 1980-90; Walmer 1990-5.92; Relief 1992-94; Bundoran 5.1994-5.95; Relief 1995-97; Weymouth 1997-98; Relief 1998-99; Clifden 1998-98; Sligo Bay 1999-2001

B-513 William McCunn & Broom Church Youth Fellowship	1973/Atlantic 21 Mk.II

William McCunn Trust and Broom Church Youth Fellowship.

Largs 9.1973-6.80; Relief 1980-88; Bangor 3.1988-11.90; Relief 1990-98

B-514 Guide Friendship I	1973/Atlantic 21 Mk.II

Girl Guides Friendship Fund.

Aberdovey 4.1974-83; Relief 1983-2000; Clacton-on-Sea 8.1984-85; Redcar 3.1986-87; Cullercoats 4.1991-10.92; Relief 1992-2000; sold 13.11.2000 to ICE-SAR Iceland

B-515 Blue Peter II/1990- Vee Webber	1973/Atlantic 21 Mk.II

Blue Peter TV Appeal.

Beaumaris 4.1976-8.85; Relief 1985-2000; Port Erin 7.1992-3.93; Flamborough 8.1993-94; Penarth 1.1996-5.96; sold 13.11.2000 to ICE-SAR Iceland

B-516 Whitstable Branch	1973/Atlantic 21 Mk.II

Kensington & Whitstable Branches.

Whitstable 6.1974-83; Relief 1983-90

B-517 Blue Peter I	1973/Atlantic 21 Mk.II

Blue Peter TV Appeal.

Littlehampton 7.1973-8.74

B-518 Sole Bay	1973/Atlantic 21 Mk.II

Anonymous gift.

Southwold 8.1973-1.85; Relief 1985-90; Falmouth 1987-11.88

B-519 Surrey Forester	1973/Atlantic 21 Mk.II

Surrey United District & Ancient Order of Foresters Society.

Lymington 8.1973-6.86; Relief 1986-90

B-520 Wildenrath Wizzer	1973/Atlantic 21 Mk.II

RAF Wildenrath, West Germany.

Appledore 1974-86; Redcar 1987-90; Relief 1990-93

B-521 Mary Livingstone	1973/Atlantic 21 Mk.II

Legacy of Mrs Mary Livingstone Sandys.

Queensferry 10.1975-81; Relief 1981-94

B-522	1973/Atlantic 21 Mk.II

KZHMRS (South Holland)

B-523 Blue Peter I	1974/Atlantic 21 Mk.II

Blue Peter TV Appeal.

Littlehampton 11.1974-9.85; Relief 1985-88; Training 10.1988-9.98

B-524	1974/Atlantic 21 Mk.II

Royal Navy

B-525 Spix's Macaw (named 1991)	1974/ Atlantic 21 Mk.II

Mr J. Anstey.

Blackpool 1975; Relief 1975-2002; Hayling Island 10.1979-11.80; Kirkcudbright 7.1988-91; Relief 1991-98; Weymouth 1998; Sligo Bay 1999; Enniskillen 2002-

B-526	1974/Atlantic 21 Mk.II

Lady D. E. G. Hunt.

Relief 1974-78; Harwich 3.1978-10.87; Relief 1987-2002; Kilkeel 1993; Hayling Island 1.1995-6.95; Clacton-on-Sea 1997-10.98; ILB Centre, Cowes 2002-04

B-527 Percy Garon	1974/Atlantic 21 Mk.II

Civil Service and Post Office Lifeboat Fund.

Southend-on-Sea 5.1976-86; Relief 1986-98; Red Bay 6.1996-9.96; Arran (Lamlash) 1.1998-12.98; sold 1998 to Finland LBS

B-528	1974/Atlantic 21 Mk.II

Relief 1974-2000; Blackpool 1976-78; Hunstanton 1982; Helvick Head 1998

B-529 Alexander Duckham	1974/Atlantic 21 Mk.II

Alexander Duckham & Co Ltd.

West Mersea 2.1976-87; Mudeford 4.1988-90; Falmouth 10.1991-93; Relief 1993-96

B-530 Guide Friendship II	1975/Atlantic 21 Mk.II

Girl Guides Friendship Fund.

Portsmouth (Langstone) 7.1975-4.81; Relief 4.1981-85; Macduff 8.1985-8.89; Relief 8.1989-11.93; scrapped 11.1993

B-531 Waveney Forester	1975/Atlantic 21 Mk.II

Court Waveney, Independent Order of Foresters Friendly Society St Peters Huntingdon, and legacies of Mr A. R. Godwin and Mrs Ethel Burton.

Gt Yarmouth & Gorleston 7.1975-11.88; Relief 1988-93; Criccieth 12.1993-6.94; Lough Swilly (Buncrana) 3.1995-10.95; Relief 1996-98; Galway 3.1996-10.96; Relief 1998-2001; Clovelly 3.1998-98; sold 23.5.2002 to Poole Harbour Commissioners

B-532 Guide Friendship III	1975/Atlantic 21 Mk.II

Girl Guides Friendship Fund.

Hartlepool 1.1976-9.86; Relief 1986-98; sold 6.1998 to Finland LBS

B-533	1976/Atlantic 21 Mk.II

St Martin's School, Walton-on-Thames.

Littlestone-on-Sea 8.1976-88; Relief 1988-90; Teignmouth 1990-91; Kilkeel 9.1992-93; Relief 1993-95; Kinghorn 6.1995-12.95; Galway 1996-10.96; sold 5.1998

B-534	1976/Atlantic 21 Mk.II

MOD (Army) Benbecula

B-535 R. A. O. B.	1976/Atlantic 21 Mk.II

Royal Antediluvian Order of Buffaloes.

Hartlepool 10.1975-6.76; Berwick 8.1976-12.92; Relief 9.1993-4.95; Kyle of Lochalsh 4.1995-8.97; sold 1999 to Ballybunion Sea & Cliff Rescue

B-536	1976/Atlantic 21 Mk.II

Peel 8.1976-89; Relief 1989-92; Sheringham 4.1992-93; Relief 1994-99; Helvick Head 2-7.1997; sold 9.1999 to Dorset Police

B-537	1976/Atlantic 21 Mk.II

Relief 1976-78; Blackpool 7.1978-6.79; Relief 1979-84; Youghal 1983-5.84; St Abbs 4.1986-88; Relief 1988-99

B class rigid-inflatable inshore lifeboats

B-538 Lord Bortherton   1976/Atlantic 21 Mk.II

Legacies of Mrs D. U. McGrigor Phillips and Mr R. K. Talbot, and Special Appeal to people of Leeds.

Staithes & Runswick 4.1978-5.89; Relief 1989-90; Teignmouth 11.1990

B-539 Lions International - District 105SE   1977/Atlantic 21 Mk.II

Mr G. A. Hodgkins, and funds raised by Lions International.

Brighton 8.1978-89; Relief 1989-98; St Catherine 10.1990-91; Sheringham 1993-94; Newquay 2.1995-8.95; sold 15.5.1998

B-540 Wolverhampton   1978/Atlantic 21 Mk.II

Wolverhampton Lifeboat Appeal.

Abersoch 3.1978-90; Relief 1990-2000; Trearddur Bay 5.1996-12.96; sold 13.11.2000 to ICE-SAR Iceland

B-541 Elizabeth Bestwick   1976/Atlantic 21 Mk.II

Bequest of Miss Edith A. Bestwick.

Relief 1976-88; Falmouth 11.1988-10.91; Berwick 12.1992-2.93; Falmouth 2.1993-3.94; Hayling Island 10.1994-1.95; Weymouth 6.1995-6.96; sold 1997 to Southern Professional Training

B-542 William Yeo   1976/Atlantic 21 Mk.II

The Family of William Yeo.

Relief 1976-87; ILB Centre, Cowes 1987-2004

B-543 Round Table   1978/Atlantic 21 Mk.II

National Association of Round Tables, Great Britain and Ireland.

Helensburgh 10.1978-90; Relief 1990-96; Weymouth 1996-97; Skerries 11.1997-6.98; Relief 6.1998-99; Clovelly 1998-10.99; Training 1999-2003

B-544 Catherine Plumbley   1979/Atlantic 21 Mk.II

Legacy of Mr R. H. Mabbs.

Minehead 7.1979-11.94; St Bees 6.1995-12.95; Relief 1996-98; Weymouth 1996; sold 7.1998 to ICE-SAR Iceland

B-545 Amelia Gregory-Armstrong   1979/Atlantic 21 Mk.II

Legacy of Mrs M. E. A. Gregory-Armstrong.

Silloth 1980-7.95; Relief 1995-98

B-546 Independent Forester Benevolence   1980/Atlantic 21 Mk.II

Independent Order of Foresters.

Lyme Regis 6.1980-9.97; Relief 1997-98; sold 1998 to Portugal

B-547 Independent Forester Liberty   1980/Atlantic 21 Mk.II

The Independent Order of Foresters.

Largs 6.1980-3.98; Relief 1998-99; sold 1999 to ICE-SAR Iceland

B-548 Aldershot   1980/Atlantic 21 Mk.II

Aldershot Branch Appeal and legacy of Doris Chartres.

Hayling Island 11.1980-10.94; Poole 11.1994-4.95; Relief 1996-98; Rye Harbour 1.1996-7.96; sold 1998 to Finland LBS

B-549 Blenwatch   1981/Atlantic 21 Mk.II

Fred Olsen Line.

New Brighton 3.1981-2.96; Relief 7.1996-9.97; Porthcawl 2.1996-7.96; Tighnabruaich 9.1997-4.98; Relief 4.1998-2001; Enniskillen 5.2001-6.03

B-550 City of Portsmouth   1981/Atlantic 21 Mk.II

Lord Mayor of Portsmouth Special Appeal.

Portsmouth (Langstone) 1981-11.96; Relief 1996-98; sold 1998 to Finland LBS

B-551 Constance MacNay   1981/Atlantic 21 Mk.II

Gift of Major R. F. MacNay.

Queensferry 1981-5.97; Relief 1997-98; Clifden 1998-99; sold 1998 to Finland LBS

B-552   1981/Atlantic 21 Mk.II

KZHMRS (South Holland) 1981-

B-553 Kirklees   1982/Atlantic 21 Mk.II

Kirklees Lifeboat Appeal.

Newbiggin 12.1981-8.98; Helvick Head 9.1998-99; sold 1999 to Sandown Inshore Rescue

B-554 American Ambassador   1982/Atlantic 21 Mk.II

American-British Lifeboat Appeal.

Atlantic College 10.1982-3.2000; Relief 2000-01; sold 6.2002 to Australia

B-555 Long Life I   1982/Atlantic 21 Mk.II

Allied Breweries Long Life Beer Promotion.

Relief 1983-99; Macduff 1985; Portaferry 1986; Falmouth 1993; St Bees 4.1995-6.95; Kilrush 4.1996-96

B-556 Spirit of America   1982/Atlantic 21 Mk.II

American-British Lifeboat Appeal.

Hunstanton 12.1982-9.98; Relief 1998-99

B-557 Weston Centenary   1983/Atlantic 21 Mk.II

Weston Branch Centenary Appeal.

Weston-super-Mare 5.1983-1.2001; sold 27.05.2002 to Finland LBS

B-558 Ramsgate Enterprise   1984/Atlantic 21 Mk.II

Ramsgate Station Branch Appeal.

Ramsgate 9.1984-7.2000; Relief 2000-01; sold 5.2.2002 to Bantry Inshore SAR

B-559 Long Life III   1983/Atlantic 21 Mk.II

Allied Breweries Long Life Beer Promotion, with the legacy of Mrs D. M. Kempton.

Aberdovey 11.1983-9.99; sold 1999 to British Virgin Islands Search & Rescue

B-560 British Diver   1983/Atlantic 21 Mk.II

British Sub Aqua Club.

Whitstable 7.1983-7.2000; sold 12.2000 to Finland LBS

B-561 Marjory Turner   1984/Atlantic 21 Mk.II

Gift of the late Mr Vincent Scott Turner in memory of his wife.

Youghal 5.1984-2.2002; sold 27.05.2002 to Finland LBS

Atlantic 21 B-513 William McCunn & Broom Church Youth Fellowship at Bangor. (Colin Watson, courtesy of RNLI)

The much travelled Atlantic 21 B-539 Lions International - District 105SE on exercise at Newquay. (Nicholas Leach)

B class rigid-inflatable inshore lifeboats

B-562 The Quiver — 1985/Atlantic 21 Mk.II
Legacy of Mrs D. Q. Presland.
Southwold 1.1985-10.98; Relief 10.1998-2002; sold 27.5.2002 to Finland LBS

B-563 Blue Peter II — 1985/Atlantic 21 Mk.II
Blue Peter TV Appeal.
Beaumaris 8.1985-9.00; Relief 2000-02; sold 27.5.2002 to Finland LBS

B-564 Blue Peter I — 1985/Atlantic 21 Mk.II
Blue Peter TV Appeal.
Littlehampton 9.1985-2001; Relief 2002-03

B-565 Manchester and District XXXII — 1986/Atlantic 21 Mk.II
Special Appeal in Manchester and District.
Appledore 3.1986-8.97; Relief 8.1997-99

B-566 Frank and Mary Atkinson — 1986/Atlantic 21 Mk.II
Gift of Mr F. Atkinson.
Lymington 6.1986-6.2002; Relief 2002; sold to KNRM 2.2003, renamed Willemtje, at Stellendam

B-567 Percy Garon II — 1986/Atlantic 21 Mk.II
A special local appeal.
Southend-on-Sea 4.1986-12.2001; Relief 12.2001-03

B-568 Burton Brewer — 1986/Atlantic 21 Mk.II
Special Appeal in Burton-On-Trent.
Hartlepool 9.1986-7.2000; Relief 2000-02

B-569 Blue Peter V — 1987/Atlantic 21 Mk.II
Proceeds from Blue Peter TV Appeal 1984/5.
Portaferry 1987-6.94; Relief 6.1994-2000; Helvick Head 1997-98

B-570 Himley Hall — 1987/Atlantic 21 Mk.II
The Himley Hall Sailing Club, Dudley; and the Mersea Island Appeal.
West Mersea 7.1987-6.2001; Relief 2001-05

B-571 British Diver II — 1987/Atlantic 21 Mk.II
British Sub Aqua Club.
Harwich 10.1987-10.2002; Relief 2002-

B-572 Dorothy and Katherine Barr — 1988/Atlantic 21 Mk.II
The Robert Barr Charitable Trust.
St Abbs 2.1988-12.2001; sold 26.2.2002 to Chilean Lifeboats

B-573 The Lady Dart and Long Life II — 1988/Atlantic 21 Mk.II
RNLI Ladies Darts League Appeal and the Long Life Beer Promotion.
Littlestone-on-Sea 6.1988-2001; sold 26.2.2002 to Chilean Lifeboats

B-574 Joseph B. Press — 1988/Atlantic 21 Mk.II
Bequests in memory of Captain Joseph B. Press, from the Manning Press family.
Gt Yarmouth & Gorleston 11.1988-2002; Relief 2002-

B-575 John Batstone — 1988/Atlantic 21 Mk.II
Round Britain Windsurf by Tim Batstone in 1984.
Peel 2.1989-92; Relief 1992-97; Clifden 5.1997-98; Relief 1998-2000; Crosshaven 6.2000-6.02; Relief 2002-05

B-576 Ellis Sinclair — 1989/Atlantic 21 Mk.II
Gift of Messrs Sinclair, Roche and Temperley, named in honour of firm's founder.
Staithes & Runswick 5.1989-10.2002; Relief 2002-

B-577 Graham Hillier and Tony Cater — 1989/Atlantic 21 Mk.II
Appeal in Surrey, and East Grinstead branch.
Brighton 7.1989-6.97; Relief 7.1997-99; sold 1999 to Sidmouth Inshore Rescue

B-578 The Rotary Club of Glasgow — 1989/Atlantic 21 Mk.II
The Rotary Club of Glasgow.
Macduff 8.1989-

B-579 Institute of London Underwriters — 1989/Atlantic 21 Mk.II
The Institute of London Underwriters.
Clacton-on-Sea 10.1989-97; Relief 1997-2001; St Abbs 12.2001-10.02; Relief 10.2002-03

B-580 Leicester Challenge — 1990/Atlantic 21 Mk.II
Leicester Branch of the RNLI.
Redcar 1.1990-11.2001; Sligo Bay 2001-02; Enniskillen 2002; Relief 2002-04; ILB Centre, Cowes 2004-

B-581 Andrew Mason — 1990/Atlantic 21 Mk.II
Gift of Mrs Janet Wilson Smith.
Helensburgh 2.1990-12.2002; Relief 12.2002-2004; Enniskillen 2004-

B-582 Borough of Solihull — 1990/Atlantic 21 Mk.II
The Borough of Solihull Lifeboat Appeal.
Abersoch 4.1990-2002; Relief 2002-

B-583 Ken Derham — 1990/Atlantic 21 Mk.II
Mudeford Lifeboat Appeal.
Mudeford 11.1990-

B-584 Youth of Ulster — 1990/Atlantic 21 Mk.II
Generosity of the people of the Province of Ulster.
Bangor 11.1990-

B-585 Peter and Grace Ewing — 1991/Atlantic 21 Mk.II
Bequest of Mrs Jan Dewar Paton.
Kirkcudbright 4.1991-12.2006

B-586 Clothworker — 1991/Atlantic 21 Mk.II
Clothworkers' Foundation.
Relief 6.1991-98; Cardigan 4.1998-99; Relief 1999-2004; Littlehampton 10.2001-6.02; Lough Derg 5.2004-

B-587 Jessie Eliza — 1991/Atlantic 21 Mk.II
Bequest of Lawrence Allan Davey.
St Catherine 9.1991-2000

B-588 Frank and Dorothy — 1991/Atlantic 21 Mk.II
Bequest of Mrs Dorothy Maud North, Purley.
Teignmouth 12.1991-8.2006

B-589 James Burgess — 1992/Atlantic 21 Mk.II
Gift of Mr and Mrs A. Burgess, as a memorial to their son James who died in 1981.
Walmer 5.1992-12.2006

B-590 Wolverson X-Ray — 1992/Atlantic 21 Mk.II
Legacy of Mr George Wolverson.
Relief 9.1992-6.93; Aberystwyth 6.1993-3.94; Relief 3.1994-96; Kilrush 1996; Galway 10.1996-9.97; Relief 1997- ; Youghal 1.2002-02; Cullercoats 3.2006-1.07

B-591 Edmund and Joan White — 1992/Atlantic 21 Mk.II
Bequest of the late Edmund White, South Shields.
Cullercoats 10.1992-3.2006; Enniskillen (Upper) 11.2006-

B-592 Ernest Armstrong — 1992/Atlantic 21 Mk.II
Legacy of Lady Alice Payne.
Relief 11.1992-12.98; Arran (Lamlash) 12.1998-1.2001; Relief 1.2001-03; Enniskillen 6.2003-11.06

B-593 Valerie Hull — 1993/Atlantic 21 Mk.II
Bequest of Mrs M. C. Hull.
Kilkeel 1.1993-11.2006

B-594 Herbert and Edith — 1993/Atlantic 21 Mk.II
Anonymous gift in memory of the late Herbert and Edith Grimwade.
Port Erin 3.1993-11.2006

B-595 Falmouth Round Table — 1993/Atlantic 21 Mk.II
Falmouth Round Table, plus bequests from Frederick Watson and Dr Gilbert Minifie, together with other gifts.
Falmouth 3.1994-

B-700 Susan Peacock — 1993/Atlantic 75
Appeal by staff from Nurdin and Peacock wholesalers.
Relief 1993- ; Burnham-on-Crouch 10.1996-2.97; Looe 8-10.2003; Burnham-on-Sea 12.2003-1.04; Relief 2004-

B class rigid-inflatable inshore lifeboats

B-701 Gordon England   1993/Atlantic 75
Gift of Mrs Florence Ashingdon, Bembridge, in memory of her cousin.
Relief 1993-2001; Littlestone-on-Sea 11.2001-6.2002; Relief 2002-

B-702 Manchester Unity of Oddfellows   1994/Atlantic 75
Gift from the Independent Order of Oddfellows Manchester Unity Friendly Society.
Sheringham 1.1994-2007; Relief 2007-

B-703 Jason Logg   1994/Atlantic 75
Memorial appeal organised by Graham Logg, of Harrogate, with kind support from
family and friends.
Flamborough 2.1994-

B-704 Enid Mary   1994/Atlantic 75
Bequest of Miss Margaret Rosalind Phillips.
Aberystwyth 3.1994-

B-705 Vera Skilton   1994/Atlantic 75
Bequest of the late Olive Vera Edith Skilton, Farnham, Surrey.
Relief 4.1994- ; temporary allocations to Appledore 8.1997-12.97; Kinsale
7.2003-12.03; Sunderland 9-11.2004; Gravesend 2005-

B-706 Blue Peter V   1994/Atlantic 75
Blue Peter TV Appeal (1993-4).
Portaferry 6.1994-

B-707 Mercurius   1994/Atlantic 75
Gift of the S. G. Warburg Group and staff, an investment banking firm.
Criccieth 6.1994-

B-708 Bessie   1994/Atlantic 75
Anonymous gift.
Minehead 11.1994-

B-709 Lucy Beryl   1994/Atlantic 75
Bequest of Mrs Lucy Beryl Stephenson, Yorkshire.
Relief 1995-10.2001; Kessock 10.2001-2.02; Relief 2.2002-

B-710 Friendly Forester II   1995/Atlantic 75
Gift of Ancient Order of Foresters Friendly Society in memory of Nora Gladys Green.
Poole 4.1995-

B-711 Helene   1995/Atlantic 75
Bequest of Helene Ranson.
Bundoran 5.1995-

B-712 Betty Battle   1995/Atlantic 75
Gift of Mr and Mrs Derrick Battle, Ashtead, Surrey.
Hayling Island 6.1995-

B-713 O E M Stone   1995/Atlantic 75
Gift of Miss Olive Emma May Stone, South Yorkshire.
Relief 7.1995-

B-714 Spirit of Cumbria   1995/Atlantic 75
The New Silloth Lifeboat Appeal and The Lake District Branch Centenary Appeal.
Silloth 7.1995-

B-715 Phyllis   1995/Atlantic 75
Anonymous gift.
Newquay 8.1995-

B-716 Gordon Mote   1994/Atlantic 75
Legacy of Gordon Robert M. Mote.
Relief 1994-2002; ILB Centre, Cowes 2002-

B-717 Daisy Aitken   1995/Atlantic 75
Bequest of Miss Margaret B. Aitken.
Lough Swilly (Buncrana) 10.1995-

B-718 Rotaract I   1995/Atlantic 75
Rotaract Clubs of Great Britain and Ireland.
Relief 11.1995-96; Blackpool 6.1996-2.98; Relief 1998- ; Crosshaven 2002

B-719 Percy Henry Patmore MBE MM   1995/Atlantic 75
Bequest of Mrs Florence Patmore.
St Bees 12.1995-

B-720 Frederick Robertson   1995/Atlantic 75
Anonymous gift.
Kinghorn 12.1995-

B-721 Rock Light   1996/Atlantic 75
An appeal initiated by the Port and City of Liverpool Branch.
New Brighton 1.1996-

B-722 Beatrice Dorothy   1996/Atlantic 75
Bequest of Mrs Beatrice Dorothy Brown.
Relief 1996-98; Blackpool 2-9.1998; Relief 9.1998-

B-723 Walters Lifeboat   1996/Atlantic 75
Bequest of Mrs Dorothy Walters.
Relief 1996-

B-724 Rotarian Dennis Cullen   1996/Atlantic 75
Rotary Club District 1110, in memory of a District Governor.
Relief 5.1996-

B-725 Spirit of Penarth   1996/Atlantic 75
Penarth Lifeboat Appeal.
Penarth 5.1996-

B-726 Giles   1996/Atlantic 75
Sunday Express lottery and RNLI funds.
Porthcawl 7.1996-

B-727 Commander and Mrs Rodney Wells   1996/Atlantic 75
Bequest of Mrs Eva Lilian Wells in memory of Commander Rodney Wells.
Rye Harbour 7.1996-

One of the last Atlantic 21s to be built, B-594 Herbert and Edith, *in rough seas off the Isle of Man. (From a photo in the author's collectionn)*

Atlantic 75 B-720 Frederick Robertson *at Kinghorn, a station which has operated D and C class inflatables, as well as an Atlantic. (Nicholas Leach)*

131

B class rigid-inflatable inshore lifeboats

B-728 Dorothy Mary   1996/Atlantic 75
Bequests of Miss Dorothy Mary Raine and Mr David Stanley Raine.
Red Bay 9.1996-

B-729 Rose West   1996/Atlantic 75
Bequest of Miss Rosemary Dora Bodenham West.
Kilrush 10.1996-

B-730 CSMA Frizzell   1996/Atlantic 75
Members of the Civil Service Motoring Association Ltd and Frizzell Financial Services.
Portsmouth (Langstone) 11.1996-

B-731 Dorothy Selina   1996/Atlantic 75
Gift of Reg Dawe, Hereford.
Trearddur Bay 12.1996-

B-732 Elizabeth Ann   1997/Atlantic 75
Legacy of Miss K. Markhan.
Relief 2.1997-

B-733 Brandy Hole   1997/Atlantic 75
Fundraising activities by Brandy Hole Yacht Club.
Burnham-on-Crouch 2.1997-

B-734 Amy Constance   1997/Atlantic 75
Legacy of Mrs Amy Constance Nunn.
Relief 4.1997-

B-735 Donald and Ethel Macrae   1997/Atlantic 75
Bequest of Mrs Jean Alison Sim.
Queensferry 5.1997-

B-736 Toshiba Wave Warrior   1997/Atlantic 75
Sponsorship of RNLI crew members who took part in the BT Global Challenge.
Relief 6.1997-2002; Gravesend 2002-04; Relief 2004-

B-737 Thelma Glossop   1997/Atlantic 75
Gift of Mr and Mrs Roy Glossop, Brighton.
Brighton 7.1997-

B-738 Dochas   1997/Atlantic 75
Galway City Appeal.
Galway 9.1997-

B-739 Peggy Keith Learmond   1997/Atlantic 75
Gift of Mrs Margaret Keith (Peggy) Learmond, Edinburgh.
Largs 3.1998-

B-740 Alexander Cattanach   1997/Atlantic 75
Anonymous gift.
Kyle of Lochalsh 8.1997-

B-741 Pearl of Dorset   1997/Atlantic 75
Local Appeal.
Lyme Regis 9.1997-

B-742 Douglas Paley   1997/Atlantic 75
Gift from Mrs Evelyn Anne Paley, Sussex, in memory of her late husband Air Commodore Douglas Paley.
Appledore 12.1997-

B-743 Alec and Maimie Preston   1998/Atlantic 75
Mr and Mrs Alec Preston, Burnley, Lancs.
Tighnabruaich 4.1998-

B-744 Robert George Alexander   1998/Atlantic 75
Legacy of the late Mr Robert George Alexander, Middlesex.
Clacton-on-Sea 10.1998-

B-745 CSMA 75th Anniversary   1998/Atlantic 75
Civil Service Motoring Association and Frizzell Financial Services.
Newbiggin 8.1998-

B-746 Phyl Clare 3   1998/Atlantic 75
Gift of Mr and Mrs Jack Cleare.
Weymouth 5.1998-

B-747 Rockabill   1998/Atlantic 75
RNLI Funds.
Skerries 6.1998-

B-748 Bickerstaffe   1998/Atlantic 75
Local Appeal.
Blackpool 9.1998-

B-749 D J S, Haverhill   1998/Atlantic 75
Bequest of David Sissons, a member of the Haverhill RNLI Guild.
Hunstanton 9.1998-

B-750 Leslie Tranmer   1998/Atlantic 75
Annie Tranmer Charitable Trust.
Southwold 10.1998-

B-751 Benjamin Downing Fairbridge   1999/Atlantic 75
Legacy from Mrs Margarete Anna Hertha Fairbridge.
Clifden 1.1999-

B-752 Tanni Grey   1999/Atlantic 75
Wales and West Mercia Regional Appeal.
Cardigan 2.1999-

B-753 City of Bradford V   1999/Atlantic 75
Appeal in City of Bradford, together with a donation from TRANSCO.
Relief 6.1999-2001; Penlee 2001-8.02; Relief 2002-

B-754 Pride of Sherwood   1999/Atlantic 75
City of Nottingham Appeal.
Relief 1999- ; St Catherine 2000-01; Mablethorpe 7.2001-1.02

B-755 London's Anniversary 175   1999/Atlantic 75
London Region 175th Anniversary Appeal.
Relief 1999- ; Salcombe 6-11.2003

B-756 Eve Pank   1999/Atlantic 75
Legacy of Lieut Colonel Pank.
Relief 6.1999-2005; St Helier 2005-1.07; Relief 1..2007-

B-757 Miss Miriam and Miss Nellie Garbutt   1999/Atlantic 75
Legacy of Miss Nellie Garbutt.
Relief 1999-

B-758 Sandwell Lifeline   1999/Atlantic 75
Sandwell Appeal, and Wales and West Mercia Regional Appeal.
Aberdovey 9.1999-

B-759 Spirit of Clovelly   1999/Atlantic 75
Clovelly Lifeboat Trust.
Clovelly 10.1999-

B-760 Alice and Charles   1999/Atlantic 75
Legacy of Charles W. Armstrong.
Helvick Head 12.1999-

B-761 Dignity   2000/Atlantic 75
Dignity Caring Funeral Services.
West Mersea 6.2001-

B-762 Jack and Joyce Burcombe   2000/Atlantic 75
Legacy of Miss Eileen J. Burcombe.
Relief 3.2000-11.05; Sunderland 11.2005-5.07; Relief 5.2007-

B-763 Colin James Daniel   2000/Atlantic 75
Gift of Mrs Brenda Daniel of Bishopstone, Berkshire.
Atlantic College 3.2000-

B-764 Oxford Town and Gown   2000/Atlantic 75
Gift of the City and University of Oxford.
Whitstable 7.2000-

B-765 Bob Turnbull   2000/Atlantic 75
Legacy from Mr Bob Turnbull, together with a donation from Mrs Jane Turnbull.
Ramsgate 7.2000-

B Class rigid-inflatable inshore lifeboats

B-731 Dorothy Selina *at speed off Trearddur Bay, one of a number of stations upgraded from operating a C or D class inflatable to an Atlantic rigid-inflatable during the 1990s. (Nicholas Leach)*

B-770 The Boys' Brigade *on exercise off the Isle of Arran, where she is based at the village of Lamlash. The Atlantic's stern arrangement of twin outboard engines and roll bar with self-righting air-bag can be clearly seen. (Nicholas Leach)*

B-776 Vic and Billie Whiffen *in the Thames Estuary off her Southend-on-Sea station. She is one of three inshore lifeboats and a hovercraft operated by the station which is amongst the busiest in the country. (Nicholas Leach)*

B class rigid-inflatable inshore lifeboats

B-766 BBC Radio Cleveland   2000/Atlantic 75
Appeal by BBC Radio Cleveland.
Hartlepool 7.2000-

B-767 Maritime Motion   2000/Atlantic 75
Shipping Appeal.
Relief 2000- ; Chiswick 2002-11.02

B-768 Blue Peter II   2000/Atlantic 75
Blue Peter TV Appeal.
Beaumaris 9.2000-

B-769 Coventry and Warwickshire   2000/Atlantic 75
Coventry and Warwickshire Lifeboat Appeal.
Weston-super-Mare 1.2001-

B-770 The Boys' Brigade   2000/Atlantic 75
The Boys' Brigade Appeal.
Arran (Lamlash) 1.2001-

B-771 Moray Dolphin   2001/Atlantic 75
An anonymous Inverness donor.
Kessock 2.2002-

B-772 Eric Rowse   2001/Atlantic 75
Gift of Mrs Denise Rowse, in memory of her husband.
St Catherine 3.2001-

B-773 Duckhams 2001   2001/Atlantic 75
Duckhams (BP Lubricants).
Relief 2001-

B-774 Braemar   2001/Atlantic 75
Fred. Olsen Cruise Lines.
Relief 2001-

B-775 Millennium Forester   2001/Atlantic 75
The Independent Order of Foresters.
Relief 2001-04; Plymouth 5.2004-

B-776 Vic and Billie Whiffen   2001/Atlantic 75
Legacy of Stella 'Billie' Whiffen, Bridport, who died in 1997.
Southend-on-Sea 12.2001-

B-777 Leicester Challenge II   2001/Atlantic 75
Leicester Branch.
Redcar 11.2001-

B-778 Joan Mary   2001/Atlantic 75
Bequest of the late Miss Evelyn Selina Wallace.
Mablethorpe 1.2002-

B-779 Blue Peter I   2001/Atlantic 75
Blue Peter Pieces of Eight Appeal 1993.
Littlehampton 6.2002-

B-780 Patricia Jennings   2001/Atlantic 75
Bequest of Patricia Jennings, late of Dorking, Surrey.
Youghal 9.2002-

B-781 Elsinore   2002/Atlantic 75
Sligo Bay Lifeboat Appeal.
Sligo Bay 2.2002-

B-782 Miss Betty   2002/Atlantic 75
Funded by Mr Clayton Love jnr.
Crosshaven 6.2002-

B-783 Dorothy and Katherine Barr II   2002/Atlantic 75
The Barr Charitable Trust.
St Abbs 10.2002-

B-784 Victor Danny Lovelock   2002/Atlantic 75
Mrs Iris Lovelock.
Lymington 6.2002-

3B-785 Fred Clarke   2002/Atlantic 75
Mr and Mrs Roy Glossop of Worthing, in memory of Fred Clarke.
Littlestone-on-Sea 6.2002-

B-786 Seahorse IV   2002/Atlantic 75
Proceeds of the Surrey Seahorse Ball and the Bisley Clay Pigeon Shooting Challenge.
Gt Yarmouth & Gorleston 7.2002-

B-787 Paul Alexander   2002/Atlantic 75
Mr and Mrs Richard Archer.
Penlee 8.2002-

B-788 Pride of Leicester   2002/Atlantic 75
Leicester Branch.
Staithes & Runswick 10.2002-

B-789 Sure and Steadfast   2002/Atlantic 75
The Boys' Brigade Appeal.
Harwich 10.2002-

B-790 Margaret Bench of Solihull   2002/Atlantic 75
Legacy of Mrs Margaret Kathleen Bench.
Abersoch 11.2002-

B-791 Gladys Winifred Tiffney   2002/Atlantic 75
Legacy of Gladys Tiffney.
Helensburgh 12.2002-

B-792 Joseph and Mary Hiley   2003/Atlantic 75
Bequest of Joseph and Mary Hiley.
Relief 12.2002-

B-793 Alan and Margaret   2003/Atlantic 75
Gift of Miss Elizabeth Beaton.
Looe 10.2003-

B-794 Joan Bate   2003/Atlantic 75
Legacy of the late Miss Joan Bate.
Salcombe 11.2003-

B-795 Staines Whitfield   2003/Atlantic 75
Gift of Mr Jonathon Whitfield.
Burnham-on-Sea 1.2004-

B-796 Miss Sally Anne (Baggy)   2003/Atlantic 75
Gift of Miss Sally Odell.
Kinsale 12.2003-

B-801 The Drayton Manor   2004/Atlantic 85
Trials 2004-06; Relief 2006-

B-802 Chelsea Flower Show   2004/Atlantic 85
Relief 2005-

B-803 William Hurst   2005/Atlantic 85
Relief 2006-

B-804 Lydia MacDonald   2005/Atlantic 85
Macduff 7.6.2006-

B-805 Jessie Hillyard   2005/Atlantic 85
Bangor 8.10.2006-

B-806 Mudeford Servant   2006/Atlantic 85
Mudeford 22.9.2006-

B-807 Mary Lewis   2006/Atlantic 85
Relief 2006-

B-808 Donald McLaughlan   2006/Atlantic 85
Walmer 14.12.2006-

B-809 The Two Annes   2006/Atlantic 85
Teignmouth 9.2006-

B-810 Tabbycat   2006/Atlantic 85
Relief 21.12.2006-

B-811 Hylton Burdon   2006/Atlantic 85
Cullercoats 9.1.2007-

B class rigid-inflatable inshore lifeboats

B-812 Frank William Walton Kilkeel 28.11.2006-	2006/Atlantic 85	**B-822** Aberystwyth	2007/Atlantic 85
B-813 Muriel and Leslie Port Erin 1.11.2006-	2006/Atlantic 85	**B-823** Criccieth	2007/Atlantic 85
B-814 Sheila Stenhouse Kirkudbright 14.12.2006-	2006/Atlantic 85	**B-024** Minehead	2007/Atlantic 85
B-815 Peterborough Beer Festival III Relief 21.12.2006-	2006/Atlantic 85	**B-825** Relief	2007/Atlantic 85
B-816 David Page St Helier 10.1.2007-	2006/Atlantic 85	**B-826** Poole	2007/Atlantic 85
B-817 Wolseley Sunderland 20.5.2007-	2007/Atlantic 85	**B-827** Bundoran	2008/Atlantic 85
B-818 The Oddfellows Sheringham 7.2007-	2007/Atlantic 85	**B-828** Hayling Island	2008/Atlantic 85
B-819 Lough Swilly	2007/Atlantic 85	**B-829** Silloth	2008/Atlantic 85
B-820 Elizabeth Jane Palmer Flamborough	2007/Atlantic 85	**B-830** Relief	2008/Atlantic 85
B-821 Newquay	2007/Atlantic 85	**B-831** Newquay	2008/Atlantic 85

B-796 Miss Sally Anne (Baggy), *the last Atlantic 75 to be built, on exercise at the mouth of Kinsale harbour in October 2004. The hull was painted with anti-fouling paint as she was kept afloat in the marina. (Nicholas Leach)*

Bangor's Atlantic 85 B-805 Jessie Hillyard *in Belfast Lough, part of the area which she covers. With seating for four crew and a host of electronic aids, the Atlantic 85 represents the RNLI's latest generation of rigid-inflatable. (Nicholas Leach)*

C class inflatable inshore lifeboats

Specifications (C-505 onwards) • length 17ft 6in (5.33m), beam 7ft 1in (2.16m), weight 1,300lbs.

In the 1970s, as the RNLI was looking for a design of inshore lifeboat that was more capable than the standard D class inflatable to enhance inshore cover, larger inflatables were trialled together with various rigid-inflatable and rigid-hulled ILBs. Five inflatables, all based on the 19ft Zodiac Mk.V except one supplied by RFD, were acquired and tested. Their most notable feature was a standing console amidships which was made from tubular steel frame for the helmsman, which raised the line of sight but was very exposed at high speeds, with two crew kneeling behind, one operating the radio. The boats had twin engines giving a speed of about twenty-five knots. The Zodiac Mk.V, although deemed to be a good sea boat, was rather punishing on the crew. By the mid-1970s, the larger Atlantic 21 had been proved and this type was more suitable for the rescues undertaken by 19ft Zodiacs at Minehead and Silloth, the two stations where the boats were deployed.

During the late 1970s, further developments with a twin-engined inflatable took place as the Institution believed a boat between the Atlantic 21 and D class inflatable was needed. The result was the C class, a boat based on the Zodiac Mk.IV inflatable, 17ft 6in in length and essentially a larger and more powerful version of the standard D class. The C class boats from C-505 (originally numbered D-505) onwards were of the Mk.IV type, fitted with twin 40hp outboard engines, and able to achieve a top speed of approximately thirty knots. Manned by a crew of three or four, the boats could be righted manually after a capsize using a system specially designed by the RNLI, with a buoyancy system which allowed the boat to continue on service even if the bow was punctured. Similar equipment to the standard D class inflatable was carried, but the C class also had a spotlight for night rescues.

When introduced in the 1970s, the twin-engined inflatables were given the D class prefix to indicate they were fully inflatable, as opposed to rigid (A class) or rigid-inflatable (B class) ILBs, and numbered D-500, D-501, etc, with the 500 suffix indicating the boats were twin-engined. The D class inflatables at the time were numbered D-1 to D-499. However, in May 1984, a review of numbering resulted in the boats being redesignated as the C class to distinguish them from their smaller single-engined sisters.

The design was developed by the RNLI to meet the requirement for a craft operating all year round day and night at a time when

D-502, one of the prototype Zodiac Mk.V inshore lifeboats, pictured when in service at Silloth. The engine controls and steering wheel were mounted on a tubular steel framework at which the helmsman stood.

One of the Zodiac Mk.V inflatables, D-503, during trials in the 1970s. She was fitted with a central console at which the helmsman stood.

many D class inflatables were only used on service during the daytime and in the summer months. The C class was also intended for service at stations where, for operational reasons, the larger Atlantic 21 was not deemed suitable. In the event, after relatively short service careers, the C class inflatables were replaced by either the Atlantic 21 or the larger Atlantic 75 rigid-inflatables, and in the 1990s the type was phased out of service altogether. A number were later used as boarding boats at stations where all-weather lifeboats were kept at exposed moorings and a large twin-engined boat was required.

D-509 sets out from Aberystwyth before the twin-engined inflatables had been redesignated the C class and renumbered accordingly. (Jeff Morris)

C-518 on exercise at Cardigan in 1996. She was one of nineteen Zodiac Mk.IV twin-engined ILBs in service during the 1980s and 90s. (Nicholas Leach)

C class inflatable inshore lifeboats

C-500   1972/Zodiac Mk.V
Minehead Rotary Club.
Trials 1972-74, Minehead 1974-79

C-501   1972/RFD 320
Trials 1972

C-502 John Gilpin   1972/Zodiac Mk.V
Gift from the John Gilpin Trust.
Trials 1973-74, Silloth 1975-9.77, Boarding Boat 1977-87

C-503   1973/Zodiac Mk.V
Trials 1973-77, Silloth 9.1977-6.79, Boarding Boat 1981-87

C-504   1973/Zodiac Mk.V
Relief 1973-86 (used as Boarding Boat at Cowes Depot)

C-505   1978/Zodiac Mk.IV
The Ruthven-Stuart family, in memory of Stella Ruthven-Stuart.
St Abbs 3.1979-4.86, Relief 4.1986-88, Red Bay 8.1986-5.87, Clifden 10.1988-2.89,
Sold locally 11.1990

C-506   1980/Zodiac Mk.IV
Legacy of Mrs M. K. Hawken.
Portaferry 5.1980-7.86, Relief 7.1986-9.87, Arran (Lamlash) 9.1987-6.88,
Relief 6.1988-5.91, Boarding Boat 1.1993-4.97, scrapped 8.1988

C-507   1980/Zodiac Mk.IV
Central London Committee.
Mudeford 1981-5.88, Relief 1989-2.90

C-508 The Chris Pirson   1980/Zodiac Mk.IV
Gifts in memory of Christopher Pirson.
Relief 1981-12.91, Ballyglass (Boarding Boat) 8.1993-10.96

C-509 Oats   1982/Zodiac Mk.IV
Rag Committee of University of Wales.
Aberystwyth 5.1983-6.93, Relief 6.1993-95, Tighnabruaich 7.1995-1.96, Cardigan
4.1996-4.98, scrapped 4.1998

C-510   1982/Zodiac Mk.IV
Bournemouth Borough's Sea Angling Festival.
Criccieth 16.9.1983-8.91, Relief 12.1991-6.95, withdrawn 1995

C-511   1982/Zodiac Mk.IV
Clubs affiliated to Rugby Football Union.
Newquay 14.12.1983-6.94, Relief 2.1995-96, became Boarding Boat

C-512   1982/Zodiac Mk.IV
Gift of Miss Diana Phillips, in memory of her parents.
Cullercoats 12.6.1984-4.91, Relief 4.1991-11.95

C-513 Sebag of Jersey   1982/Zodiac Mk.IV
Gift of Frederick E. Cohen, in memory of his father Sebag Cohen.
St Catherine 14.4.1984-10.90, Relief 8.1991-7.95

C-514   1984/Zodiac Mk.IV
Promotion by Ind Coope Alloa Brewery Co Ltd and the Co-op in Scotland.
Kinghorn 16.6.1984-8.93, Relief 1993-6.95, Red Bay 1996-97, Clifden 10.1997-6.98

C-515   1985/Zodiac Mk.IV
Bequest of the late Mrs Peggy Patria Clowes, in memory of her husband.
St Bees 9.1985-3.95

C-516 The Belsize Charitable Trust No.1   1986/Zodiac Mk.IV
The Belsize Charitable Trust, in memory of Eric David Jackson.
St Ives 2.10.1986-10.95

C-517   1984/Zodiac Mk.IV
The Lewes and District Lifeboat Appeal.
Rye Harbour 1986-96, Relief 1996-97

C-518   1984/Zodiac Mk.IV
Gift of Mrs Nany Lynda Hopkinson, Windermere.
Cardigan 29.3.1987-6.97

C-519 Thomas Corbett   1984/Zodiac Mk.IV
Red Bay 25.6.1987-7.95, Relief 11.1995-1.96, Tighnabruaich 1.1996-9.97

C-520   1986/Zodiac Mk.IV
Relief 2.1988-96

C-521 Prince of Arran   1988/Zodiac Mk.IV
Fred Olsen Shipping Line, through passengers of cruiseship Black Prince.
Arran (Lamlash) 6.1988-1.98, sold 27.1.1998

C-522   1988/Zodiac Mk.IV
Bequest of Peter and Steve Laban.
Clifden 7.1989-10.97, Rosslare Harbour (Boarding Boat) 10-12.1997, publicity 7.1988

C-523 British Diver IV   1990/Zodiac Mk.IV
Special Appeal organised by the British Sub-Aqua Club.
Relief 1-12.1991, Criccieth 12.1991-7.93, Tighnabruaich 4-9.1994, Red Bay
28.7.1995-4.96, Cardigan 6.1997-5.98, sold 1998

C-522, the penultimate C class inflatable, outside the lifeboat house at Clifden, where she was stationed from 1989 to 1997 as the first station lifeboat. Transported on a road-going trailer, she could be taken to different sites in the area to be launched, depending on the position of a casualty. (Nicholas Leach)

D class inflatable inshore lifeboats

The introduction of the inshore lifeboat in the early 1960s was one of the most significant developments in the history of the lifeboat service. In 1960, no small inflatable lifeboats were in service, but within forty years their numbers had increased to such an extent that they were the most numerous type in service. The inshore lifeboat was introduced as a result of changing demands made on lifeboats as the type of casualty changed. During the two decades after World War II, more and more people used the sea for leisure purposes as incomes and leisure time increased. As a result of the expansion of the leisure industry, the number of inshore incidents to which lifeboats were called increased. Conventional lifeboats were not well suited to such work and a simple, fast rescue craft for working inshore would be much more effective.

The RNLI bought an inflatable boat in 1962 for trials, and a delegation visited France, where similar boats were in operation, to obtain further advice and see the boats in action. Following these initial steps, the first inshore rescue boats were introduced in the summer of 1963 when eight were sent to stations around the country. Such was their success that in each of the following years more and more places began to operate the boats.

The 16ft inflatable lifeboats, made from tough nylon coated with neoprene/hypalon, were crewed by two, powered by a 40hp outboard engine, and could be launched quickly and easily. The advantages of these boats were their speed, which at twenty knots was considerably faster than any lifeboat in service during the 1960s, their ability to go alongside other craft or persons in the water without causing or suffering damage, the short time taken to launch them, and their low running costs.

In the first year of operation, the eight inshore lifeboats launched thirty-nine times and saved ten lives. The following year, nineteen more entered service and by 1966 the number of inshore lifeboats on station had risen to seventy-two, of which thirty-two remained on station throughout the year with the rest operating only during the summer.

As the RNLI's inshore fleet expanded, so did the technical expertise applied to the design. Modifications were made as the ILB was developed: an inner tube was fitted to prevent air leaking out; floorboards able to take the strain of high speeds were developed; and foam rubber mattresses were installed to improve the safety and comfort of the crew. Because of the pounding the boats gave their crews, an age limit of 45 was imposed and new young recruits were found. Equipment was added to the craft to

The first inshore rescue boat outside the quayside house at Aberystwyth from where she was operated in 1963. (Jeff Morris)

make them more effective rescue tools. This included VHF radio, first aid kit, flares, compass, a spare propeller and an anchor.

The first boats were made by RFD, a company well known for supplying life-rafts on board ships, of the PB16 type, 15ft 6in in length with a beam of 6ft 3in, and weighed 550lbs. A handful of 15ft 6in Zodiac Mk.III boats were also used during the 1980s and 90s. The RFD PB16 served many stations throughout the country, and was a distinctive boat with black tubes and orange patches. However, by the early 1980s, further advances in design and technology resulted in the RNLI developing a new and slightly larger ILB in conjunction with Avon Inflatables. The new type was 16ft 3in long with a 6ft 7in beam, and weighed 745lbs.

Between 2000 and 2003, the RNLI's naval architects examined the design of the inshore lifeboat again with the intention of producing a replacement for the existing boats. As a result, the design was completely re-engineered and an ILB was produced which was faster, incorporated the latest advances in material and equipment technology, and was more consistent in its performance, better equipped and easier to maintain. Designated Inshore Boat 1 (IB1), the new ILB had a 50hp engine with electric startup, and the floor sections and transom were fabricated from composite materials which were as strong and stiff as plywood, the material used hitherto for ILBs, but lighter and easier to maintain. The hull was made from hypalon-coated polyester which gave a more consistent boat shape and performance. A new stowage pod, designed to allow the anchor to be stowed ready-rigged for deployment, provided housing for other equipment. The new design was trialled in 2002-3 and the production version was introduced into service in August 2003.

The first inshore rescue boat at Great Yarmouth and Gorleston, D-9, was a rudimentary craft compared to modern inshore lifeboats of the twenty-first century. (From an old photo supplied by Ivor Steadman)

One of the IB1 type inflatable lifeboats, D-637 Aldergrove II, from Newcastle in Co Down. The IB1 ILBs incorporated advanced technology which made the early inflatable rescue craft of the 1960s seem somewhat basic. (Nicholas Leach)

D class inflatable inshore lifeboats

D-1   1963/RFD PB16
Aberystwyth 5.1963-9.63; Gt Yarmouth & Gorleston 1.1965-6.65

D-2   1963/RFD PB16
Whitstable 5.1965-7.65

D-3   1963/RFD PB16

D-4   1963/RFD PB16
Mudeford 6.1963-10.63

D-5   1963/RFD PB16
St Ives 4.1964-10.64; West Mersea 1964-5.65

D-6   1963/RFD PB16
Southwold 7.1963-10.63; Redcar 10.1963-9.64; North Sunderland 3.1966-10.66

D-7   1963/RFD PB16
Mudeford 1964

D-8   1963/RFD PB16
Bembridge 5.1964-10.64; Wells 8.1965-8.66

D-9 [became D-1-P]   1963/RFD PB16
Gorleston 5.1963-8.64; Blackpool 6.1965-8.65; Wells 8.1965-65; St Ives 4.1966-7.67

D-10   1963/RFD PB16
Worthing 3.1964-10.64; Aberdovey 5.1965-8.65

D-11   1963/RFD PB16
Wells 6.1963-10.64; Mudeford 3-9.1965; Hastings 9.1965-7.67

D-12 [became D-2-P]   1963/RFD PB16
Aberdovey 11.1963-64; Redcar 5-10.1965; Tynemouth 4-5.1965; Redcar 3-6.1967;
Abersoch 1968-70

D-14   1964/RFD PB16
Walmer 4-10.1964; Southwold 5-7.1965; West Mersea 1965; West Kirby 3-9.1967;
Harwich 1968; Brighton 1969

D-15 [became D-3-P]   1964/RFD PB16
Barrow 4-6.1964; Skegness 6-7.1964

D-16   1964/RFD PB16
Pwllheli 4-10.1964; St Ives 6.1965-4.66; Bournemouth 7.1967-6.68; Arbroath
8.1968-6.69; Relief 1969-72

D-17   1964/RFD PB16
Broughty Ferry 4.1964-8.67

D-18 [became D-4-P]   1964/RFD PB16
Bembridge 4.1965-7.67

D-19   1964/RFD PB16
Aberystwyth 3-10.1964; Aberdovey 8.1965-5.67; Reserve 1967-70; Aberdovey 1970

D-20   1964/RFD PB16
Yarmouth 7-10.1964; West Mersea 1965; Pwllheli 6.1965-10.66; Scarborough
7-10.1967; Mudeford 7.1968-10.70; Relief 1971-72

D-21   1964/RFD PB16
Hastings 4.1964-10.64; Southend-on-Sea 5-6.65; Torbay 6-10.1965; Broughty Ferry
10.1965-5.66; Walmer 5-7.1966; Mudeford 9-11.1967; Relief 1967-72

D-22 [became D-5-P]   1964/RFD PB16
Yarmouth 3.1965-6.67; Relief 1969

D-23   1964/RFD PB16
Torbay 4-10.1964

D-24   1964/RFD PB16
Whitstable 7.1965-9.65; Walmer 7-10.66; Bembridge 3.1969-5.71; Relief 1971-74

D-25   1964/RFD PB16
Southwold 3.1964-10.64; Hastings 3.1965-8.65; Torbay 3.1966-8.66;
Pwllheli 3.1967-10.67; Wells 7.1968-10.69; Relief 1969-72

D-26   1964/RFD PB16
Walmer 4.1965-10.65; Gorleston 8.1967-7.68; Cromer 1970-10.71

D-27 [became D-10-P]   1964/RFD PB16
Hastings 1965; Worthing 8.1965-10.67

D-28   1964/RFD PB16
Barrow 6-10.1964; Whitstable 4-5.1965; Worthing 7-8.1965; Aberystwyth 4.1969-70

D-29   1964/RFD PB16
Wells 5-8.1965; Atlantic College 1966

D-30   1964/RFD PB16
Aberystwyth 8.1965-6.67; St Agnes 6-7.1968; Bournemouth 1969-69

D-31   1964/RFD PB16
Redcar 9.1964-5.65

D-32   1964/RFD PB16
Gt Yarmouth & Gorleston 1964; Eastbourne 6.1965-5.66; West Mersea 5-10.1966

D-33   1964/RFD PB16
Atlantic College 1965-11.66

D-34   1964/RFD PB16

D-35   1964/RFD PB16
Southend-on-Sea 1966-

D-36   1965/RFD PB16
Southwold 7.1965-9.70; Worthing 5.1965-7.65

D-37   1965/RFD PB16
Redcar 6.1966-10.66; Yarmouth 3.1966-6.66; North Sunderland 3.1967-10.67;
Relief 1968-72; Littlestone-on-Sea 8.1968-9.68

D-38   1965/RFD PB16
Atlantic College 7.1965-66; Relief 1966-73

D-39   1965/RFD PB16
Brighton (Pier) 4.1965-10.67; St Agnes 4.1968-6.68; Relief 1969-72

D-40   1965/RFD PB16
Bangor 5.1965-3.68; Scarborough 3.1968-10.69

D-41   1965/RFD PB16
Lymington 1965-70; Relief 1970-73

D-42 [became D-12-P]   1965/RFD PB16
Mudeford 9.1965-9.67; Relief 1968-73; New Brighton 6.1973-8.74; Relief 1974-77

D-43   1965/RFD PB16
Barrow 5.1965-6.72; Relief 1972-74

D-44   1965/RFD PB16
Mumbles 5.1965-8.72

D-45   1965/RFD PB16
Whitstable 9.1965-3.68; Whitstable 7.1969-5.70; Relief 1970-73

D-46   1965/RFD PB16
Largs 5.1965-9.67; Poole 9.1967-1.70; Aberdovey 1970

D-47   1965/RFD PB16
Bournemouth 5.1965-7.67; Weston-super-Mare 4.1969-5.70

D-48   1965/RFD PB16
Eastney 5.1965-5.70; Relief 1970-71

D-49   1965/RFD PB16
Tynemouth 5.1965-3.66; Torbay 9.1966-8.67; Whitstable 3.1968-7.69; Filey 3.1970-
8.72; Relief 1972-79

D-50   1965/RFD PB16
Cullercoats 5-10.1965; Tynemouth 3.1966-10.68; Littlestone 3-7.1970; Relief 1970-
73

D-51 [became D-4-P]   1965/RFD PB16
Blyth 5.1965-10.65; Amble 5.1966-4.70

D-52   1965/RFD PB16
Porthcawl 5.1965-9.70; Relief 1970-73

D-53 [became D-11-P]   1965/RFD PB16
North Sunderland 5.1965-10.65; Blyth 3.1966-10.72

D-54   1965/RFD PB16
Llandudno 6.1965-10.66; Moelfre 8.1969-10.69; Amble 4.1970-72; Relief 1972-77

D-55   1965/RFD PB16
Newquay 7.1965-7.67; Torbay 9.1967-10.69; Relief 1970-71

D class inflatable inshore lifeboats

D-56	1965/RFD PB16
Humbermouth 5.1965-10.72; Relief 1973-77	
D-57	1965/RFD PB16
Blackpool 5.1965-10.70; Relief 1970-71	
D-58	1965/RFD PB16
Skegness 7.1965-10.72; Relief 1972-74; Withernsea 1974; Relief 1974-77	
D-59	1965/Dunlop
D-60	1965/Dunlop
Southend-on-Sea 8.1965-10.66	
D-61	1965/Dunlop
Mablethorpe 5.1965-8.65; Eastbourne 7.1966-10.66	
D-62	1965/Dunlop
Moelfre 8.1965-6.66; Southend-on-Sea 4.1967-8.69	
D-63	1965/Dunlop
Southend-on-Sea 3.1967-4.67	
D-64	1965/Dunlop
Kinghorn 6.1965-8.65	
D-65	1965/Dunlop
West Mersea 6-10.1965; Relief 1965-67; Kinghorn 4-10.1967; Kippford 3-10.1970	
D-66	1965/Dunlop
Helensburgh 6.1965-2.68	
D-67	1965/Dunlop
Moelfre 7-8.1965; Mablethorpe 8.1965-10.66	
D-68	1965/Dunlop
Scarborough 1965; Kinghorn 8.1965-4.67	
D-69	1965/Dunlop
Poole 1965-9.67	
D-70	1965/RFD PB16
Abersoch 6.1965-9.69; Relief 1969-70	
D-71	1965/RFD PB16
Harwich 5.1965-10.71; Coverack 6-10.1972; Relief 1972-83	
D-72 [became D-7-P]	1965/RFD PB16
Happisburgh 6.1965-10.72; Relief 1972-75	
D-73 [became D-8-P]	1965/RFD PB16
Gt Yarmouth & Gorleston 6.1965-67; Relief 1967-69; Burnham-on-Crouch 3.1969-73	
D-74	1965/RFD PB16
Tramore 6.1965-67; Weston-super-Mare 1968-10.72; Relief 1973-78	
D-75	1965/RFD PB16
Relief 1965-77	
D-76	1965/RFD PB16
On board 70-001 1966; Relief 1967-71	
D-77 [re-numbered Y-1]	1967/RFD 320
Boarding boat 1967-80	
D-78 [re-numbered Y-2]	1967/RFD 320
Boarding boat 1967-76	
D-79 [re-numbered Y-3]	1967/RFD 320
Boarding boat 1967-81	
D-80 [re-numbered Y-4]	1967/RFD 320
Boarding boat 1967-83	
D-81	1967/RFD PB16
Port St Mary 1967-72; Lytham St Annes 1975	
D-82	1966/RFD PB16
Wells 8.1966-7.68; Relief 1968-71	
D-83	1963/RFD PB16
Weston-super-Mare 5.1966-68; Relief 1968-71	
D-84	1966/RFD PB16
Whitby 5.1966-10.70; Relief 1970-77	

D-85 [became D-7-P]	1966/RFD PB16
Scarborough 4.1966-7.67; Relief 1967-75	
D-86	1966/RFD PB16
Filey 4.1966-10.69; Relief 1970-71	
D-87	1966/RFD PB16
Cullercoats 3.1966-10.68; Relief 1968-71; Kippford 3.1971-10.71	
D-88	1966/RFD PB16
Port Talbot 1966-9.71; Relief 1971-77	
D-89	1966/RFD PB16
Exmouth 5.1966-7.72; Relief 1972-73	
D-90	1966/RFD PB16
Littlestone-on-Sea 5.1966-10.69; Relief 1969-77	
D-91	1966/RFD PB16
Fleetwood 5.1966-7.70; Relief 1970-75; on board 70-001 1975	
D-92 [became D-21-P]	1966/RFD PB16
Bridlington 4.1966-70; Relief 1970-77; on board 70-002 1977-80; flood relief 1980-3	
D-93 [became D-15-P]	1966/RFD PB16
Morecambe 5.1966-10.72; Burnham-on-Crouch 3.1974-10.75	
D-94	1966/RFD PB16
Sunderland 5.1966-10.76	
D-95	1966/RFD PB16
Burnham-on-Crouch 5.1966-10.68; Relief 1968-73	
D-96	1966/RFD PB16
Bude 5.1966-8.75; Relief 1975-80	
D-97	1966/RFD PB16
Conwy 6.1966-8.71; Relief 1971-75	
D-98	1966/RFD PB16
Kippford 1966-10.69; Relief 1969-71	
D-99	1966/RFD PB16
Margate 5.1966-8.75	
D-100	1966/RFD PB16
West Kirby 6.1966-10.66; Boulmer 3-10.68; Cullercoats 3.1969-10.74; Relief 1975-80	
D-101 [became D-19-P]	1966/RFD PB16
Cromer 3.1967-70; Bembridge 6.1971-10.75; Relief 1976-82	
D-102	1966/RFD PB16
Moelfre 6.1966-8.69; Torbay 1970-70	
D-103	1966/RFD PB16
Borth 6.1966-10.75	
D-104 [became D-19-P]	1966/RFD PB16
Flint 6.1966-8.76; Relief 1976-80; flood relief 1980-83	
D-105	1966/RFD PB16
Rye Harbour 6.1966-10.75; Relief 1976-84; Boarding Boat 1984-?	
D-106	1966/RFD PB16
Crimdon Dene 6.1966-10.74	
D-107	1966/RFD PB16
Clacton-on-Sea 7.1966-6.78; Relief 1978-80	
D-108	1966/RFD PB16
West Mersea 3.1967-10.72; Withernsea 3-10.75; Howth 9.1977-10.78; Relief 1978-80	
D-109	1966/RFD PB16
Llandudno 3.1967-10.76; Relief 1976-79	
D-110	1966/RFD PB16
Newquay 7.1967-8.68; on board 70-002 1969; Aberdovey 1970; St Abbs 6.1974-10.75; Relief 1975-80; flood relief 1980-83	
D-111	1966/RFD PB16
Berwick 4.1967-8.76; Aldeburgh 7.1977-80	
D-112 Blue Peter III	1966/RFD PB16
North Berwick 4.1967-10.72; Relief 1973-84; display from 1984	

D class inflatable inshore lifeboats

D-113   1966/RFD PB16
Eastbourne 3.1967-6.68; Gorleston 7.1968-12.69; Wells 3.1970-5.76; Relief 1976-80

D-114   1966/RFD PB16
Mablethorpe 3-6.1976; Whitby 6.1976-10.77; flood relief 78-83; Boarding Boat 83-87

D-115 Blue Peter I   1966/RFD PB16
Littlehampton 4.1967-6.72; Relief 1972-75

D-116   1966/RFD PB16
Holyhead 4.1967-7.76; Blackpool 1979-82; Boarding Boat 1983-?

D-117   1966/RFD PB16
Criccieth 4.1967-10.71; Blackpool 3.1972-81; Relief 1981-83

D-118 [re-numbered Y-6]   1966/RFD 320
Boarding boat 1966-80

D-119 [re-numbered Y-7]   1966/RFD 320
Boarding boat 1966-76

D-120 [became D-17-P]   1966/RFD PB16
Lytham St Annes 4.1967-10.76; Relief 1977-80; Penarth 6.1980-8.81

D-121   1966/RFD PB16
Stonehaven 4.1967-10.74; Relief 1975-80

D-122   1966/RFD PB16
New Quay 3.1967-10.75

D-123   1966/RFD PB16
Kinghorn 3.1968-5.76; Relief 1976-80

D-124 [became D-18-P]   1966/RFD PB16
Little & Broad Haven 5.1967-10.75; Relief 1976-82

D-125   1967/RFD PB16
Lyme Regis 5.1967-10.68; Relief 1969-75

D-126   1967/RFD PB16
Trearddur Bay 3.1967-10.77; Relief 1978-90; Hunstanton 3.1980-10.81

D-127   1967/RFD PB16
Beaumaris 5.1967-3.76

D-128 [became D-8-P]   1967/RFD PB16
Southend-on-Sea 4.1969-3.70

D-129   1967/RFD PB16
Howth 4.1967-9.77; Relief 1977-83; Boarding Boat 1983-87

D-130   1967/RFD PB16
Plymouth 5.1967-7.68; Craster 8.1969-6.75

D-131 [became D-28-P]   1967/RFD PB16
On board 70-001 1968-74; Relief 1975-78; flood relief 1978-83

D-132   1967/RFD PB16
Helensburgh 2.1968-10.71; Relief 1971-74; Relief 1974-84; Stranraer 6.1974-10.74

D-133   1967/RFD PB16
Yarmouth 6.1967-9.68; Moelfre 3.1970-10.74

D-134 [became D-24-P]   1967/RFD PB16
Tighnabruaich 5.1967-7.79; Relief 1979-83

D-135   1967/RFD PB16
Walmer 3.1967-10.70; Kippford 3.1972-10.77

D-136   1967/RFD PB16
Redcar 6.1967-10.78; flood relief 1978-83

D-137   1967/RFD PB16
Barmouth 6.1967-10.78; flood relief 1978-83; Boarding Boat 1983-?

D-138   1967/RFD PB16
Aberdovey 5.1967-12.67; Relief 1968-70; Selsey 7.1970-10.80; Relief 1980

D-139 [became D-25-P]   1967/RFD PB16
Port Isaac 6.1967-10.77; flood relief 1977-83

D-140   1967/RFD PB16
Aberystwyth 6.1967-9.68; Aberdovey 1969-70 and 1971-4.74; Criccieth 8.1974-8.80; Relief 1980-84; ILB Centre, Cowes 1984-88

D-141 [became D-14-P]   1967/RFD PB16
Rhyl 7.1967-10.75

D-142 [became D-26-P]   1967/RFD PB16
St Ives 7.1967-10.77; flood relief 1978-83

D-143   1967/RFD PB16
Hastings 7.1967-4.75; Relief 1975-79; Boarding Boat 1979-?

D-144   1967/RFD PB16
Bembridge 7.1967-10.68; Tynemouth 3.1969-10.69; Silloth 3.1970-4.75; Relief 1975-77; Moelfre 3.1977-5.80; Relief 1980-84

D-145   1967/RFD PB16
Queensferry 7.1967-4.71; Sheerness 7.1972-10.76; Relief 1977-80; on board 70-003 1980-81

D-146   1967/RFD PB16
Silloth 8.1967-10.69; Southend-on-Sea 5.1970-11.75

D-147   1967/RFD PB16
Shoreham 7.1967-5.70; Relief 1970-73

D-148   1967/RFD PB16
St Agnes 7.1968-8.72; Relief 1972-80

D-149   1967/RFD PB16
Relief 1967-70; on board 70-002 1970-75

D-150 [became D-16-P]   1967/RFD PB16
Broughty Ferry 8.1967-6.68; Relief 1968-71; Varne Lightvessel 1971-72; Relief 1972-78; Southend-on-Sea 1975-76

D-151   1967/RFD PB16
Largs 9.1967-8.73

D-152   1967/RFD PB16
Bournemouth 6.1968-10.72; Hartlepool 5.1973-7.73; Boarding Boat 1975-78

Inshore Rescue Boat No.32 putting out on exercise from the beach at Eastbourne in July 1965. (Jeff Morris)

D-115 Blue Peter I at Littlehampton. The lifeboats funded by Blue Peter TV programme raised the profile of ILBs. (RNLI)

D class inflatable inshore lifeboats

D-153	1967/RFD PB16
Pwllheli 3.1968-5.78; Boarding Boat 1978-83	
D-154	1967/RFD PB16
Relief 1967-71	
D-155	1967/RFD PB16
West Kirby 9.1967-7.75	
D-156	1967/RFD PB16
Relief 1967-69; Lyme Regis 1969-70; Blackpool 1971	
D-157 [became D-10-P]	1967/RFD PB16
North Sunderland 3.1968-7.80; Relief 1980-84	
D-158	1967/RFD PB16
Brighton (Pier) 4.1968-10.68; Southend-on-Sea 8.1969-7.75	
D-159	1967/RFD PB16
Eastbourne 6.1968-7.78; Relief 1978-84	
D-160	1967/RFD PB16
Relief 1967-71	
D-161 [became D-15-P]	1967/RFD PB16
Aberdovey 1.1968-3.69; Yarmouth 5.1969-10.75	
D-162 [became D-27-P]	1967/RFD PB16
Bangor 3.1968-10.69; Shoreham 7.1970-10.78; Relief 1979-84	
D-163	1967/RFD PB16
Tramore 3.1968-3.78	
D-164 [became D-9-P]	1967/RFD PB16
Selsey 3.1968-7.70; Relief 1970-72	
D-165	1967/RFD PB16
Horton & Port Eynon 6.1968-7.80; Relief 1980-84; ILB Centre, Cowes 1984-?	
D-166	1967/RFD PB16
Hartlepool 5.1968-4.72; Coverack 5-6.1972; Coverack 3.1973-10.78; Relief 1979-85	
D-167 [became D-20-P]	1967/RFD PB16
St Catherine 10.1969-10.79; Blackpool 1981-3.82	
D-168	1967/RFD PB16
Aberdeen 1968-81; Relief 1981-?	
D-169	1967/RFD PB16
Dunbar 7.1968-83; Relief 1983-84; Boarding Boat 1984-?	
D-170	1967/RFD PB16
Arbroath 6.1969-10.72; Weston-s-Mare 4.1973-81; Relief 1981-84; St Agnes 1984-85	
D-171	1967/RFD PB16
Newquay 3.1969-8.79	
D-172	1967/RFD PB16
Yarmouth 9.1968-5.69; Tynemouth 3.1970-81; Relief 1981-?	
D-173	1967/RFD PB16
Broughty Ferry 6.1968-12.83; Relief 1984-?	
D-174	1970/RFD PB16
Porthcawl 9.1970-83; Relief 1983-87; Boarding Boat 1987-?	
D-175 Alan Thurlow Ashford	1970/RFD PB16
Bangor 3.1970-83; Relief 1983-85; Boarding Boat 1985-?	
D-176	1970/RFD PB16
Queensferry 4.1971-9.72; Relief 1972-89; Boarding Boat 1989-91	
D-177	1970/RFD PB16
Minehead 4.1970-83; Relief 1983-?	
D-178	1970/RFD PB16
Brighton (Pier) 3.1970-10.74; Relief 1974-82; Blackpool 1982-83; Relief 1983-?	
D-179 Blue Peter IV	1970/RFD PB16
Gorleston 6.1970-6.77; Tramore 3.1978-10.79; Relief 1979-81; St Agnes 10.1981-84	
D-180	1970/RFD PB16
St Bees 9.1970-9.85; Relief 1985-	
D-181	1970/RFD PB16
Lymington 1970-8.73; Relief 1973-79; Hunstanton 6-10.1979	
D-182	1970/RFD PB16
Whitstable 5.1970-6.74; Margate 10.1975-6.84; Relief 1984-87;	
Cleethorpes 5-6.1987; Relief 1987-?	
D-183 Young People of Scarborough	1970/RFD PB16
Scarborough 3.1970-84; Relief 1984-	
D-184	1970/RFD PB16
Eastney (Portsmouth) 5.1970-84; Relief 1984-	
D-185	1970/RFD PB16
Arran (Lamlash) 6.1970-84; Relief 1984-87	
D-186	1970/RFD PB16
Aberystwyth 6.1970-5.83; Relief 1983-	
D-187	1970/RFD PB16
Fleetwood 7.1970-84; Relief 1984-	
D-188 The Lord Feoffees	1970/RFD PB16
Bridlington 6.1971-10.83; Relief 1983-87	
D-189	1970/RFD PB16
Littlestone-on-Sea 7.1970-3.72; Port Talbot 3.1972-84; Relief 1984-85	
D-190	1970/RFD PB16
Mudeford 10.1970 81; Relief 1981	
D-191	1970/RFD PB16
Southwold 9.1970-8.73; Relief 1973-	
D-192	1970/RFD PB16
Abersoch 3.1971-12.77; Newquay 8.1979-10.80; Relief 1980-82 and 1984-?	
Blackpool 5.1982-84	
D-193	1971/RFD PB16
Whitby 3.1971-6.77	
D-194	1971/RFD PB16
Cardigan 7.1971-87	
D-195	1971/RFD PB16
Sold to Spain 1971	
D-196	1972/RFD PB16
Red Bay 3.1972-87; Boarding Boat 1987-	
D-197	1972/RFD PB16
Cromer 3.1972-84; Relief 1984-87; Boarding Boat 1987-	
D-198	1972/RFD PB16
Barrow 7.1972-4.86; Relief 1986-87; Boarding Boat 1987-	
D-199	1972/RFD PB16
Mumbles 8.1972-86; Relief 1986-	
D-200	1971/Avon 650 S
Walmer 3.1971-10.76	
D-201	1971/Avon 650 S
Harwich 1.1971-12.73	
D-202	1972/RFD PB16
Filey 8.1972-7.86; Relief 1986-?	
D-203	1972/RFD PB16
Amble 1972-84; Boarding Boat 1984-?	
D-204	1972/RFD PB16
Tenby 7.1972-86; Sheringham 1986-86	
D-205	1972/Zodiac Mk.II
Conwy 8.1971-3.76; Relief 1976-87	
D-206	1971/Zodiac Mk.II
Relief 1971-74; Harwich 1.1974-12.75; Relief 1976-	
D-207	1971/Zodiac Mk.II
Criccieth 3.1972-8.74; Relief 1974-	
D-208	1972/RFD PB16
Morecambe 3.1973-10.85; Relief 1985-87; Boarding Boat 1987-?	
D-209	1972/RFD PB16
Port St Mary 3.1973-87	

D class inflatable inshore lifeboats

D-210 1972/RFD PB16	**D-231** 1975/Zodiac Mk.II
Blyth 3.1973-87	Burnham-on-Crouch 3.1976-11.86; Relief 1986-87
D-211 1972/RFD PB16	**D-232** 1975/Zodiac Mk.II
Humbermouth 3.1973-2.80; Relief 1980-	Bude 8.1976-8.87
D-212 1972/RFD PB16	**D-233 Onslaught II** 1975/Zodiac Mk.II
Skegness 3.1973-87; Relief 1987-	Borth 3.1976-6.87
D-213 1972/RFD PB16	**D-234 [became D-8-P]** 1975/Zodiac Mk.II
Happisburgh 3.1973-87	Stonehaven 3.1975-10.84; Amble 3.1985-8.86; Relief 1987
D-214 1972/Zodiac Mk.II	**D-235 GUS Jnr** 1975/Zodiac Mk.II
Exmouth 7.1972-77; Relief 1976-87	St Abbs 3.1976-10.78; Tighnabruaich 7.1979-9.87
D-215 Blue Peter IV 1972/RFD PB16	**D-236** 1975/Zodiac Mk.II
St Agnes 3.1973-10.81	Southend-on-Sea 7.1975-87
D-216 Blue Peter III 1972/RFD PB16	**D-237** 1975/Zodiac Mk.II
North Berwick 3.1973-85; Dun Laoghaire 1986; Relief 1986-8; Boarding Boat 1988-9	Crimdon Dene 3.1975-7.87
D-217 1972/RFD PB16	**D-238 Hemel Hempstead Round Table** 1975/Zodiac Mk.II
Relief 1972-77; Sunderland 3.1977-87; ILB Centre, Cowes 1987-?	New Quay 3.1976-9.87
D-218 1972/RFD PB16	**D-239** 1975/Zodiac Mk.II
Relief 1972-76; on board 70-003 1976-86	Conwy 3.1976-87
D-219 1972/RFD PB16	**D-240** 1975/Zodiac Mk.II
Arbroath 3.1973-87	Harwich 1.1976-2.78; Relief 1978-10.87; sold to Red Cross, sent to Bangladesh 1988
D-220 1972/RFD PB16	**D-241** 1975/Zodiac Mk.II
Burry Port 3.1973-87	Rye Harbour 3.1976-86; Relief 1986-87
D-221 1972/Avon 650 S	**D-242** 1975/Zodiac Mk.II
Relief 1972-73	Little & Broad Haven 3.1975-8.87; Relief 1987-
D-222 1972/Avon 650 S	**D-243 [became D-13-P]** 1975/Zodiac Mk.II
Relief 1972-73	Rhyl 3.1976-5.87; Relief 1987-88
D-223 1972/Zodiac Mk.II	**D-244** 1976/Zodiac Mk.II
Relief 1972-	Bembridge 3.1976-87
D-224 1975/Zodiac Mk.II	**D-245 Alick Mackay** 1976/Zodiac Mk.II
Stranraer 3.1975-83; Relief 1983-	Kinghorn 5.1976-7.85; Relief 1986-7.87; Boarding Boat 1987-90
D-225 1975/Zodiac Mk.II	**D-246 Spirit of Rotary** 1976/Zodiac Mk.II
Moelfre 3.1975-76; Relief 1978-87; Southend-on-Sea 4-10.1987; sold to Red Cross	Wells 5.1976-87
D-226 1975/Zodiac Mk.II	**D-247** 1976/Zodiac Mk.II
Hastings 5.1975-10.82; Relief 1983-88	Mablethorpe 6.1976-88
D-227 1975/Zodiac Mk.II	**D-248** 1976/Zodiac Mk.II
Withernsea 3.1976-83; Relief 1983-1.87	Yarmouth 3.1976-10.78; Relief 1979-
D-228 [became D-33-P] 1975/Zodiac Mk.II	**D-249 Caribbean I** 1976/Zodiac Mk.II
Craster 6.1975-83; Relief 1983-87	Holyhead 7.1976-88
D-229 1975/Zodiac Mk.II	**D-250** 1976/Zodiac Mk.II
Cullercoats 1975-84; Relief 1984-6.88	Llandudno 3.1977-88
D-230 Miss Winfield 1975/Zodiac Mk.II	**D-251** 1976/Zodiac Mk.II
West Kirby 7.1975-12.86; Relief 1986-87	Lytham St Annes 3.1977-88

Inshore Rescue Boat No.152, later numbered D-152, at Bournemouth on exercise, July 1969. (Jeff Morris)

D-256 Lion Club 1 was one of the Zodiac Mk.II type inflatables of which only a relatively small number were built. (RNLI)

D class inflatable inshore lifeboats

D-252	1976/Zodiac Mk.II
Flint 8.1976-88	

D-253	1976/Zodiac Mk.II
Sheerness 3.1977-88	

D-254	1976/Zodiac Mk.II
Walmer 3.1977-88	

D-255	1977/Zodiac Mk.II
Exmouth 3.1977-88	

D-256 Lion Club 1	1977/Zodiac Mk.II
St Ives 3.1978-87; Relief 1987-	

D-257	1977/Zodiac Mk.II
Port Isaac 3.1978-88	

D-258	1977/Zodiac Mk.II
On board 70-003 1978-88; Boarding Boat 1988-	

D-259	1977/Zodiac Mk.II
Trearddur Bay 3.1978-88; Boarding Boat 1988-	

D-260 Gwynaeth	1977/Zodiac Mk.II
Whitby 3.1978-88; Boarding Boat 1988-93	

D-261	1977/Zodiac Mk.II
Kippford 3.1978-88; Boarding Boat 1988-93	

D-262 Clacton Round Table	1977/Zodiac Mk.II
Clacton-on-Sea 7.1976-12.83; Relief 1984-8.88	

D-263	1977/Zodiac Mk.II
On board 70-003 (at Kirkwall) 1978-88; sold to Iceland 6.1989	

D-264	1978/RFD PB16
Shoreham Harbour 3.1979-10.87; Relief 1987-9.89; Training 1989-9.94	

D-265	1978/RFD PB16
Pwllheli 3.1979-88; Boarding Boat 1990-92	

D-266	1978/RFD PB16
Eastbourne 7.1978-9.86; Relief 1986-3.90	

D-267	1978/RFD PB16
Redcar 3.1979-88	

D-268	1978/RFD PB16
Barmouth 3.1979-88; Relief 1989-90	

D-269	1978/RFD PB16
Tramore 3.1980-88; Relief 1989-90	

D-270	1979/Zodiac Mk.II
Aldeburgh 3.1980-88	

D-271	1979/Zodiac Mk.II
North Sunderland 7.1980-88	

D-272	1979/Zodiac Mk.II
Criccieth 8.1980-83; Relief 1983-89	

D-273	1979/RFD PB16
Howth 3.1979-89; Boarding Boat 1989-92	

D-274	1979/RFD PB16
St Catherine 2.1980-4.84; Relief 1984-88	

D-275	1979/RFD PB16
Horton & Port Eynon 7.1980-88; Relief 1989-90; Boarding Boat 1990-95	

D-276 Gillian Powell	1979/RFD PB16
Moelfre 5.1980-89; Boarding Boat 1990-96	

D-277 Sea Lion	1980/RFD PB16
Selsey 3.1981-89; Boarding Boat 1991-94	

D-278	1980/Zodiac Mk.II
Newquay 10.1980-84; Relief 1984-89	

D-279	1981/Zodiac Mk.II
Penarth 1981-89; Boarding Boat 1989-91	

D-280	1981/Zodiac Mk.II
Tynemouth 1981-7.89	

D-281 Sewing Machine Times	1981/Zodiac Mk.II
Aberdeen 1981-9.89	

D-282	1981/Zodiac Mk.II
Weston-super-Mare 1981-89	

D-283	1981/Zodiac Mk.II
Skerries 1981-89	

D-284	1981/Humber
Boarding Boat 1981-93	

D-285	1981/Humber
Boarding Boat 1981-93; Barmouth 1982	

D-286	1982/RFD PB16
Relief 1982-87; Torbay 5.1987-88; Boarding Boat 1988-93	

D-287	1982/Zodiac Mk.II
Stranraer 1982-89	

D-288 Cinque Ports I	1982/Zodiac Mk.II
Hastings 1983-89	

D-289	1982/Zodiac Mk.II
Withernsea 1983-2.90	

D-290	1983/Zodiac Mk.II
Craster 1983-10.89	

D-291 Donald Digby Middleton	1983/RFD PB16
Porthcawl 1983-3.89; Relief 1989-91; Boarding Boat 1991-94	

D-292 Castle House	1983/RFD PB16
Dunbar 1983-89; Marazion 4.1990-91; Relief 1991-92; Boarding Boat 1992-95	

D-293	1983/RFD PB16
Broughty Ferry 1984-89; Relief 1989-92	

D-294 Bill Mellis	1983/RFD PB16
Margate 6.1984-89	

D-295	1983/RFD PB16
Minehead 3.1984-4.92; Boarding Boat 1992-96	

D-296	1983/RFD PB16
Portsmouth (Langstone) 1984-4.92	

D-297	1983/RFD PB16
Port Talbot 1984-90; Relief 1990-92; Boarding Boat 1992-94	

D-298	1983/RFD PB16
Fleetwood 1984-92; Boarding Boat 1993-95	

D-299 Lord Feoffees	1983/RFD PB16
Bridlington 3.1984-92	

D-300 Lodge of Peace No.322	1983/RFD PB16
Blackpool 12.1983-93; Boarding Boat 1993-95	

D-301 Alan Thurlow Ashford	1983/RFD PB16
Bangor 1984-88; Relief 1988-93; Boarding Boat 1993-95	

D-302	1983/RFD PB16
Clacton-on-Sea 1.1984-92; Relief 1992-93; Boarding Boat 1993-96	

D-303	1983/RFD PB16
Arran (Lamlash) 1984-87; Relief 1988-	

D-304	1983/RFD PB16
Scarborough 1984-92; Boarding Boat 1992-93	

D-305 Blue Peter IV	1983/RFD PB16
St Agnes 1985-94; Relief 1994-95	

D-306 Blue Peter III	1983/RFD PB16
North Berwick 1985-6.93; Boarding Boat 1993-11.96	

D-307 Spirit of Round Table	1983/RFD PB16
Cromer 1984-92; Relief 1992-95	

D-308	1983/RFD PB16
Relief 1984-86; Kilkeel 1986-10.92; Boarding Boat 1992-96	

D-309	1983/RFD PB16
Relief 1984-95	

D class inflatable inshore lifeboats

D-310	1983/RFD PB16
Blackpool 11.1984-7.93; Relief 7.1993-95	

D-311 The Holgate	1983/Avon/Evans EA16
Relief 1985-86; Trials 1986-97; Training 1997-99	

D-312 Court Henbury	1984/Zodiac Mk.II
Relief 1985-92	

D-313 [became D-35-P]	1984/Zodiac Mk.II
Relief 1985-92; Display 1992-95	

D-314 Tricentrol I	1984/Zodiac Mk.II
Relief 1985-89; Display 1989-94	

D-315 Charlie B	1985/Avon/Evans EA16
Tenby 1986-4.93; Display 1993-95	

D-316	1985/Avon/Evans EA16
Morecambe 1986-5.93; ILB Centre, Cowes 5.1993-95	

D-317	1985/Avon/Evans EA16
Dun Laoghaire 1986-5.93	

D-318 Modeller I	1985/Avon/Evans EA16
Barrow 4.1986-4.93	

D-319	1985/Avon/Evans EA16
Mumbles 1986-11.94	

D-320 Filey Lion	1985/Avon/Evans EA16
Filey 7.1986-6.93; Relief 6.1993-95	

D-321 Rose Elizabeth Lawrence	1985/Avon/Evans EA16
Amble 1986-6.93; Relief 1993-95	

D-322 Humphrey and Nora Tollemache	1986/Avon/Evans EA16
Eastbourne 9.1986-93; Relief 1993-95	

D-323 Gus	1986/Avon/Evans EA16
Port St Mary 1987-7.94; Relief 1994-96	

D-324 BBC Radio Newcastle II	1986/Avon/Evans EA16
Blyth 1987-7.94; Relief 1994-96	

D-325 Tricentrol II	1986/Avon/Evans EA16
Cleethorpes 6.1987-94; Relief 1994-95	

D-326 Michel Philippe Wolvers	1986/Avon/Evans EA16
Skegness 1987-94; Larne 9.1994-95	

D-327	1986/Avon/Evans EA16
Happisburgh 1987-9.94	

D-328 Stephen Willoughby	1986/Avon/Evans EA16
Relief 1987-93	

D-329 BBC Radio Newcastle I	1986/Avon/Evans EA16
Sunderland 1987-94	

D-330	1986/Avon/Evans EA16
Arbroath 1987-10.94	

D-331 Dorothy Way	1986/Avon/Evans EA16
Burry Port 1987-9.94; Relief 1994-96	

D-332	1986/Avon/Evans EA16
West Kirby 1986-12.94; Display 1995-97	

D-333	1986/Avon/Evans EA16
Relief 1987-90; Courtown 5.1990-91; Relief 1991-93; Newcastle 1-11.1994	

D-334	1986/Avon/Evans EA16
Relief 1987-96	

D-335	1986/Avon/Evans EA16
Burnham-on-Crouch 1987-5.97	

D-336	1986/Avon/Evans EA16
Relief 1987-94; Angle 5.1994-96	

D-337 Norman Victor Hickling	1986/Avon/Evans EA16
Crimdon Dene 1987-93; Relief 1993-96	

D-338 Bruce's Bonus	1986/Avon/Evans EA16
Relief 1987-96	

D-339	1986/Avon/Evans EA16
New Quay 8.1987-95; St Ives 4-12.1995; Relief 1995-96	

D-340 Rotherham Grammar School	1986/Zodiac Mk.II
Relief 6.1987-94	

D-341	1986/Zodiac Mk.II
Southend-on-Sea 1987-88; Relief 1988-93; Boarding Boat 1993-94	

D-342	1986/Zodiac Mk.II
Relief 1987-92	

D-343	1987/Avon/Evans EA16
Bude 8.1987-96	

D-344 Onslaught	1987/Avon/Evans EA16
Borth 6.1987-6.95; Relief 1995-98; Boarding Boat 1998-99	

D-345 Douglas MacMillan Drew	1987/Avon/Evans EA16
Tighnabruaich 1987-4.94; Relief 1994-96	

D-346 Yachting Monthly	1987/Avon/Evans EA16
Conwy 1987-95; Boarding Boat 1998-2000	

D-347	1987/Avon/Evans EA16
Little & Broad Haven 9.1987-7.95; Relief 1995-96	

D-348 Banks' Staff I	1987/Avon/Evans EA16
Rhyl 1987-7.95; Relief 1995-96; Boarding Boat 1997-99	

D-349	1987/Avon/Evans EA16
Southend-on-Sea 1987-7.95; Relief 1995-96	

D-350	1987/Avon/Evans EA16
Relief 1987-94; Rock 3.1994-95; Relief 1995-96	

D-351 Rotary Club of Sutton	1987/Avon/Evans EA16
Shoreham Harbour 1987-96; Relief 1996-97	

D-321 Rose Elizabeth Lawrence *at Ilfracombe. (Nicholas Leach)*

D-326 Michel Philippe Wolvers *on duty at Larne, 1995. (Nicholas Leach)*

D class inflatable inshore lifeboats

D-352 Jane Ann	1987/Avon/Evans EA16
Wells 1988-11.96	

D-353	1987/Avon/Evans EA16
Bembridge 1988-6.96; Relief 1996-97	

D-354 Alfred George Martin	1987/Avon/Evans EA16
Torbay 1988-96; Relief 1996-97	

D-355	1987/Avon/Evans EA16
Relief 1988-96	

D-356	1987/Avon/Evans EA16
Lough Swilly (Buncrana) 1988-6.96	

D-357 Braemar	1987/Avon/Evans EA16
Mablethorpe 1988-7.96; Relief 7.1996-97	

D-358	1987/Avon/Evans EA16
Holyhead 1988-8.96; Relief 8.1996-99	

D-359 41 Club 1	1987/Avon/Evans EA16
Llandudno 1988-10.96	

D-360	1987/Avon/Evans EA16
Lytham St Annes 1988-10.96; Relief 10.1996-98	

D-361 Tangent I	1987/Avon/Evans EA16
Flint 1988-10.96; Relief 10.1996-97	

D-362 Kensington Rescuer	1987/Avon/Evans EA16
Sheerness 1988-96; Relief 1996-97	

D-363	1988/Avon/Evans EA16
Walmer 1988-1.97; Relief 1997	

D-364 Clubs of the River Exe	1988/Avon/Evans EA16
Exmouth 1988-5.97; Relief 5.1997-99	

D-365	1988/Avon/Evans EA16
Relief 1988-97	

D-366 Peter and Mollie Tabor	1988/Avon/Evans EA16
Port Isaac 6.1988-5.97; Relief 5.1997-11.98; Port Isaac 11.1998-99	

D-367 Sea Horse	1988/Avon/Evans EA16
Trearddur Bay 6.1988-5.96; Relief 1996-2002	

D-368 Douglas Cameron	1988/Avon/Evans EA16
Southend-on-Sea 8.1988-10.97; Relief 10.1997-98	

D-369	1988/Avon/Evans EA16
Whitby 8.1988-7.97; St Davids 1997-12.98; Relief 1998-99	

D-370 41 Club II	1988/Avon/Evans EA16
Kippford 8.1988-99	

D-371 41 Club III	1988/Avon/Evans EA16
Relief 9.1988-2000	

D-372 The Lion	1988/Avon/Evans EA16
Pwllheli 7.1988-8.97; Relief 8.1997-98; Boarding Boat 1998-2001	

D-373	1988/Avon/Evans EA16
Redcar 6.1988-7.97; Relief 7.1997-99	

D-374	1988/Avon/Evans EA16
Barmouth 9.1988-8.97; Relief 8.1997-98	

D-375 Alice	1988/Avon/Evans EA16
Tramore 11.1988-12.96; Relief 12.1996-97	

D-376	1988/Avon/Evans EA16
Aldeburgh 12.1988-6.97; Relief 1997-99	

D-377	1988/Avon/Evans EA16
North Sunderland 1988-11.97; Relief 1997-99	

D-378	1988/Avon/Evans EA16
Relief 12.1988-93; Portrush 7.1993-94; Relief 1994-2000	

D-379	1988/Avon/Evans EA16
Howth 1.1989-4.98; Relief 1998-2001	

D-380	1988/Avon/Evans EA16
Horton & Port Eynon 11.1988-97; Relief 1997-99	

D-381 Douglas	1989/Avon/Evans EA16
Moelfre 2.1989-6.98; Relief 1998-99	

D-382	1989/Avon/Evans EA16
Selsey 5.1989-5.98; Port Isaac 9.1998-9.98; Relief 9.1998-99	

D-383 Sea Tiger	1989/Avon/Evans EA16
Relief 6.1989-99	

D-384 John Cresswell	1989/Avon/Evans EA16
Penarth 7.1989-6.98; Relief 6.1998-99	

D-385	1989/Avon/Evans EA16
Tynemouth 7.1989-98; Relief 1998-99	

D-386 Trevor Edwin Jones	1989/Avon/Evans EA16
Aberdeen 9.1989-7.98; Relief 1998-99	

D-387 Boto-X 87	1989/Avon/Evans EA16
Weston-super-Mare 1989-7.98; Relief 7.1998-99	

D-388 Crusader	1989/Avon/Evans EA16
Stranraer 7.1989-10.98; Relief 1998-99	

D-389 Captain Colin	1989/Avon/Evans EA16
Broughty Ferry 9.1989-9.98; Relief 1998-99	

D-390 Tiger D	1989/Avon/Evans EA16
Porthcawl 8.1989-2.96; Fowey 8.1996-97; Relief 1997-99	

D-391 Lifeline	1989/Avon/Evans EA16
Relief 9.1989-98	

D-392 Cecile Rampton	1989/Avon/Evans EA16
Hastings 10.1989-10.98; Relief 1998-99	

D-393 Helen Mitchell Scrimgeour	1989/Avon/Evans EA16
Skerries 12.1989-11.97; Relief 1997-98	

D-394 Banks' Staff II	1989/Avon/Evans EA16
Withernsea 2.1990-1.99	

D-395 Bob	1989/Avon/Evans EA16
Craster 2.1990-99; Relief 1999-2001	

D-396 Starting Point	1989/Avon/Evans EA16
Relief 11.1989-93; Kessock 6.1993-94; Looe 1994; Relief 1994-99	

D-397 Banks' Staff III	1989/Avon/Evans EA16
Dunbar 12.1989-3.99; Relief 1999-	

D-398 Victory Wheelers	1989/Avon/Evans EA16
Relief 11.1989-94; Montrose 4.1994-95; Hayling Island 3.1995-3.96; Relief 1996-99	

D-399 Bertha	1989/Avon/Evans EA16
Relief 12.1989-99	

D-400 Tigger	1989/Avon/Evans EA16
Margate 12.1989-5.99; Relief 1999	

D-401 Banks' Staff Appeal IV	1990/Avon/Evans EA16
Relief 5.1990-2001	

D-402 Warwick	1990/Avon/Evans EA16
Port Talbot 7.1990-8.99; Relief 1999-2000	

D-403 City of Peterborough	1990/Avon/Evans EA16
Relief 6.1990-93; Campbeltown 4.1993-94; Relief 1994-2000	

D-404 Ann Speed	1990/Avon/Evans EA16
Relief 5.1990-99; Fenit 7.1999-2000	

D-405 British Diver III	1990/Avon/Evans EA16
Relief 6.1990-93; Looe 1993-94; Relief 1994-99	

D-406 Phyl Clare	1990/Avon/Evans EA16
Relief 8.1990-93; Swanage 4.1993-94; Newquay 9.1994-4.96; St Davids 1997-98; Relief 1998-2001	

D-407 The Marlborough Club, Didcot	1990/Avon/Evans EA16
Relief 7.1990- including Dunbar 2002 and Calshot 2-12.2003	

D-408 City of Derby	1990/Avon/Evans EA16
Relief 8.1990-2001	

D class inflatable inshore lifeboats

D-409 Taipan 1990/Avon/Evans EA16
Relief 8.1990-2000

D-410 Bacchus 1991/Avon/Evans EA16
Relief 3.1991-97; Alderney 7.1997-99; Relief 1999-2002

D-411 1991/Avon/Evans EA16
Marazion 3.1991-11.99; Relief 1999-2000; Marazion 2000-01; Relief 2001-04

D-412 B P Service 1991/Avon/Evans EA16
Courtown 3.1991-7.99; Relief 1999-2001

D-413 Billy Mills and George Ralph 1991/Avon/Evans EA16
Relief 1991-2001

D-414 Fairlands Lady 1991/Avon/Evans EA16
Relief 1991-

D-415 Pride of West Kingston 1991/Avon/Evans EA16
Relief 1991-95; Fishguard 4.1995-96; Relief 1996-2001

D-416 1991/Avon/Evans EA16
Relief 1991-2000

D-417 Douglas Hurndall 1991/Avon/Evans EA16
Relief 1991-94; Swanage 1994-95; Relief 1995-2001

D-418 1991/Avon/Evans EA16
Relief 1991-2002; Calshot 6.2002-2.03; Relief 2003-04

D-419 Sarah Helena 1991/Avon/Evans EA16
Relief 8.1991-

D-420 Leslie D 1992/Avon/Evans EA16
Minehead 4.1991-7.99; Relief 1999-2000

D-421 Lord Raglan 1991/Avon/Evans EA16
Portsmouth (Langstone) 4.1992-9.2000; Relief 2000-04

D-422 Alec Dykes 1992/Avon/Evans EA16
Ilfracombe 3.1992-2000; Relief 2000-04; Bude 2004; Relief 2004-

D-423 John Edmunds 1992/Avon/Evans EA16
Relief 1992-

D-424 City of Chester 1992/Avon/Evans EA16
Fleetwood 4.1992-2000; Relief 2000-03; Burnham-on-Sea 12.2003-

D-425 Strickson 1992/Avon/Evans EA16
Relief 3.1992-

D-426 Lord Feoffees II 1992/Avon/Evans EA16
Bridlington 4.1992-9.2000; Wexford 11.2002-1.04; Relief 2004-

D-427 Storrs 1992/Avon/Evans EA16
Relief 1992-98; Sligo Bay 1998-99; Relief 1999-2004

D-428 St Vincent Amazon 1992/Avon/Evans EA16
Relief 1992-97; Whitby 1997; Relief 1997-2004

D-429 R. J. M. 1992/Avon/Evans EA16
Blackpool 6.1992-2000; Calshot 1.2001-6.02; Relief 2002-

D-430 Rotherham Grammar School 1992/Avon/Evans EA16
Relief 5.1992-

D-431 Veronica 1992/Avon/Evans EA16
Clacton-on-Sea 7.1992-2000; Relief 2000-03; Littlehampton 2003-04; Relief 2004-

D-432 Ordnance Survey Bosun 1992/Avon/Evans EA16
Relief 6.1992-95; Wicklow 6.1995-5.97; Relief 5.1997-2004

D-433 Marjorie 1992/Avon/Evans EA16
Relief 6.1992-95; Berwick-upon-Tweed 5.1995-96; Relief 1996-2002; Fowey 2.1997-9.97; Littlehampton 6.2002-03; Relief 2003-

D-434 John Wesley Hillard 1992/Avon/Evans EA16
Scarborough 7.1992-2.2001; Relief 2001-

D-435 Table 32 1992/Avon/Evans EA16
Relief 8.1992-94; Shoreham Harbour 1994-95; Relief 1995-2001

D-436 Chloe 1992/Avon/Evans EA16
Cromer 8.1992-6.2001; Relief 6.2001-03; Eastbourne 2003; Relief 2003-

D-437 Jill Gatti 1992/Avon/Evans EA16
Relief 1.1993-

D-438 Arthur and Georgina Stanley Taylor 1993/Avon/Evans EA16
Tenby 4.1993-1.2001; South Broads 7.2001-04

D-439 Phyllis Mary 1993/Avon/Evans EA16
Relief 1.1993-95; Montrose 1995; Larne 1995-6.96; Relief 1996-

D-440 Brenda Reed 1993/Avon/Evans EA16
Morecambe 5.1993-5.2001; Relief 2001-02; Trearddur Bay 2002-04; Relief 2004-

D-441 Irish Diver 1993/Avon/Evans EA16
Dun Laoghaire 5.1993-2001; Trearddur Bay 7.2001-10.02; Relief 2002-

D-442 Edgar Law 1993/Avon/Evans EA16
Blackpool 7.1993-7.2001; Relief 2001-

D-443 Modeller II 1993/Avon/Evans EA16
Barrow 4.1993-10.2001; Relief 2001-

D-444 Sharpes Classic All Seasons 1993/Avon/Evans EA16
Relief 2.1994-

D-445 AXA Life Inshorer 1993/Avon/Evans EA16
Relief 1993-7.96; Fethard 7.1996-97; Relief 1997-

D-446 Holme Team 1993/Avon/Evans EA16
Filey 6.1993-2001; Relief 2001-

D-447 Thomas Campbell 1993/Avon/Evans EA16
Amble 6.1993-10.2001; Relief 2000-03; Wexford 1.2004-7.05; Relief 2005-

D-448 Sea Ranger 1993/Avon/Evans EA16
Relief 1993-95; Sennen Cove 1995-96; Relief 1996-2004

D-449 Humphrey and Nora Tollemache II 1993/Avon/Evans EA16
Eastbourne 8.1993-10.2001; Relief 2001-04; South Broads 2004-05; Relief 2005-

D-450 Anthony 1993/Avon/Evans EA16
Relief 1993-94; Sennen Cove 1994-95; Relief 1995-

D-362 Kensington Rescuer *at Sheerness. (Nicholas Leach)*

D-418 on relief duty at North Berwick, 1997. (Nicholas Leach)

D class inflatable inshore lifeboats

D-451 Jeanne Frances	1993/Avon/Evans EA16
Relief 1993-	

D-452 Blue Peter III	1993/Avon/Evans EA16
North Berwick 3.1994-9.2003; Relief 9.2003-	

D-453 Blue Peter IV	1993/Avon/Evans EA16
St Agnes 2.1994-2004	

D-454 Blue Peter VI	1993/Avon/Evans EA16
Cleethorpes 2.1994-2004; Relief 2004-	

D-455 Spirit of Kintyre	1994/Avon/Evans EA16
Campbeltown 3.1994-10.2001; Relief 2001-	

D-456 Jonathan Simpson	1994/Avon/Evans EA16
Portrush 3.1994-2.2002; Relief 2002-	

D-457 Elsie Frances I	1994/Avon/Evans EA16
Relief 3.1994-	

D-458 Maureen Samuels	1994/Avon/Evans EA16
Relief 5.1994-2004; Littlehampton 2004; Relief 2004-	

D-459 Margaret and Fiona Wood	1994/Avon/Evans EA16
Kessock 5.1994-10.2001; Relief 10.2001-04	

D-460 Leicester Fox	1994/Avon/Evans EA16
Skegness 6.1994-2.2002; Relief 2.2002-03; New Quay 2003-04; Relief 2004-	

D-461 Spirit of the RAOC	1994/Avon/Evans EA16
Looe 8.1994-3.2002; Relief 2002-05; Workington 6-8.2004; Anstruther 4.2005-06	

D-462 Frances	1994/Avon/Evans EA16
Port St Mary 7.1994-4.2002; Relief 4.2002-	

D-463 Nellie Grace Hughes	1994/Avon/Evans EA16
Mumbles 11.1994-7.2004; Relief 2004-	

D-464 Wren	1994/Avon/Evans EA16
Blyth 7.1994-11.2003; Relief 11.2003-	

D-465 Palmer Bayer	1994/Avon/Evans EA16
Relief 6.1994-2006	

D-466 Phyllis Mary II	1994/Avon/Evans EA16
Relief 8.1994-2004; St Agnes 2004-05; Relief 2005-	

D-467 Kathleen Scadden	1994/Avon/Evans EA16
Relief 9.1994-98; Cardigan 9.1998-6.99; Relief 1999-	

D-468 Colin Martin	1994/Avon/Evans EA16
Happisburgh 9.1994-10.2003; Troon 1.2004-06	

D-469 Winifred and Cyril Thorpe	1994/Avon/Evans EA16
Relief 10.1994-99; Alderney 2-9.1999; Relief 1999-2002; Wexford 2002-11.02; Relief 2002-04; Ballyglass 2004-	

D-470 Landlubber	1994/Avon/Evans EA16
Sunderland 9.1994-11.2003; Relief 11.2003-	

D-471 Coachmakers of London	1994/Avon/Evans EA16
Arbroath 10.1994-8.2004; Relief 2004-07	

D-472 Kip and Kath	1994/Avon/Evans EA16
Burry Port 10.1994-9.2003; Relief 9.2003-	

D-473 Thomas Jefferson	1994/Avon/Evans EA16
West Kirby 12.1994-12.2003; Relief 2003-	

D-474 G. C. H. Fox	1994/Avon/Evans EA16
Relief 12.1994-2003; Eastbourne 2003; Relief 2003-07	

D-475 Phyl Clare 2	1995/Avon/Evans EA16
Swanage 4.1995-8.2003; Relief 8.2003-	

D-476 Corydd	1995/Avon/Evans EA16
New Quay 5.1995-2003; Relief 2003-07	

D-477 Pride of Nuneaton and Bedworth	1995/Avon/Evans EA16
Relief 5.1995-1999; Kippford 1999-2001; Teddington 1.2002-05; Relief 2005-	

D-478 Aldergrove	1995/Avon/Evans EA16
Newcastle 5.1995-2005	

D-479 May	1995/Avon/Evans EA16
Borth 6.1995-5.2004; Relief 5.2004-	

D-480 The Craft Club	1995/Avon/Evans EA16
Relief 1995-	

D-481 Holme Team 3	1995/Avon/Evans EA16
Montrose 7.1995-8.2004; Relief 2004-	

D-482 Arthur Bate	1995/Avon/Evans EA16
Conwy 6.1995-10.2004; Angle 12.2004-6.05; Relief 6.2005-	

D-483 C. John Morris DFM	1995/Avon/Evans EA16
Relief 1995-	

D-484 Sybil	1995/Avon/Evans EA16
Little & Broad Haven 7.1995-8.2004; Relief 2004-	

D-485 Stafford with Rugeley	1995/Avon/Evans EA16
Rhyl 7.1995-10.2004; Relief 2004-	

D-486 Eleanor and Catherine	1995/Avon/Evans EA16
Relief 1996-2005; South Broads 2005-	

D-487 Foresters London Pride	1995/Avon/Evans EA16
Southend-on-Sea 7.1995-2005	

D-488 Mabel	1995/Avon/Evans EA16
Relief 1995-2000; Fenit 2000-01; Relief 2001-	

D-489 Dolly Holloway	1995/Avon/Evans EA16
Rock 9.1995-2005	

D-490 Spirit of the ACC	1995/Avon/Evans EA16
Sennen Cove 3.1996-2004; Relief 2004-	

D-491 Cetrek	1995/Avon/Evans EA16
Relief 1996-	

D-492 Lawnflite	1995/Avon/Evans EA16
Relief 1996-2002; Cardigan 3-9.1998; Ballyglass 2002-04; Relief 2004-	

D-472 Kip and Kath *at Burry Port. (Nicholas Leach)*

D-531 Walter Grove *breaks through surf off Horton beach. (Nicholas Leach)*

D class inflatable inshore lifeboats

D-493 Isabella Mary		1995/Avon/Evans EA16
Angle 3.1996-2004; Relief 2004-05; South Broads 2005-		
D-494 Sunrise		1995/Avon/Evans EA16
Berwick upon-Tweed 3.1996-2005; Relief 2005-		
D-495 Elsie Frances II		1995/Avon/Evans EA16
Bude 3.1996-12.2003; Burnham-on-Sea 5.2004-		
D-496 Leonard Stedman		1996/Avon/Evans EA16
Hayling Island 3.1996-2005; Relief 2005-		
D-497 Lord Daresbury		1996/Avon/Evans EA16
Newquay 4.1996-2005; Relief 2005-		
D-498 Fred Croker		1996/Avon/Evans EA16
Relief 1996-		
D-499 Jean and Paul		1996/Avon/Evans EA16
Larne 6.1996-2005		
D-500		1996/Avon/Evans EA16
Relief 1996-2004; Anstruther 2004-4.05		
D-501 Forest Row Choir		1996/Avon/Evans EA16
Shoreham 5.1996-8.2005; Relief 8.2005-		
D-502 Inis-Eoghain		1996/Avon/Evans EA16
Lough Swilly (Buncrana) 6.1996-		
D-503 Criddy and Tom		1996/Avon/Evans EA16
Bembridge 6.1996-8.2005; Relief 2005-		
D-504 Spirit of the RPC		1996/Avon/Evans EA16
Torbay 9.1996-		
D-505 Arthur Bygraves		1996/Avon/Evans EA16
Fishguard 7.1996-2006; Flint 9-12.2006; Relief 12.2006-		
D-506 Patrick Rex Moren		1996/Avon/Evans EA16
Mablethorpe 7.1996-11.2005; Relief 11.2005-06; Troon 7.2006-		
D-507 Spirit of Bedworth and Nuneaton		1996/Avon/Evans EA16
Holyhead 8.1996-11.2005; Relief 11.2005-06; Ballyglass 6.2006-		
D-508 John Saunderson		1996/Avon/Evans EA16
Llandudno 10.1996-11.2006; Relief 2006-		
D-509 John Kennedy		1996/Avon/Evans EA16
Lytham St Annes 10.1996-4.2006; Relief 2006-		
D-510 Marjorie Helen		1996/Avon/Evans EA16
Flint 10.1996-9.2005; Relief 9.2005-		
D-511 Margaret		1996/Avon/Evans EA16
Tramore 12.1996-6.2005; Relief 6.2005-		
D-512 Jane Ann II		1996/Avon/Evans EA16
Wells 11.1996-1.2007; Relief 2007-		
D-513 Seahorse I		1996/Avon/Evans EA16
Sheerness 10.1996-9.2006; Relief 2006-		
D-514 Lord Kitchener		1996/Avon/Evans EA16
Walmer 1.1997-12.2006; Relief 2006-		
D-515 Spirit of the RCT		1996/Avon/Evans EA16
St Ives 5.1997-2.2007; Relief 2007-		
D-516 Spirit of the Exe		1996/Avon/Evans EA16
Exmouth 5.1997-9.2006; Relief 2006-		
D-517 Spirit of the PCS RE		1997/Avon/Evans EA16
Port Isaac 5.1997-98		
D-518 Inbhear Deas		1997/Avon/Evans EA16
Wicklow 5.1997-2.2007; Relief 2007-		
D-519 Ernest and Rose Chapman		1997/Avon/Evans EA16
Burnham-on-Crouch 5.1997-2007; Relief 2007-		
D-520 Bob Savage		1997/Avon/Evans EA16
Aldeburgh 6.1997-5.2007; Relief 2007-		
D-521 OEM Stone II		1997/Avon/Evans EA16
Whitby 7.1997-2007; Relief 2007-		
D-522 City of Chester II		1997/Avon/Evans EA16
Pwllheli 8.1997-		
D-523 Peterborough Beer Festival 1		1997/Avon/Evans EA16
Redcar 7.1997-		
D-524 Pilgrim		1997/Avon/Evans EA16
Barmouth 8.1997-		
D-525 Holme Team IV		1997/Avon/Evans EA16
Clifden 5.1998-		
D-526 Olive Herbert		1997/Avon/Evans EA16
Fowey 9.1997-		
D-527 Ethel Royal		1997/Avon/Evans EA16
Southend-on-Sea 10.1997-		
D-528 Arthur Harris		1997/Avon/Evans EA16
Fethard 3.1998-		
D-529 Martin, John and Ann		1997/Avon/Evans EA16
Seahouses 11.1997-		
D-530 Marguerite Joan Harris		1997/Avon/Evans EA16
Howth 4.1998-		
D-531 Walter Grove		1998/Avon/Evans EA16
Horton & Port Eynon 5.1998-		
D-532 Kingsand		1998/Avon/Evans EA16
Moelfre 6.1998-		
D-533 Peter Cornish		1998/Avon/Evans EA16
Selsey 5.1998-		
D-534 Severn Rescuer		1998/Avon/Evans EA16
Penarth 6.1998-		
D-535 The Cromer Smuggler		1998/Avon/Evans EA16
Tynemouth 8.1998-		
D-536 Margaret II		1998/Avon/Evans EA16
Aberdeen 7.1998-		
D-537 Faith		1998/Avon/Evans EA16
Weston-super-Mare 7.1998-		
D-538 Tom Broom		1998/Avon/Evans EA16
Stranraer 10.1998-		
D-539 Hartlepool Dynamo		1998/Avon/Evans EA16
Broughty Ferry 9.1998-		
D-540 Cecile Rampton II		1998/Avon/Evans EA16
Hastings 10.1998-		
D-541 Brian and Margaret Wiggins		1998/Avon/Evans EA16
Withernsea 1.1999-		
D-542 A. B. One		1999/Avon/Evans EA16
Craster 2.1999-		
D-543 Saint David Dewi Sant		1999/Avon/Evans EA16
St Davids 12.1998-		
D-544 The Hastings		1999/Avon/Evans EA16
Dunbar 5.1999-		
D-545 Tigger Too		1999/Avon/Evans EA16
Margate 5.1999-		
D-546 Spirit of the PCS RE II		1999/Avon/Evans EA16
Port Isaac 6.1999-		
D-547 Society of Societies		1999/Avon/Evans EA16
Cardigan 6.1999-		
D-548 Star of the Sea		1999/Avon/Evans EA16
Courtown 7.1999-		
D-549 George and Christine		1999/Avon/Evans EA16
Minehead 7.1999-		
D-550 Gwenllian The Rotary Club of Port Talbot		1999/Avon/Evans EA16
Port Talbot 8.1999-		

D class inflatable inshore lifeboats

D-551 Spirit of Alderney	1999/Avon/Evans EA16
Alderney 8.1999-	
D-552 Global Marine	1999/Avon/Evans EA16
Marazion 11.1999-2000; Relief 2000 03; Anstruther 5.2003-04, Relief 7.2004-05;	
Burnham-on-Sea 8.2005-12.06; Relief 12.2006-	
D-553 David Whitehead	1999/Avon/Evans EA16
Kippford 7.2001-	
D-554 Heyland II	1999/Avon/Evans EA16
Portsmouth (Langstone) 9.2000-	
D-555 Deborah Brown	1999/Avon/Evans EA16
Ilfracombe 8.2000-	
D-556 Saddleworth	1999/Avon/Evans EA16
Fleetwood 9.2000-	
D-557 Lord Feoffees III	1999/Avon/Evans EA16
Bridlington 9.2000-	
D-558 William and Rose Nall	1999/Avon/Evans EA16
Blackpool 9.2000-	
D-559 Seahorse II	1999/Avon/Evans EA16
Clacton-on-Sea 10.2000-	
D-560 John Wesley Hillard II	1999/Avon/Evans EA16
Scarborough 2.2001-	
D-561 Cursitor Street	2000/Avon/Evans EA16
Fenit 3.2001-	
D-562 Georgina Stanley Taylor	2000/Avon/Evans EA16
Tenby 1.2001-	
D-563 Rotary District 1120	2000/Avon/Evans EA16
Filey 3.2001-	
D-564 Peter Bond	2001/Avon/Evans EA16
Morecambe 5.2001-	
D-565 Tony Heard	2001/Avon/Evans EA16
Dun Laoghaire 7.2001-	
D-566 Norah Cadman	2001/Avon/Evans EA16
Blackpool 7.2001-	
D-567 Spirit of Tamworth	2001/Avon/Evans EA16
Barrow 8.2001-	
D-568 Seahorse III	2001/Avon/Evans EA16
Cromer 6.2001-	
D-569 Rosemary Palmer	2001/Avon/Evans EA16
Amble 10.2001-	
D-570 Joan and Ted Wiseman 50/Roger B. Harbour	2001/Avon/Evans EA16
Eastbourne 10.2001-8.2003; North Berwick 9.2003-7.04; Ballyglass 2004-6.06	
D-571 Three Brothers	2001/Avon/Evans EA16
Campbeltown 10.2001-	

D-572 Ken and Mary	2001/Avon/Evans EA16
Portrush 2.2002-	
D-573 Leicester Fox II	2001/Avon/Evans EA16
Skegness 2.2002-	
D-574 Regina Mary	2002/Avon/Evans EA16
Looe 3.2002-	
D-575 Hounslow	2002/Avon/Evans EA16
Port St Mary 4.2002-	
D-576 Spirit of the Thames	2002/Avon/Evans EA16
Teddington 6.2002-	
D-600 Metcap	2002/IB1
Trials 2002-03; Training 2003-	
D-601 Jenny Topham	2002/IB1
Trials 2002-03; Relief 2003-	
D-602 Gilbert Goble	2002/IB1
Trials 2002-04; Relief 2004-	
D-603 Forever Forward	2002/IB1
Trials 2002-04; Relief 2004-	
D-604 Marie Turner	2002/IB1
Trials 2002-04; Relief 2004-	
D-605 Joan and Ted Wiseman 50	2003/IB1
Eastbourne 8.2003-	
D-606 Jennie B	2003/IB1
Blyth 11.2003-	
D-607 Spirit of Berkhamsted	2003/IB1
Happisburgh 10.2003-	
D-608 Helen and Ian Tytler	2003/IB1
Sunderland 11.2003-	
D-609 248 Squadron RAF	2003/IB1
Calshot 12.2003-	
D-610 Catterick	2003/IB1
Relief 1.2004-	
D-611 The Young Watsons	2004/IB1
Burry Port 9.2003-	
D-612 Dave and Trevor Jones	2004/IB1
West Kirby 12.2003-	
D-613 Jack Cleare	2004/IB1
Swanage 8.2003-	
D-614 Flo and Dick Smith	2004/IB1
Trearddur Bay 1.2004-	
D-615 CSMA Frizzell 80th Anniversary	2004/IB1
Relief 2004-	

One of the first of the IB1 type D class inflatables, D-605 Joan and Ted Wiseman 50, *on exercise off Eastbourne. (Nicholas Leach)*

D-617 Henry Philip *in the surf just off Bude beach, north Cornwall, conditions for which the D class ILB is ideally suited. (Nicholas Leach)*

D class inflatable inshore lifeboats

D-616 Amy Lea		2004/IB1
New Quay 2.2004-		
D-617 Henry Philip		2004/IB1
Bude 5.2004-		
D-618 Blue Peter VI		2004/IB1
Cleethorpes 7.2004-		
D-619 Blue Peter III		2004/IB1
North Berwick 7.2004-		
D-620 Edna May		2004/IB1
Relief 2004-		
D-621 Duncan Ferguson		2004/IB1
Arbroath 8.2004-		
D-622 May II		2004/IB1
Borth 5.2004-		
D-623 Peterborough Beer Festival 2		2004/IB1
Mumbles 7.2004-		
D-624 Spirit of the RLC		2004/IB1
Sennen Cove 7.2004-		
D-625 John Charles Raybould		2004/IB1
Relief 2004-		
D-626 David Leslie Wilson		2004/IB1
Montrose 8.2004-		
D-627 Arthur Bate II		2004/IB1
Conwy 8.2004-		
D-628 Austin Burnett		2004/IB1
Little & Broad Haven 8.2004-		
D-629 The Shannock		2004/IB1
Workington 8.2004-		
D-630 Langley Muir		2004/IB1
Relief 12.2004-		
D-631 Spirit of Juniper		2004/IB1
Littlehampton 10.2004-		
D-632 Godfrey & Desmond Nall		2004/IB1
Rhyl 10.2004-		
D-633 Pride of London Foresters		2004/IB1
Southend-on-Sea 1.2005-		
D-634 Rusper		2004/IB1
Rock 1.2.2005-		
D-635 Semper Paratus		2004/IB1
Relief 8.2004-		
D-636 Valery Wilson		2005/IB1
Newquay 2.2005-		
D-637 Aldergrove II		2005/IB1
Newcastle 3.2005-		
D-638 Richard John Talbot Hillier		2005/IB1
Angle 6.2005-		
D-639 Howard and Mary Broadfield		2005/IB1
Berwick-on-Tweed 7.2005-		
D-640 Mabel Davies		2005/IB1
Relief 3.2005-		
D-641 Blue Peter IV		2005/IB1
St Agnes 3.2005-		
D-642 Amanda James and Ben		2005/IB1
Hayling Island 5.2005-		
D-643 Tra Mhor		2005/IB1
Tramore 6.2005-		
D-644 Phillip Booth		2005/IB1
Wexford 7.2005-		

D-645 Martin Jolly		2005/IB1
Relief 2004-		
D-646 Hannabella Ferguson		2005/IB1
Larne 8.2005-		
D-647 Barry Lazell		2005/IB1
Shoreham Harbour 8.2005-		
D-648 Spirit of Mortimer		2005/IB1
Teddington 5.2005-		
D-649 Dorothy Beatrice May Gorman		2005/IB1
Bembridge 8.2005-		
D-650		2005/IB1
Relief 2005-		
D-651 John William Hirst		2005/IB1
Torbay 2005-		
D-652 Team Effort		2005/IB1
Fishguard 4.2006-		
D-653 William Hadley		2005/IB1
Mablethorpe 11.2005-		
D-654 Angel of Holyhead		2005/IB1
Holyhead 11.2005-		
D-655 Guardian Angel		2005/IB1
Relief 17.11.2005-		
D-656 William Robert Saunderson		2005/IB1
Llandudno 22.11.2006-		
D-657 Sally		2005/IB1
Lytham St Annes 18.4.2006-		
D-658 Sir Y Flint		2005/IB1
Flint 19.12.2005-		
D-659 George Godfrey Benbow		2005/IB1
Howth 7.2.2006-		
D-660 City of Leeds		2006/IB1
Relief 22.2.2006-		
D-661 Jane Ann III		2006/IB1
Wells 9.1.2007-		
D-662 Eleanor		2006/IB1
Sheerness 27.9.2006-		
D-663 Duggie Rodbard		2006/IB1
Walmer 13.12.2006-		
D-664 Puffin		2006/IB1
Burnham-on-Sea 11.12.2006-		
D-665		2006/IB1
Relief 2006-		
D-666		2006/IB1
[Number not allocated]		
D-667 The Rotary Centennial Queen		2006/IB1
Anstruther 30.11.2006-		
D-668 Colin Bramley Parker		2006/IB1
St Ives 5.2.2007-		
D-669 George Bearman		2006/IB1
Exmouth 28.9.2006-		
D-670		2006/IB1
Relief 2006-		
D-671 Sheringham Shanty Men		2007/IB1
Wicklow 21.2.2006-		
D-672 Ernest and Rose Chapman II		2007/IB1
Burnham-on-Crouch 2007-		
D-673 Christine		2007/IB1
Aldeburgh 1.5.2007-		

E class Tiger fast response boats

Constructed 2001-2002, 6 built.
Specifications • length 9m, beam 2.8m, draft 1m, weight 3.5 tonnes fully fuelled.

In January 2001, the RNLI announced that it would be operating lifeboats on the tidal river Thames in response to a request from the Maritime and Coastguard Agency (MCA). The criteria required lifeboat to operate along the Thames between Canvey Island and Teddington Lock. In order to achieve the criteria, the RNLI determined that a fast, highly manoeuvrable craft was required. As no lifeboat in the fleet was capable of achieving the required speed, which was about 40 knots, and timescales for designing such a craft were tight, a suitable vessel was sourced from commercial manufacturers and six fast rescue craft, with lightweight aluminium alloy hulls, were purchased. The planing hull was fitted with a collar fabricated from a polyurethane-coated closed cell foam and the type was categorised as E class lifeboats.

The E class, introduced in January 2002 for exclusive use at the three Thames lifeboat stations of Gravesend, Tower Pier and Chiswick, were based on a 9m fast response craft design from Tiger Marine Ltd, a company based at Trearddur Bay in Anglesey. In total six boats were built, ensuring a back-up for each of the three station boats. Built at FBM Babcock Naval Shipyard, Rosyth, the Tiger Marine boats, with a speed of almost forty knots, enabled incidents to be reached within fifteen minutes.

They were powered by twin Steyr/Bukh turbo diesel engines, each delivering 230hp at 4,000 to 4,400rpm via drive-shafts connected to Hamilton 241 water jet units. The craft have an open transom and a large working deck for easy survivor recovery. Aerials, warning siren, navigation lights and righting bag were located on an A-frame mounted aft. The electronics fitted included a VHF radio, Metropolitan Police radio, echo sounder, radar and chart plotter, GPS satellite navigation, and mobile phones. They were self-righted in the event of a capsize and carried a full inventory of lifesaving and safety equipment, searchlights and bilge pumps. They were designed to operate at full speed with a minimum endurance of four hours, day or night, with a crew of three and capacity for up to twenty survivors.

The boats were not permanently assigned to any station but operated in a pool between the three stations, and cycled through to build up operational hours on each. Maintenance was partly undertaken by RNLI staff and partly by the Metropolitan Police boatyard at Wapping, under contract, about ten miles from Chiswick. This yard also acted as the storage depot for the boats when they were not in use.

E class lifeboat E-002 Olivia Laura Deare leaving Gravesend on exercise with some volunteer crew. (Nicholas Leach)

E-001, E-002 and E-004 are put through their paces at Tower Pier in front of the Tower of London on 2 January 2002, the day the Thames lifeboat service was officially launched. (Nicholas Leach)

During the boats' initial year in service, problems with the design were soon evident so the RNLI undertook a rectification and modification programme to improve the boats' operational effectivenenss and make them more reliable. The Technical Office undertook a detailed survey to determine what improvements were needed and also gathered a 'wish list' from the crews. The programme highlighted the unreliability of the electrics and the need for an improved fuel system and tanks. Improvements were also required to the bilge system, the deck hatches and the seating console configuration. The roll-cage and radar platform also needed to provide navigation and emergency lights with an improved radar installation and better deck access. The design review took place at the Inshore Lifeboat Centre (ILC) in Cowes and involved technical and engineering staff from the RNLI's head office, the ILC and the coast, together with representatives from the Thames stations.

The modifications were implemented during 2003 and 2004. Along with full engine instrumentation, a sophisticated intercom/radio set-up, which allows communications between crew and external agencies, was fitted, together with radar/plotter, two VHF radios, a Metropolitan Police radio, navigation/blue flashing/deck flood lights and an electric bilge pump. E-002, the first boat to be modified, was delivered to the Thames during July 2003. After a number of areas were highlighted for further improvements, these, coupled with ideas from the crews operating the boats, were introduced on E-001 and subsequent boats as they were refitted. E-001 was launched in November 2003 and delivered to the Thames a month later with the other boats following in 2004.

E class Tiger fast response boats

E-001 Public Servant (Civil Service No.44)	2001/Tiger Marine		**E-004 Ray and Audrey Lusty**	2001/Tiger Marine
CISPOTEL Lifeboat Fund.			Legacy of Raymond and Audrey Lusty, Farnham.	
Thames (Tower Pier) 1.2002-			Thames (Chiswick) 1.2002-	
E-002 Olivia Laura Deare	2001/Tiger Marine		**E-005 Legacy**	2001/Tiger Marine
Bequest of Olivia Deare, Gravesend.			Bequest of Lieut Philip F. S. King.	
Thames (Gravesend) 1.2002-			Thames (Relief) 2.2002-	
E-003 Chelsea Pensioner	2001/Tiger Marine		**E-006 Joan and Kenneth Bellamy**	2001/Tiger Marine
Bequest of Dr Patricia Mary Martyn Baguley, High Lorton, Cockermouth.			Bequest of Joan and Ken Bellamy.	
Thames (Relief) 1.2002-			Thames (Relief) 2.2002-	

E class lifeboat E-005 Legacy setting out from Tower Lifeboat Station, and heading under Waterloo Bridge. The full-time crews employed at Chiswick, Tower and Gravesend were supplemented by volunteers organised along the same lines as lifeboat stations round the coast. (Nicholas Leach)

Chiswick's E class lifeboat E-006 Joan and Ken Bellamy on patrol near Battersea Power Station on the Thames in March 2007, after being modified and rebuilt. The twin jet drives are just visible in this photo. (Nicholas Leach)

Inshore rescue hovercraft

Introduced 2002, still in production, 6 built.
Specifications • length 7.6m (25ft), crew 4, seats for 6-8.

The inshore rescue hovercraft was introduced to meet the demand for a rescue craft capable of crossing terrain such as tidal marshes and mudflats that dry out at low tide and which can be inaccessible by boat. The RNLI began assessing whether hovercraft could be used as effective rescue tools in 2001. During the assessment, it was specified that the hovercraft must operate safely in different terrains and volunteer crews had to be able to master 'flying' it. The commercially available Griffon 470TD hovercraft built by Griffon Hovercraft of Southampton was trialled. The 470TD had two propeller-fans over the stern, driven by twin 85hp 1.9-litre Volkswagen intercooled and turbo-charged diesel engines. The craft, capable of speeds in excess of 30 knots, had seating for between six and eight people, including the pilot, or could carry a total of 470kgs (1,036lbs) of payload.

During the evaluation trials in Poole, the hovercraft showed that it could withstand damage, was easy to prepare for launch, worked well over sand and mud and crew training was comparable to that undertaken by inshore lifeboat crews. Limitations included its carrying capacity, a maximum of 450kg, an inability to work on porous surfaces and a weather restriction to wind speeds of less than twenty-five knots and wave heights less than 0.6m (2ft).

Following the trials at Poole and as part of the hovercraft pilot scheme, the craft was taken to five lifeboat stations, selected because they had handled incidents in which a hovercraft might have been of use and because extensive sand or mudflats in the

Profile of the Griffon 470TD hovercraft, which was trialled at Poole, and then taken to five lifeboat stations in 2001 to assess its suitability. Its subsequent success led to its introduction at selected stations. (Scott Snowling)

stations' areas of operation inhibited the ability of existing water-borne lifeboats. Trials were held at Hunstanton, which covers the sandbanks of the Wash; Morecambe, which covers the treacherous Morecambe Bay; Flint and West Kirby which deal with incidents on the rivers Dee and Mersey near Liverpool; and Southend-on-Sea, where mudflats of the Thames Estuary can cause problems.

Once all the tests had been completed, a report was submitted to the RNLI's executive committee in November 2001 which subsequently led to the decision to introduce hovercraft to the RNLI's fleet, to be co-located at existing lifeboat stations. Morecambe became the first station to have a hovercraft in December 2002 when H-002 The Hurley Flyer was declared operational. Three further hovercraft were ordered from Griffon and, by the end of 2004, Hunstanton, Southend-on-Sea, and New Brighton were all operating the craft.

H-001 Molly Rayner	2002/Griffon 470TD
Bequest of Mr Donald Rayner, Buckinghamshire.	
Trials 2001-02; Relief 12.2002-	
H-002 The Hurley Flyer	2002/Griffon 470TD
Gift of Mrs Kay Hurley, MBE.	
Morecambe 23.12.2002-	
H-003 Hunstanton Flyer (Civil Service No.45)	2003/Griffon 470TD
CISPOTEL Lifeboat Fund.	
Hunstanton 25.7.2003-	

H-004 Vera Ravine	2004/Griffon 470TD
Bequest of Mrs Vera Ravine.	
Southend-on-Sea 10.7.2004-	
H-005 Hurley Spirit	2004/Griffon 470TD
Gift of Mrs Kay Hurley, MBE.	
New Brighton 23.6.200-	
H-006 John Russell	2005/Griffon 470TD
Bequest of John Russell.	
Relief 2005-	

H-001 Molly Rayner *returning to the RNLI Depot at Poole during a crew training course, May 2004. (Nicholas Leach)*

H-002 The Hurley Flyer *at Morecambe in December 2002 on the day she become the first hovercraft in RNLI service. (Nicholas Leach)*

Inshore rescue hovercraft

H-003 Hunstanton Flyer (Civil Service No.45) *being taken through the sand dunes at Hunstanton and towed onto the beach by Land Rover. She is used to cover the sanbanks of the Wash. (Nicholas Leach)*

H-004 Vera Ravine *from Southend-on-Sea on exercise in the Thames Estuary, July 2004. (Nicholas Leach)*

H-005 Hurley Spirit, *the second hovercraft funded by Mrs Kay Hurley, during the craft's official naming ceremony at New Brighton, June 2005. Although H-005 arrived in October 2004, she was not officially placed on station until 23 June 2005 after several months of training and evaluation. New Brighton was deemed the best location from which to operate a hovercraft to most effectively cover the Mersey and Dee estuaries. (Nicholas Leach)*

Appendix 1 • Motor lifeboats sold abroad

ON	Sold	Named	Stations
Australia (Royal Volunteer Coastal Patrol)			
1002	1999	P&O Nedlloyd Stratheden	Botany Bay (NSW) 1999-
1003	1999	P&O Nedlloyd Strathmore	Narooma (NSW) 1999-
1005	1999	P&O Nedlloyd Strathallan	Ulladulla (NSW) 1999-
1006	1999	P&O Nedlloyd Rawalpindi	Sydney (NSW) 1999-
1011	1993	Anl Sea Guardian	Woolongong (NSW) 1993-98, St Helens (Tasmania) 2.1998-
1029	1999	P&O Nedlloyd Strathaird	Trial Bay (NSW) 2002-
1035	1999	P&O Nedlloyd Strathnaver	Batemans Bay (NSW) 1999-
1056	1999	PV Danial Thain	Port Stephens (NSW) 1999-
1058	2002	P&O Nedlloyd Encounter	Mosman, Sydney 7.2002-
Canada (Canadian Lifeboat Institution)			
1033	1999	1A 001	Roberts Bank, Vancouver 1999-
Chile (CVBS)			
705	1955	Cap Christiansen	Valparaiso 1955-98, now demo
860	1980	Valparaiso 3	1980-98, now back in England
1051	1998	Capitan Eduardo Simpson Roth	Valparaiso 10.1998-
China (Rescue and Salvage Bureau)			
1081	2005	Hua Ying 393	Fuzhou 2006-
1082	2005	Hua Ying 398	Donghai, Shanghai 8.2005-
1093	2005	Hua Ying 396	Shenzhen 2006-
1098	2005	Hua Ying 397	Zhangjiang 2006-
1106	2006	Hua Ying 395	Dalian 2006-
1107	2005	Hua Ying 394	Dalian 2006-
1123	2005	Hau Ying 399	Wenzhou, Zhejiang 12.2005-
1143	2005	Hua Ying 392	Shantou 2006-
Estonia (Eesti Vetelpaasteuhingu)			
998	1993	Anita	Haapsalu 1993-
1009	1994	Anni	1994-
Faroe Islands (Nodoya Bajargingarfelag)			
1103	2005		
Finland (Suomen Meripelastusseura)			
1049	1999	Mac Elliott	Porkkala, Helsinki 1999-
1059	2001	Arvinsilma/2005- Russaro	Turku 4.2001-02; Hanco 2002-
1076	2002	Torbay	Kaskinen 10.2002-
1098	2002	Janne Malén	Uusikaupunki 2002-

ON	Sold	Named	Stations
Guatemala			
734	1959	George Shee	1959-
781	1959	W.R.A.	8.1958-
Iceland (Association for Search and Rescue)			
988	1988	Henry A. Halfdansson	Rekjavik 6.1989-2002
1050	1998	Oddur V. Gislason	Grindavik 11.1998-
1053	2002	Björg	Rif 6.2002-
1057	2002	Ásgrímur S. Björnsson	Reykjavík 6.2002-
1061	2000	Gunnar Fridriksson	Ísafjörður 9.2000-
1070	2003	[Destined for Raufarhofn, but wrecked during passage 12.2003]	
1078	2003	Einar Sigurjónsson	Hafnarfjördur 8.2003-
1100	2007		
1108	2005	Ingibjorg	Höfn 2005-
1113	2004	Hafbjörg	Neskaupstadur 5.2004-
1118	2004	Gunnbjörg	Raufarhöfn 10.2004-
1135	2006	Vörður II	Patreksfjörður 9.2006-
1136	2005	Hunabjorg	Skagaströnd 2005-
Madeira			
1067	2003		Madeira 2003-
1077	2003		Madeira 2003-
Namibia			
1026	1996	The Spirit of Standard Bank	Walvis Bay 2000-5; Luderitz 2005-
Netherlands (KNZHRM)			
779	1946	Rosabella	Terschelling 1946-55, sold 1955
780	1946	Rosilee	Vlieland 1946-59, sold 1959
New Zealand (Sumner LBI or Royal NZCG Federation)			
1028	1999	Westgate Rescue	New Plymouth (CG) 1999
1032	1998	P&O Nedlloyd Rescue	Lyttleton (Sumner) 9.1998-
1043	1998	Nicholsons Rescue/ Trust Porirua Rescue	Mana (CG) 4.1998-
1045	1999	P&O Nedlloyd Rescue	Waiheke (CG) 4.1999-
1048	1995	Ivan Tulley Rescue	West Coast Buller Marine, Greymouth (CG) 7.1995-
1060	1999	Hamilton Rotary Rescue	Raglan (CG) 12.1999-
1065	1999	Legend	Napier (CG) 1999-2004; sold to become pleasure boat
1079	1999	John Barton Acland Rescue	Kiakoura (CG) 7.1999-6.2004; sold to become pleasure boat
South Africa (National Sea Rescue Institute)			
1088	1994	South Star (Redding 17 10-05)	Hermanus 1994-
1089	2003	Spirit of Nadine Gordimer	Hout Bay 2006-
1090	2003	Spirit of Safmarine III	Cape Town 2006-
1101	1997	Spirit of Toft	Algoa Bay, Port Elizabeth 1997-
1102	1997	Sanlan Rescuer	Gordon's Bay 1997-
1104	2003	Eikos Rescuer II	Durban 2003-
Tenerife			
1021	1992	Sea Lion/Solent Sealion	Tenerife 1992-2001, sold
Uruguay (ADES)			
704	1957	Ades 1, Captain Francisco Alvarez	Retired in dry dock at Colonia, Montevideo
934	1984	Ades 2 Sudelmar	Puerto de Sauce 1984-
1012	1995	Ades 14 ILC 95	Puerto de Colonia 1995-
1019	1993	Ades 12, I.M. De Maldonado	Punta Del Este 1993-
1044	1997	Ades I6	Puerto Del Bucoe 1998-
1068	1994	Ades 13 Agustin Carlevaro	Puerto De Carmelo 1995-

Ásgrímur S. Björnsson (ex-ON.1057) moored at Reykjavik, Iceland. The Icelandic lifeboat service brought a number of lifeboats from the RNLI, starting with a pulling lifeboat in the late 1920s. As well as 52ft Aruns, the service also bought a number of Atlantic 21s between 1998 and 2004. (Gary Markham)

Appendix 2 • Motor lifeboats on display

Barrow

Herbert Leigh (ON.900) is on display outside the Dock Museum where she has been since 1994.

Blackgang Chine, IOW

Friendly Forester (ON.915) is displayed outside at the Blackgang Chine Museum.

Buckie

The Doctors (ON.983) was displayed outside at the Buckie Drifter Centre since April 1995, although the Centre closed in 2005 leaving the boat with an uncertain future.

Charlestown

Amelia (ON.979) has been on display outside the Shipwreck and Heritage Museum, Charlestown, Cornwall, since 1993.

Chatham

The Chatham Historic Dockyard in Kent houses the Lifeboat Collection. This includes of the following motor lifeboats: B. A. S. P. (ON.687), Helen Blake (ON.809), Susan Ashley (ON.856), St.Cybi (Civil Service No.9) (ON.884), North Foreland (Civil Service No.11) (ON.888), Grace Darling (ON.927), J. G. Graves of Sheffield (ON.942), The Will and Fanny Kirby (ON.972), Edward Bridges (C.S.& P.O.No.37) (ON.1037) and the prototype 44ft Wavenet 44-001. In addition, Mary Gabriel (ON.1000) is kept afloat in the river and used by Chatham volunteers for publicity and fund-raising purposes.

Cromer

H. F. Bailey (ON.777) has been displayed inside the old No.2 lifeboat house since 1994, but during 2005 a new purpose-built centre was constructed for her.

Donaghadee

Sir Samuel Kelly (ON.885) is on display in a car park near Donaghadee harbour.

Duxford

Jesse Lumb (ON.822) is one of the exhibits at the Imperial War Museum, Duxford.

Gorleston-on-Sea

John and Mary Meiklam of Gladswood (ON.670) has been on display inside the former Gorleston lifeboat house since June 1994.

Hartlepool

Princess Royal (C. S. No.7) (ON.828) has been restored and is based at the Marina. Also in the marina, but kept out of the water, is Robert and Dorothy Hardcastle (ON.966).

Harwich

Valentine Wyndham-Quin (ON.985) has been kept inside the old lifeboat house, which is now used as a maritime museum, at the Green since July 1995.

Hoylake

Thomas Corbett (ON.862) has been undergoing restoration at the Laird Foundation, Birkenhead, for eventual display at Hoylake.

Hythe Marina, Southampton

Ruby and Arthur Reed (ON.990) has been outside on display at Hythe Marina since 1990 in the middle of a roundabout in the car park.

Irvine

T. G. B. (ON.962) is displayed inside the Scottish Maritime Museum.

Kirkleatham

Sir James Knott (ON.975) is displayed at Kirkleatham Old Hall Museum, near Redcar.

Land's End

James and Catherine Macfarlane (ON.989) is displayed outside at the Land's End complex where she has been since June 1988.

Longhope

Thomas McCunn (ON.759) is kept inside the lifeboat house at Brims, Hoy, and forms the centrepiece of the Longhope Lifeboat Museum. She has been at Longhope since 2000 having been privately owned between then and her sale from service in 1972.

Marchwood

Lucy Lavers (ON.832), one of the Dunkirk Little Ships, had been under restoration at the B.M.P.T. Husbands Boatyard, Marchwood, but in 2005 this closed down leaving the boat with an uncertain future.

Moelfre

Birds Eye (ON.996) is displayed inside the Sea Watch Centre at Moelfre, where she has been since May 1991.

Newbiggin-by-the-Sea

Mary Joicey (ON.984) was moved in 2005 from the Child Beale Wild Life Trust, Reading, where she had been displayed since November 1989, to Newbiggin for restoration and future display.

Newport IOW

Langham (ON.676) is under restoration at the Classic Boat Museum along .

Poole

Thomas Kirk Wright (ON.811) is kept inside the old lifeboat house on Poole Quay and plans were announced in 2007 to open the building up as an information centre.

Sheringham

Former Sheringham lifeboats Foresters Centenary (ON.786) and Manchester Unity of Oddfellows (ON.960) are displayed at the 'Mo' bandstand area in the town.

Spalding

The hull of Mary Pullman (ON.981) has been on display at Baytree Garden Centre, Weston, Spalding, Lincolnshire, since March 1993.

Swansea

Currently in storage for future display at Swansea's Maritime Museum are William Gammon – Manchester and District XXX (ON.849) and Watkin Williams (ON.922).

Ulster

William and Laura (ON.870) is in storage at the Ulster Folk and Transport Museum, Cultra, Ulster, for possible future display.

Valentia

Rowland Watts (ON.938) is undergoing restoration for display at Valentia.

Walton-on-the-Naze

One of the four lifeboats converted to motor during the first trials with engines, James Stevens No.14 (ON.432), has been under restoration at Titchmarsh Marine for display at the Walton Lifeboat Museum since 2003.

Longhope lifeboat Thomas McCunn *(ON.759) on the slipway outside the lifeboat house at Aith Hope that serves as the Longhope Lifeboat Trust's Museum. (Nicholas Leach)*

Index

Index

Index

The individual lifeboat entries are indexed by the table number and the entry within the table, e.g. 4/10.
Where lifeboats have 'The' in their name, this has been omitted in the index.
p indicates a photograph of the lifeboat.
Inshore lifeboats have not been indexed, but photos of individual ILBs have.
The tables are correct as of 30 June 2007.

Bibliography

Barnett, James R. (1933, 2nd edition 1950): *Modern Motor Life-boats* (Blackie, Glasgow).

— (1940): Fifty Years of Life-boat Design, in *The Lifeboat*, April 1940, pp.233-235.

Cameron, Ian (2002): *Riders of the Storm* (Weidenfeld & Nicolson, London).

Cox, Barry (1998): *Lifeboat Gallantry* (Spink & Son Ltd, London).

Dawson, Major A. J. (1923): *Britain's Life-boats: The Story of a Century of Heroic Service* (Hodder & Stoughton, London).

Farr, A. D. (1973): *Let Not The Deep: The story of the Royal National Lifeboat Institution* (Impulse Books, Aberdeen).

Farr, Grahame (1981): *Papers on Life-boat History, No.5: The Steam Life-boats 1889-1928* (Grahame Farr, Bristol).

Fry, Eric C. (1975): *Life-boat Design and Development* (David & Charles, London).

Hudson, F. D., Hicks, I. A. and Cripps, R. M. (1993): The design and development of modern lifeboats, in *Proceedings of the Institute of Mechanical Engineers*, vol.207.

Kirton, Tim (1989): The Watsons: variations on a theme, in Lifeboat Enthusiasts' Society *Newsletter*, No. 87, pp.8-13.

Leach, Nicholas (2001): *The Waveney Lifeboats: An illustrated history of the RNLI 44ft Waveney lifeboats 1967-1999* (Bernard McCall, Portishead, Bristol).

— (2001): *A Saviour of Souls: William and Kate Johnston, the story of a legendary prototype lifeboat* (N&SRG).

— (2003): *Sennen Cove Lifeboats: 150 Years of Lifesaving* (Tempus Publishing Ltd, Stroud, Gloucestershire).

— (2003): *Oakley Lifeboats: An Illustrated History of the RNLI's Oakley and Rother Lifeboats* (Tempus Publishing Ltd, Stroud, Gloucestershire).

Leach, Nicholas and Russell, Paul (2004): *Cromer Lifeboats 1804-2004* (Tempus Publishing Ltd, Stroud, Gloucestershire).

Morris, Jeff (1994): *Lists of British Lifeboats Part 3: Steam Lifeboats 1888-1901 and Motor Lifeboats 1904-1993* (Lifeboat Enthusiasts' Society).

— (1995): *The History of the Tynemouth Lifeboats*.

— (1999): *The Story of the Newhaven Lifeboats* (2nd edition).

Swann, F. R. H. (1973): Technical Developments in the Life-boat Service, in *The Lifeboat*, April 1973, pp.446-452.

Warner, Oliver (1974): *The Life-boat Service: A History of the Royal National Life-boat Institution 1824-1974* (Cassell, London).